Modern Theology

This book offers a clear introduction to modern Christian theology (1789–present) and is accessible for undergraduates on a wide range of courses in theology and religious studies.

The 'long nineteenth century' saw enormous transformations of theology, and of thought about religion, that shaped the way both Christianity and 'religion' are understood today. Muers and Higton provide a lucid guide, giving students a critical understanding of their own 'modern' assumptions, of the origins of the debates and the fields of study in which they are involved, and of major modern thinkers.

Modern Theology:
- introduces the context and work of a selection of major nineteenth-century thinkers who decisively affected the shape of modern theology
- presents key debates and issues that have their roots in the nineteenth century but are also central to the study of twentieth- and twenty-first-century theology
- includes exercises and study materials that explicitly focus on the development of core academic skills.

This valuable resource also contains a glossary, timeline, annotated bibliographies and illustrations.

Rachel Muers is Senior Lecturer in Christian Studies at the University of Leeds, UK. Her recent books include *Theology on the Menu* with David Grumett (Routledge, 2010).

Mike Higton is Academic Co-Director of the Cambridge Inter-faith Programme and Senior Lecturer in Theology at the University of Exeter, UK. His recent books include *A Theology of Higher Education* (2012).

Modern Theology

A Critical Introduction

Rachel Muers and Mike Higton

Routledge
Taylor & Francis Group

LONDON AND NEW YORK

First published in 2012
by Routledge
2 Park Square, Milton Park, Abingdon, Oxon OX14 4RN

Simultaneously published in the USA and Canada
by Routledge
711 Third Avenue, New York, NY 10017

Routledge is an imprint of the Taylor & Francis Group, an informa business

British Library Cataloguing in Publication Data
A catalogue record for this book is available from the British Library

Library of Congress Cataloging in Publication Data
Muers, Rachel.
Modern theology : a critical introduction / Rachel Muers and Mike Higton.
p. cm.
Includes index.
1. Theology. I. Higton, Mike. II. Title.
BT28.M84 2012
230--dc23
2012004225

ISBN: 978-0-415-49584-4 (hbk)
ISBN: 978-0-415-49585-1 (pbk)
ISBN: 978-0-203-10477-4 (ebk)

Typeset in Gentium
By Saxon Graphics Ltd, Derby

Printed and bound in Great Britain by the MPG Books Group

C ontents

Illustrations

Acknowledgements

We are very grateful to Lesley Riddle at Routledge for her immense enthusiasm, patience and support through what proved to be a longer and more complex process than we had initially hoped; without her, this book would never have seen the light of day. We are indebted to the anonymous readers who provided detailed comments on chapter drafts, to Charles Twombly for his input at various stages and to Alice E. Wood for her help with the introductory chapters. We thank Rhiannon Grant for her extensive work on the glossary and the timeline. Katherine Ong and other members of the staff team at Routledge have consistently provided invaluable, prompt and efficient assistance.

Our experience of teaching courses in modern theology to undergraduates at the Universities of Exeter and Leeds was crucial in the development of this book. We are grateful to the students on those courses for – knowingly or unknowingly – testing the material and helping us to improve it. In particular, Rachel Muers would like to thank students on THEO 2400, especially Stanley Pearson and Jenny Wong, for reading and offering comments on several draft chapters. We also acknowledge with gratitude the support of our colleagues at the Universities of Exeter, Leeds and Cambridge.

Every effort has been made to trace copyright holders and obtain permission to reproduce material. Any omissions brought to the attention of the publisher will be remedied in future editions.

Introduction

What is modernity?

AIMS

By the end of this chapter, we hope that you will:

- understand what is meant by the term 'modern' in the context of this textbook

- know about some of the controversies around the definition and assessment of 'modernity'

- know some of the major issues that have engaged theological thought in the modern period, and be better prepared to reflect on them in relation to specific thinkers and movements.

Studying modernity: about this book

The word 'modern' has specific meanings in academic and theological contexts, as we shall see in this chapter, but these meanings are not completely separate from its general use. When we study modernity, it is important to examine our background assumptions about what it means to be modern. Before you begin this chapter, pause to jot down:

• what words and images come to mind when you read the phrases: 'modern life'; 'the modern Church'; 'modern art'; 'modern people'
• any synonyms you can think of for the word 'modern'
• any antonyms (opposites) you can think of for the word 'modern'.

Keep these notes and refer back to them as you go through the chapter. How do the ideas you automatically associate with being 'modern' relate to the account of modernity we are giving here?

Studying religious thought often involves learning to understand contexts and beliefs that are very different from our own. Students of religion have to learn the skill of *intellectual empathy* – thinking from inside someone else's head, understanding the world from the point of view of someone whose assumptions and ways of reasoning are not one's own. For most people reading this textbook, however, the study of 'modern theology' is not just an exercise in seeing things from someone else's point of view. It is an exercise in seeing how *our own* 'point of view' – our own set of assumptions and ways of thinking – came to be as it is. We study modernity, then, in order to understand better why certain questions about theology bother us so much today, while others seem irrelevant; why some kinds of argument are accepted and others are not; why 'theology' and 'religion' are defined in certain ways and given certain roles, and so forth.

This critical introduction to modern theology focuses on how modern theological ideas arose, and were given the formulations that continue to influence and shape thinking today. When we use 'modern' in our title we do not just mean 'contemporary' but we do hope to give you some ways of being *critical* about contemporary theology and contemporary thought about religion, through an *introduction* to their history and context.

What does it mean to be 'critical' and why is this a critical introduction? Being critical is not the same as being negative or identifying problems; this work is not straightforwardly 'critical' of modernity in that sense. In an academic context, to be critical is to make reasoned and argued *judgements* about something. This book is 'critical' because we are presenting you with our judgements about the texts, thinkers and movements we describe. We are not claiming simply to 'tell you all the facts and let you make up your own mind'; we do not think that is possible. We have made judgements about what is important and what is unimportant; we have made judgements about the connections between different texts and thinkers; we have made judgements about various aspects of the 'big story' of modernity. We have tried to make sure that our key judgements are pointed out and justified in the text.

The presence of judgement – the fact that this is a 'critical introduction' – need not, in itself, mean that our account is biased (although of course it *is* bound to be biased, and you should use your own critical abilities to seek out and identify our biases). It also need not mean that our account is controversial – although on some points it might be.

What is modernity?

What are we talking about when we say 'modernity'? We want to suggest three possible ways of answering this question.

The most obvious way is to name, firstly, a *specific historical period* and then to start a debate about exactly when modernity begins. You will find several different starting dates given for the modern period. Different academic disciplines have different conventions – although within any given discipline there will also be debates about when modernity begins.

Thus, for example, historians often date modernity from the mid-fifteenth century, or even earlier; 'early modern' history covers the beginning of this period. One event that is often taken to mark the beginning of the modern period is the fall of Constantinople in 1453. In English history, the Wars of the Roses (1455–1487) have sometimes been regarded as marking the transition from medieval to modern. A slightly different view would place the beginning of modernity in Europe at the Reformation and the Wars of Religion (thus, in the second half of the sixteenth century). By contrast, in music, literature and art, the label 'modern' is usually associated with the Modernist movement in the late nineteenth and early twentieth centuries. Again, sociological accounts of modernity would usually associate the 'modernisation' of Britain (for example) with the **Industrial Revolution** of the early nineteenth century.

In this book, we focus our account of modernity on a period that both social historians and historians of ideas generally agree is very important for modernity. Our focal period in the first part of the book is the so-called 'long nineteenth century'

– which begins at or around the time of the American and French Revolutions (1774 and 1789) and ends with the First World War (1914–1918). In the second part of the book, we look at twentieth- and early twenty-first-century thought in the light of what happened in the long nineteenth century. Of course, as we will explore in the next chapter, this 'modern' period needs to be understood in the light of what went before it.

Two questions arise from what we have just said. First, does modernity have an end as well as a beginning – or are we still in modernity? The idea of *post*modernity, and of the *end* of modernity, will be discussed at several points in this book. For most purposes, however, we think it is important to see modernity as open-ended. Even if some or all of us do not share all the characteristically modern concerns described in this book, early-twenty-first-century readers have so much in common with the 'moderns' that it is not particularly helpful to talk about modernity as something in the past.

Second, and more importantly, how are these dates chosen? Asking that question makes us realise that 'modernity' cannot be *just* the label for a period of time (like 'last year' or 'my grandmother's lifetime'). The only reason it is possible to argue about when 'modernity' begins is that 'modernity' means something more than a set of dates.

This brings us to our next suggestion for defining modernity; modernity is a *set of social phenomena.* 'Modernity' could designate ways of life, and ways of thinking about life, that only became possible or widespread at a certain time in history. Some candidates for the distinguishing features of 'modernity' might be: **industrialisation** and urbanisation; the development of (various forms of) democracy and the rise of nation-states; the development of science (as a set of practices, institutions and ways of thinking about knowledge); and the emergence of religious pluralism and the idea of a '**secular**' public sphere.

Much more could be said about all of these phenomena. Think, for example, about the complex effects of modern ways of producing goods, and modern uses of land – the development of factories and of industrial cities. The movement from the villages to the cities meant a whole set of different ways of relating: to other people, to the natural environment, to people's own work (and to fellow workers and machines), to food and goods and money, to time, to churches and religious communities and so forth.

When we are studying theological and philosophical texts, these social phenomena sometimes come into view directly, because the authors discuss them. Sometimes, however, they come into view more indirectly. The attitudes and assumptions that are reflected in modern *society* are also reflected in modern *thought*. The questions that are being worked out theoretically in the texts we read are often those that are being worked out practically in the society of the time. So we may find it helpful to think of modernity, thirdly, as a *set of attitudes or ideas* – remembering always that these attitudes and ideas never float free from particular social and historical circumstances.

> There is an interesting, ongoing – and distinctively modern – question about the relationship between the development of ideas, on the one hand, and the economic and political development of society, on the other. (See the discussions of 'idealism' and of Marx in Chapter 5 for one set of modern debates on the subject.) In this book, we aim to show that these developments *are* related in some way, without settling on one answer to the question of *how* they are related.

In the next section of this chapter, we discuss at more length some of the key ideas that animate *religious* thought in modernity. Probably the most widely recognised, and the broadest, characteristic of modern thought is a focus on the human being and the human subject. It is the rise of **humanism**, from as early as the twelfth century, which leads some scholars to put the origins of modernity much further back in history than we do here. Modern people are interested in understanding what it is to be human; they are interested in exploring, theoretically and practically, what human beings are capable of; and they are interested in questions about who we are, what we can know, what we can do, what we can be. These are the questions that constitute the modern *turn to the subject.*

> That is 'subject' as in the grammatical subject of a verb. *I* write a book about modern theology, *you* try to understand it, *she* decides not to bother. It is a characteristically modern attitude, reflective of the 'turn to the subject', to be interested in the *I*, the *you* and the *she* in that sentence. Who am *I* to think I can tell *you* something about modern theology? How do *you* understand it? And should *she* decide not to bother?
>
> It is not an accident, incidentally, that we have only used singular subjects of sentences in this example (no *we* or *they*). Individualism is another attitude frequently cited as a characteristic of modernity. The 'subject' to whom modern questioning turns is typically singular.

Another distinctively 'modern' attitude, which is equally important for our discussion of theology and religious thought, comes to light if we think about the *opposites* of 'modern' (see the exercise at the beginning of this chapter). Calling something 'modern' tends to be a way of contrasting it with what went before, and/or with what is stable, established or unchanging – modern as opposed to ancient or outdated; modern as opposed to traditional or classic. Modernity, then, is preoccupied with change. To be able to talk about 'modernity' we need to have the assumption that things can change – that the basic conditions of human life, thought and activity are not always the same. If we combine this with the modern emphasis on 'what human beings can do', we can see the basis for a modern interest, not just in the fact that 'things change' but in the fact that human beings *can change things for themselves.*

Note that once we have said this, we have already set up a conflict between 'modern' thought, on the one hand, and tradition – recognising texts, ideas and practices from the past as having authority in relation to present ways of life – on the other. Note also that one of the reasons it is important to study modern thought is the modern belief, often acted out in modern history, that human *thought*, combined with human action, can change things. In modernity, ideas matter.

In this book, we will use many 'isms' in our discussion of modern thought, trying to show how particular texts and thinkers fit into larger movements of thought, that in turn relate to larger political and social movements. We will talk, for example, about nationalism, feminism, idealism, socialism, pluralism, deism, creationism, liberalism … Not all of our 'isms' refer only to modernity, but it is still true that modernity is the great age of 'isms' – the age when 'big ideas' about humanity and the world are thought to be worth naming, identifying yourself with, organising around and fighting for – literally as well as metaphorically. Some would argue that this age of 'isms' is now over, for better or worse, that the contemporary world is deeply mistrustful of these 'big ideas' and the movements they name. It could certainly be argued that, in public discourse (about politics, economics, 'ethics', religion), 'isms' are more often used to label one's opponents than to label oneself. See Chapter 17 for further discussion of this (supposed) change.

One of the reasons we begin our discussion of modernity with the American and French Revolutions is that these represent the first attempts to change, comprehensively and fundamentally, the shape of human life and society according to ideas that people can understand and formulate. Particularly in the case of the French Revolution, we can see a new vision of human life set in sharp and violent confrontation with tradition. As we will see in Chapters 3 and 5, this posed an enormous and distinctive challenge for religious and philosophical thought.

Thinking about revolutions brings us to a further issue. Once we start to talk about fundamental changes in the conditions of human life, we are unlikely to be talking about something that can be viewed dispassionately. Are these changes *for the better* or changes *for the worse*? Is it a good thing to be modern? 'Modern' is not simply a description, it is an evaluation, and one that carries different connotations in different contexts. For much of the period we shall be discussing, 'modern' was often a positive self-designation, an identity people wanted to claim for themselves; but it was, and is, also used to label and condemn unwanted change.

We have said that we are focusing on the long nineteenth century, which ends (by historians' convention) with the First World War. The First World War represents, in many ways, a crisis for the *positive* view of 'modernity'. As we shall see, however, the picture is very complicated. Look back at the notes you made before reading this chapter, and consider whether your words and images associated with 'modernity' are positive or negative. Were you assuming that 'modern' was a good way to be?

At this point we should introduce a term you will come across frequently in discussions of modernity, and that may sometimes appear as a near-synonym for modernity – Enlightenment. When historians refer to 'the Enlightenment', they normally mean the period immediately before the one on which this book focuses – the late seventeenth and eighteenth centuries. 'Enlightenment' was how some of the thinkers of this period – and later commentators – chose to describe the process of intellectual and social change of which they believed they were part. It is clearly a positive self-designation and one that gives a very negative portrayal of the preceding age, as an age of 'darkness'. Unlike some commentators, we do not think modernity is *all* about the Enlightenment and its effects but we do think the Enlightenment is a key aspect of modernity. We discuss this further in the next section, and in Chapter 2.

Some key issues in modern thought

In this section, we discuss five distinctively 'modern' themes that constitute the agenda for much of modern theology and modern thought about religion. They are distinctively modern, not just because they arise within the (broad) time period we have specified as 'modern', but because they relate closely to both the social and political changes and the intellectual changes that constitute modernity.

Our first theme is *reason*. By the beginning of the long nineteenth century, the idea of a new, reforming, anti-traditional 'Age of Reason' was already well established and widely discussed. The late seventeenth and eighteenth centuries – the time of the Enlightenment – are also often termed the 'Age of Reason'. Reason – in various forms and with various shades of meaning, some of them linked to linguistic differences – had been a key part of philosophical and theological vocabulary for centuries. There was nothing new, or distinctively modern, about praising reason, describing human beings as rational, calling people to live in accordance with right reason or setting out rules for judging whether an idea was reasonable.

> [People] have always used reason to make things intelligible for want of anything better, and most people who write prose or ... think about the larger issues of the world and the universe can lay claim to using some form of reason to help guide their thoughts and construct their arguments. It is difficult to see that Thomas Hobbes [1588–1679, a representative of the Age of Reason] was any more reasonable than Thomas Aquinas [1225-1274].
>
> John Redwood, *Reason, Ridicule and Religion:*
> *The Age of Enlightenment in England, 1660-1750*
> (London: Thames and Hudson, 1976), p13.

Nonetheless, philosophical and traditional discourse about reason changed in modernity and reason took centre stage in a new way. The modern question about reason begins as a question about what any and every 'rational' human being can know, understand or prove, *without* reference to traditions or external authorities.

To some extent, this modern view of reason is bound up with developments in science. The rise of scientific societies meant the rise of new methods for fixing knowledge and establishing truth – the emergence of the 'scientific method'. Again to some extent, the development of modern reason was linked to the development of new institutions, spaces and media where reasoning could go on: more printed material more widely available, a larger educated middle class who gathered to discuss ideas.

One of our claims in this book, however, is that the modern question about reason originated with an urgent question about *peace*, in the wake of a series of devastating 'religious' wars in Europe (including the Thirty Years' War and the English Civil War). How can people of different local and religious traditions live together? What can possibly unite people in a way that will not lead to violent conflict? The creation of 'reason' had much to do with the creation of an agreed basis for common life. As we will see, this still affected debates about 'reason' in the long nineteenth century.

For Christian theology, modernity poses the critical question, is Christianity rational? Would it 'make sense' to any and every rational person even if its truth were not taken on authority? What can be made of those aspects of the Bible and of traditional doctrine that strike us as 'contrary to reason'? If the answer is that Christianity is *not* rational (or, not rational in the sense intended by the question), the further question is 'does it matter?' What is the status of reason within religious thought, and what can be said theologically about reason in human life more generally? *Are* we in fact only, or mainly, reasoning beings?

This leads on to our next theme – *knowledge of God.* In modernity, questions of **epistemology** – of the nature of knowledge, how we can claim to know anything – assume great importance. For theologians, the question that arises is: how can any thinking or talk about God have any 'purchase' on God? If human beings claim to know God, on what basis do they make that claim? And what other forms of human knowledge does the knowledge of God resemble?

Again, this central question of modernity arises well before the nineteenth century. As we shall see in the next chapter, it was approached from numerous angles in the eighteenth century, drawing on different philosophical frameworks for understanding knowledge. In the nineteenth century, the key framework for understanding knowledge was Kant's thought (see Chapter 3). Following Kant, one particular approach to answering the question of the 'knowledge of God' – closely associated with Schleiermacher (see Chapter 4) – was very influential. It takes *religious life* as the starting point for assessing and understanding knowledge of God. The theologian can look at religion – at human thinking about God, experience of God, awareness of God, faith in God – and ask 'what is it, about God and about humanity, that makes this religion possible?'

The critical response to this approach is just as important for modern theology as the approach itself – and we shall explore both in the following chapters. Note at this point, however, that the question of 'how God can be known' still matters. Does studying religion tell us anything about God, or only something about human beings? How much relevance does a 'scientific' approach to knowledge have to questions about God?

Some of these contemporary questions point us to a third focal theme for our discussion of modern theology. *Suspicion of religion* is an important part of the context in which modern theology is done. Again, opposition to religion (either in general, or in specific forms) was nothing new in the nineteenth century. It was the late seventeenth century, for example, that saw an enormous upsurge in England of pamphlets and books warning about the dangers of '**atheism**' (and a rather smaller number of pamphlets and books that actually promoted anything that we might now call atheism).

The distinctive feature of nineteenth-century thought is the development of several different, although connected, ways of *explaining* religion as a purely human phenomenon – explaining it, that is, in a way that made the truth or otherwise of its claims (about God, humanity, the world and so forth) irrelevant. Paul Ricoeur termed the key promulgators of such readings of religion the 'masters of suspicion'. It is important to note that suspicion of religion, as we use it here (following Ricoeur), is not just opposition to religion. It is the claim to look past what religion *claims* to be (e.g. a set of ways of relating to God and knowing God) and see that it is *really* something different (e.g. a way of maintaining the economic and political *status quo*).

Ricoeur's 'masters of suspicion', all of whom are discussed in this book, were Ludwig Feuerbach, Karl Marx, Friedrich Nietzsche and Sigmund Freud.

As we will see, theological responses to suspicious readings of religion do not have to consist of denials, and some suspicious readings of religion can, in fact, be put to powerful theological use. In any case, modern theology – now no less than in the nineteenth century – has to engage with these suspicious readings. Almost at the same time as theologians (such as Schleiermacher) began to take the human phenomenon of religion as a starting point for theological thought, proponents of other, 'modern', forms of knowledge – history, economic and political science, psychology – became interested in studying and explaining religion on their terms. The question still arises as to whether that kind of analysis – for example, the sociology of religion or the psychology of religion – in explaining religious belief, explains it *away*.

Our fourth theme takes us directly into the political arena. Modernity is concerned with *freedom*. The idea of freedom was, of course, central to the French and American Revolutions, and to the thought of the Enlightenment. Perhaps even more than 'reason', freedom, in modernity, names the highest human value. In modern arguments about ethics or politics, nobody usually questions that it is a good and important thing to be free. It is more common to see arguments about what 'true' freedom is, what the best or most important kind of freedom is and whether someone else's vision of freedom is 'really' freedom at all.

Philosophically, theologically and politically, this naming of freedom as the highest value creates a whole series of questions. How is freedom to be defined? What, in practice, does the life of the free person look like, and what does the life of free *people* – a shared life built on freedom – look like? At the beginning of the period we are discussing there was a widely-held belief that religion, or at least some of its aspects and manifestations, represented a threat to human freedom. Alongside this, there was a well-developed, and politically significant, debate about *religious* freedom. Where should religion fit into a political system that held human freedom among its highest goals? And what account of human freedom could Christianity itself offer?

Our final theme is one that comes to the fore especially in the long nineteenth century – although in many ways it is central to the idea of modernity. Modernity is interested in *history, and historical change*. As we have said, the very word 'modern' implies a contrast with what went before. Modernity sees increased interest in the idea that human life is historically conditioned and can change through history. Although history-writing is not itself modern, the academic discipline of history as we now know it is a modern development. Nineteenth-century thinkers were, very often, interested in the human subject as a *historical* subject. To understand why human beings think and act as they do, and what they are or are not capable of achieving, they sought to understand humans within history.

Of course, this 'historical turn' raises questions for all the other themes we have discussed. Does 'reason' change through history? And if so, what real prospect is there for reaching stable rational *agreement*? Is the process of historical change something that makes God known? Can we understand and accept what people of different historical ages have claimed about God? Does a historical view of religion, and the recognition that religion changes over time, explain religion away? And if we are shaped by our history, how can we also say that we are free?

For Christian theology, history is bound to matter; at the centre of the Christian creed is a human story that is located within human history, and the Bible is dominated by 'history-like' narratives. An emphasis on historical change and the historical conditioning of human life, then, is not straightforwardly a problem for theology. It does, however, bring a specific set of questions and challenges. For example, what unites 'Christianity' as it changes through history? What are the implications of giving, to a set of texts that reflect a particular historical context and outlook, authority in relation to *all* subsequent historical contexts? And what about Jesus' own relationship to his particular historical context – does it limit his significance for people who do not share that context, and if not, why not?

There is also the question of the evaluation of change. From the eighteenth century until at least the early twentieth century, the dominant 'reading' of historical change was that it was change *for the better* – 'enlightenment', a movement from darkness to light. The assumption was that human knowledge, especially scientific knowledge, could and would make progress; societies could and would become more 'civilised', rational and free; the conditions of human life could and would improve. Although, as we shall see, there were many exceptions, it is fair to characterise the long nineteenth century as a time of optimism about historical change.

How ought Christian theology to view and assess stories of historical progress or of historical decline? The question of the relationship between Christian hope for the coming of the kingdom of God, on the one hand, and modern optimism, on the other, has remained controversial. It relates to a wider issue brought up by our whole discussion: is 'modernity', as we have characterised it, best described as a *Christian* phenomenon, as something *anti*-Christian or as neither?

This idea of progress is so widely assumed, even now, that it is worth remembering that it was not always around. Towards the beginning of what historians term the modern period, the assumption tended to be that society and human nature *began* in a state of perfection and deteriorated over time. The best hope humanity had, on this view of history, was to undo the effects of historical development, the growth of more and more harmful 'customs', and try to get back to the original, natural condition of human life. Both the Reformation and the Renaissance were characterised, not by the desire to 'move on', but by the desire to go *back* to ancient and pure sources of knowledge. Historical change, for radical or reforming thinkers well into the eighteenth century, was generally not a good thing.

Here, for example, is John Milton writing to the English Parliament in 1643, in an appeal for Church reform, blaming the wrongs and injustices of his society on historically-acquired 'custom':

> ... who of all Teachers and Masters that have ever taught, hath drawn the most Disciples after him, both in Religion and in Manners? ... Custom ... which not only in private mars our education, but also in public is the common climber into every chair, where either Religion is preached, or Law reported: filling each estate of life and profession, with abject and servile principles; depressing the high and Heaven-born spirit of Man, far beneath the condition wherein either God created him or sin hath sunk him ... Error supports custom; custom countenances error.
>
> John Milton, *The Doctrine and Discipline of Divorce* (1643)

Assessing modernity: some debates

As you might expect, given what we have said about modernity's 'historical turn', there are an enormous number of histories of modernity. In fact, histories of modernity began to be written near the beginning of the modern period. Especially in those histories that focus on the development of ideas, religion is often an important 'player' in these histories.

A very influential, and until recently dominant, way of telling the story of modernity was in terms of the decline of religion (specifically, of Christianity). Modernity was about the progressive 'loss of faith', the loss of the influence of religion, the **secularisation** of more and more aspects of life and the retreat of religion into a largely irrelevant and anachronistic sideshow. As we shall see, this is the story that at least some of the 'Enlightenment' thinkers of the eighteenth century, and at least some of the 'masters of suspicion', wanted to tell. Later, the work of Max Weber (1864–1920), whose story of the progressive disappearance of religion began with the Reformation, gave further theoretical weight to this account of modernity.

The 'secularisation thesis', as it is often called, has been widely challenged in contemporary social science; it still has many proponents and has been modified in various ways. Debates within the social sciences tend to focus on the contemporary situation – does the evidence suggest that modern societies *are* becoming progressively less religious?

Scholarly discussions of secularisation include Peter Berger, *The Sacred Canopy: Elements of a Sociological Theory of Religion* (Garden City: Doubleday, 1967). See also Berger's later work, in which he argued against his own early belief in secularisation; Steve Bruce, *God is Dead: Secularization in the West* (Oxford: Blackwell, 2002); Rodney Stark and William Bainbridge, *The Future of Religion: Secularization, Revival and Cult Formation* (Berkeley: University of California Press, 1986).

For the purposes of this book, we are less interested in the contemporary social-scientific issue – is religion actually declining now? – and more interested in the historical and theological issue – was modernity, from the start, 'against' Christianity? Here, the picture is even more complicated. In recent years, Christian theologians in the West have often told the story of modernity as a story of loss. Even if Christian institutions and practices have not disappeared, they argue, modern concerns and themes have tended to distort Christian belief, or to promote visions of humanity and the world that are basically opposed to Christianity. 'Modern theology' often appears, in these accounts, as a set of unsuccessful and/or disastrous compromises with a flawed intellectual and social project.

Examples include Michael Buckley, *At the Origins of Modern Atheism* (New Haven: Yale University Press, 1987); John Milbank, *Theology and Social Theory: Beyond Secular Reason* (Oxford: Blackwell, 1990).

For a similarly critical reading of the modern project – without the same theological agenda – see Stephen Toulmin, *Cosmopolis: The Hidden Agenda of Modernity* (Chicago: University of Chicago Press, 1990).

Another, contrasting, theological approach to telling the story of modernity presents a story of modern progress for theology itself. Theological thought confronts the challenges of modernity, and the radical changes it undergoes constitute an improvement, not a decline.

> This is the approach taken, for example, by James P. Mackey in *Modern Theology: A Sense of Direction* (Oxford: Oxford University Press, 1987); and also by Philip Kennedy in *Modern Introduction to Theology: New Questions for Old Beliefs* (London: I. B. Tauris, 2006).

One key point to take from these critical accounts by recent thinkers is that the story of modernity can be told as a story of change and debate within Christianity (and to some extent within other religious traditions), not just as something that happened outside Christianity. Modern questions, in other words, can be seen as theological questions. It is hard to deny that most of the people who can be credited, or blamed, with bringing about the modern transformation of the world held religious beliefs. Many of them, even when they were arguing for what we might now call 'secularisation', framed their arguments explicitly in theological terms. This does not, of course, necessarily mean that they were *right* to do so or that their theology is good theology. It does mean, however, that we cannot understand them on their own terms unless we take their religion seriously. There is no reason to assume that the religious content of modern texts and modern political movements is irrelevant, or not meant seriously – unless we have already decided, on other grounds, that religion is irrelevant or not worth taking seriously.

In this book we assume that there are substantive theological issues at stake within modern debates about reason, the knowledge of God, the suspicion of religion, freedom and historical change. We do not assume that theology stops mattering once the process of modernisation starts; and we do not assume that 'modern' theology is by definition problematic. We also do not assume that the story of modern theology is a story of progress. In other words, we try not to adopt a position for or against modernity as a whole, we want to show that modernity is highly complex, and that we cannot separate ourselves from it, even (or especially) as theologians.

Bibliography

Introductions and overviews: 'long nineteenth century' theology and religious thought:

James C. Livingston, *Modern Christian Thought: vol 1, The Enlightenment and the Nineteenth Century* (Minneapolis: Fortress, revised edition 2006). The best available introduction to our focal period.

David Fergusson (ed.), *The Blackwell Companion to Nineteenth-Century Theology* (Oxford: Blackwell, 2010). Collection of essays by leading scholars on specific thinkers and movements, including many of those discussed in this book.

Claude Welch, *Protestant Thought in the Nineteenth Century*, 2 vols (New Haven: Yale University Press, 1972). A very readable introduction, somewhat dated but very important and still well worth consulting.

Ninian Smart (ed.), *Nineteenth-century Religious Thought in the West*, 3 vols (Cambridge: Cambridge University Press, 1985). A major collection of essays – many of the authors are themselves significant figures in twentieth-century religious thought.

John Elbert Wilson, *Introduction to Modern Theology: Trajectories in the German Tradition* (Louisville: Westminster John Knox Press, 2007). Despite the title, this is not really an introductory work, it is useful for more detailed discussion of some of the figures we look at in Section A.

Karl Barth, *Protestant Theology in the Nineteenth Century: Its Background and History*, edited by Colin E. Gunton (Grand Rapids: Eerdmans, 2002). This is worth reading, not only for the detail it provides on a subset of the thinkers discussed in this book, but also to give you a sense of Barth's own approach to the nineteenth century.

Don Cupitt, *The Sea of Faith* (London: SCM, new edition 2003). Very positive reading of developments in modern religious thought, extremely lively and readable, caused controversy when it first appeared (especially in the context of Cupitt's other work).

Introductions and overviews: the nature of modernity and modern theology:

Gareth Jones (ed.), *The Blackwell Companion to Modern Theology* (Oxford: Blackwell, 2007). Introduction discusses the issue of how to define 'modernity'.

Gary Dorrien, *The Word as True Myth: Interpreting Modern Theology* (Louisville: Westminster John Knox Press, 1997). Introduction and first few chapters give a very readable overview of modern theology, focused on questions of knowledge, biblical interpretation and 'myth'.

Philip Kennedy, *A Modern Introduction to Theology: New Questions for Old Beliefs* (London: Tauris, 2006). Makes a sustained case for a particular 'modern' approach to theology and in the process offers historical and conceptual accounts of the nature of modernity.

Some further reading on modernity (particularly in relation to religion):

Charles Taylor, *A Secular Age* (Cambridge, MA: Harvard University Press, 2007).

Stephen Toulmin, *Cosmopolis: The Hidden Agenda of Modernity* (Chicago: University of Chicago Press, 1992).

Zygmunt Bauman, *Modernity and the Holocaust* (Ithaca: Cornell University Press, expanded edition 2000). The best known of Bauman's many, very influential, critical accounts of modernity.

Historical Introduction

Approaching the revolution

AIMS

By the end of this chapter, we hope that you will:

- understand some of the major developments in religious thought, and thought about religion, in the late seventeenth and eighteenth centuries, which affected theology in the 'long nineteenth century' and beyond

- understand what is meant by 'the Enlightenment' and why it is important

- know about some changes in religious practice, and the place of religion in society, in the late seventeenth and eighteenth centuries that affected the 'long nineteenth century'

- have had the chance to reflect on the relationship between the history of theology and other aspects of history.

An age of reason?

> It was the best of times, it was the worst of times, it was the age of wisdom, it was the age of foolishness, it was the epoch of belief, it was the epoch of incredulity, it was the season of Light, it was the season of Darkness, it was the spring of hope, it was the winter of despair, we had everything before us, we had nothing before us ... It was the year of Our Lord one thousand seven hundred and seventy-five.
>
> Charles Dickens, *A Tale of Two Cities*
> (1859; reprinted Harmondsworth: Penguin Popular Classics, 2007, p1)

The famous opening passage of Charles Dickens' *Tale of Two Cities*, set at the time of the French Revolution, depicts Europe in the late eighteenth century as riddled with contradictions and paradoxes, caught between extremes – an age of wisdom *and* an age of foolishness. Dickens is, of course, telling a story, setting up his tale of two cities by presenting pairs of opposites, so we might not take his depiction at face value. He does, however, provide a useful reminder that describing just one context, one movement or one set of ideas will fail to do justice to eighteenth-century thought.

As we said in the last chapter, the historical period immediately before the French Revolution (hence, immediately before the period on which this book focuses) has often been referred to, in historical shorthand, as the 'Age of Reason'. As we will see in this chapter, 'reason', in a new and distinctively modern form, *is* a key feature of religious thought in this period. There is a great deal of 'rational' and rationalising theology, and 'rational' critique of religion. However, we cannot ignore the very important theological and ecclesial developments that went in the other direction – *against* the claims of 'reason', affirming religious life as something more than, or other than, rational.

See also Karl Barth, in his introductory summary of eighteenth-century thought:

> must we not continue to ask whether the whole concept of 'Enlightenment' ... is enough to characterize one aspect of the century ... could we not with almost as much justice call it the age of mystery?
> (*Protestant Theology in the Nineteenth Century*, translated by Brian Cozens and John Bowden, new edition, London: SCM, 2001, p21).

It is worth watching your language when you are discussing eighteenth-century 'reason'. Not all eighteenth-century thinkers who believed strongly in the power and importance of *reason* were, strictly speaking, **rationalists.** The debate between rationalist and **empiricist** approaches to knowledge was important for eighteenth-century philosophy and theology – and all those involved, including those who were not rationalists, would have regarded themselves as advocates of reason.

By the late seventeenth century, much of Europe was experiencing the aftermath of 'religious' war. Particularly significant was the Thirty Years' War (1618–1648), the name generally given to a series of wars in central Europe, in which confessional divisions (between Catholics, Lutherans and Calvinists) were the major focus of conflict. In German-speaking Europe, numerous towns and cities were destroyed, and the effects of the war were exacerbated by widespread plague and famine. The English Civil Wars (1642–1651), in which religion was a significant and complex factor, also gave rise to long-lasting social and political upheaval in England, Wales and Scotland, and to devastation on an enormous scale in Ireland.

A note about Germany: Since many of the thinkers we discuss in this book were German, it is worth remembering that 'Germany' means very different things at different historical points. Until 1871, Germany did not exist as a state. For most of the eighteenth century, 'Germany' did not even really exist as an idea, nor did 'German' exist as an identity that people would claim. What is now Germany was many small and medium-sized states, sharing a language, but not a political identity. 'Germany' was a geographical expression (like, for example, 'central Europe' today). The modern idea, and thus the modern state, of Germany is itself one of the enduring legacies of eighteenth-century and early nineteenth-century thought.

As we suggested in the first chapter, *reason* emerged, in the years following the wars of religion, as a possible new basis for common life. The existing structures of religious and political authority had suffered a crisis, and in some respects at least had failed. The perceived problem was social and political – what could maintain peace and enable people to live together? – and also a problem of knowledge – what sources could be trusted to give assured and stable knowledge of the world and of God?

For the late-seventeenth- and eighteenth-century thinkers who identified themselves as part of the Enlightenment, the crisis of existing authority was an opportunity, not simply a disaster. There was the opportunity to emerge from the 'darkness' of traditional authority into the 'light' of universal reason. This light of reason would enlighten – so the many protagonists of the Enlightenment argued – not merely the minds of individuals, but the shared life of communities and states. The Enlightenment was a project of re-founding social and political order, and re-founding knowledge, on the basis of *reason*. In later sections of this chapter, we will see how this project – and responses to it, and the limitations to it that became apparent – shaped the context for nineteenth-century theology. However, in order to understand the various ways in which Christianity related to the turn to 'reason', we first need to take a step back and consider some important aspects of how Christianity itself was understood in this period.

A key modern assumption: Christianity as knowledge

'Religion', today, is often assumed to mean 'belief' – in a sense that links 'belief' very closely to 'knowledge'. A common way of defining religion is in terms of things that certain people believe or hold to be true. For example: 'Christianity is believing that God is Father, Son and Holy Spirit, that God created the world, that Jesus Christ is God incarnate ...'. If we have that kind of definition of Christianity – in which Christianity is about believing a list of non-obvious or improbable things – a sensible response to me, if I said I was a Christian, would be to ask me about proofs, evidence, sources, processes of reasoning and so forth (such as you might ask for from me if I said, for example, that I believed that my colleague was an undercover Secret Service agent and my missing cat had been abducted by extra-terrestrials). *If religion is mainly about believing certain things – or holding certain things to be true – then questions, assumptions and ground rules about how we judge what is true, how we decide what to believe or how we can know are going to be very important in debates about religion.*

> If you have studied the 'philosophy of religion' at school or undergraduate level, you have almost certainly worked with, and perhaps internalised, the assumption that religion is a set of beliefs or truth-claims. The philosophy of religion, as ordinarily studied and taught (at least in the English-speaking world at present), is the philosophy of 'things that religious people hold to be true'. 'Religion', for its purposes, is defined in terms of beliefs or truth-claims.

It was not always widely assumed that 'religion' meant 'things people hold to be true', nor that questions and rules about knowledge were central to religious debates. Broadly speaking, this is a modern idea and its origins are complex. One of its sources is the greater emphasis, in Protestant thought following the Reformation, on individual 'faith', reflected on and made explicit in each person's life. Alongside this emphasis on the individual's faith (and 'faith' meant far more than 'holding the right things to be true') came the development and wide circulation of 'confessions', summaries of the main articles of Christian belief.

The most famous example in English is the Westminster Confession (1646), which begins with a discussion of the 'knowledge of God' as given through Scripture:

> Although the light of nature, and the works of creation and providence do so far manifest the goodness, wisdom, and power of God, as to leave men unexcusable; yet are they not sufficient to give that knowledge of God, and of His will, which is necessary unto salvation. Therefore it pleased the Lord, at sundry times, and in

divers manners, to reveal Himself, and to declare that His will unto His Church; and afterwards for the better preserving and propagating of the truth, and for the more sure establishment and comfort of the Church against the corruption of the flesh, and the malice of Satan and of the world, to commit the same wholly unto writing; which makes the Holy Scripture to be most necessary.

'Protestant orthodoxy' and 'Protestant scholasticism' are terms often used to describe one dominant form of Christian theology in the years following the Reformation – that is, in the period preceding and overlapping with the Enlightenment. The terms suggest a preoccupation with right belief ('orthodoxy') – with systematising Christian beliefs and demonstrating their connections with each other, with clarifying concepts and resolving disputes over the exact meaning and nature of central Christian claims. Scholastic theology, both before and after the Reformation, was interested in Christian theology as a body of knowledge, and in using tools of logical enquiry – taken, at least to some extent, from Aristotle and his successors – to explore how that body of knowledge made sense, and how it related to other forms of (supposed or real) knowledge. *Protestant* scholasticism had certain distinctive aims within this – for example, a concern to make the rationality of Christian belief evident, at least in principle, to each individual believer.

The nature and value of 'Protestant scholasticism' is contested, and debates about it are shaped by different evaluations of the later theologies that reacted *against* it. It is sometimes seen as the 'bad old days', when theologians were only concerned to defend their own systems, and when theology became divorced from the reality of religious life; it is sometimes seen as the 'good old days' when the full content of traditional Christian belief was robustly affirmed; and of course it is sometimes seen as the first sign of modernity corrupting Christian theology! It was under sustained attack during the late seventeenth and eighteenth centuries – but it has had a lasting influence on theological thought, not least in establishing the 'shape' of *systematic* theology, within Protestantism at least. Contemporary systematic theologies are often still organised under the headings, and answer many of the questions, developed by the Protestant scholastics. In fact, Protestant scholasticism is quite likely to have influenced the shape and syllabus of any introductory course to Christian theology that you have studied.

   Recent works on Protestant scholasticism include Brian Armstrong, *Calvinism and the Amyraut Heresy: Protestant Scholasticism and Humanism in Seventeenth-century France* (Madison: University of Wisconsin Press, 1969); Richard A. Muller, *After Calvin: Studies in the Development of a Theological Tradition* (Oxford: Oxford University Press, 2003). See also Gary J. Dorrien, *The Remaking of Evangelical Tradition* (Louisville: Westminster John Knox, 1998), Chapter 2.

It is possible to see, in this context, how people might come to associate 'being a Christian' with 'knowing certain things about God', or 'holding a particular set of propositions to be true' (rather than, for example, 'being part of a particular community', 'worshipping God in a particular way', 'being in a particular relationship to God', 'having particular attitudes').

For whatever reasons, during the period we are discussing in this chapter, the idea of religion as (debatable) *knowledge*, 'holding things to be true', was very prominent – particularly among the relatively small, but growing, number of highly educated people. It was not the *only* way in which Christianity was understood. Indeed, as we will see, there were movements within eighteenth-century Christianity that radically de-emphasised 'holding the right things to be true'. It was, however, generally the case that when eighteenth-century people spoke or wrote about 'Christian religion' they meant 'the things Christians think are true'. The obvious question to ask was, why do Christians think these things are true? Or, more pointedly and urgently in the context of confessional divisions, if different groups hold different things to be true, on the subjects to which Christian beliefs relate, how do we decide who is right?

It is worth recognising that this was a question *internal* to Christianity, as well as a question posed, at various points in the eighteenth century, by people who did not identify themselves as Christian. The mere fact that different groups of Christians believe different things was not automatically seen as a reason to reject Christianity, or to give up the search for 'right belief'. The main point to note at this stage was that Christian theology – particularly Protestant Christian theology – was very focused in this period on how to resolve questions of 'right belief', and that this fitted into a context in which the nature and scope of reason was a major intellectual issue.

A question to think about: Is working out how to distinguish true belief from false belief a good way to stop religious conflict? At least some eighteenth-century religious thinkers believed that it was, and this motivated their theological and philosophical enquiry.

Reason, nature and natural religion

But how exactly was 'reason' supposed to provide firm ground for making judgements about religion? One influential line of thought relates to another central theme of seventeenth- and eighteenth-century thought – *nature*. We noted in the first chapter that early modern thinkers often contrasted the bad effects of history and 'custom' with the goodness, simplicity and rationality of humanity in its original and 'natural' state. For many Enlightenment thinkers, to follow reason is to live in accordance with one's nature, and vice versa. Moreover, reason directs us to a *common* human nature, something we share and can recognise in each other. This shared 'nature' might not, of course, appear as a set of agreed beliefs; it might be, for example, a set of moral principles or ways of acting that we accept as 'natural' to humanity.

> The idea that we can and should go back 'before' social conditioning, historical accident, upbringing, education and so forth, in order to find out what humanity is 'really' *meant* to be like, plays a role in various public and popular debates today. Consider, for example, the use of evolutionary psychology to discuss whether altruism, co-operation and so forth are 'natural' human characteristics, and the endless arguments about whether there are 'natural' differences, in character, abilities and so forth, between men and women.

The emphasis on 'nature' is, of course, also linked to the development of the natural sciences. With the rise of science, 'nature' – the given physical world – appeared both as an *object* of human knowledge (that could be observed and studied without recourse to external authorities) and as a *source* of knowledge. By studying nature in its parts, people could learn about the whole, about themselves and about God.

What does this mean in theological terms? There is enormous interest, in seventeenth- and eighteenth-century writing, in *natural religion*. This is itself an idea with a long history. There is a classical distinction in Christian theology between natural and revealed knowledge of God – the former being the knowledge of God that is possible for humanity by virtue of being *created* the way we are, the latter being the knowledge of God that is given in God's revelatory acts. In this view, of course, God is the source of both natural and revealed knowledge (because God is the creator as well as the revealer) and there is, or should be, no contradiction between them. Note also that 'natural knowledge', for theologians, means not only the knowledge that people can gain about God by studying human or non-human nature – it also means the knowledge that they can gain about God by using their 'natural', created reason.

Many of the accounts of 'natural religion' produced in the seventeenth and eighteenth centuries fit, to a greater or lesser extent, within this classical Christian framework. They describe the *coherence* of 'natural religion' (what could be known about God on the basis of creation) and 'revealed religion' (what could be known about God on the basis of revelation), and often they argue for the importance of 'natural' religion within Christian thought. Many texts on this theme were produced in Britain as part of Christian opposition to deism (see below) – one of the most famous and influential being Joseph Butler's *Analogy of Religion Natural and Revealed* (1736).

Particularly following the Reformation, the question of whether we *can* in fact have true 'natural' knowledge of God is a key area of controversy. If sin distorts the originally good human 'nature', and the capacity for knowing God with which human beings were created, it is clear that any 'natural' knowledge of God claimed by sinful humanity will be untrustworthy and subject to error. The Reformers agreed that knowledge of God *was* 'natural' to humanity, but argued that fallen and sinful humanity could not use this natural knowledge.

Thus Calvin: 'That there exists in the human mind, and indeed by natural instinct, some sense of Deity, we hold to be beyond dispute ... but ... in regard to the true knowledge of [God], all are so degenerate, that in no part of the world can genuine godliness be found.' (*Institutes of the Christian Religion*, book 1, ch 3, 4; Grand Rapids, MI: Eerdmans, 1989, pp43, 46).

As we shall see, a distrust of unaided 'natural knowledge of God', in the light of sin's corruption of all natural knowledge, did not stop Protestant theologians from arguing that theology could and should be *rational*. It also did not stop the production of numerous works on 'natural religion' by Protestant theologians in the period we are studying. Humanity aided and guided by God's revelation *could* recognise God in nature, even if this would have been impossible without God's aid and guidance.

In the German context, one very influential account of the relationship between natural and revealed religion, which accorded 'reason' a central role, was developed by the philosopher Christian Wolff (1679–1754). Wolff was a rationalist in the strict sense, committed to basing knowledge on what could be demonstrated logically through a method analogous to mathematics – without, for example, using evidence from the world or from experience. So his 'natural theology' consisted of arguments for the existence and nature of God that everyone ought to be able to understand through the use of reason alone. (It was 'natural theology', not because he was studying 'nature', but because he was arguing from the rationality that we all 'naturally' possess.)

Wolff accepted that there were numerous claims about God and the world, made within Christian theology, that did *not* work in this way – that could not be known through unaided reason. He proposed, firstly that there was a considerable overlap between 'natural' and 'revealed' ideas of God, and secondly, that 'revealed' theology could and should be shown to cohere with reason. Indeed, for Wolff, a theologian could or should be able to demonstrate rationally that any given revelation 'beyond reason' was necessary for human salvation and well-being.

In some ways, Wolff's was not a particularly radical or new position. It was, as we shall see, controversial in its particular context; but the coherence of reason and revelation, and the idea that (at least to some extent) reason enabled human beings to recognise the 'rightness' or 'fittingness' of revelation, had a long history. However, at least some of his successors drew more radical conclusions from his thought and argued that numerous doctrines thought to be part of 'revealed' Christianity must be rejected as contrary to reason or to the well-being of humanity. (We discuss the development of the latter group of arguments – attacking Christian doctrines as dangerous to humanity's well-being – in Chapter 17.)

Wolff's starting-point was the coherence of 'natural' and 'revealed' religion. However, the late seventeenth and eighteenth centuries also saw the development of a view of 'natural religion' that set it over *against* 'revealed religion'. This is the approach known as **deism**. A few very well-known deist texts, and the whole idea of 'deism', aroused enormous controversy – to the point where it is hard to tell how important an influence deism actually had on religious thought.

Against religion? Deism, atheism, anti-clericalism

The first known use of the word 'deism' is from sixteenth-century France. The idea of deism did not, however, come to prominence until the late seventeenth and eighteenth centuries. As with all such terms, the definition of deism is controversial. In general, deism is associated with the attempt to develop a religion of reason, based solely on 'nature', a religion that would be universally acceptable to rational persons, and in accord with a fully rational morality and politics.

Deist thought involved direct opposition to Christianity and its institutions, including its political institutions. For the deists, *all* (so-called) revealed religion was an unacceptable addition to, and corruption of, rational belief. For John Toland – generally accepted as a prominent English deist, although his exact beliefs and aims at different stages of his career are uncertain – this meant that Christianity could only be 'true religion' if all claims contrary to reason or exceeding the scope of reason were eliminated from it. This is the argument of his most famous or notorious work, *Christianity Not Mysterious* (1696).

Note that although Toland's work was attacked as anti-Christian, he used the terms 'Christianity' and 'Gospel' positively, to denote the true religion of reason. At other times in his life, he more clearly identified himself as a Christian, explaining and defending the rationality of (a particular reading of) Christianity.

In England, there was an enormous outpouring of anti-Deist writings in the period we are discussing. Deism, as an attack on Christian institutions and traditions, was perceived and presented in public as a major religious, political and social threat. 'Atheism', likewise, was identified and attacked as a threat – although there are very few authors from this period who explicitly claimed not to believe in God. The political dimensions of the controversies are easier to see in a context where the state and the Church are closely allied – and where the Church has come to be more closely associated with its beliefs. An attack on religious belief could be portrayed as an attack on state and public order – and, indeed, vice versa. When eighteenth-century English Church leaders talked about the dangers of 'atheism', they were as likely to be talking about young upper-class men behaving badly, threatening public order and ignoring the needs of the state, as about philosophers who argued against the existence of God.

In France, eighteenth-century deism and atheism is most closely associated with the *philosophes* – a term that simply means 'philosophers', but in this context refers to a more diverse grouping of intellectuals who wrote and spoke on political, social and religious themes. Voltaire (real name François-Marie Arouet, 1694–1778), Denis Diderot (1713–1784) and Jean-Jacques Rousseau (1712–1778) are the best-known figures associated with this 'movement' – although, especially given the very strong disagreements between Rousseau and his fellow *philosophes*, it would be wrong to describe it as a coherent school of thought.

Figure 2.1 Voltaire

Voltaire's criticisms of Christian irrationality and 'superstition', and his writings in favour of religious toleration, are among the most famous products of the French Enlightenment. He perceived the French regime of his day – a monarchy supported by, and supporting, the Catholic Church hierarchy, frequently suppressing religious and political dissent – as a barrier to the rational and peaceful progress of humanity. His slogan *'écrasez l'infâme'* – 'destroy the infamous' – may have referred to religious 'superstition' in general or to the French political and religious establishment in particular. Anti-clericalism, his opposition to the power of the clergy, is a powerful theme in his writings.

One of Voltaire's best-known quotations is: 'I disagree with what you say, but I will defend to the death your right to say it.' Unfortunately, it appears that he did not actually say this (even if he had the right to say it).

He did write, speaking of religious difference in his essay *On Toleration*, that '[it] would be the height of folly to pretend to bring all men to have the same thoughts'.

He also wrote, 'If God did not exist, it would be necessary to invent him' (*Letter to the Authors of the Treatise of the Three Impostors*, 1762). He argued on several occasions that the preaching of Christianity to the uneducated classes was necessary to secure social order.

Voltaire was, on most definitions, a deist. He frequently affirmed his belief in God, and equally frequently affirmed his belief that religion could and should be fully rational. His attacks on the Church establishment, on the power of the clergy and on religious intolerance found widespread support among people who did not necessarily share his deism. In a context of religious plurality and conflict, there were many Christians who had a strong interest in promoting tolerance and criticising government attempts to control religion. For example, the Jansenists, a reforming movement within Catholicism, gained widespread support across French society in the eighteenth century, in the face of government and papal opposition. Voltaire's eloquent calls for religious toleration and scathing attacks on the religious establishment – like those of the English deists – resonated, at least, to some extent, with *religious* dissenters.

The relationship between 'deism' and the origins of the American Revolution is complex. Thomas Paine (1737–1809), one of the intellectual inspirations behind the Revolution, was a significant proponent of the 'religion of reason' against traditional and institutional Christianity (see for example his tract *The Age of Reason*, 1794). The term 'deist' has been applied to – and contested for – many of the Founding Fathers of the United States, including most notably, and plausibly, Thomas Jefferson. Benjamin Franklin stated in his autobiography that he had been convinced of the truth of deism by reading English anti-Deist sermons, 'for the arguments of the Deists, which were quoted to be refuted, appeared to be much stronger than the refutations'.

'Deism' is often also used to describe the thought of Hermann Samuel Reimarus (1694–1768). In works published during his lifetime, Reimarus defended the coherence of 'natural' and 'revealed' religion, but in a collection of 'fragments' published posthumously by Gotthold Lessing (the 'Wolfenbüttel Fragments', 1774) he argues that much of Christian revelation, as found in the Bible, is contrary to reason and must be rejected.

Reimarus' major influence on later theology came through these posthumous fragments, and related not so much to his idea of reason as to his view of history. The 'irrationality' of the Bible, as described in the Wolfenbüttel Fragments, lies in the implausibility of the events it claims to describe. In a 'fragment' on the Gospels, Reimarus argues that the New Testament's claims about the miracles and the divinity of Jesus have a plausible historical explanation – they are the creation of Jesus' disciples, a fraudulent attempt to conceal the failure of Jesus' mission and the disappointment of his hopes for the coming of God's kingdom. Although Reimarus' claims about deliberate falsification by Jesus' followers have rarely found much support, the methodological move he makes here – explaining the content of the Gospels by reference to the context and needs of the early Christian communities – has been enormously important for later biblical criticism. (See Chapter 10.)

Religion beyond reason

So a significant dimension of eighteenth-century religious thought was the drive to make religion rational or to establish in what respects it could be regarded as rational. There was, however, another side to religious development and innovation in this period – one that stood in some ways directly in opposition to the 'religion of reason', and was in other ways unexpectedly similar to it.

By the beginning of the eighteenth century, **Pietism** was firmly established as a major religious force in the German-speaking countries, and especially in Prussia. Developing from the ministry and writings of Philipp Jakob Spener (1635–1705), the Pietist movement emphasised individual prayer and devotion, the conversion experience and the feeling of inner, **subjective**, religious certainty. Roughly speaking, Pietists were concerned about the 'faith by which I believe', in contrast to the scholastic emphasis on the 'faith [content] that is believed'. Equally, however, they were concerned about the implications of Christian faith for the moral life; the Pietist was encouraged to make the whole of his or her life holy.

Spener and his followers encouraged the study of the Bible and the formation of small groups ('conventicles') meeting usually in private houses for prayer, Bible study and reflection on Christian life. In fact, besides its theological significance, Pietism was a significant social movement. Pietist 'conventicles' and the connections between them proved to be major sites of social and political influence; Pietism was particularly popular with the educated middle classes. Calls for social and political reform during this period were often associated with Pietist groups. Notably, Pietist conventicles were one context in which women could develop their interpretations of the Bible, lead worship and participate in debate.

As we will see, Pietism was an influence on the thought of many of the nineteenth century's major theologians. But was Pietism *for* or *against* the Enlightenment? On the one hand, it was often explicitly anti-rational, downplaying the role of reason in religion and emphasising instead emotional conviction and the non-rational (or more-than-rational) act of individual faith. The most notorious example of Pietist anti-rationalism was the successful campaign by Pietist theologians to have Christian Wolff dismissed from his academic post, after the publication of his system of natural and revealed religion.

On the other hand, however, Pietism clearly represents another form of the modern 'turn to the subject' – with its intense interest in the individual person's faith, emotions, devotional practice and way of life. The movement was also perceived – both by its opponents and by many of its adherents – as being opposed to traditional patterns of religious authority (in particular, the close alliance of Church institutions with the state). Pietists were concerned about freedom, even if, unlike some of the Enlightenment thinkers, they saw no need to equate freedom with some particular model of reason.

Other major religious developments in the eighteenth century stand in a similar tension to the central themes of the Enlightenment. In England, from the 1730s onwards, the phenomenon initially called the 'Evangelical Revival' led to the emergence of Methodism. John Wesley (1703–1791) described his own 'conversion' experience in a famous passage that sets the tone for the Methodist movement:

> I went very unwillingly to a society ... where one was reading Luther and preface to the Epistle to the Romans. About a quarter to nine, while he was describing the change which God works in the heart through faith in Christ, I felt my heart strangely warmed. I felt I did trust in Christ, Christ alone for salvation, and an assurance was given me that he had taken away my sins, even mine and saved me from the law of sin and death.
>
> John Wesley, *Journal*, vol 1, pp449–484;
> reprinted in Albert C. Outler (ed.),
> *John Wesley* (Oxford: Oxford University Press, 1980, p68).

Note how central *feeling* is to Wesley's 'conversion'. He was, at this time, an ordained priest of the Church of England, with a thorough training in theology and philosophy; the experience he describes added nothing to his knowledge of central Christian doctrines, and he does not describe it in terms of new rational understanding. What comes to him for the first time, according to Wesley, is the 'assurance' that these doctrines apply to him; and this assurance is given through what might be described as emotional experience.

It was this kind of conversion – a change of 'heart' – that Wesley and the other preachers of the Methodist revivals invited and hoped for. Wesley preached to large crowds, often of mainly working-class people, proclaiming a universal offer of divine grace and calling on his hearers to accept it. Like the Pietists, Wesley saw the holy life – what he called 'Christian perfection' – as a consequence of conversion. He also established 'societies' for prayer, bible study and mutual support. His brother Charles (1707–1788) wrote hymns for the use of the Methodist societies that express equally clearly the nature of the faith around which Methodism centred – its intensely personal and emotional character, its focus on the assurance of God's forgiveness and its promise of holiness:

> Love divine, all loves excelling,
> joy of heaven, to earth come down;
> fix in us thy humble dwelling;
> all thy faithful mercies crown!
> Jesus thou art all compassion,
> pure, unbounded love thou art;
> visit us with thy salvation;
> enter every trembling heart ...
> Finish, then, thy new creation;
> pure and spotless let us be.
> Let us see thy great salvation
> perfectly restored in thee.
>
> Charles Wesley, 1747

The Wesleys' co-worker George Whitefield (1714–1770) conducted extensive preaching tours in America, and was among the leaders of the revival now known as the 'First Great Awakening'. In both Britain and America, the eighteenth-century revivals were major public events. The revival preachers, especially Whitefield, often attracted enormous audiences (contemporary reports suggested as many as 30,000 at one of Whitefield's sermons) and the reported effects of their preaching are dramatic both in scope and in nature. There were reports of thousands of people experiencing the 'new birth' of conversion; of extreme manifestations of emotion (fainting, uncontrollable weeping, outbursts of joy), and, particularly important to Wesley, of people whose lives were transformed into images of 'holiness'.

Figure 2.2 George Whitefield

The reasons for the success of the revival movements are complex. Theologically, we can see that the Protestant emphasis on individual faith – and on the necessary connection between salvation and faith – made the questions of what faith was, who had faith and how faith was acquired very pressing. Indeed, as we shall see, the revival movements themselves led to further controversy around these central questions of the nature of faith and salvation.

Socially, the revivals happened at a time when, in both Britain and America, there were particular reasons to be concerned about the state of Christian 'faith'. In America, the colonies founded on the Puritan ideal of a holy commonwealth – a political order formed by people who were 'saints', convinced Christians – now, one or two generations on, had many people who did not profess that personal conviction. In Britain, industrialisation was leading to movements of population, creating widespread concern about social unrest – and new working-class communities that were not served by existing Church structures.

Not surprisingly, there was extensive criticism of the revival movements. The accusation made most often was that these movements were mere enthusiasm. The word has a long history in Protestant polemics; Martin Luther used its German equivalent (*Schwärmerei*) to denounce the **Anabaptists** and other representatives of the '**Radical Reformation**' for their failure, as he saw it, to pay proper attention to scripture, reason or public order. For eighteenth-century critics of revivalism, 'enthusiasm' meant emotional religion that exceeded all limits – including the limits of reason and the limits of right belief. Many of the proponents of revivalism – including, notably, Jonathan Edwards, whose work we discuss below – were anxious to defend it against charges of 'enthusiasm' by demonstrating its coherence both with reason and with Christian tradition.

If it was not (all) about reason, was revivalism about *freedom?* Theologically, 'freedom' became a source of contention within the revival movement. George Whitefield entered public controversy with the Wesleys over their contention that people had the *free choice* to accept or to reject God's offer of salvation – a claim that they did not invent, but that (at least as Whitefield saw it) ran counter to a central Calvinist tenet, that the salvation of any person was eternally predestined by God and in no way dependent on human choices.

The Wesleys' position was often described, at least by their opponents (including Whitefield), as **Arminianism** – after Jacobus Arminius (1560–1609). Jonathan Edwards (see below) began his 'revival' preaching with a series of sermons against Arminianism.

More generally, the revivals could be read as a triumph of freedom – freedom for individuals to live transformed lives, freedom from the limits of existing Church structures and of rationalising accounts of Christian faith. They could also – by critics in their time and by many critics since – be read as suppressing freedom, precisely by downplaying people's rational faculties, and hence encouraging the uncritical acceptance of Christian claims (along with the personal authority of the preachers).

The relationship between the American revivals and the American Revolution is an area of continuing scholarly controversy, in which the meaning of 'freedom' – as it is enshrined in the founding documents of the United States – is a key issue. Alan Heimert, in *Religion and the American Mind: From the Great Awakening to the Revolution* (1969), argued that the revivals were directly linked to the Revolution, promoting a democratic spirit and an openness to social and political change. Highly controversial in its time, Heimert's thesis continues to be both attacked and defended. There are many issues at stake, about the role of religious ideas in political history, about the ways in which ideas have 'influence' – and, perhaps most importantly, about the relationships between the story of modernity, the story of the United States and the story of evangelical Christianity.

Jonathan Edwards (1703–1758) was best known in his lifetime as a preacher in, and public defender of, the revivals in New England. His reputation as a theologian grew after the posthumous publication of many of his theological works – though it still stands alongside his fame, or notoriety, as a 'hell-fire preacher'. Edwards offers the best example of an *intellectual* theological defence of the 'emotional' phenomenon of the revivals – one that sought to engage with Enlightenment criteria of knowledge and rationality. For Edwards, the central transformation that occurs with the gift of faith is not simply of the mind and understanding, nor simply of the emotions, but of the *affections* – the direction of a person's love. Put more simply, to receive the divine gift of faith is to love God. Love, Edwards argued, is closely bound up with knowledge and perception; we cannot love something without perceiving and understanding it in a certain way. Nonetheless, love is not only a matter of right understanding; one can know, as it were theoretically, that something is good or valuable, without loving it.

In Edwards' work, the love people have for God is linked to their perceiving, and rejoicing in, God's glory and beauty – a glory and beauty that is reflected in the natural order, as well as in God's ordering of human lives, communities and history. Edwards has, in other words, an account of 'natural theology' and he believes it is possible to give a reasoned account of how God's glory can be seen in the natural and human worlds.

Thinking about 'beauty' can be a way to bring together the reason and the emotions, as ways of knowing and relating to the world – at least if you accept, as Edwards (and his contemporaries) thought you had to, that beauty is not *only* in the eye of the beholder. Beauty also has to be related to the emotions and affections; to call something beautiful is to *feel* a certain way about it, to be affected by it in a certain way. But it is also possible to discuss, explain, or reason about, what makes something beautiful. Kant's work (see Chapter 3) also finds in aesthetic judgements – judgements about beauty and taste – a way beyond some of the oppositions of the Enlightenment.

However, Edwards entirely rejects the idea that human beings can do anything, or know anything, *for themselves* that will help to bring them to the true love of God. So simply being presented with a reasoned account of how God can be known, understanding it and accepting it as true, would not, in itself, give someone the 'faith' associated with salvation, the love of God for which humanity is intended. That faith remains, for Edwards, a gift of God – and God's own 'glory', displayed as justice, requires God to condemn and destroy whatever is opposed to God, including the faithless human being.

> Edwards is still best known for his sermon 'Sinners in the Hands of an Angry God' (1741), focused on human beings' absolute inability to save themselves:
>
>> [W]hatever pains a natural man takes in religion, whatever prayers he makes, till he believes in Christ, God is under no manner of obligation to keep him a moment from eternal destruction. So that, thus it is that natural men are held in the hand of God, over the pit of hell; they have deserved the fiery pit, and are already sentenced to it; and God is dreadfully provoked ... the devil is waiting for them, hell is gaping for them, the flames gather and flash about them ... they have no refuge, nothing to take hold of ...
>>
>> Johnathan Edwards, 1741; reprinted in *Sinners in the Hands of an Angry God and Other Puritan Sermons* (Mineola, NY: Dover, 2005).
>
> By way of contrast, here is his description of what his wife Sarah (*née* Pierpoint, 1710–1758) experienced following her conversion during the revivals:
>
>> Where the affections of admiration, love, and joy, so far as another could judge, have been raised to the highest pitch ... the soul has been as it were perfectly overwhelmed, and swallowed up with light and love, a sweet solace, and a rest and joy of soul altogether unspeakable ... So that (to use the person's own expressions) the soul remained in a kind of heavenly elysium, and did as it were swim in the rays of Christ's love, like a little mote swimming in the beams of the sun that come in at a window. The heart was swallowed up in a kind of glow of Christ's love coming down as a constant stream of sweet light, at the same time the soul all flowing out in love to him ...
>>
>> Jonathan Edwards, *Some Thoughts Concerning the Present Revival of Religion in New England*, 1742 book 1, section 5. Reprinted in *The Works of Jonathan Edwards*, vol 1 (Edinburgh: Banner of Truth Trust, 1974).

Telling the story

This chapter was intended to give you some sense of where the thinkers we discuss in the rest of this book were 'coming from', what problems they were seeking to address and how their central concerns were affected by a long social, political and intellectual history. Inevitably, our account of the eighteenth century has been highly selective, as is our account of the long nineteenth century and of subsequent theological development. If you imagine trying to write a narrative of the factors affecting religious thought in our own time – even if you limit it to just one country – you will gain some sense of the level of selection and omission that has been necessary. Before beginning our detailed accounts of the long nineteenth century, we suggest that you reflect on the project we are engaged in – trying to understand the history of religious thought – and how it interacts with other aspects of history.

Look back over our chapter and consider what aspects of eighteenth-century history we have focused on and which we have omitted. What have we omitted that might be relevant to understanding the religious thought of the time? What might have influenced or been influenced by theological developments?

Here are some examples of areas we have not discussed and of what might have been discussed within them:

- Exploration and colonisation by European countries: James Cook's voyages to New Zealand and Australia (1768–1771); conflicts between Britain and France over trading rights and influence in India; war in Canada (Battle of Quebec, 1759).
- Technology: James Watt's development of steam engines (1760s onwards).
- Literature: Daniel Defoe's *Robinson Crusoe* (1719), Henry Fielding's *Tom Jones* (1749), Pierre Choderlos de Laclos' *Les Liaisons Dangereuses* ('Dangerous Liaisons') (1782).
- Music: Transition from the baroque to the classical era; Johann Sebastian Bach (1685–1750), Wolfgang Amadeus Mozart (1756–1791).
- Architecture: The development of *neoclassical* architecture from the mid-eighteenth century.

Bibliography

James Byrne, *Glory, Jest and Riddle: Religious Thought in the Enlightenment* (London: SCM, 1996). Very readable account, focused on issues of religion and reason; the best starting-point for studying this period.

Carter Lindberg (ed.), *The Pietist Theologians: An Introduction to Theology in the Seventeenth and Eighteenth Centuries* (Oxford: Blackwell, 2005). Includes chapters on Wesley and Puritan theologians, as well as European Pietists. Note the large number of female theologians discussed.

Karl Barth, *Protestant Theology in the Nineteenth Century*, Chapters 1–6. See previous chapter's Bibliography for comments on the importance of this work. Barth offers a particularly useful introduction to rationalism and Pietism in Germany.

Carl R. Trueman and R. Scott Clark, *Protestant Scholasticism: Essays in Reassessment, Studies in Christian Thought and History* (Milton Keynes and Waynsboro: Paternoster, 1999).

Robert Jenson, *America's Theologian: A Recommendation of Jonathan Edwards* (Oxford: Oxford University Press, 1988). As the title suggests, an accessible introduction to Edwards that is also an argument for his theological importance.

Henry Rack, *Reasonable Enthusiast: John Wesley and the Rise of Methodism* (London: Epworth Press, 1989). See especially the Prelude, on the religious context of eighteenth-century England.

Section A

Key Thinkers

In this first section, we introduce the work of seven thinkers from the 'long nineteenth century'. These are people whose ideas and writings have set the agenda for academic theology into the twentieth and twenty-first centuries. We also want to argue, however, that the questions they raise and the ways they deal with them are of very wide importance, beyond universities and beyond churches. Studying these thinkers helps us to see how today's everyday assumptions were formed – particularly around the themes of freedom, reason, history, knowledge of God and the criticism of religion.

You will see that the first five chapters in this section discuss thinkers from very similar social and church contexts. All of them are Western European Protestants, four of them are German-speaking. Moreover, all of them are men and all are highly educated at a time when access to education was much more limited than it is now. They cannot possibly tell the 'whole story' of religious thought in the long nineteenth century. We have chosen to focus on them because we think that – for better or worse – it is their social and academic tradition that has made the most difference to subsequent theology, certainly in the North and the West and hence (to some extent) worldwide. Theirs is the story of modern theology that has most often been told, retold, revisited, criticised and conversed with. You need to understand their story in order to understand what has happened since.

In the following two chapters, however, we introduce some of the other stories that have helped to shape modern theology and some of the different perspectives that might emerge if we focused on them instead of on the established 'key thinkers'. We hear voices from outside Europe, outside the Protestant churches, outside the educated elite. In Section B, when we begin to consider broader themes in modern theology, more of these 'other' voices can be heard.

One of our aims in this section is to enable you to work with confidence with the primary texts – the writings of our 'key thinkers'. We do not intend our chapters to be substitutes for reading what these thinkers actually wrote. Studying theological and philosophical writing from the 'long nineteenth century' is challenging, particularly when you have to read at least some of the texts in translation. However, it is an essential part of understanding modern theological thought. Many of these texts are classics, by which we mean not just 'texts everyone ought to read' but 'texts that go on generating new meaning and new conversations'. We have included a range of 'reading aids' in these chapters, such as notes on vocabulary and structure, and exercises designed to help you to analyse complex texts.

3

Immanuel Kant

AIMS

By the end of this chapter, we hope that you will:

- understand why Kant is important for religious thought after the Enlightenment

- know about his approach to philosophy, how he applies it to religion and what the results are – in particular, the relationship between morality and religion in his thought, and his objections to arguments for the existence of God

- have thought about the implications of his work for modern understandings of what religion is, and how it relates to the public sphere.

Introduction

Immanuel Kant (1724–1804) led a notoriously dull life, but he lived in exciting times, when the modern West – its ideals, its political forms and its understanding of human life – took shape. As a thinker in and of those times, Kant has probably been more influential on modernity and postmodernity than any other philosopher. His thought on religion is no exception; although few would describe him as a theologian, modern theology has been decisively shaped by his work.

Kant's life work was to think through the implications of the philosophical moves made by Enlightenment thinkers in the eighteenth century. He spelled out the philosophical justification for, and implications of, these moves, and explored their limitations. In doing this, he developed the work of many others – Descartes, Rousseau, Locke, Hume and others – but went beyond them in important respects.

Kant has been called 'the philosopher of the French Revolution', and it is important to read his work as emerging from a context of revolution – and also from a context shaped by a recent history of religious war. Dramatic political, social and religious change, planned and executed to fit with *ideas* about how human society should work, had become possible in Kant's time to an extent and on a scale that had never been seen before. Philosophy and theology were both significantly intertwined with politics and, as we shall see, Kant was treated, at times, as politically dangerous.

When we consider Kant's thought on religion, it is important to look at the political aspects of what he says. He was particularly influential in shaping the modern relationship between religion and politics, or religion and 'public life' more generally. Contemporary debates about the place of religion in the state, in education, in ethical arguments and so forth, take place in the context that Kant's thought created. We will explore this further in the exercise at the end of this chapter.

Figure 3.1 Immanuel Kant

Before studying Kant's thought, it is worth knowing about one major religious influence on him – and on several of the other thinkers studied in the first section of this book. Kant was brought up in a devout Pietist family. Pietism was an enormously influential religious movement in the German-speaking countries in the eighteenth century – particularly among the middle classes. It emphasised individual conversion, moral integrity and personal religious experience of an intensely emotional kind. Kant, as we shall see, retained some Pietist themes in his religious thought, while deliberately distancing himself from others.

Kant's key works

- He is best known for the 'three critiques': *Critique of Pure Reason* (1781), *Critique of Practical Reason* (1788), *Critique of Judgement* (1790).
- *Groundwork for the Metaphysics of Morals* (1785) – the source of the famous 'categorical imperative'; also important for his religious thought.
- Numerous shorter political essays, including 'An Answer to the Question "What is Enlightenment?"' (1784).
- *Religion within the Limits of Reason Alone* (1793) – his most controversial work, which led to his being forbidden by the King of Prussia to write on religious questions.
- *The Conflict of the Faculties* (1795) – written in the wake of that controversy and representing an indirect response to it.

Kant's situation: the problem of speaking in public

The Enlightenment, the 'age of reason', had much to do with creating new kinds of public space where 'men of reason' explored ideas and decided together how to order their societies. (We say 'men' deliberately, although the participation of women in those spaces was already a matter for debate – see the discussion of Mary Wollstonecraft in Chapter 9.) In these public spaces, what mattered was not whether an idea fitted with some existing traditional scheme, but whether it met with the requirements of reason. Reason was assumed, by its nature, to cross all sorts of boundaries – geographical, temporal and religious; any 'rational being' from any country or community could take part in the discourses of reason.

Kant's essay 'An Answer to the Question "What is Enlightenment?"' (1784) sets out one vision of what this idea of 'universal reason' might mean for society. Kant presents a vision of Enlightenment as a social and political project – with freedom at its centre, and religion as the key area in which freedom needs to be worked out. It was written in a 'revolutionary' context – between the American and the French

Revolutions, at a time when the power of Enlightenment thought to shape political relationships was a major issue.

> The Enlightenment set up a basic dichotomy – an either-or for thought – that was social and political as well as intellectual. When you make a claim, are you basing it on *universal, public reason(s)* that any rational person can share; or on reasons that come from some particular community or tradition?
>   Note some features of this dichotomy:
>
> - It is, of course, not value-neutral and it had major political implications. The philosophers of the Enlightenment saw 'universal reason' as the future of society and of humanity.
> - 'Universal reason', although it sounds as if it should be *communal* (because everyone can, in principle, follow and agree with it), is in fact very focused on the *individual*. For the purposes of universal reason, it does not matter whether you are part of any particular community, or any community at all. Thinking on your own, for yourself, you can come to the same conclusions as any other rational being.
> - In fact, you will have to distance yourself from your community and its traditions – from all sources of knowledge that might not be accepted by 'any rational being' – in order to enter the new 'rational' public space.

In his essay, Kant famously sums up Enlightenment in the Latin motto *Sapere aude* – 'dare to know'. He glosses this as 'have the courage to use your own reason' – and refuse to let anyone else think on your behalf. His essay contrasts (on the one hand) freedom, maturity and reason, with (on the other hand) imprisonment, immaturity and irrationality. The challenge he puts to the rulers of his day is 'allow the people to grow up, by giving them the freedom to reason for themselves'.

What does 'reason' have to do with 'freedom'? As Kant sees it, we are most truly ourselves when we are most free; freedom is central to what it means to be human. The freedom that matters most here is freedom from external constraints on the exercise of reason – including, and especially, practical reason, moral decision-making. It is the freedom that you have when 'nobody is telling you what to do', 'nobody is forcing you to do anything' – and when you are not being swayed by your emotions, or by anything else that is subject to external pressure. At that point, you are free to think for yourself – and you can be rational.

There are, obviously, social and political conditions that encourage this kind of freedom, and Kant explores them in the essay. For example, there have to be public spaces that are not subject to censorship or other forms of imposed constraint on speech and reasoning; there have to be places where 'nobody is telling you what to say' and 'nobody is telling you what to think'. Freedom is also, however, a condition of the mind; you have to learn to be 'free' from external pressures and to use your own reason. In this sense we can say that adults are more free than children, and educated people are more free than less educated people – always assuming that education is training in the use of reason, rather than training in compliance with a defined set of external authorities.

We will see, later in the chapter, what all of this means for the social and political place of religion. First, however, we need to look more closely at the nature of 'universal reason'. It is all very well to say that we should use reasons that are acceptable to 'any rational being' and not accept arguments that are based on traditional authority. But what kinds of reasons *are* acceptable to any rational being? What sorts of things can and should we all agree on, and how does that agreement arise from our reason? Recent advances in the natural sciences seemed to show that reason was capable of producing agreement about all kinds of claims about the physical and natural world. But is reason capable of producing agreement about religion, or about morality, or about politics? To answer these kinds of question, Kant embarked on a *critique* of reason – an attempt to ask how reason works, what its limits are and what kinds of agreement it can and can't produce. He asked, how do we, as rational beings, know anything and how can we be sure of our knowledge?

These are the questions that animate Kant's major works and to which we now turn.

How Kant thinks

How do we know anything and how can we be sure of our knowledge? Kant focuses on the aspects of these questions that relate to the knower. He is interested in what it means to say that we are 'rational beings' and what that implies about 'what we can all agree on'. In this, he thinks through, and within, what is often referred to as the 'turn to the subject' in modernity. Modern thought – here understood broadly, from the Reformation onwards – is interested in understanding human beings as thinkers, knowers and agents. Modern thinkers ask questions, not just (or not mainly) about 'what there is' and 'what happens', but about 'who knows what there is (and how)' and 'who acts (and how)'.

As we saw in the introduction, the eighteenth century produced a range of answers to the question 'how do we know?' Kant rejects the idea, which he found in the empiricist philosophers of the eighteenth century (Hume, Locke), that we are mainly passive recipients of sensations from the outside world. But he is also very sceptical about the rationalist idea that we have innate knowledge, accessed through reason.

Kant's breakthrough is to focus on how the mind processes and organises the sensations it receives from the outside world. He argues that there are some general structures of thought that are necessary for us to be able to think about, understand or conceptualise anything at all. These general structures are shared by *all* rational beings; they constitute the rational mind.

Notes on terminology:

- Kant's very famous and influential method for investigating any aspect of human thought or experience is the **transcendental** method. Looking at some specific thought, concept or experience, he asks 'what has to be there for this thought, concept or experience to be possible? What are its preconditions?' 'Transcendental' should not be confused with the more commonly-used theological term, 'transcendent'. It has a specific meaning and application in Kant's philosophy and in works that draw on Kant's philosophy, and is not usually found anywhere else.
- What we are calling 'general structures of thought' have several different names in Kant's philosophy because they work in several different ways. (The differences are not relevant to our discussion here, which is why we have employed a catch-all term.) For example, in the literature on Kant, you may find references to 'categories' and 'necessary postulates [of reason]' – both of which are 'general structures' of the kind described here.

How does this work? For example, you can think about (imagine, describe, define) all sorts of different objects, but you cannot think about any objects at all without thinking about them taking up space. 'Space' is an idea that you need in order to think about objects. You cannot think about, or experience, 'space itself' in the way that you think about or experience 'objects in space' (you cannot draw a picture of or measure 'space itself'). But you cannot make sense of the world without some kind of understanding of 'space' and how it works. (We do not, for instance, Kant says, learn *from experience* that two objects cannot occupy the same space, or that an object cannot be in two places at once; we have those ideas already in place, and we use them to interpret our experience.) By analysing how you think about objects-in-space, you can say a bit about how 'space' works.

Here is another example, more relevant to Kant's ideas on religion. Consider the relationship between cause and effect. Hume argued that we get our ideas of cause and effect from experience; we see that one event consistently follows another and we learn to associate them and give the name of 'cause and effect' to that association.

Kant suggests that this is not how it works; we have a *prior* idea of 'cause and effect' and we use this to explain what we observe.

As a third example, the key general structure that makes *moral* or *practical* reasoning possible is 'free will'. We do not learn by experience that we have free will; we simply act on the 'assumption' that we have free will. As we will see, this is particularly important for Kant's religious thought, it will be discussed in more detail later.

The first important point about Kant's general structures – such as space, cause and effect and free will – is that they are features *of the mind*, not of the world.

What does this mean? First, that we cannot get away from them. We cannot just decide to stop perceiving the world in terms of space, time, cause and effect and so forth, and we cannot just decide to stop acting as if we have free will. Without these general structures, we could not experience anything, think about anything or do anything.

The fact that these general structures are features of our minds means, second, that they themselves are not usually open to our critical examination; our minds do not automatically notice them. We do not usually think *about* these general structures, we think *through* them. They are not objects of thought, they are what we use to think with. You do not, ordinarily, see 'space', you see how different objects move or are positioned in space. You do not ask yourself 'am I free to choose what I do?', you ask yourself 'should I do this or that?'

But, third, because these general structures are features of the mind and not of the world, we sometimes *need* to be aware of them, so that we are not misled about the world. The fact that we 'cannot get away from them' does not mean that they correspond to anything outside us. We are going to make mistakes if we start to think and act as if these features of our minds are features of the real world. So it is useful to develop an awareness of what our general structures of thought are, how they work, and how they shape our knowledge. This is the critique that Kant undertakes.

I am very short-sighted and have severe astigmatism; luckily, I have glasses. Without my glasses, the world would be a meaningless blur to me. I do not *see* my glasses when I am wearing them. Normally, I forget that they are there and get on with seeing the world through them.

But, as with Kant's general structures of thought, if I forget *completely* that my glasses are there, and start to think that everything I see is an effect of the world rather than an effect of my glasses, I could start jumping to false conclusions. If I see a large dark spot on the wall, I should probably check that my glasses are clean before I reach for the scrubbing-brush, and if that road-sign looks fuzzier this week than it did last week, I should probably seek help from my optician rather than from the city council.

> Kant's insight is that all rational thinking and perceiving occurs through 'glasses'. All our experience comes to us filtered through the 'lenses' of reason. We cannot take these glasses off. But we can understand a bit about how they work and thus we can stop ourselves reaching false conclusions about the world beyond the lenses.

The second important point about Kant's general structures is that they are features of any and every rational mind, not contingently (i.e. it does not 'just happen' by coincidence or by historical accident that we all think the same way) but necessarily (i.e. to have these general structures *is* just what it means to be rational). So, our individual reasoners leave their particular traditions and communities behind and come into the new, Enlightenment, public square to work out what they have in common. And they discover that what they have in common is the way their reasoning minds work.

> Here the 'glasses' analogy breaks down. My glasses only affect me. But for Kant, everyone sees the world through the same 'lenses'. In fact, that is the *only* thing we all have in common.

But this in turn seems to mean that reason – universal public reason – cannot tell us anything about the world as it actually *is*, it can only tell us about how and why things *appear* to us. We cannot think outside or beyond our reasoning minds and so there is no way to reach reliable conclusions, conclusions that everyone can accept, about what is 'really there'. There is an unbridgeable gulf between 'things as they appear to us' and 'things as they are in themselves'. (For a more extended discussion of all this, see Allen Wood, *Kant* (Oxford: Blackwell, 2005), Chapter 3.)

Here is another way of looking at the limits of Kantian reason: we can agree, in Kant's public sphere, on anything that has to do with how reason works. We can get a long way, for example, with agreeing procedures for rational decision-making. We can also say quite a lot about what is *not* a 'reason-able' subject, something about which it is not possible to agree. If you imagine the Enlightenment public sphere as a meeting, Kant's version of reason will give you a clear (if short) agenda and a clear set of rules for how to run the meeting. What has been up for debate since Kant is whether, and how, reason on its own will let you reach any substantive conclusions within the meeting.

How Kant thinks about religion

What can't be said

One of the biggest issues on Kant's own agenda, for many reasons, was religion. There are two main reasons for this. First, Kant believed that 'reason' had much to say about religion, both negatively and positively. Bad religion was an enemy of reason, but reason could reform religion. Religion (both its doctrines and its institutions) had many elements that *could not* be 'reasonable' and some that might impede the proper use of reason, but also (as we have already seen) elements that were closely linked to reason.

Second, Kant's Europe had been shaped by the wars of religion after the Reformation and by the peace settlements that enshrined the principle of *cuius regio, eius religio* ('whose region, his religion' or 'for each region, its own religion'). In the sixteenth and seventeenth centuries, it was widely assumed that a ruler had the power to determine the religion of the people within his jurisdiction; a Lutheran monarch would be the head of a Lutheran state, and so forth. It was also assumed that rulers must protect the rights of religious minorities within their states. In Kant's Prussia there was still a very close connection between religion and state power. The (Lutheran) clergy were servants of the state and monarchs would take action to maintain and enforce religious orthodoxy within the 'official' Church. Kant himself later fell foul of the Prussian state for his views on religion. In this context, the development of new public spaces where matters of religion were debated according to principles of 'universal reason' was politically controversial.

So, where does Kant's account of 'reason' leave knowledge of God? Traditionally, God is 'located' *beyond* the forms of knowledge that we have just been discussing. For example, God is not in space, not in time and not part of the inner-worldly chains of cause and effect. So if we cannot know or understand anything without general structures like space, time and cause and effect, how can we claim to know or understand God?

Kant, in fact, uses his way of looking at reason to demolish certain traditional 'proofs' of the existence of God, in particular, the cosmological argument. This is, roughly, the argument that reasons from the chains of cause and effect within the world to a 'First Cause'. Kant argues that, to make this argument work, we need to treat 'cause and effect' as a real property of things 'out there', and not just a property of the mind; and that we have, and can have, no basis on which to do that.

> Back to the glasses analogy: Kant thinks that arguing from our understanding of cause and effect to God as First Cause is a bit like me, wearing my dirty glasses, speculating about who might have put that spot on the wall. It is based on the false assumption that a feature of how we know things is a feature of the things that we know.

Furthermore, Kant notes that we do not need to believe in a First Cause to be able to make sense of our experience in terms of cause and effect. The First Cause is not itself a general structure of thought, nor is it an essential aspect of our thinking about 'cause and effect'. This is going to be important when we look at the 'argument for the existence of God' that Kant *is* prepared to use.

Notice, before we move on, what has happened here. In pre-modern Christian thought, *God* was the source of space, time and cause-and-effect, but Kant has made *the mind* the source of space, time and cause-and-effect. He does not say 'there's nothing real out there' or 'it's all in your mind' but he does say that you cannot move from your perceptions of order, in the way you experience the world, to any order that exists 'out there'.

What can be said

Can any more positive claims about God be made using Kant's approach? In Kant's outline of *Religion within the Limits of Reason Alone*, the 'reason' that is relevant to religion is not primarily reason about the world but reason about ourselves as moral agents.

So far, most of our examples of Kant's thought have related to our reasoning about 'what there is' – the material covered in his *Critique of Pure Reason*. But Kant also undertook the critique of 'practical reason', that is, reasoning about what we *do*, reasoning about morality. Here, too, he found general structures of thought that are 'built in' to the reasoning mind and are the necessary preconditions for all our particular ideas and decisions about right and wrong. And the idea of God is, for him, part of the general structures of thought that make morality possible.

How does this work? Anyone who has studied ethics has heard of Kant's *categorical imperative*. It has various formulations, one of the most famous being 'Act as if the maxim of your action were to become through your will a general law' – very roughly, 'act as everyone ought to act'. For our purposes, the important point is not the content or the consequences of the categorical imperative, but the fact that it exists at all. Kant thinks that there is an 'ought' (an *imperative*) built into the structure of the reasoning mind (the *categories*). We are inescapably subject to an 'ought', to which our reason leads us and which our reason will not let us ignore. And this – remembering our discussion above – is a *universal* 'ought', just because it comes from reason. Each rational person can and should discover this moral 'ought' for herself, but when she discovers it, she discovers something that is equally binding on her and on every other rational being. An action or a principle of action only counts as 'moral', Kant says, if it can be recognised as universally binding in this way.

For example: I tell a lie, and feel guilty about it even if nobody ever finds out. The fact that I feel guilty tells you that I have a sense that there is a moral order, a set of moral claims on me, a set of 'oughts' and that I do not have the freedom simply to change those 'oughts'.

Nobody, in this example, has imposed moral guilt on me from outside. My perception of what I 'ought' to do has come from my own free reasoning. As a free and rational being, I can work out this law for myself. But when I work it out, I perceive it as a genuine constraint on my actions, not something I just made up. And I recognise it as an 'ought' that is binding on any and every moral being, not just on me. When I say 'lying is wrong', I do not just mean 'I, personally, shouldn't lie' but 'nobody should lie'.

One of the important consequences of this line of thought is that, for Kant, morality is something about which we *can* say at least something 'in public'. The general structures of reason that we all share *will* enable us to agree on (a limited range of) moral claims. We can get to these moral claims by understanding our own reasoning minds, without having to bring in any assumptions about the 'world out there'. As you will see if you study Kant's ethics and its interpretation, there is considerable debate about just how far the 'categorical imperative' and associated ideas will take you into substantive moral reasoning. The point is simply that morality, for Kant, is firmly on the public 'agenda', and this, for Kant, is how religion also comes onto that agenda.

How does this work? Belief in God, Kant says, arises from a tension within our moral experience, a tension that begins from our inescapable experience of the universal 'ought'. Here is how the tension arises:

- Kant thinks, first, that it is obvious that to say to someone 'you ought to do x' necessarily implies that they *can* do x. *Ought implies can.* For example, if I say to you 'you ought to give £100 to charity', I clearly believe that you have £100, otherwise what I am saying makes no sense.
- Now, that inescapable rational 'ought' – the one that comes to us when we recognise that a certain action is right or wrong – presents itself to us as something that 'ought' to be obeyed all the time, by everyone everywhere.
- But we know that we do not, and cannot, always obey the moral 'ought' – either because of the way the world is or because of the way we are.
- And we also know that even if we obey the moral 'ought', the world as a whole does not. Bad things happen to good people and our moral reason responds 'it's not fair – that ought not to happen'.

So we are caught in a contradiction. Logically, 'ought implies can', but there are real 'oughts' that seem impossible to fulfil. We know that we *ought* to do the right thing all the time and we also know that this is impossible. Likewise, goodness *ought* to be rewarded, but it is impossible to ensure that that happens. Both of these 'oughts' – our doing the right thing all the time and goodness always being rewarded – would only be possible if human beings and the world were changed radically.

There is another way to look at it. Without God, Kant thinks, we might end up having to choose between morality and happiness, with no prospect of ever reconciling the two. (The political activist can stand up against an unjust and powerful government and be tortured to death or she can give up her protest, co-operate with the regime and have a long and comfortable life.) But it is rational to want happiness and it is rational to want to be moral. Morality, with its unconditional 'ought', will always trump happiness (we can see that it is better for the activist to resist injustice, even at the cost of her happiness) but if we see someone having to choose between the two, we will be dissatisfied, and it will be reasonable for us to be dissatisfied. This is unless we believe that, beyond the present world, her good action will be rewarded with the happiness that is 'rightly' hers.

Of course, we might respond to that example by saying 'the answer to that problem is not to invent heaven for the dissident, but to reform the society'. And Kant is, in fact, very interested in social and political progress and the ways in which the enormous political changes in his day might make it easier for people to be both moral and happy. Some of his works express great political optimism. But he is still concerned, first, about where that leaves the individual in an unjust society (who will be dead long before her moral action reaps any earthly 'rewards' for her successors) and, second, about the fact that people still, despite everything (even in a reformed society), go on doing wrong and injustices still persist.

This in turn means, however, that for Kant what really matters about belief in God is justice done to the individual - the reward for moral goodness. He is still very interested in the idea of the perfectly just society, the society in which the moral law (which is the same as the 'will of God') is universally followed. But he does not need to believe that this society will really come about, only that God will reward people who live as members of this society. The 'kingdom of ends' – the perfectly moral society – is, in Kant's terms, a 'regulative ideal'. In other words, it is an ideal that people can think about and look towards when they make moral decisions, without needing or expecting it to exist in practice.

In fact, perfect goodness and the perfect reward for goodness would only be possible in a world that is in accord with the will of a perfectly good being. We ourselves lack the power to bring about that world, but the tension within our moral reason demands that that world should be possible. In order to stop our moral reasoning collapsing into contradiction, we need to believe that the world and human life *can* be reshaped according to the will of a perfectly good being. We need, in other words, to believe in God, whose will is to 'be done on earth as it is in heaven' (Matthew 6:10).

But how is this different from the 'cause and effect' example, discussed above? As Kant sees it, our everyday thinking about cause and effect gets on fine, is internally consistent and enables us to operate in the world, without a First Cause. By contrast, our thinking about right and wrong is liable to grind to a halt without a perfectly good being who is also the sovereign of the world.

It is important to realise that in Kant's work this is quite a strong claim. It means that belief in God is inescapable. Morality is universal – as we have seen, the categorical imperative is valid for all rational beings. It is 'subjective' to the extent that everything is 'subjective' for Kant (there is always a subject doing the knowing). But you do not 'make it up as you go along', and you cannot change it at will, it is part of the glasses you wear. You cannot opt out of rationality, you cannot opt out of *practical* reasoning (reasoning about what you ought to do) and so you cannot, without living in an intolerable rational contradiction, opt out of belief in God. This is something about which an Enlightened society, basing itself on reason, can properly agree.

> It is not difficult to see the traces of Kant's Pietist upbringing in his intense reverence for the dictates of conscience and the 'moral law', absolutely binding on each person and calling each person to a holy life. Famously, he wrote that genuine awe was inspired by 'the starry heavens above me and the moral law within me'.

But although it is strong, Kant's claim is also strictly limited – and it is not very surprising that it proved controversial. Belief in God, we have seen, arises from the general structures of thought – from the 'categorical imperative'. It is, to use the earlier analogy, part of the spectacles we wear. We cannot escape this belief, but we can have no knowledge of how, or indeed whether, it relates to things 'in themselves'. And why should the way our moral reasoning is constituted, and the belief in God that this necessarily produces in us, tell us anything about God as God really is?

A further problem is that 'reason alone', as we have discussed it so far, gives a very minimal account of God. God, according to reason, is the guarantor of the moral law, who rewards moral goodness beyond earthly existence, but we cannot deduce very much more about God from this line of reasoning. So, much of what Christians want to affirm about God is excluded from this account of religion: it is not material that an Enlightened society could properly agree about, so it can play no role in the rational, public ordering of such a society.

In *Religion within the Limits of Reason Alone*, Kant proposes that the gap between his religion arising from 'practical reason', and religious belief as we know it, is filled by **revelation**. Revelation, he argues, must be *compatible* with 'reason' in order to be recognisable and acceptable by rational beings, but it does not have to come 'within the limits of reason', it does not have to be *deducible* from reason. Furthermore, because Kant has restricted the powers of 'reason' so much, one could argue – and Kant did argue, in response to attacks on his work – that he has left room for the whole of traditional Christianity outside the 'limits of reason'.

Consider this in the context of Enlightenment philosophers' wholesale attacks on Christian particularity and historical revelation - the idea that the particular historical person Jesus of Nazareth, and the texts about him could define people's knowledge of God. Kant appears, at first glance, to have found a space for revelation even in the context of a 'religion of reason'. There are huge areas of religious life about which reason can say nothing, and that can proceed on the basis of revelation.

Nonetheless, the place of revelation remains ambivalent in this scheme. For Kant, the critical test of religious truth is still, always, universal reason, to which each individual has access by virtue of being a rational being. Universal reason 'trumps' particular revelation. So:

- revelation, to co-exist with universal reason, must make no claims that directly *contradict* it;
- and, where revelation and universal reason positively coincide (i.e. where revelation tells you something that your reason could have told you), universal reason is still the judge of particular revelation. For example, in Kant's under-standing of Christianity we accept Christ as the perfect moral exemplar, and become his followers, because our practical reason *tells* us that he is a moral exemplar. Particular revelation (Jesus Christ) is judged by universal reason (the moral law).

This may sound rather abstract, but it had important social, political and institutional consequences because, as we have already seen, the debate about what 'reason' could and could not do was also a debate about what 'reasons' could have power and authority in what contexts. In the next section, we look at how Kant's ideas about reason and revelation in religion contributed to the shaping of the modern state.

Religion and the state

We have already noted that Kant's essay 'An Answer to the Question "What is Enlightenment?"', in discussing the social and political forms of life in an 'age of enlightenment', focuses on religion as the key example of a sphere in which the role of public reason needs to be carefully defined. Here, and in his later essay on the 'Conflict of the Faculties', he sets out the place of religion according to the divisions established in his philosophical work. There is, for Kant, as we have seen, a part of religion that falls 'within the limits of reason alone', closely linked to moral reasoning; and there is a part that *cannot* be 'reasoned' about, but can only be believed on the basis of some external authority.

Now, this division of religion becomes, in 'What is Enlightenment?' and 'Conflict of the Faculties', a division of spheres of activity and a division of labour within the state. Very importantly, Kant maps this division within religion onto the division between the *private* and the *public*. As we have already suggested, for Kant to be 'public' is to speak and argue according to what can be accepted on the basis of reason; so whatever does not or will not subject itself to the criteria of reason is classed as 'private'. In 'private', Kant says, people can subject themselves to external authorities, and can make and defend 'irrational' claims, but if they want to speak and be heard in 'public', they must do so on 'enlightenment' terms, freely and in accordance with reason. You can, as it were, believe what you like and accept any authority you like, in your own home or your own little community, but you should not expect anyone else, anyone you might meet in the 'public' square, to automatically accept your beliefs as valid starting-points for an argument.

Notice, before we go on, what has happened to the church in this discussion. The church, for Kant, is a 'private' space, because it is a space within which arguments and claims can be based on something other than universal reason. The same, as we will see, can be said of any space – like, for example, a theology faculty – wherein the Church's claims are examined on their own terms. If religion is going to be discussed in public, that cannot mean in church!

What does this mean in a context in which, as we have seen, the state is closely linked to the Church? Note, first, that in Kant's vision of 'enlightenment' there is a certain tension in the idea of the state. The state makes laws and imposes them on people, which, on the face of it, prevents them from 'using their own reason'. This is necessary in order for social life to continue. Furthermore, Kant thinks that, in the interests of social order, the state might need at any given time to enforce laws that cannot be fully explained or justified in rational terms, or even to enforce laws that are contrary to universal reason. All of this seems to suggest that the state can have nothing to do with universal reason, and that the new Enlightenment 'public sphere' is bound to be critical of the state. In fact, state regulation is, in Kant's terms, concerned *only* with people's 'private' lives! (But remember that 'private' covers a very wide range here – it means everything that cannot be established on the basis of universal reason).

But, at the same time, Kant thinks that the state can and should be committed to preserving and strengthening a 'public sphere' for universal reason *for the state's own good*. The state needs to create a space where free reasoning is possible, where nobody dictates in advance what the conclusions of argument can and cannot be. It needs this so that it can itself gradually become more rational, so that its laws and policies can be brought into line with universal reason.

In the case of religion, Kant likewise believes that it is useful, often necessary in the interests of good order, for there to be regulation – for the state, or the state-run Church, to tell people what they may or may not say. The Church, as a 'private' sphere, can be regulated by the state. The king, he suggests in 'What is Enlightenment?', can legitimately tell clergy what they may and may not teach *in church*. What neither state nor Church should do, he thinks, is restrict freedom of thought and speech about religion *in public*. People should be free to argue in public about the Church's teachings, even if they are obliged to maintain the 'official' teachings in their sermons and services. In the long run, this will lead to revisions to the 'official' teachings, bringing them more into line with universal reason. Thus, Kant says, the enlightened ruler tells his subjects: 'Argue all you like and about whatever you like, but obey!'

> He uses the example of the army. Army officers, *as officers*, are obliged to obey all the king's orders, or the army cannot function. But, as long as they go on obeying the orders, they should be free to argue rationally and critically, in public, about whether the orders are good. That is the only way to ensure that good and rational orders are given in future.

We have suggested that, for Kant, it is in the state's interests actively to promote public and rational debate. Importantly, this might mean that the state sometimes has to act to defend the 'public sphere' against threats to its 'publicness' or its rationality. The state may have to limit the power and authority of the Church or similar bodies, in order to keep the 'public sphere' free from external and imposed authority. In modern states founded on the principles of Enlightenment – most notably France – we see the principle of 'secularity' legally enshrined and legally enforced. Appeals to religious authority are specifically and actively excluded from the public sphere.

For Kant in Prussia, however, there was no immediate prospect of a 'secular' state. We have seen that, for him, there needed to be public spaces in which religion could be freely discussed on 'rational' terms, rather than on the terms set out by a particular religious tradition. Where, in a state with an established Church, might such public spaces be found? This was a personal as well as a theoretical problem for Kant, whose 'space' for speaking and writing about religion was repeatedly under threat. After he published his *Religion within the Limits of Reason Alone*, he was forbidden by the King of Prussia to write on religious issues. His response to the ban is found in the essay published (with some shorter companion pieces) as 'The Conflict of the Faculties'.

The core essay in 'The Conflict of the Faculties' is a defence of the public space from which Kant himself wrote about 'religion within the limits of reason alone' – the philosophy faculty of a university. For Kant, the philosophy faculty is the space in which any and every subject, including religion, can and should be discussed from the perspective of universal reason. As such, and provided that it continues to do that job and no other, its work should not be regulated, censored or controlled by the state (so the state reaction to Kant's own writings was illegitimate). Rather, the state should protect the philosophy faculty, as a space from which further 'enlightened' reforms of the state and its institutions might come.

In Kant's university of Königsberg, as elsewhere, the philosophy faculty existed alongside a faculty of theology. Kant's argument for the philosophy faculty's freedom to reason about religion sits alongside a claim that the theology faculty is concerned with 'revealed' religion. The theology faculty's work – interpreting and transmitting revealed religion – lies outside the 'limits of reason alone', as Kant has defined them. Its work, therefore, is not 'public' in Kant's sense and, thus, may legitimately be regulated by the Church and the state.

While this division of 'religion' has many implications beyond the university, it is worth bearing it in mind as an important challenge *to* the university. Kant's understanding of the roles of the faculties – in particular, his idea of maintaining, within the university, a space free from, and critical of, religious traditions – helped to shape subsequent debates about the place of religion and theology in universities. As we shall see, this was a key issue that Schleiermacher confronted.

Table 3.1

Faculty	Philosophy	Theology
Main subject matter	'Pure religious faith' 'Natural' religion	'Ecclesiastical' faith 'Revealed' religion
Main source of authority	Practical reason	Bible and tradition
Sees religion as ...	Universal Moral	Particular, historical Moral *and* historical, cosmological, metaphysical, etc.
Studies the ...	'Core' of religion	'Vehicles' of religion
Its role is ...	Public	Private
State can and should ...	Protect it in the interests of rational progress	Regulate it in the interests of good public order

Exercise: religion and state after Kant

This exercise is designed to help you to think about the contemporary relevance of Kant's thought and to encourage you to look for the contemporary relevance of the other thinkers considered in this section of the book. It will help if you have read the essay 'An Answer to the Question "What is Enlightenment?"', but you can think through the issues on the basis of our summary. Consider this news story:

BBC News, 18 July 2006

Home Secretary John Reid has decided to proscribe, or ban, four organisations which he believes are involved in, or linked to, terrorism. Two of the organisations are UK-based Islamist groups and are being outlawed for 'glorification' of terrorism.

The two groups ... are successors to Al Muhajiroun, a small organisation ... widely known for inflammatory interviews and hijacking ordinary Muslim events.

Shortly after the London bombings [*in July 2005*], Prime Minister Tony Blair pledged to ban the successors of Al Muhajiroun and another organisation called Hizb ut-Tahrir (HT). This group has not yet been banned.

Hizb ut-Tahrir is an Islamic political party that draws most of its support from university students. HT says it wants to create an Islamic government in Muslim lands, including the end of Israel. It opposes parliamentary democracy as un-Islamic, but insists that it is committed to non-violent means of achieving its goals ...

Inayat Bunglawala of the Muslim Council of Britain, one of the main umbrella groups, said months of patient lobbying of ministers had paid off. 'We have our disagreements with Hizb ut-Tahrir but we do not believe that banning the group would help – it would drive it underground,' said Mr Bunglawala. 'If you want to defeat an organisation, then you do it through open dialogue, through ideas. Banning political parties is the kind of action you would see in a Middle East dictatorship rather than a confident democracy like ours.'

Mr Bunglawala said that despite concerns over anti-terrorism laws, most Muslims would have little sympathy for Al Muhajiroun's offshoots.

Dominic Casciani

Ask yourself: what issues about religious freedom, religion and reason, and the relationship between religion and the modern state, arise here? What assumptions are made (by the writer, the government or the interviewees) about these topics?

What, on the basis of what you have read so far, would Kant think about this story? Would it confirm or challenge his views?

Now try to identify a few more recent news stories that raise related issues – about religion in public, religion and the state, religion and reason – and answer the questions in relation to them.

Conclusion: after Kant

During, and immediately after, his own lifetime, Kant's influence was strongest in the German-speaking world but has spread far wider since then. As we shall see in subsequent chapters, theologians and philosophers of religion since his time, at least in Europe and to a large extent in North America, have had to engage with the questions he posed. Perhaps more important, however, is the insight we gain from the study of Kant into how the wider public sphere is constructed and how religion is located within it. Not only academic ideas but everyday assumptions about religion in modernity are very often 'Kantian'. Studying Kant enables us to understand the history of some of what we take for granted – not necessarily to prove it wrong, but to see that it was not always accepted as obvious and necessary.

In the late twentieth and early twenty-first centuries, Kant's legacy has often been assessed negatively – as part of a widespread critique of 'modernity' and its effects. (See, for example, Chapter 17, 'Becoming postmodern'). However, even the critics of Kant find it difficult to avoid engaging with his questions.

Bibliography

Primary sources discussed in this chapter (recommended translations):

Immanuel Kant, *Critique of Pure Reason*, ed. and trans. Paul Guyer and Allan W. Wood (Cambridge: Cambridge University Press, 1998).

Immanuel Kant, *Groundwork for the Metaphysics of Morals*, ed. and trans. Allan W. Wood (New Haven: Yale University Press, 2003).

Immanuel Kant, *Kant: Political Writings*, ed. H.S. Reiss, trans. H.B. Nisbet (Cambridge: Cambridge University Press, 1991).

Immanuel Kant, *The Conflict of the Faculties*, ed. and trans. Mary J. Gregor (New York: Abaris Books, 1990).

Secondary reading:

Manfred Kuehn, *Kant* (Cambridge: Cambridge University Press, 2001). The definitive biography.

Paul Guyer, *Kant* (London: Routledge, 2006). See especially Chapter 6 on Kant's religious thought.

C.D. Broad, *Kant: An Introduction* (Cambridge: Cambridge University Press, 1978).

Allen Wood, *Kant's Moral Religion* (Ithaca: Cornell University Press, 1970). Clear and readable account that places Kant's religious contribution at the centre of his philosophy.

George di Giovanni, *Freedom and Religion in Kant and his Immediate Successors: The Vocation of Humanity, 1774-1800* (Cambridge: Cambridge University Press, 2005). Presents an argument for the innovative character of Kant's work in its particular context, useful for the history of debates around 'freedom and religion'.

Gordon E. Michalson, *Kant and the Problem of God* (Malden: Blackwell, 1999). Puts forward a provocative alternative reading of Kant as a forerunner of modern atheism rather than of modern theology.

Ronald M. Green, *Religious Reason: The Rational and Moral Basis of Religious Belief* (New York: Oxford University Press, 1978), Part 1. Uses Kant as the starting-point for a contemporary theory of religion, based in moral reasoning.

4 Friedrich Schleiermacher

AIMS

By the end of this chapter, we hope that you will:

- understand why and how Friedrich Schleiermacher's thought has been important for modern theology and modern thought about religion, including how it has affected contemporary thought

- understand some key concepts for Schleiermacher's theology, and how he uses them

- have a basic understanding of the central ideas and themes of the Romantic movement and how it influenced Schleiermacher's theology

- have thought through one approach to reading a 'difficult' primary text in theology and feel more confident about reading other primary texts.

Introduction

Friedrich Schleiermacher (1768–1834) has become known as the 'father of modern theology', mainly because he was the first, or at least the first influential, theologian to rethink Christian thought in direct response to Kant. He was both a leading intellectual figure and a leading figure in the Protestant Church, at a time when religion was unfashionable in intellectual circles. In studying Schleiermacher's work, and especially when reading critical assessments, it is worth remembering both 'sides' of his story and noticing how he brings together the different communities and ways of thinking to which he was committed.

Schleiermacher's academic achievements place him among the shapers of modern thought. For example, he was a key figure in the foundation of the University of Berlin – the first major university of the modern era and an attempt to shape an institution around the modern understanding of knowledge. He was at the centre of the intellectual and cultural life of Berlin at the height of the Romantic movement in philosophy, literature and art, and was close friends with leading figures of German Romanticism. He was a supporter of the early movement for German national unification. Besides his theological and Church work, he is known for his classical scholarship – as a translator of Plato's dialogues – and for his very influential work on hermeneutics and the philosophy of language.

Schleiermacher's religious commitments are important for understanding his work. Unlike the other individuals we discuss in this section, he was ordained; he wrote his most famous book (*On Religion*) while working, not as an academic, but as a

Figure 4.1 Friedrich Schleiermacher

pastor, and he retained his role as a pastor while holding a professorship at the University of Berlin. Like Kant, Schleiermacher was influenced by the Pietist movement – in his case, the strongest influence was that of the Moravian Brethren (*Herrnhuter*), who were also important in John Wesley's spiritual and theological development. Brought up within this community, Schleiermacher later rejected much of their theology, but retained their emphasis on 'piety', religious inwardness and holy living. He was involved in the complex politics of the Protestant Churches, seeking to promote a single vision of 'Protestant' theology and liturgy that would unite Lutherans and Reformed but also opposing the creation, by royal decree, of a unified 'Protestant' state Church.

Schleiermacher's major theological works:

- *On Religion: Speeches to its Cultured Despisers* (1799) – the book that made Schleiermacher famous. It is particularly important to remember, when studying this book, that it was written for a specific purpose and audience (see below).
- *Brief Outline of Theology as a Field of Study* (1811, 1830) – his theological 'syllabus'. It appears in various translations, including various translations of the title (e.g. *Brief Outline of the Study of Theology*).
- *The Christian Faith* (1821, 1830) – his systematic theology. It is worth looking at Schleiermacher's comments on the contents and reception of *The Christian Faith*, in his 'open letters' to a friend and colleague: *On the Glaubenslehre: Two Letters to Dr Lücke* (1829). Note that, partly because of the title under which Schleiermacher's letters to Lücke were published, *The Christian Faith* is often referred to as '*the Glaubenslehre*' ('doctrine of faith'), which is not the German title, but a description of the contents.

Schleiermacher was an excellent translator (most notably, of Plato) and this is relevant to his theological work as well. In his writings he is always 'translating', between traditional Christian language and philosophical terminology or between the language the Church understands and the language the 'cultured despisers' of religion understand. If you think he has not mentioned a certain theological idea in his writing, it is worth asking whether it is actually there, but just expressed in another 'language'. Of course, you should then also ask whether anything has been lost in the translation.

Schleiermacher's legacy is most clearly seen in those modern theologies that look for correspondences between Christian teaching and wider human culture and experience. The fiercest criticisms of his work have come from those who want to defend Christian teaching as unique and irreducible to other forms of human knowledge, Christianity as (potentially or actually) 'counter-cultural' and Christian knowledge of God as beyond human capacities or understanding.

We begin with a discussion of a major background influence, without which it is impossible to understand what Schleiermacher was trying to achieve.

Romanticism

Romanticism was a broad intellectual and cultural movement in the late eighteenth and early nineteenth centuries. It can be interpreted as a continuation of the modern 'turn to the subject' (see Chapter 3 for more on this term) and of the Enlightenment's call for freedom and also as a protest against the Enlightenment's concentration on reason and on universals. For the Romantics, what matters is not what is true of everyone, or every rational being, but what is true of this particular individual. The uniqueness of the person – or the nation, or the landscape, or the work of art – was their focus. Freedom was not, mainly, 'freedom to be rational', but 'freedom to be yourself'. Furthermore, what mattered was the individual as a whole – not only the mind, but also the body; not only the reason, but also the emotions, the passions and, crucially, the imagination. Art could tell the truth about individuality in a way that more 'rational' forms of expression could not. In many ways, the paradigm of freedom was the artist's free creativity.

The political radicalism of many Romantic thinkers was grounded in their love of freedom – the freedom to be oneself without external control, as a person or (crucially) as a nation. Movements for national and cultural self-determination – with appeals to pre-modern histories and mythologies – found support among the Romantics. One of the most famous English Romantics, Lord Byron, died in Greece while working for the Greek army in its war of independence against the Ottoman Empire. The German Romantics, among them the Brothers Grimm (famous collectors of folklore and fairy tales), were at the origins of German nationalism; they developed the idea of a distinctively German spirit, culture and history. The Romantics in general were interested in the pre-modern and particularly the Middle Ages. This was in contrast to the Enlightenment's derision of medieval 'superstition'. The Romantics sought to remember, record and learn from past ages that were in danger of being effaced by relentless rational and technological progress.

The contemplation of wilderness and untamed nature was another strand of Romantic thought and experience. The idea that an uninhabited, un-ordered, 'irrational' landscape could be beautiful was a Romantic innovation that we now take for granted. It is often said that the English Romantics 'invented' the Lake District – as the American Romantics later 'invented' the landscapes of the Hudson River valley. For many Romantic writers and artists, the encounter with wild nature was seen in religious terms. Contemplating nature, they experienced unity with the transcendent and awe in the face of the 'sublime'.

Traditional religion was an object of attack for many Romantic thinkers, as a source of repressive laws that constrained and stifled the human spirit – think of William Blake's outcries against 'Nobodaddy'. But they were equally opposed to the various eighteenth-century attempts to preserve and defend religion by making it more 'rational' and hence, in the view of many Romantics, even more inhuman and lifeless.

Schleiermacher, in late 1790s Berlin, was an oddity among the Romantic intellectuals with whom he spent so much time – a Christian pastor among people who, for the most part, despised all religion. This was the position from which he began his reworking of Christian theology. His work *On Religion: Speeches to its Cultured Despisers* was written for his friends, whose 'cultured' outlook, like his own, was shaped by Romanticism.

Figure 4.2 Portrait of Henrietta Herz (1778) by Anna Dorothea Therbusch

Reason, feeling and the knowledge of God

We might expect a Romantic thinker like Schleiermacher to disagree with Kant – the great advocate of religion 'within the limits of *reason* alone'. But for all Schleiermacher's disagreements with Kant, his starting-point in thinking about religion is basically a Kantian one. Schleiermacher assumes that, in order to talk about God, we will have to talk about human beings and how they know or experience God. We cannot start by talking about 'God in Godself', because we can have no access to that. Even the titles of his major works reflect this – he writes *On Religion* and on *The Christian Faith*, not 'on God'. Particularly in *On Religion*, but also in his later work, he asks Kant's question about religion – what has to be true about the human mind for human beings to be able to know God, or to be religious?

Where he parts company with Kant is not in the questions he asks but in the answers he gives. Kant, as we have seen, located the core of religious knowledge in morality or practical reasoning. Schleiermacher thought this gave much too limited an account of religion and of God. Morality, he explained in *On Religion*, is only a part of human life and experience. Knowledge of God comes from something more basic than morality, that relates to the whole of human life.

That 'something more basic' Schleiermacher termed *Gefühl*, which is normally translated as 'feeling'. It means a response of the whole person to a situation or experience (remember his links to Romanticism and think about a person's response to a work of art or a wild landscape).

In at least some of the contexts in which Schleiermacher uses *Gefühl*, a better translation is 'mood'. Religion is not, for Schleiermacher, an occasional overwhelming sensation – it is a way of being-in-the-world, which affects everything a person does. An angry person does and thinks everything angrily; a religious person, as Schleiermacher describes it, does and thinks everything religiously. It is important to remember that when Schleiermacher talks about religious 'feeling' he is usually talking about something very deep-seated, which is present all the time – whether you notice it or not. In a similar way, you can be (for example) in a bad mood, or under stress, without really noticing it, even though your mood will affect everything you do and think.

So Schleiermacher thinks that knowledge of God comes to a person, not first through her capacity to reason but through her capacity to feel – or, more precisely, her capacity to be affected as a whole person by a whole situation. In *On Religion*, Schleiermacher locates religious knowledge in 'intuition'. Intuition is a form of knowledge but it is *non-discursive* knowledge, i.e. knowledge that you possess without having thought it through and without being able to explain it. What is known intuitively is grasped 'all at once' rather than being achieved through reasoning. It is felt before it is understood.

'Intuition', as used in everyday English, is in fact a fairly good translation of the term Schleiermacher uses, although we are unaccustomed to seeing it in academic work. Consider this everyday claim to intuitive knowledge: 'As soon as she walked into the room I knew that something was wrong.'

What is claimed here is a perfectly valid sort of 'knowledge' of the world. It is one that we normally trust, without even thinking about it. (How often have you been aware of, and acted on, an instant impression of a person or a situation?) It is an instant response to the other person as a whole, as I become aware of her. It is not about weighing up evidence, constructing arguments or presenting proofs. It is knowledge that I probably cannot trace back to any 'part' of me – did it come from something I saw, something I heard, something I thought? Notice, however, that it is still a knowledge of *her*, of something in the 'real world' that is other than me, it is emphatically *not* something that only came from me, or something that I simply invented.

This is, roughly, how Schleiermacher thinks religion begins. It begins in a more-than-rational response of the whole person to something beyond them, that gives the person knowledge of that 'something-beyond-them'.

Note also that in this example:

- My intuitive reaction to the other person – 'something is wrong' – will affect how I behave towards her and how I feel about her, even if I do not really understand or think about my intuition. So my intuition will form my 'mood' in my interactions with her. You might not be able to pinpoint its effects in anything specific that I do – you might, for example, just pick it up in my tone of voice or my body language.
- Having said that: I can, and probably will, *reflect rationally* on my intuition ('something is wrong'). I might, for example, try to work out what is wrong with her. I might also *express* my intuition, I might ask her what is wrong or tell someone else that I am worried about her. None of that would change the fact that I have experienced and trusted that original more-than-rational and non-verbal intuition. Schleiermacher thinks that his job, as a theologian, is to *reflect rationally* on religious intuitions and on how they are *expressed* by the people who have them.

What kind of 'feeling' or 'mood' is religion? Basically, it is the feeling of being in relation to God – the 'mood' brought about in a person by relation to God. If we ask 'but what kind of feeling is *that*?' we find slightly different answers in different parts of Schleiermacher's work. In *On Religion* he writes of intuitions of 'the universe' – awareness of being in relation to, and connected with, the whole of reality. (Remember that this is a book specifically aimed at making links with the 'cultured despisers' of Christianity – Schleiermacher deliberately avoids or downplays theological language.)

However, the most famous description Schleiermacher gives, in *The Christian Faith*, of religious feeling is a 'feeling of absolute dependence'. In religion we become aware, Schleiermacher says, that we do not cause ourselves and do not make ourselves what we are. Everything about us and our lives has an aspect of contingency, of 'givenness', of 'could have been otherwise'. We are constantly aware that we depend on something other than us to make us what we are. 'Dependence' here means not just 'needing something', but more generally 'being shaped or affected by something', as in 'my mood in the mornings *depends on* the news I hear on the radio when I wake up'.

Sometimes what we are aware of is our dependence on particular things within the world. I am aware of how the people around me affect me, how I need them and how they determine what is possible for me. This is a *relative* dependence. There is no one person and no one aspect of the world on whom or which I depend absolutely for everything, and I am 'depended on' myself by those on whom I depend. I make a difference to the world even as it makes a difference to me. Even if I recognise how I depend on 'the world' as a whole – my entire physical environment – I am still aware that I can affect the environment in some small way.

But we also become aware, Schleiermacher says, that we and the world *as a whole* are 'given', 'could be otherwise', depend on something else. We have an awareness of *absolute*, not relative, dependence – dependence on something that we *cannot* affect because it is not simply part of our world.

If you have studied the philosophy of religion, you may see comparisons here with the Cosmological Argument and the idea of a chain of causal 'dependence' leading back to a First Cause. The important point to note, when thinking through this comparison, is that Schleiermacher is not making an *argument* for absolute dependence. He does not think that people '*work out*' that they are absolutely, as well as relatively, dependent; he thinks that they know it intuitively.

To get a handle on this in the contemporary context, you could think about the way in which the language of 'gratitude', 'thankfulness' or 'counting your blessings' is used, even by people who are not explicitly religious. (On a quick web search I found someone expressing 'gratitude' for 'having the courage to be an agnostic'!) You might see here some evidence that could support Schleiermacher's claims. He might say that these everyday expressions of 'gratitude', even without reference to God, are acknowledgements of a feeling of absolute dependence. He would then also say, of course, that they are, as such, really acknowledgements of God – whether or not the people concerned know it.

Building theology on piety

The 'feeling of absolute dependence, or, which is the same thing, of being in relation to God' was for Schleiermacher the basis of piety – the core of a person's religious life. This was also, for him, the starting point for theological thought. Knowledge of God, and knowledge of everything else in relation to God, began from this experience of 'absolute dependence' – 'God-consciousness'. This may sound very abstract and not easy to link to religion as we know it. Schleiermacher has frequently been criticised for basing Christianity on something that is not recognisably Christian at all.

To assess this criticism, it is worth paying a little attention to the structure of his main systematic work, *The Christian Faith*. Schleiermacher is a very 'architectural' thinker. Structure matters to him. In particular – and appropriately enough – relationships of dependence matter to him. He wants to know what the *foundations* of a system of thought are, what ideas *build on* or *rest on* what others, what ideas are needed to *support* what others. It is well worth looking at the contents pages of *The Christian Faith* to gain a sense of how he thinks Christian belief is structured. But be aware that the structure does not necessarily show you what matters most to Schleiermacher. Just because something is not 'foundational' does not mean it is not important. The foundations of your house are no more important than the roof (although they might be harder to change or replace). So, Schleiermacher thinks that the feeling of absolute dependence is foundational for Christianity, but that does not mean that it is the whole of Christianity or even that it is the most important part of Christianity.

The discussion of the 'feeling of absolute dependence' in *The Christian Faith* is in the introduction, where Schleiermacher expressly states that he is not doing theology. In order to do theology, he would have to be talking about some specific religious community and how its relationship to God is expressed. When he is talking about the 'feeling of absolute dependence' in general, in abstraction from any religious community, he is not yet doing theology, he is doing philosophy. Theology, for him, is *systematic reflection on the piety of a particular religious community and how it is expressed*. And in fact, Schleiermacher says, although philosophers can say a little about 'God-consciousness' in general, without referring to its manifestation and expression in specific religions, nobody ever actually experiences 'God-consciousness' *in general*, so philosophy will not give you a very full or useful account of religion. God-consciousness is always experienced in and through some particular religious community. In *The Christian Faith*, the 'theology', and the discussion of real religion (as opposed to a purely theoretical, generic version of religion), only starts when Schleiermacher starts to discuss Christianity.

His account of Christianity is centred on Jesus Christ as Redeemer. What defines Christian life and faith, for Schleiermacher, is the awareness that humanity's relationship with God is imperfect, that people cannot overcome this imperfection by their own efforts and that Jesus Christ both enacts and makes possible a perfected relationship with God. He talks about this both in the traditional language of sin and redemption, and in the newer language of God-consciousness. We know, he says, that we constantly fail to recognise and live out our 'absolute dependence' on God; our God-consciousness is fundamentally impaired, we exist in sin. In Jesus we see a person whose God-consciousness is perfect, whose mind and will are fully united with God, who lives every moment in the light of the feeling of absolute dependence. In him, the sinfulness of human nature is overcome. The Church as a community maintains, communicates and forms in its members the same God-consciousness that Jesus had, through the presence and work of the Holy Spirit. To be joined to the Church is to share in Jesus' relationship with God.

It is important to remember that 'God-consciousness' here does not just mean 'ideas about God'. God-consciousness *is* the presence of the self-revealing God to a person or a community. Schleiermacher's theology is 'subjective', in that – like Kant – he is interested in the human 'subject' who knows God. But the whole point of the 'feeling of absolute dependence' is that the human subject does not invent God. In 'absolute dependence', we really experience our relation to God – and it is really God who is experienced.

It is also important to see that, in Schleiermacher's work, Jesus is *not* simply a model of perfect God-consciousness, an example for everyone to follow. You cannot, of your own free will, acquire a different kind of God-consciousness, because God-consciousness operates at such a deep level of human existence. Perfect God-consciousness is only possible through a transformation of human life, which human beings cannot achieve for themselves. Jesus' life and the life of the Church are this transformation of human life, which is the work of God that continues through the history of the Church.

Schleiermacher's close relationship to Romantic thought becomes particularly apparent towards the end of *The Christian Faith*, where he writes of the world as 'an absolutely harmonious divine work of art' (p733), centred around the life of Christ and around the Church. Like the Romantics, Schleiermacher defines art in terms of 'self-presentation'. Artistic activity is aimed at the expression of some aspect of the 'inwardness' of the individual. The work of art is characterised by coherence and by the reciprocal relation of the parts and the whole. To speak of the world, and world-history, as a 'divine work of art' is to see it as a single complex reality in which God expresses Godself. Christians, in expressing their faith, share in the creation of the work of art; the Holy Spirit that acts in and through the Church is the 'ultimate world-shaping power'.

As might be apparent from this, Schleiermacher's theological scheme does not accord any importance to the idea that human beings were originally perfect and lost this perfection in the Fall. (In fact, he argues that we could not make sense of the claim that Adam had a perfect 'God-consciousness' because 'consciousness' as we know it develops in community and through language, and Adam had neither.) His account of sin and redemption is, to use broad and sometimes inaccurate categories, 'Irenaean' and 'Scotist'.

> Irenaean: after St Irenaeus of Lyon (c.120–c.200). Scotist: after John Duns Scotus (c.1266–1308). For a critical discussion of Schleiermacher's account of Christ, sin and redemption, which emphasises its 'Irenaean' and 'Scotist' characteristics, see R. Kendall Soulen, *The God of Israel and Christian Theology* (Minneapolis: Fortress Press, 1996), pp68–78.

It is 'Irenaean' because for him the original human creation (Adam) is not complete, not perfect, rather it is 'ready to be perfected' in Christ. It is 'Scotist' because for him the Incarnation was always part of God's plan of creation and was not a response to the Fall. The history of the world, God's 'work of art', is a single coherent piece of work, oriented from the beginning towards Jesus Christ. Schleiermacher does speak of Christianity as a religion centred on 'redemption', but for him redemption does not presuppose an earlier state of perfection from which humanity fell.

Theology in the university

Besides the 'cultured despisers' of religion, Schleiermacher had another important audience for his reconstruction of Christian theology – the government ministers and the scholarly community who were establishing the new University of Berlin. The institutional structure of the older universities accorded theology an exalted status. It was the 'queen of the sciences', the highest among the 'higher faculties' of the university, the discipline that was served by all the others – after all, what form of knowledge could be more important than the knowledge of God? This positioning of theology was, of course, called into question by the Enlightenment's rethinking of 'knowledge'. By the time the conversations about the foundation of the University of Berlin began in the early nineteenth century, theology was seen as a problem within the university. It did not look like a proper academic discipline. It was subject to external authorities and free investigation was constrained; it made claims that could not be tested out by the normal methods of academic enquiry; it repeated old knowledge, rather than developing new knowledge. It was 'unscientific' – in German, *unwissenschaftlich*. It might be socially useful (for the training of pastors, for example) but it could not play a major role in the university's core mission, the pursuit of knowledge.

Wissenschaft often appears untranslated in secondary literature on German thought. 'Science' is probably the best translation, but you have to remember that it includes 'social' and 'human' sciences as well as 'natural' sciences. In our period, it means 'valid knowledge and the valid pursuit of knowledge' – valid according to post-Enlightenment criteria. It was a key and contested term in Schleiermacher's day – there were debates around what counted as *Wissenschaft* and how to define *Wissenschaft* (compare contemporary debates about which claims, techniques, etc. count as 'scientific').

Schleiermacher entered this debate about the place of theology in the new university with a vigorous defence of theology as *Wissenschaft* – as an academically defensible field of study and indeed an important area of research and enquiry. His vision of the university and theology's place in it was reflected in what eventually happened. Berlin ended up with a faculty of theology alongside, but not superior to, its other faculties.

Schleiermacher's key move was to define theology as systematic reflection on piety – on religious life and how it is expressed. This did not, he thought, exclude the traditional idea that theology was knowledge of *God*, because, he said (recalling Kant here) we cannot think about God without also thinking about how people know and experience God. It did mean, however, that theology had an object of study – piety, religious life – that was open to all the modern forms of enquiry. Piety could be studied historically and analysed philosophically, as well as being developed 'practically' by pastors. In fact, there was no special method of enquiry that belonged only to theology, so theologians in the modern university would have to learn to do both history and philosophy in order to give a good account of their subject matter.

In his *Brief Outline of Theology as a Field of Study* – his 'syllabus' for theological education, an enormously influential text – Schleiermacher divided theology into three main fields: philosophical, historical and practical. 'Historical' theology included, not only biblical studies and Church history, but also systematic theology, which, as Schleiermacher understands it, describes the beliefs and practices of the present Christian community in the same way that Church history describes the past. 'Practical' theology, for Schleiermacher, applies philosophical and historical knowledge to the present guidance and development of the Christian community. His syllabus emphasises the development of a 'scientific' (*wissenschaftlich*) spirit in the theologian, which can then be put to practical service within the Church community. For him, the 'practical' aspects of theology are the main point, but the philosophical and historical aspects have their own value as fields of academic study.

If many aspects of Schleiermacher's vision of theology in the university sound uncontroversial now, that is because most university 'religion' departments in Europe and North America today (even those that were founded before Berlin) owe at least something to Schleiermacher's work. Schleiermacher did not exactly invent 'religious studies' but he defined theology in terms of the study of religious life and thus opened up 'religion' as an object of academic enquiry. Furthermore, with his work on religious 'feeling', he offered a broad definition of religion that was (apparently) applicable to non-Christian religions and that made religion an important and distinctive part of all human life. If Schleiermacher was right about religion, it made sense for universities to do not only *theology* but also *religious studies*.

In fact, Schleiermacher also developed schemes for the categorisation and comparison of religions. For example, in the introduction to *The Christian Faith* he describes Christianity thus: 'Christianity is a monotheistic faith, belonging to the teleological type of religion, and is essentially distinguished from other such faiths by the fact that in it everything is related to the redemption accomplished by Jesus of Nazareth.' Note how the terms used in this description enable comparisons and contrasts with *other* religions – for example, Christianity is described as 'monotheistic' (*as opposed to* 'polytheistic' religions, but *like* some other religions).

Aspects of Schleiermacher's legacy

We have already suggested that Schleiermacher's influence was immense – not just on the content of theology but on theological method and on how the interconnected fields of 'theology' and 'religious studies' developed within modern universities. By starting from the post-Enlightenment, Kantian question, 'how can human beings have knowledge of God?', Schleiermacher located theology firmly among the 'human sciences' within the university, where it has largely stayed. He also set an agenda for theology that permitted, indeed encouraged, theologians to respond positively to historical, cultural and intellectual change. This was the 'liberal' theology that dominated the European Protestant scene in the nineteenth century, but its influence has been much wider and deeper. For example, contextual theologies, theologies that take as their starting point the experience of particular communities, theologies engaging with 'modernity's' challenges to faith – all these, in the twentieth and twenty-first centuries, owe much to Schleiermacher's reshaping of the theological task.

However, in the twentieth and twenty-first centuries, it has also become very difficult to read Schleiermacher other than through the work of Karl Barth (1886–1968). Barth developed his theological project in direct, and highly critical, response to Schleiermacher and the tradition of liberal theology. His well-known polemics against liberal theology, informed by his close (and often surprisingly sympathetic) study of Schleiermacher's work, have set the tone for critiques of Schleiermacher.

Karl Barth, *The Theology of Schleiermacher*, trans. Geoffrey W. Bromiley (Edinburgh: T&T Clark, 1982) – a course of lectures Barth gave at Göttingen – is a very important secondary work on Schleiermacher, not because it gives an 'impartial' account of his theology but because it shows how and why the reaction against him occurred. It is also worth reading as a good (not perfect!) model of critical engagement with theologians with whom you disagree. Barth profoundly disagrees with Schleiermacher on the basis of a careful reading of his work and a real attempt to understand his major concerns and assumptions.

One cannot, wrote Barth, speak about God by speaking about humanity in a loud voice; the whole attempt to find a path from human experience and knowledge to claims about God is fundamentally misguided. It is all very well, he says, to claim that a certain human 'feeling' is an experience of God, but that is, after all, simply a claim, which is easily open to reductionist challenges. If you are going to start with human feelings, what is to stop someone from saying that these are *just* human feelings and that talk of God is redundant? So, for the influential and still-developing streams of theological thought in Europe and North America that originate from Barth's work, Schleiermacher's project represents a blind alley. However, debates around Schleiermacher's work and legacy continue, both attempting to resolve questions about his own theological positions and thinking through his relevance for the contemporary world.

Exercise: reading Schleiermacher

The summaries of thinkers provided in these chapters are not intended to be a substitute for reading the primary texts. Many of the primary texts of modern theology are, however, quite challenging to read, so it will always be tempting to rely too heavily on secondary literature. This exercise is intended to provide you with some 'tools' that will give you the confidence to approach difficult primary texts. It is also intended to help you to assess some of the claims we have made here about Schleiermacher's thought.

Our focus is an extract from *The Christian Faith*, which has been deliberately selected because: (a) it relates directly to some of the issues discussed in this chapter; and (b) it is very, very difficult – if you can make some sense of this, you can make some sense of most of the other primary texts relevant to this book. What follows are, firstly, some suggestions about how to approach a text of this kind, and, secondly, an annotated 'narrative' about one person studying the text.

First Part of the System of Doctrine: introduction

§32. The immediate feeling of absolute dependence is presupposed and actually contained in every religious and Christian self-consciousness as the only way in which, in general, our own being and the infinite Being of God can be one in self-consciousness.

1.

The fact that the whole Christian religious consciousness is here presupposed is entirely legitimate, for here we abstract entirely from the specific content of the particular Christian experiences, and what we have stated is in no way affected by these differences. Hence nothing can be deduced from the above proposition either for or against any dogmatic formulation of such specific content. But if anyone should maintain that there might be Christian religious experiences in which the Being of God was not involved in such a manner, i.e. experiences which contained absolutely no consciousness of God, our proposition would certainly exclude him from the domain of that Christian belief which we are going to describe. Our proposition appeals, therefore, against such a person to the religious self-consciousness as it appears and is recognized everywhere in the Evangelical (Protestant) Church: that is, we assert that in every religious affection, however much its special contents may predominate, the God-consciousness must be present and cannot be neutralized by anything else, so that there can be no relation to Christ which does not contain also a relation to God. At the same time, we also assert that this God-consciousness, as it is here described, does not constitute by itself alone an actual moment in religious experience, but always in connection with other particular determinations; so that this God-consciousness maintains its identity through its particular moments in all manifestations of Christian piety, just as in life generally the self-consciousness of an individual does in the different moments of his existence. Hence the view that in every Christian affection there must be a relation to Christ does not in the least contradict our proposition. Much more is this the case when the pious feeling comes to expression as an actual moment in the form of pleasure of pain. For the Christian faith, however, the incapacity implied in religious pain must be ascribed to lack of fellowship with the Redeemer, while, on the other hand, the ease in evoking pious feeling which goes along with religious pleasure is regarded as a possession which comes to us from this fellowship. Thus it is evident that, within the Christian communion, there can be no religious experience which does not involve a relation to Christ.

3.
... it may be objected that the foregoing statement is not pertinent to our subject, because it is not so much peculiarly Christian as characteristic of monotheism in general. The answer is that there is no purely monotheistic piety in which the God-consciousness alone and by itself forms the content of religious experiences. Just as there is always present in Christian piety a relation to Christ in conjunction with the God-consciousness, so in Judaism there is always a relation to the Lawgiver, and in Mohammedanism to the revelation given through the Prophet. In our Holy Scriptures for this reason God is constantly referred to by the name of the Father of our Lord Jesus Christ. The saying of Christ also (John 14:7–9) implies that every relation to Christ includes also the God-consciousness.

Translated by H.R. Macintosh and J.S. Stewart

How do we approach this text? Here is a plan you might follow.

Stage 1

Read the text through once. At this stage, do not worry AT ALL about how much of it you do or do not understand; it is important to know what is there.

Stage 2

Read it again. Think about, and write brief notes on:

A) The structure and approach – what kind of text is this?
- For example, in this case: what is the bit in bold type at the beginning, and how does it relate to the rest of the text?
- Is this a single continuous argument, or a set of smaller arguments related to a general theme? Are there parts that seem more or less important?

B) The subject matter – what is it about?
- You may also be able to say *what it is arguing* – but do not worry if you cannot work that out at this stage.

C) The point of writing this – who is this for, why is it being written?
- What is important or controversial about what the author is saying? Who is in the target audience, and what do they have to be persuaded of?

Before you read on, try Stages 1 and 2 for our text. Here are some responses, from one reader, to the questions in Stage 2 – what do you think of them?

A) The sentence in bold type is the claim with which Schleiermacher wants his readers to agree; the rest of the text is where he defends it against possible objections. I notice there are a lot of expressions like 'But if anyone should object ...'.

B) The text seems to be about the nature of Christian religious experience and Christian consciousness of God, and how this relates to Jesus Christ.

C) He clearly expects what he is saying to be controversial – or why mention all these 'objections'? He seems to be writing for Christians, because he is talking about 'objections' that are couched in Christian language.

There also seems to be some discussion of how Christianity relates to other religions; perhaps he thinks that some people reading this might be non-Christians, or at least interested in non-Christian religions.

Stage 3

The chances are that, when you did Stage 2, you still could not understand large sections of the text, so now we are going to work through it more slowly and try to understand more of it.
   Some useful hints for this stage of reading:

- Don't panic. Assume that you can understand this. It was written for people like you.
- Take a leaf from Schleiermacher's own book – pay attention to the structure. Use this to determine your reading strategy. Pay attention to the structure, not just of the whole piece, but of each paragraph and each sentence. For example, what follows from what (where are the 'therefore's and the 'I conclude that's)? What is a statement of somebody else's point of view and what is a statement of the author's own point of view? Which sentences are unnecessary asides? Which are repetitions of earlier points ('in other words ...'). Prioritise as you go along.
- Start with what you *do* understand, and use the resources you have – but use them to work towards an overall understanding of the text.
- Make guesses, as you go along, about what the text means. Form hypotheses, test them and be prepared to revise or abandon them.
- Look out carefully for oppositions and identities. That is, pay special attention if you get the sense that the author is *contrasting* two things. Start drawing up a list of what he places on one side of the contrast and what he places on the other. And pay

special attention if you get the sense that the author is using all sorts of different phrases to refer to the *same* thing. Again, try drawing up a list of all the terms that he uses for this one idea. You may well find that, even though there are all sorts of phrases that you don't yet understand, there are enough items on the lists that you do understand to enable you to make a good guess at the items that still baffle you.

- Assume the text makes sense and does not contradict itself; if you think you have found a contradiction, ask yourself, is it more likely that there is a real contradiction here or that I have not fully understood what is going on?

1 Finding somewhere to start

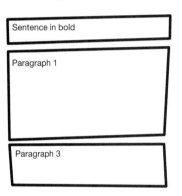

In this case, I decided (looking at my answer to question A, above) that the sentence in bold type was what I really needed to understand – but I couldn't make head or tail of it. So I decided to hunt around for something I *could* understand, and start with that.

> Pay attention to the overall structure and use this to decide your reading strategies.

> Don't panic.

I started with the last paragraph of the text (Paragraph 3), because it seemed much less abstract and philosophical – and in fact I started with the last two sentences.

> In our Holy Scriptures for this reason God is constantly referred to by the name of the Father of our Lord Jesus Christ. The saying of Christ also (John 14:7–9) implies that every relation to Christ includes also the God-consciousness.

First, I looked up John 14:7-9 and found:

> 'If you know me, you will know my Father also. From now on you do know him and have seen him'. Philip said to him, 'Lord, show us the Father and we will be satisfied'. Jesus said to him, 'Have I been with you all this time, Philip, and you still do not know me? Whoever has seen me has seen the Father. How can you say, "Show us the Father"?'

> Use the resources available to you! Biblical references in theological texts are often a good way to get a clue to what's going on – but remember that they are themselves open to multiple interpretations.

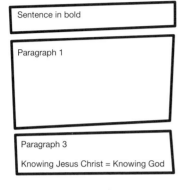

So, with that biblical text to help me understand the last sentence, I think these two sentences are making two complementary points. The first says that, in Christianity, God is 'constantly' spoken of in connection with Jesus Christ; you can't relate to God without relating to Jesus. The second says that 'knowing Jesus Christ equals knowing God' or 'being in relation to Jesus Christ equals being in relation to God'; you can't relate to Jesus without relating to God. It goes both ways.

On the basis of these sentences, I form the hypothesis: **Schleiermacher is saying something in this passage about how Christians know or relate to God**; and he's saying something about how **Christians, specifically, can't think about God without thinking about Jesus Christ**.

> Form hypotheses about what is going on in the *whole* passege.

I test my hypothesis by reading 'back' a little way. Well, it seems to be supported by the rest of that paragraph, where he suggests that every religious community – Judaism, 'Mohammedanism' [*Islam – but he can't have known much about it if he used that term*] – has specific ways of naming and thinking about God. He seems to be saying that although the monotheistic religions all talk about 'God', each talks about God in a distinctive way. And the distinctive way of talking about God, in each case, seems to be linked to history and to revelation – you talk about God by talking about the people, the books, etc. that show you God. So, for Christians, you have to talk about Jesus Christ in order to talk about God.

> Bear in mind that you are working with extracts from a larger text, and be wary of assuming that an issue is 'ignored' (it might well be discussed somewhere else).

- *An aside: interesting – he seems to put the three monotheistic religions very much 'on a level' here; he doesn't argue for why Christianity is better, or special. (Must find out later: does he argue for the superiority of Christianity anywhere else?)*
- *Another aside: I don't really think what he says about Judaism is true – not everything in Judaism refers to Moses. (Does that matter? He mainly wants to make a point about Christianity here – see my earlier thoughts about the overall aim of the text. But is it OK if he misrepresents Judaism while doing so? Must think about that.)*

> Think about your criticisms of the text and the argument – and decide whether they are criticisms of the core of the argument or of side points.

2 Back to the beginning

I'm not much further forward on how this relates to the rest of the text, though. Time to go back to the beginning, and reread the sentence in bold type.

> **The immediate feeling of absolute dependence is presupposed and absolutely contained in every religious and Christian self-consciousness as the only way in which our own being and the infinite Being of God can be one in self-consciousness**

Right, this is puzzling – it does not mention Jesus Christ at all. Does it have *anything* to do with what I have just said? What about 'our own being and the infinite Being of God can be one'? That sounds a bit like Jesus in John's Gospel saying 'I and the Father are one' … let's try to understand this phrase.

Schleiermacher's talking about *us* here, not about Jesus. But how can *we* be 'one' with 'the infinite being of God'? Well, it must matter that it's 'in self-consciousness'. Maybe we are 'one' with God in some sense when we know or experience God – which is bringing together 'me' and 'God' in one place (my consciousness)? That would fit my hypothesis about the overall meaning of the text (that it's about how Christians know or relate to God).

So let's try assuming that 'our own being and the infinite being of God can be one in self-consciousness' means, roughly, 'we can know God'.

The sentence would now read

> **The immediate feeling of absolute dependence is presupposed and absolutely contained in every religious and Christian self-consciousness as the only way in which [we can know God]**

the … feeling of absolute dependence is … the only way we can know God

Paragraph 1

For Christianity, specifically…
Knowing Jesus Christ = Knowing God

So – 'the immediate feeling of absolute dependence is [something I'll work out later] the only way we can know God'?

> Pay attention to sentence structure – here I am breaking the sentence up into units and trying to understand each one.

I still don't understand the whole of that sentence, but I've got far enough to see roughly what it might be saying: the immediate feeling of absolute dependence is the only way we can know God.

3 Into the middle

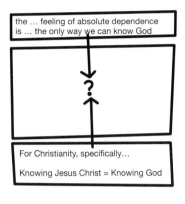

the … feeling of absolute dependence is … the only way we can know God

?

For Christianity, specifically…

Knowing Jesus Christ = Knowing God

But hang on – compare that with what I said about the final paragraph. Surely the immediate feeling of absolute dependence has nothing to do with Jesus Christ? But the last paragraph was all about how Christian knowledge of God is always related to Jesus Christ! So there seems to be a contra-diction.

> You think you have found a contradiction – give the author a good chance to explain him/herself before you conclude that the text is *really* contradictory.

Maybe this is what Schleiermacher addresses in the first long paragraph, which I've been ignoring because it looked difficult.

I look for references to 'Christ' and find this sentence:

> Hence the view that in every Christian affection there must be a relation to Christ does not in the least contradict our proposition.

I assume that by 'our proposition' he means the bit in bold at the beginning that he's just been discussing. This sounds promising – he's talking about the same 'contradiction' that I identified, and denying that it exists.

There's a 'Hence' there, so the bit immediately beforehand must explain why there isn't a contradiction.

> Pay attention to paragraph structure – what depends on what?

Here he says something about how God-consciousness is

> not … by itself alone an actual moment in religious experience, but always in connexion with other particular determinations

the … feeling of absolute dependence is … the only way we can know God

never get feeling of absolute dependence on its own, but always in some particular way

For Christianity, specifically…

Knowing Jesus Christ = Knowing God

I remember from the textbook that 'God-consciousness' is another way of saying 'feeling of absolute dependence', and vice versa.

All else being equal, trust the secondary literature – but use it as a way into the primary texts, not a substitute for reading them.

Here he seems to mean that you never just experience 'God' but always God 'in some particular way' (which for Christians is always linked to Jesus Christ).

Be aware of words and phrases with equivalent, or nearly equivalent, meaning; this can help you to follow an argument. Here I've got the idea from the textbook, but I might also have deduced it from the passage.

There's also something about different 'moments of existence' such as 'pleasure and pain' – there are different forms of religious experience, which if you're a Christian are all always linked back to Christ (and presumably, for other people are linked to other ways of talking about God).

- *An aside: it is striking how much language about feelings he uses in this text – 'pain', 'pleasure', 'affection', etc. He obviously wants to emphasise that religion starts with feeling.*

The language used is not irrelevant to the meaning of the text; think about how the ideas are conveyed. BUT be wary when reading texts in translation (like this one) – if you hang too much on the precise meaning and connotations of a specific word, you might find out that the word in the original language has completely different shades of meaning and connotations.

BUT he wants to say that these experiences also have to be linked back to this underlying feeling of absolute dependence, this God-consciousness that everyone has, or they don't count as religious.

4 Putting it all together

OK, but why is that important? What is the point of this whole discussion?

Stop occasionally to think about your understanding of the big picture as well as the details. This is where secondary literature can be particularly useful because it will give you an account of the 'big picture', which you can test against your reading of this specific passage.

- From the textbook, I know that Schleiermacher is interested in how people can possibly know God, and his answer is 'through *feeling*' (because he doesn't agree with Kant – he doesn't think you have access to God through reason). He locates a 'feeling of absolute dependence' and says 'that's where you have access to God'.

It makes sense that he would then want to explain 'how does this vague and general feeling-of-absolute-dependence get you to *Christian* belief in God?'

And what he says in this extract, to start off his explanation, is:

> Here is my current best guess about what the extract means, based on the discussion so far.

- you can never have the 'feeling of absolute dependence' (which is God-consciousness) on its own, it's always channelled through a particular religion and through your individual experiences ...
- and if you are a Christian, insofar as you have 'God-consciousness', you have consciousness of God *as* 'the Father of our Lord Jesus Christ', and of your own relationship to God *through* fellowship with Christ ...
- but the underlying 'feeling of absolute dependence' will be shared with people who are not Christians ...
- even though, if you are a Christian, you won't be able to talk about, or even experience, that 'feeling of absolute dependence' apart from your relationship to Jesus Christ. Muslims, Jews, etc. will also have their own distinctive forms of the 'feeling of absolute dependence'/God-consciousness.

Hmm – this could be controversial! Is he trying to have his cake and eat it – all religions are the same 'underneath' *and* they're all different? Don't Christians think Christianity is more 'different', more distinctive, than that? And has he completely run away from the issue of whether what Christians say about God and Jesus Christ is actually *true*? Does he care whether God is *really* the Father of Jesus Christ, or only whether some people 'experience' God that way?

> I am *now* in a position (having formed a clear idea of what the text says) to raise some critical questions. I am not necessarily in a position to say how Schleiermacher would answer them. I should try to find out – by studying this text and/or by wider primary and secondary reading.

When I have thought further about these last questions, I am in a position to write at least a brief summary of the passage, using some direct quotations *that I understand and of which I can explain the meaning*; to relate it to what I know about Schleiermacher's work as a whole, from my (limited) secondary reading; and to discuss and evaluate some possible criticisms of what he says here.

Bibliography

Primary sources

The series *Schleiermacher: Studies and Translations* edited by Terrence N. Tice is of very high academic quality and importance – but the books are expensive! Older, but still usable, translations of several of Schleiermacher's works are available online.

Friedrich Schleiermacher, *On Religion: Speeches to its Cultured Despisers*, trans. Richard Crouter (Cambridge: Cambridge University Press, 1996). See also Crouter's very useful introduction – probably the best place to start for secondary reading on the Speeches.

Friedrich Schleiermacher, *The Christian Faith*, ed. and trans. Hugh Ross Mackintosh *et al.* (Edinburgh: T&T Clark, 1928, reprinted 1999). A very useful 'reader's guide' is available at <http://people.bu.edu/wwildman/schl/cfguide/cfguide.htm>.

Friedrich Schleiermacher, *Brief Outline of Theology as a Field of Study*, trans. Terrence N. Tice (Lewiston: Edwin Mellon, 1989).

Friedrich Schleiermacher, *On the Glaubenslehre: Letters to Dr Lücke*, trans. James Duke and Francis Fiorenza (New York: American Academy of Religion, 1981).

Friedrich Schleiermacher, *Christmas Eve: Dialogue on the Incarnation*, trans. Terrence N. Tice (Lewiston: Edwin Mellon, 1991). Although not an 'academic' work, this is well worth reading; written as a conversation among friends on Christmas Eve, it gives a clear sense of Schleiermacher's theological priorities, and particularly of the importance of Romanticism for his thought.

Secondary reading

Keith Clements, *Friedrich Schleiermacher: Pioneer of Modern Theology* (London: Collins, 1987). Introductory work, including biographical material.

Richard Crouter, *Friedrich Schleiermacher: Between Enlightenment and Romanticism* (Cambridge: Cambridge University Press, 2005). Detailed scholarly account of Schleiermacher's works and context, particularly interesting on how Schleiermacher related to his times.

Brian M. Gerrish, *A Prince of the Church: Schleiermacher and the Beginnings of Modern Theology* (London: SCM, 1984). Another introductory text by a very influential scholar of Schleiermacher. Gerrish interprets Schleiermacher firmly within the Reformed tradition, as a 'Church' theologian. He argues this case in *The Old Protestantism and the New: Essays on the Reformation Heritage* (Edinburgh: T&T Clark, 2000).

Stephen Sykes, *Friedrich Schleiermacher* (Woking: Lutterworth Press, 1971). For more on how Sykes locates Schleiermacher in the history of theology, and particularly for a theological discussion of his idea of 'religion', see *The Identity of Christianity: Theologians and the Essence of Christianity from Schleiermacher to Barth* (London: SPCK, 1984).

David Jasper (ed.), *The Interpretation of Belief: Coleridge, Schleiermacher and Romanticism* (Basingstoke: Macmillan, 1989).

Jacqueline Marina (ed.), *Cambridge Companion to Schleiermacher* (Cambridge: Cambridge University Press, 2005). See especially the essay by Robert Adams on faith and knowledge.

Richard R. Niebuhr, *Schleiermacher on Christ and Religion* (New York: Scribner's, 1964). An older work, seeking the 'rehabilitation' of Schleiermacher. Niebuhr reads Schleiermacher as standing in strong continuity with the theological tradition, and focuses particularly on the importance of Christology in his thought.

Terrence N. Tice, *Schleiermacher* (Nashville: Abingdon Press, 2006). Particularly valuable introduction to Schleiermacher, including discussion of his influence and scholarly reception.

5

G.W.F. Hegel

AIMS

By the end of this chapter, we hope that you will:

- understand some of the ways in which Hegel's thought has been important for modern theology and modern thought about religion

- understand some reasons why it might still be worth studying his work

- know, and have explored through some examples related to religion, a few key concepts and patterns in his philosophy

- understand, at least on a basic level, why he called Christianity the 'religion of truth and freedom'.

Introduction: life and context

Georg Wilhelm Friedrich Hegel (1770–1831) was, by the end of his life, a celebrity – one of the best-known public figures in the rapidly-developing state of Prussia, and especially in its capital, Berlin. His lectures on philosophy pulled in large crowds (although at least some of those who attended were only hoping to catch one of his famously witty put-downs, or marvel at his notoriously bad lecturing style). His views on the issues of the day were sought out and discussed throughout the city. When he died, at the age of 61, his funeral was a major public event. His philosophy shaped the intellectual life of Europe for years after his death.

For much of his life, however, Hegel had looked like a failure. He had started out by training for the Lutheran pastorate, but had rebelled against the conservative and restrictive attitudes of the institution where he was sent to train. His early attempts at establishing a career in academic writing failed. He held jobs as a private tutor, as a newspaper editor and as the director of a *Gymnasium* (a 'high school') before he secured an academic post.

While Hegel was building up his career, Europe was undergoing enormous political change. Famously, he finished the book that made his name, *Phenomenology of Spirit*, in a city (Jena) that was under siege from Napoleon's armies. The Battle of Jena secured, for Napoleon, control over the small German city-states of the 'Holy Roman Empire'. This was the beginning of a reorganisation of all aspects of how the German-speaking countries were governed and run. It was not just a transfer of power – it was a transfer to a different *kind* of power, a different way of organising life. States acquired new constitutions and new codes of law.

Figure 5.1 G.W.F. Hegel

For Hegel, this was basically good news. He was strongly influenced by Romantic thought, a supporter of the French Revolution, and an advocate of political and religious freedom – and what he saw in Napoleon was someone who could make that freedom *real* throughout Europe. He wanted to know what the 'freedom' promised by the French Revolution looked like in practice, in the long run. One way to read Hegel's philosophy is as a reflection on the French Revolution and its aftermath – if you remember that we are still living in the aftermath of the French Revolution.

Among philosophers, Hegel is normally discussed alongside the *German Idealists* – Fichte, Schelling and others. He was part of a set of philosophical conversations in the late eighteenth and early nineteenth centuries that took up both the advances Kant made and the continuing problems he posed. Kant, as we saw in the first chapter, emphasised the active role of the mind in knowing the world – we do not just receive sensations passively, we actively 'make sense' of the world. We cannot understand anything without understanding our own act-of-understanding. This opened the way for philosophical systems that sought to explain *reality as a whole* starting from *the knowing and thinking self* – the 'I'; systems for which ideas, mind, reason and meaning were ultimately important.

Terminology: 'Idealist', used of philosophers, does not have its ordinary English-language meaning ('somebody who has ideals') – although many of these thinkers were 'idealists' in our sense as well. Idealist philosophers are those who take *ideas*, the activity of the thinking mind, as the ultimate reality. Very roughly, idealists are philosophers who explain 'matter' in terms of 'mind' – as opposed to materialists, who explain 'mind' in terms of 'matter'.

As we will see, Hegel's name for ultimate reality is 'mind' or 'spirit'; so he is normally classed as an idealist. However, this does not mean that he says 'matter doesn't really exist' or 'the world only exists inside your head'. He is an **objective** idealist. He says that the world really exists, apart from the individual who happens to be thinking about it. But he is still an idealist, because he thinks that everything is explicable in terms of reason, thinking and spirit – as the outworking of *absolute* reason, thinking and spirit. We will explore what this means, later in the chapter.

Hegel is most famous for his *Phenomenology of Spirit*, which is where the basic structure of his thought is first set out. The final sections give an account of 'religion'. A more detailed, and in some ways more accessible, source for his views on religion is his *Lectures on the Philosophy of Religion*, particularly the sections on 'absolute religion'.

Reading Hegel: how he thinks

Hegel's philosophy is notoriously complex – so notoriously complex that most people do not bother to read it. However, its complexity is built up from a few simple patterns. What makes it complex is that the patterns repeat, over and over again. Its complexity is like the complexity of a fractal.

The most basic pattern in Hegel's thought is *alienation and reconciliation*, or *alienation and going-beyond*. He thinks of:

- a simple unit (an idea, a situation, an aspect of the world)
- that splits (alienation)
- and comes back together (reconciliation), in a way that doesn't *lose* the two parts but brings them together in a larger and more complex unity.

This is the *Hegelian dialectic.* Put like that, it sounds very abstract – but Hegel works it through in real-life examples, of everything.

- You're listening to a lecture on Hegel's philosophy. You are not really understanding it, but you are writing down everything the lecturer says anyway. There's a simple unity between your listening and note-taking, on the one hand, and what the lecturer says, on the other.
- Then suddenly you stop and think: 'What she just said was complete rubbish, and there's no point in writing it down.' You stop writing.
- Briefly, you do not know what to do next. That's a moment of alienation; your listening and note-taking process is suddenly set 'over against' what the lecturer is saying.
- And then, perhaps, you start taking notes again – only now you are thinking as you write and recording the lecture in a way that makes more sense to you, and incorporates your critical reflections on what is said. That is reconciliation.
- Note that what you are doing now is more *complex* than the original 'simple unity' (when you were transcribing everything the lecturer said without thinking about it). It is also – which will become important later in the chapter – a lot more *rational*, and a definite sign of *progress*.

One of Hegel's major problems with Kant's philosophy was the lack of any move to 'reconciliation' or 'going-beyond'. He thought Kant had stopped with 'alienation'. As we saw in the previous chapter, Kant often produces pairs of opposites – for example, 'things in themselves' over against 'things as they appear to us', 'moral faith' over against 'ecclesiastical faith', 'philosophy' over against 'theology' – and does not say anything about how we get past that point of contradiction. Hegel was looking for ways to think and speak about the next step, beyond the pair of opposites.

You will probably come across accounts of Hegel that describe the dialectic as 'thesis-antithesis-synthesis' – where the 'thesis-antithesis' corresponds to what we have here called 'alienation', and the 'synthesis' to 'going-beyond alienation'.

We have chosen not to use thesis-antithesis-synthesis here: first, because these terms and ideas do not appear very much in Hegel's own writings; and second, because 'thesis-antithesis' implies that something [thesis] is being contradicted or challenged by something completely separate *from outside itself* [antithesis]. This is not how Hegel thinks. He is interested in *internal* tensions and contradictions within concepts and societies, and how they work themselves out.

The term we have expressed here as 'reconciliation or going-beyond' – *Aufhebung* in German – is notoriously difficult to translate into English. It contains the ideas of *keeping* the contradictory terms that result from alienation, and of *changing* them so that you no longer have a simple contradiction. The German word, in ordinary usage, can mean both 'preserve' and 'remove'! In older translations of Hegel you will find *Aufhebung* rendered as 'sublation', which is not very helpful. 'Transcending' is a little more helpful. 'Reconciliation' works very well for some purposes. The most literal translation is 'upheaval'.

Hegel's basic pattern is recognisably a Christian pattern. God creates the world, which is 'alien' to God's self, and then becomes united with it. There is a stage of alienation and a stage of 'getting beyond' alienation. Creation becomes alienated from God and is reconciled to God in Christ through the Holy Spirit. The incarnation brings together God and humanity in one person's life and makes possible the 'bringing together' of the whole of creation with God. This correspondence between the pattern of Hegel's thought and the pattern of Christian theology is, as we will see, no accident

Using this basic pattern, Hegel put forward a *total* philosophy, a philosophy that claimed to say something about nature, science and human activity, world history, religion – everything, as a whole. He presents everything as one vast interconnected process that exhibits the basic pattern at every level.

The term that, in Hegel's philosophy, covers the whole of reality is *Geist*. This is, again, notoriously hard to translate – it means 'spirit', but is also close in meaning to 'mind' or 'reason'.

When Hegel uses the word *Geist* for 'the whole of reality', this means that he believes that reality is *rational*. And, if reality is rational, rationality and reasoning is 'real'. Our thought-processes are part of the process by which ultimate reality develops. As thinkers and reasoners, we are not just spectators – we are an active part of what we reason about.

Reading tip: One of the features that makes Hegel hard to read is his tendency to use the word 'spirit' (= *Geist*) over and over again (e.g. 'Spirit is only spirit when it is for spirit'). That is because 'spirit' for him means *everything*. He is trying to describe the 'internal' processes of the universe – how the universe relates to itself. You might come up with similarly repetitive sentences if you were trying to describe your own thought-processes: e.g. 'I asked **myself** what I should do next'. One tip for interpreting these sentences is to forget about the nouns and focus on the verbs and the prepositions.

We are now ready to say a little more about what it means for Hegel to be an 'idealist'. Someone who is *not* an idealist will tend to think of the universe as fundamentally material. She will, of course, acknowledge that some parts of the universe happen to be *thinking* material (your and my brains, for instance). Part of the universe happens to be so constructed that it can look at and think about the rest of the universe, and it happens to find that the rest of the universe *can* be looked at and thought about.

Now, our non-idealist would probably say that these facts – that there are thinking bits of the universe, and that the universe turns out to be thinkable by them – are interesting but not particularly important. Hegel, on the other hand, puts these facts at the centre of his account of the universe. The universe is a something-that-thinks – a context in which consciousness emerges and develops. It is, in its way, a conscious reality. All the bits of thinking going on in your head and my head are not simply accidental facts about a material universe; they are parts of the universe's way of being conscious. And this same universe is at the same time a something-that-can-be-thought. The most important fact about the universe is that it is a *something that is conscious*, and what it is conscious of is itself. The story of the universe, for Hegel, is the story of the emergence and development of the universe-as-self-conscious.

Another way of putting it would be: Hegel, as an objective idealist, thinks that *the universe makes sense*. It 'makes sense' in that it can be thought about and understood ('this makes sense to me') and it also 'makes sense' in that it thinks and understands ('I can make sense of this').

It is also important to realise the 'making-sense' part of the story does not just happen inside the brains of individuals; it happens through societies and cultures. A society and a culture is a way of 'making sense of' the universe. More accurately, individuals, societies and cultures are all parts of the great process whereby the universe 'makes sense of itself', by which everything becomes both fully knowable and fully known.

One of Hegel's most famous sayings, from the *Philosophy of Right* is 'the real is the rational, and the rational is the real'. Before reading on, think about this sentence and your response to it. Why might some people object to this claim?

It has been argued that Hegel meant 'everything is all right and makes sense just as it is' – reality *as it is* is fully rational, and anything that doesn't fit into the rational system we have can't be real. Obviously that is problematic – on many levels, not least the political, because it sounds like a way of denying that anything (e.g. the state) could be improved.

This may not actually be what Hegel meant (see the discussion, below, of 'left' and 'right' Hegelians). At a minimum, he is saying that everything can be thought about and 'made sense of' over time – nothing real is unthinkable. And he is saying that thinking about things makes a real difference. There are not two separate spheres, 'thought' and 'reality', which fail to interact; there is one process, the universe-thinking-itself.

Another way of putting it: Hegel thinks that the universe makes sense to us, and that we make sense of the universe. But he does not assume that these two sorts of 'making sense' automatically coincide at any given time or in any given situation. In fact, he is very interested in the story of how they keep failing to coincide, how we keep misunderstanding the universe and how the universe keeps frustrating our expectations.

Various twentieth- and twenty-first-century (and some earlier) commentators have reacted against this aspect of Hegel's thought on ethical and political grounds. It can be argued that, by making everything 'thinkable' within one philosophical system, Hegel makes it impossible to encounter or acknowledge anything, or anyone, that is genuinely different from what we already know. Whatever does not fit in is either ignored or destroyed; it is a recipe for totalitarianism. On the other hand, there are twentieth- and twenty-first-century religious thinkers who think Hegel was not trying to make everything fit neatly together – rather, he was drawing attention to the difficult and ongoing *process* of 'thinking things through', the pervasiveness of conflict and the repeated need for reconciliation. Rowan Williams is one theologian who reads Hegel this way and draws extensively on his work. See his 'Logic and Spirit in Hegel' in Mike Higton (ed.), *Wrestling with Angels: Conversations in Modern Theology*.

Theology

We can deduce, from this overview of Hegel's thought, certain key ideas about the nature of human life and history that would also affect his religious thought. First, he believes in 'progress'; he tells a story of historical change, and tells it as a story of the *advance* of Spirit and of humanity. Second, his vision is not one of easy, obvious or predictable progress. For Hegel, progress only occurs in and through struggle; alienation is an inevitable and necessary aspect of human life and world history. We are always in the middle of the process of 'going-beyond'; our life always has elements of contradiction and conflict. Third, although Hegel is interested in individuals and their stories, and in the processes of alienation and reconciliation that go on between individuals and societies, ultimate truth and meaning is found in the whole, not in the individual.

This has major theological implications. We have seen that Hegel's story of alienation and reconciliation is the Christian story; he thinks he is giving philosophical expression to the Christian vision of world history. However, in Hegel's account, alienation and struggle are *necessary* – they are the means by which Spirit advances. So, theologically, for him, the Fall is necessary; humanity has to become alienated from God so that a higher reconciliation of God and humanity will be possible. The story of Adam and Eve's sin is the story of a 'happy fault'.

> This was not a new idea. Medieval theology and piety had developed the idea of the 'happy fault' (*felix culpa*): 'O happy fault, that merited such redemption and such a Redeemer!' If redemption in Christ is a good that exceeds the goodness of the original created state, has humanity not gained as a result of the sin that led to that redemption?

We are now in a position to examine Hegel's philosophy of religion. In order to understand what he means by 'philosophy of religion' and why religion is so important to his philosophy, we have to challenge some pervasive assumptions. In the English-speaking world today, 'philosophy of religion' is usually taken to mean using philosophical tools to think about some specific religious claims (such as immortality of the soul, creation and so forth). That works in a context in which 'philosophy' mainly means 'clarifying concepts' and 'deciding whether arguments make sense' – a context shaped by the twentieth-century tradition of *analytic* philosophy.

But, for Hegel, philosophy is about understanding the meaning of life, the universe and everything – and so is religion. The main difference between them is that they do it in different ways – philosophy explains and religion 'represents'. Very roughly, religion tells you a story, philosophy tells you what the moral of the story is. Religion is 'picture-thinking', philosophy translates the pictures into concepts. So when Hegel does 'philosophy of religion', he is using philosophy to explain what religion has always been about; he is making religion more 'philosophical'.

Then it is important to realise that Hegel thinks that religion – at least, Christianity – *really does* get to the meaning of life, whether Christians fully understand it or not. So his philosophy is not, in his view, going to prove religion wrong. In fact, he claims that philosophy is more orthodox, more conservative about traditional Christian doctrine, than much of Christianity. Christians who do not really understand their own religion are likely to reject or downplay doctrines that, from a philosophical point of view, are very important.

For example, Hegel's thought is thoroughly Trinitiarian. For him, the doctrine of the **Trinity** is key to understanding how God's life can include alienation and reconciliation, and how God can be involved in the process of world history while still being the one eternal God. Thus, God is present in Jesus Christ, experiencing alienation in the heart of God's own self in the crucifixion and death of Jesus. At this point of ultimate contradiction, Hegel is prepared to say, 'God Himself is dead'. Again, God the Spirit completes the work of reconciliation – bringing about the eschatological 'Kingdom of the Spirit' to succeed and perfect the present 'Kingdom of the Son'. Hegel does break with theological tradition, or side with a historical minority, on several points – such as his interpretation of the Fall, discussed above, and indeed his strong reading of the 'death' of God on the cross – but he always claims that he is presenting a genuine and plausible rereading of Christian scripture and tradition.

But there is a tension here. If religion is a set of stories or pictures, and philosophy tells you the meaning of the stories or pictures, do you still need the religion once you have the philosophy? Do you need to believe in the historical truth of the Christian stories, and do you need to express these truths about the meaning of life in Christian terms? In the *Phenomenology of Spirit*, Hegel argues that after the development of Christianity there needs to be a final movement of 'going-beyond' – Christianity needs to be transformed into philosophical understanding, beyond its 'picture-thinking'. This does not, however, mean that there will be no religious practice, no religious stories and no religious community. Religion as such is not abolished by the move to 'philosophy of religion' – in fact, it is valued more, because people have a deeper understanding of why it is true and important. At least, that appears to be Hegel's view – but it is easy to see why at least some of his successors thought that his philosophy called them to dispense with traditional Christianity.

In his lectures on the philosophy of religion, Hegel calls Christianity the 'religion of truth and freedom'. What does he mean by this?

Religion and freedom

In Douglas Adams' *Life, the Universe and Everything*, the intergalactic adventurer Zaphod Beeblebrox, having acquired a fast spaceship and enormous power, confronts an experience that Hegel would term *abstract freedom*.

> 'Freedom,' he said aloud.
> Trillian came onto the bridge at that point and said several enthusiastic things on the subject of freedom.
> 'I can't cope with it,' he said darkly [...]
> 'Here I am, Zaphod Beeblebrox, I can go anywhere, do anything ...

'I am,' he added, 'one hell of a guy, I can do anything I want. I just don't have the faintest idea what.'

He paused.

'One thing,' he further added, 'has suddenly ceased to lead to another,' in contradiction of which he had another drink and slid gracelessly off his chair.

Douglas Adams, *Life, the Universe and Everything*
(Pan Macmillan, 1982), Chapter 8, p54–55.

As Hegel saw it, human beings in modernity were liable to end up in Zaphod Beeblebrox's situation. More precisely, he thought they *had* already done so with the French Revolution, which was the point at which human beings declared, collectively, that they could do anything they wanted, and then slid gracelessly into the Reign of Terror.

A pessimistic response to this might be to say: 'So, freedom is clearly a bad thing. Let's forget all attempts to assert our freedom over against the systems of rules that we have inherited; it only leads to anarchy and destruction. Let's just go back to authoritarian rule.' That is not Hegel's response. He thinks that there *can* be freedom but that real freedom, 'concrete' freedom, is much more complex than just saying 'I can do anything I want'.

The problem is that abstract freedom, freedom to do 'anything I want', cutting loose from all constraints, will always come up against its opposite – the need to do *something* in particular, and the real constraints we operate under as finite, historical human beings. If we do not acknowledge and think through that contradiction, we are trapped in it. We are stuck with an abstract freedom that we do not know how to use, and meanwhile we are at the mercy of forces that we cannot avoid because we have not acknowledged their power over us. (Zaphod has another drink and slides off the chair; revolutionary France collapses into authoritarianism and violence.) The solution, Hegel says, is to 'go beyond' abstract freedom.

What does this look like? Consider a small-scale but pertinent example: someone who is brought up as a follower of a particular religious tradition and who, as she grows up, participates in its practices, repeats its stories and so on, because that is what she has always done. Then imagine that at some point – perhaps in adolescence – she rebels. She rejects the religion in which she was brought up. She sees its rules, practices and beliefs as *alien* to her, and she resolves to get away from them completely. Now, she says, 'I can do anything I want'.

In practice, though, she is still the person who was shaped by that religious upbringing. What she does and thinks now is still affected by it. Even how she chooses to express her 'freedom' is shaped by what she is trying to free herself from; she is always in rebellion against her religious background. On the one hand, she says 'I can do anything I want'; on the other hand, what she in fact does is being affected by her past. She has, in Hegel's terms, discovered abstract freedom – but she is not yet really living a free life.

Later in life, perhaps, she realises what is going on. She recognises how this religious upbringing shaped her life and personality and she makes conscious decisions about how to live with that past. She makes her religious upbringing 'her own' by acknowledging it and working with it. Perhaps she returns to the religious tradition she left (with a changed attitude, what we might call a 'mature faith') or perhaps she does not. In either case, she has now gone beyond 'abstract freedom' through reconciliation – reconciling her exercise of freedom with her particular circumstances. The free person in whom Hegel is most interested is, not the teenager (or the intergalactic playboy) who says 'I can do anything I want – so what shall I do?', but the adult who says 'Now I really *know* who I am and what I want to do'.

Incidentally, it is not a coincidence that stories about people growing up are so useful for explaining Hegel's ideas. The 'maturity' of modern humanity, contrasted to the 'childhood' of the past, was a common image for Enlightenment thinkers. (Recall Kant in 'An Answer to the Question "What is Enlightenment?"'). Hegel's own *Phenomenology of Spirit* has been compared to the 'coming-of-age novel' (*Bildungsroman*), a genre that was newly popular at this time.

So what makes Christianity the 'religion of freedom'? Hegel believes that freedom is integral to Christianity, and that the modern discovery of freedom is not a step away from Christianity but a stage in Christian history. Christianity teaches *and practises* the increase of real freedom – not just freedom to 'do what you want' but freedom gained through making history, rules, beliefs, material conditions and so forth your own. Other religious traditions, as he presents them, ask you to subject yourself to 'alien' rules and a God who always remains 'other'. Christianity, on the other hand, speaks of laws that are 'written on the heart' and of a God who becomes human. Within Christianity, as Hegel sees it, the life of God is not simply something that goes on 'over there' beyond our knowledge. It is something taking place in our world, catching people up into it. God's life is being 'made real' in the lives of Christians. For Christians, 'following God's commandments' (which sounds like obeying external dictates) and 'living out your faith' (which sounds like making and acting out your own decisions) come to mean the same thing.

Furthermore, recall what we said earlier about Hegel's interest in societies and cultures as ways of 'making sense'. Christianity is not merely an individual reality, but also and importantly a social one. Hegel takes up the Christian idea of the Body of Christ as a union in which each person freely contributes her own individual gift of the Spirit to the building up of the whole.

See 1 Corinthians 12, for example verses 4 and 7: 'Now there are varieties of gifts, but the same Spirit ... to each is given the manifestation of the Spirit for the common good.'

In the Christian community, Hegel says, each person is more free the more he learns to contribute what is specifically his to each other person, and receive from each other person what is specifically that other person's.

Revelation

The history of becoming-free is, for Hegel, exactly that: a history. It is a process that includes changes over time and specific developments in particular times and places. You cannot describe it or understand it without talking about those specifics. Those specifics are how truth and freedom become real for us – how they are *given* to us.

This is why, for Hegel – unlike Kant, and many of Kant's philosophical predecessors – belief in revelation is an indispensable part of Christianity. There have to be specific times, places and events through which truth and freedom become real within history, and through which they are given to humanity. Christianity, says Hegel, is the 'religion of truth' not just because what it says is true, but because it explains *how it is possible* to know and speak the truth. Christians say: God reveals God's self and therefore people can know God and say true things about God. God is revealed in the Word and through the work of the Holy Spirit – and the whole story of world history is the story of God's self-revelation.

Hegel argues that this is theologically valid, but it is also philosophically important. The true God must be *self*-revealing, because otherwise there is no way to overcome the alienation between 'God in God's self' and 'God according to human knowledge'. If God doesn't reveal God's self to us, there's always an unbridgeable gap between our thoughts about God and the 'real' God. And if this alienation cannot be overcome, Hegel thinks, the move towards truth and freedom is cut off; at some point our efforts to 'think everything through' will meet a brick wall, something we just have to accept or reject but can never understand. For Hegel, it is enormously important that what is given to the world, in revelation, is *God's own self*. Christians, who receive the Holy Spirit and become part of the Body of Christ, are not just people who know something about God; they are people who are part of God's own act of knowing.

The point about 'revelation' that really bothered Kant and his predecessors is that it is given to people from an external authority. Hegel's important insight here, which has implications for politics and culture as well as religion, is that 'everything must come to us from outside' (*Lectures on the Philosophy of Religion*, Lectures of 1827, p252 (Hodgson trans.)). Everything we have is given to us from an external authority – which does not mean that it cannot also be 'reasonable', or worth reasoning about. Revelation is not opposed to reason, but is its prerequisite.

But does the acceptance of revelation, as Kant thought, place a limit on freedom? Freedom, truth and reason are as closely linked for Hegel as they are for Kant. Recall that, for Kant, a person is most free when she is using her reason. The same is true for Hegel – but the difference is that he is interested in what that person is reasoning *about*. If you only had your reason, without external influences, you would have no thoughts, because you would have nothing to think about. The interesting question for Hegel is not 'what can reason do on its own?' but 'what can reason do with what is given to it?'

This leads Hegel to his interest in history – which could be his most important contribution to modern thought about religion. He is probably the first person to place 'reason' fully in history, taking seriously the idea that reasoning (including the reasoning of whoever is writing this and whoever is reading it) always happens in a particular time, place, culture, language and set of circumstances. Nowadays this is a throwaway line – hard to argue with, even if its implications are not always thought through. Hegel, however, was living in the very early days of the study of history. It was a relatively new idea that the past might be different from the present, in any way that was worth studying. The term *Zeitgeist* (spirit of the age) – expressing the idea that different periods of history have different 'ways of thinking' – was coined a few decades prior to Hegel's work, and taken up in Hegel's own thought.

His philosophy and his theology is not an account of 'how things are and always have been', but an account of 'how things came to be as they are, and where they are going'. Again, he argues that this makes theological sense; Christianity is a story, a story that is still going on and in which Christians claim to participate. The history of the world is a history of the activity of (the Holy) Spirit and both the philosopher and the theologian have to make sense of this history.

For Hegel, Christianity needed to be a 'positive religion' – by which he meant that it had to 'posit', to take as given, specific texts, events and stories. An idea or theory that corresponded to nothing in history could not really be 'true', however interesting or plausible it might be – just as a person with no way of relating to her historical situation could not really be free. Here again, Christianity appears as the 'religion of truth', the religion in which ultimate meaning becomes present in history and history is given meaning. The gap between a meaningless set of brute facts and an otherworldly realm that gives them meaning is overcome.

Hegel was not, then, concerned to separate out the 'natural' from the 'revealed' or the timeless from the 'historical' in Christianity. He wanted to use philosophy to explain the universal and world-historical significance of Christianity's 'positive' content. Again, he found theological justification for this move. The resurrection and ascension of Jesus preserves Jesus' particular human life while 'going beyond' it; and the sending of the Holy Spirit enables this history to be related to each and every other particular history.

Hegel's legacy

The scale and scope of Hegel's influence meant that there were bound to be debates over the interpretation of his thought. Analyses of his legacy tend to divide his followers into two groups: Left Hegelians (such as Feuerbach, Marx, D.F. Strauss) and Right Hegelians (such as Martensen, a key influence on Kierkegaard's intellectual context).

We have already seen where the fault-line between the two groups might lie. Hegel can be read as a political and religious radical, or at least as supplying the basis for radicalism. His claim that Christianity as 'representation' or 'picture-thinking' needed to be gone beyond, through philosophy, could easily become a call for the end of Christianity. Thus, in Marx's thought, religion is understood as a form of **alienation**, which needs to be overcome in the name of full human freedom. On the other hand, Hegel's own defence of 'orthodox' Christian doctrines (revelation, the Trinity) could be seen as giving philosophical justification for maintaining the religious *status quo*. In the same way, Hegel's interest in historical processes, and the historical development of reason, can be read in (at least) two ways – as a call for more revolutions to bring the process of world history closer to fulfilment, or as an affirmation of *this* historical situation as the culmination of reason's development.

Given the later course of European history, it is not really surprising that Hegel, with his attempt to provide a 'philosophy of everything', is now often read as the predecessor of one or another form of political totalitarianism – either of Marx and hence of communism, or of extreme German **nationalism** and hence of Nazism. His own political sympathies and interests, as we have seen, were with those who were trying to work out how the Enlightenment ideals of reason and freedom could be made real in history. Many of the more sympathetic recent discussions of Hegel focus not on the 'end point' – the political or religious vision that supposedly results from his philosophy – but on how he describes intellectual, religious or social processes.

Exercise

In the chapter on Schleiermacher, we introduced some approaches to reading difficult primary texts. When studying thinkers such as Kant, Schleiermacher and Hegel, it is important to spend plenty of time with the primary texts – but you also have access to numerous secondary sources, providing summaries and critiques of the primary texts. These secondary sources are (we hope) based on much longer and more detailed study of the primary texts than you are able to undertake. They are also, inevitably, shaped by their authors' particular interests, assumptions, aims and backgrounds, and they often contradict each other. So how should you use these secondary sources? How do you evaluate and engage with what they say about the primary texts and reach your own critical judgements?

In this exercise, we aim to help you to feel more confident about reading and evaluating critical accounts of major historical thinkers and about raising your own critical questions both to the secondary and to the primary sources.

We will look at short extracts from two accounts, by twentieth-century scholars, of Hegel's philosophy of religion.

Step 1

The first thing you will need to do is read the extracts and go through something like the process for 'reading difficult texts' described in the Schleiermacher chapter. For each extract, try to:

a) determine whether the author is 'for' Hegel, 'against' Hegel or neither;
b) summarise in your own words the main points the author makes about Hegel;
c) determine – with the help of the bibliographical information – as much as you can about what sort of secondary source this is. For what purpose is the author writing about Hegel? Is the main aim to give an account of what Hegel says or to argue some wider point? In real life, of course, you would generally have far more information available to you than we have provided here, because you would have the book or article from which the extract is taken. Even here, though, you can probably find out more information about the authors and their books.

Do this for yourself before reading on to Step 2.

A.
Hegel is ... 'unorthodox' because he posits a prior 'moment' of relatively unrealised and merely abstract subjectivity in God. He is also 'heretical' because, in gnostic fashion, he conceives of creation as a negation which results in a self-alienation, and so as itself a 'fall', both for God and for humanity. This means that, unlike orthodox tradition, he makes evil a necessity ... [footnote: Hegel, *Lectures on the Philosophy of Religion*, ed. Peter Hodgson, vol. 3, pp296ff, 304–316]
John Milbank, Theology and Social Theory, revised edition
(Oxford: Blackwell, 2006), p159 in chapter 'For and Against Hegel'.

B.
Hegel offers a vision of God as the encompassing, inexhaustible sphere of all that is – intellectual and material, eternal and temporal, infinite and finite. Nothing is outside of God, even the most trivial or despicable. God encompasses what is not-God within God. All that comes about in the world, great good and terrible evil, is preserved within the divine life, even if as negated or overcome ... [Hegel's]

holism of the spirit honours the inexhaustible generative power of God as well as the irreducible wealth of the world.

> Peter Hodgson, *Hegel and Christian Theology: A Reading of the Lectures on the Philosophy of Religion* (Oxford: Oxford University Press, 2005), pp272–273 in final chapter 'The Theological Significance of Hegel Today'.

Step 2

My summaries read:

A (John Milbank)
a) Against Hegel.
b) Hegel is not an orthodox Christian, for three reasons: (1) he thinks God needs to develop over time; (2) he thinks creation is a 'fall'; (3) he thinks evil is necessary. (NB: if your summary of A did not include all these points, don't worry; this is not the main point of the exercise.)
c) Part of a larger project that isn't only about Hegel (*Theology and Social Theory*); this is a chapter that is aiming to evaluate Hegel's usefulness for that project ('For and Against Hegel').

B (Peter Hodgson)
a) For Hegel.
b) Hegel thinks God includes everything, and nothing (not even evil) is outside God.
c) Part of a close study of Hegel – this is the concluding chapter, which is focused not on the details of Hegel's work, but on his importance for theology *now*.

At this point you are already in a position to start making judgements about how to evaluate and use the sources. For example, you know that both of them are reading Hegel from within Christian theology, addressing audiences of Christian theologians (possibly alongside others). That affects the questions they ask about Hegel and the criteria on which they evaluate him – note, for example, the discussion of whether Hegel is 'heretical'.

You also know that Hodgson is emphasising those aspects of Hegel that he thinks are most relevant to theological thought *today* (rather than, for example, those aspects of Hegel that were most interesting in Hegel's own time), so you would probably not quote this extract in a discussion of Hegel's historical context. You also know that Milbank's evaluation is part of a larger theological project of his own and you might need to find out more about the aims and outcomes of that project in order to be able to judge his reading of Hegel. You know that neither author is 'unbiased' – but hopefully you knew or expected that before you started!

The next step is to set yourself up to evaluate the authors' claims, to put yourself in a position where you can join in a conversation with them about Hegel, rather than simply restating what they say. For each extract, write down:

a) At least one claim *about Hegel* that is made here (using your summary); whether you think, on the basis of your reading so far, that that claim is justified; any queries you have about it; and how you might test or investigate it further.

b) At least one claim or assumption about *something else* that is important to what the author is saying about Hegel; whether you think, on the basis of your existing knowledge, that that claim or assumption is justified; any queries you have about it; and how you might test or investigate it further.

Step 3

Many answers are possible – here are some examples:

A (John Milbank)

a) Claim: Hegel thinks creation is a 'fall' for both God and the world. This makes some sense, because, according to what I have read about Hegel, creation (the separateness of God and world) is linked to 'alienation', which is something you have to overcome, not straightforwardly a good thing. Test the claim by reading the passages given in the footnote – is Milbank summarising them well, are other interpretations possible? Could also check other secondary literature for discussions of Hegel and creation, to see whether most scholars agree.

b) Claim: Orthodox Christian theology does not say that creation is a 'fall'. Again, this sounds plausible – e.g. the Fall comes *after* creation in the biblical narratives. But I am not sure how much of a problem it really is, in Christian theology, to put creation and 'fall' together – perhaps others besides Hegel do this? I might need to read more of what Milbank says on the subject; or I might need to consult a textbook, or revisit notes from other courses, about 'creation' in Christian theology.

B (Peter Hodgson)

a) Claim: Hegel thinks God includes everything (see above). This sounds plausible, in that Hegel's philosophy of religion is a 'total' philosophy, i.e. including everything. But I do not really understand what it means – is he saying that Hegel is a pantheist? Test the claim, first, by reading more of Hodgson's book – this is the final summary chapter, and he must explain this in more detail elsewhere (consult the index and the contents page). Then check the passages of Hegel to which he refers, and see if his summaries are reasonable and if other interpretations are possible. Perhaps also look for reviews of Hodgson's book and see what others say about it – is his a very controversial interpretation of Hegel, or one that is widely accepted?

b) Assumption: It is a good thing to have a theology in which God 'includes' everything – including evil. This assumption is not stated in the extract, but it comes across in the style of Hodgson's presentation. I am not convinced – why should we want God to 'include' evil, isn't God supposed to be good? Test the assumption by reading this passage in context, to see whether Hodgson puts forward a plausible defence.

Having reached this point, you know what you need to do in order to join the conversation about Hegel. If you have been keeping a record of your reflections, you now have a *good* set of notes on your secondary sources – notes that will enable you to do more than simply rehash what various secondary sources say. On some points (for example, (b) on Hodgson, above), you can join in the conversation simply by questioning the assumptions, or the reasoning process, of the secondary sources, without going back to the primary texts. On most substantive points, you will have to go both to the primary texts and to other secondary sources, building up your own picture of Hegel to which you can relate the secondary sources' claims. And in order to make this a manageable task, you will have to decide (as these authors have decided) which conversations you want to join – which issues in the interpretation of Hegel are interesting or important and which you can leave aside.

As a final step in this exercise, we suggest you think back over this chapter and go through the same process in relation to some of the claims and assumptions *we* make – summarising them, working out how you would evaluate them and preferably testing them through reference to relevant sources. This might sound rather like a process of alienation and reconciliation – and that might not be a coincidence.

Bibliography

Primary sources

The most relevant works for our purposes are:

G.W.F. Hegel, *Phenomenology of Spirit*, trans. A.V. Millar with notes by J.W. Findlay (Oxford: Oxford University Press, 1979). You may also have access to the translation by J.B. Bailey, *Phenomenology of Mind* (London: Dover Books, reprinted 2004); we recommend the Millar translation, not least because of the way it translates the key term *Geist*.

G.W.F. Hegel, *Lectures on the Philosophy of Religion*, ed. Peter C. Hodgson, trans. R.F. Brown *et al.* (Berkeley: University of California Press, 1985).

Secondary reading

Terry Pinkard, *Hegel: A Biography* (Cambridge: Cambridge University Press, 2000). Not only gives a very engaging account of Hegel's life, but also discusses all the key aspects of his philosophy. See also Pinkard, *Hegel's Phenomenology: The Sociality of Reason* (Cambridge: Cambridge University Press, 1996), for further exposition of the structure of Hegel's philosophy.

Peter Singer, *Hegel: A Very Short Introduction* (Oxford: Oxford University Press, 2001). Accessible introduction to Hegel, contains some material on religion.

Frederick Beiser, *Hegel* (London: Routledge, 2005). Has a useful section on 'the religious dimension' of Hegel's thought, and surveys the development of his ideas on Christianity.

William Desmond, *Hegel's God: A Counterfeit Double?* (Aldershot: Ashgate, 2003). An extended critique of Hegel by a philosopher of religion; a dense book, but the preface gives a useful account of the overall argument.

Lawrence Dickey, 'Hegel on Religion and Philosophy', in Frederick Beiser (ed.), *Cambridge Companion to Hegel* (Cambridge: Cambridge University Press, 1993). Focuses on the historical context of Hegel's views on religion, and his place in the controversies of his day.

Peter C. Hodgson, *Hegel and Christian Theology: A Reading of the Lectures on the Philosophy of Religion* (Oxford: Oxford University Press, 2007). Sympathetic and readable take on Hegel's importance for Christian theology, by a Hegel scholar who is also a theologian.

Andrew Shanks, *Hegel's Political Theology* (Cambridge: Cambridge University Press, 1991). Not an easy read, but an interesting constructive argument for Hegel's contemporary relevance.

Rowan Williams, *Wrestling with Angels: Conversations in Modern Theology*, ed. Mike Higton (London: SCM, 2007), Chapter 3. Williams' theology is influenced at several points by (a particular reading) of Hegel; this essay presents his assessment of Hegel's theological and political importance.

6

Søren Kierkegaard

AIMS

By the end of this chapter, we hope that you will:

- understand some of the ways in which Kierkegaard's work has been important for modern theology

- know how to approach Kierkegaard's pseudonymous writings

- understand what Kierkegaard says about truth and subjectivity

- be able to distinguish different versions of Kierkegaard in recent theological and philosophical writing.

Introduction: Kierkegaard's life

It is easy to become fascinated by Kierkegaard's life, and to turn a discussion of his theology into an analysis of his biography. There is something odd about such an approach, however. It is true that Kierkegaard is deeply concerned with the way in which Christian faith becomes passionately real in an individual life, but it is equally true, as John Caputo says, that he 'sought a way to excite Christian passion in his readers *without interposing himself between the individual and God*' (*How to Read Kierkegaard*, London: Granta, 2007, p6, our emphasis). He went to fairly elaborate lengths to secure this, as we shall see.

Figure 6.1 Søren Kierkegaard

Søren Aabye Kierkegaard's short life (1813–1855) would make a good novel – though the novel would be better if it could also include the story of his father, Michael Pedersen Kierkegaard. Søren was born into urban comfort and financial stability, but his father had been born into rural poverty, and his route from that poverty to wealth had not been smooth. Shortly before he died, Michael revealed to his 25-year-old son a secret he had been carrying around for nearly 70 years: once, when a miserable shepherd boy, he had cursed God for burdening him with such a fate. All the prosperity and stability that had followed, Michael had understood against the background of that sin – as he saw it, an unforgivable sin against the Holy Spirit. He believed that God had given all this only in order to take it all away. His first wife had died and by the time he was himself close to death five of his seven children had too; he did not expect the two who remained (Søren and his brother Peter) to outlive him.

Søren's upbringing was, as far as we can tell, affectionate, but his father's beliefs about his sin and its consequences seem to have lent it a serious, even melancholy air – a moral and religious earnestness and a deep seriousness about the gravity of sin. When a student at the University of Copenhagen, following his father's intention that he should study theology and then enter the Lutheran priesthood, Søren rebelled for a time and became (at least by his family's austere standards) rather self-indulgent and pleasure-seeking, but in 1838 he experienced some kind of reawakening to his Christian faith, and reconciliation with his family and with his father's seriousness – just a month before the latter died. Kierkegaard wrote, 'I regard his death as the last sacrifice of his love for me, because in dying he did not depart *from* me but he died *for* me, in order that something, if possible, might still come of me' (*Journals and Papers* 5: *Autobiographical, Part One: 1829-1848*, eds. Howard V. Hong and Edna H. Hong, Bloomington: Indiana University Press, 1978, p122).

As well as being shaped by his relationship to his father, however, Kierkegaard's life and work were shaped by his relationship to Regine Olsen. He met her in 1837, they became engaged in 1840, and Kierkegaard broke off the engagement in 1841. The reasons for the break remain obscure but seem to include a sense that he should not burden her with his persistent underlying melancholy, and that he was called to a life of Christian service that would require of him an almost monastic existence. It was in the days after the break – distraught, fully aware of his cruelty, and yet determined – that Kierkegaard began writing in earnest and his career as a theologian and philosopher properly began.

For the rest of his life, despite a plan (later abandoned) to become a pastor, Kierkegaard remained an independent author, producing an astonishing volume of writing in the 14 years between 1841 and his death in 1855, at the age of 42. He sought in that writing to fulfil the vocation that his father's death had confirmed for him and for which he had abandoned the engagement to Regine: a vocation to examine and communicate what it means to be a Christian and to fight against false accounts of what Christian life involves – especially accounts that water down and make something easy and comfortable out of the life-encompassing demand that he believed Christianity makes on each person.

Kierkegaard was not trying in his writings to set out a theory, or to communicate in the abstract to 'any rational human being' – but, in the first place, to make possible a transformation among the specific people who surrounded him. He was living in what has become known as the Danish Golden Age – a period of artistic and intellectual flourishing prompted in part by the influence of Romanticism. (Kierkegaard was, for instance, a contemporary of Hans Christian Andersen – indeed, Kierkegaard's first publication was a review of one of Andersen's novels.) More particularly, he was writing in a context of confident state Christianity, where to be a citizen meant being a baptised Lutheran, and where the state Church was home to what Kierkegaard saw as an undemanding form of Enlightenment Christianity in which no serious tension was admitted between faith and reason or between devotion and citizenship. Danish Christianity was certainly shot through with veins of Pietism but, to Kierkegaard's eye, it seemed to be quite possible to combine even this Pietism with state Christianity without undue anxiety.

Kierkegaard's writings were an attempt to unsettle his readers from this comfortable rut and to tip them into something quite different. Safe Christendom had, he thought, been mistaken for dangerous Christianity, and the idea that Christian commitment might make awkward, overwhelming and intemperate demands had been lost.

His writings against the compromises of Christendom became increasingly sharp over the years and the last years of his life were consumed by a fierce attack on and break with the state Church. On his deathbed, he refused to take Communion from a Lutheran pastor, saying:

> I have made my choice ... The pastors are civil servants of the Crown and have nothing to do with Christianity ... [Y]ou see, God is sovereign, but then there are all these people who want to arrange things comfortably for themselves ... Then they are the sovereign, and God's sovereignty is finished.
>
> in Bruce H. Kirmmse (ed.), *Encounters with Kierkegaard: A Life as Seen by His Contemporaries*, trans. Bruce H. Kirmmse and Virginia R. Lauren, Princeton: Princeton University Press, 1996, p126.

There is a problem here for many who read Kierkegaard today. It is very easy to cheer along – to side quickly with him against the compromise, self-satisfaction and hypocrisy of the Church he was attacking. In other words, it is very easy to read in such a way that the stabs of Kierkegaard's prose are all taken to hit a target *over there* and to leave us, the readers, untouched. It is worth recognising, if we read like this, that we have become a kind of reader that Kierkegaard absolutely did not want.

Kierkegaard's writings

Kierkegaard's writings fall into two distinct camps. On the one hand, there are a number of writings produced in his own voice, under his own name – mostly 'edifying discourses' (that is, more or less, extended sermons, written with pastoral intent). On the other hand, there are the better-known and more voluminous writings published under a variety of pseudonyms. One of the central challenges facing anyone who begins reading Kierkegaard is that of knowing how to approach these pseudonymous writings.

Kierkegaard's use of pseudonyms appears to have been deliberate and strategic. He did not want to present the world with 'Kierkegaard's theology', but to provoke a journey of reflection and change in his readers. Rather than presenting his readers with a finished theory, he presents a series of explorations, each examining as if from within one way that life and faith might look from some waypoint on that journey. So, for instance, in the first half of *Either/Or*, the book he began writing after breaking with Regine, he explores from within what he calls the 'aesthetic' approach to life – exploring both what it means to live this approach consistently and reflectively, and showing his readers (rather than telling them) how unsatisfactory a life such an approach yields. In the second half of the book, under a different pseudonym, he writes from a different waypoint on the journey – the 'ethical' approach to life – and again explores that approach from the inside, showing how it is able to respond to and resolve some of the failings of the aesthetic approach, but also making it clear that the ethical approach has inadequacies of its own.

The various pseudonymous viewpoints can't be neatly arranged along a single line, and they don't all work in the same way. He chooses different genres for different viewpoints; some are more parodic than others; in some the problems with the viewpoint emerge from within, in some they are problems that are only visible to someone looking at this form of life from without. The overall pattern, however, is clear: Kierkegaard is attempting to write in such a way that his readers can't simply settle back and think they've 'got' his take-home message and can now rest content. The process is, quite deliberately, not one that leads to an easy finishing point: one can't simply select the final viewpoint in the journey, discard the rest and declare that one has at last arrived at Kierkegaard's theology. Rather, his readers are handed a series of mirrors for self-examination, and invited to an ongoing process of transformation.

One way of understanding the nature of Kierkegaard's authorship more precisely is by comparing him to Hegel (see Chapter 5). Hegel's work, as we have seen, was full of descriptions of the ways in which contradictions emerge within any given pattern of society and thought, including within the pattern of relationships between individuals and the whole made possible by that form of society. And his work is full of descriptions of the ways in which later patterns of society and thought could resolve those earlier contradictions by drawing the conflicting elements into a deeper resolution – a process for which, as we saw, he used the word *Aufhebung*. Hegel presented these transformations as leading in the direction of a greater integration: a unity of thought and world, individual and society. Kierkegaard's pseudonymous works can be seen as setting out a kind of internalised, individualised Hegelianism. It is not now whole social symphonies that are explored from the inside and shown to have their clashing themes brought to resolution in a new composition. It is individual patterns of life and commitment that are explored from the inside and shown to have their inadequacies overcome in other, truer patterns. And where they lead is not to a whole system in which the individual and society, thought and world are reconciled but to an individual life shaped in a certain way in response to God's sovereignty.

> Something similar might be said about Karl Barth's commentary on Romans, particularly the famous second edition of 1922. Barth's writing is not designed to give the reader an easily graspable overview of Paul's theology (or of Barth's). Rather, it is designed to push and pull at the reader, to needle her, to unsettle her and so to provoke her into a new way of thinking. Such a strategy doesn't make for easy reading, but neither Kierkegaard nor the early Barth was much concerned with making things easy. (For more on Barth, see Chapter 10.)

The aesthetic, the ethical and the religious

The *structure* of Kierkegaard's work may resemble Hegel's in this way, but in other respects his work is marked by a decisive rejection of Hegel. We may grasp something of that rejection if we examine the role Kierkegaard gives to ethics.

Although he has other and more complex ways of arranging his presentations, Kierkegaard sometimes talks as if there were three main settlements on the journey that he is describing: the aesthetic, the ethical and the religious. The aesthetic pattern of individual life is found when someone does not realise or deliberately refuses to acknowledge that his decisions about how to live can be given any deeper shape than the pursuit of pleasure or gratification. The aesthete is someone who lives for such pleasure and whose greatest enemy is boredom – the ennui that saps all pleasures becomes too familiar. The only shape that such a person's life can take on is that of an ongoing struggle against boredom. As mentioned above, Kierkegaard pseudonymously describes the aesthetic life from within in the first part of *Either/Or*.

Kierkegaard's second pattern of individual life is the ethical. The ethical person recognises that in her decisions she is *responsible*; there are demands upon her that shape how she may appropriately respond and she is called to shape a life that responds to those demands. Kierkegaard's description of the ethical, notably in the second part of *Either/Or*, has more than a whiff of Hegel about it. It has to do with a person discovering how to live well in her various social roles: as wife, mother, worker and citizen. The ethical person works to fit well into a social order that makes good space for her; it is a matter of social duties and obligations willingly owned and undertaken.

Whereas Hegel's work might be seen as seeking for the perfection of the ethical in something like this sense, a fitting unity between the individual and the social order, Kierkegaard regards this way of shaping one's life as inadequate, just as the aesthetic approach is inadequate. The more we explore it, the more we discover, not that an ever more perfect synthesis is possible, but that meeting all the obligations that face us is impossible. This discovery is not so much, in Kierkegaard's presentation, a matter of uncovering an inherent contradiction in the heart of ethical life; it is, rather, a matter of encountering a higher standard, beside which the ethical looks tawdry. For instance, Judge William, the pseudonym Kierkegaard uses to explore the ethical in *Either/Or*, presents a largely untroubled and confident view of the possibility of ethical life – but he undermines that presentation by including at the end of the book a sermon from a pastor friend, entitled 'Ultimatum: The Upbuilding that Lies in the Thought that in Relation to God We Are Always in the Wrong'. Continued exploration of what is demanded of us by way of ethical life in a Christian milieu leads to the discovery that we are incapable of living as we ought. It is because of this that the ethical cannot be the end of the journey, and we must pass on to the religious.

Kierkegaard as Christian theologian

Kierkegaard considered, when preparing the second edition of *Either/Or*, adding a note declaring 'I hereby retract this book. It was a necessary deception in order, if possible, to deceive men into the religious, which has continually been my task all along' (*Journals and Papers* 6: *Autobiographical, Part Two: 1848-1855*, eds. Howard V. Hong and Edna H. Hong, Bloomington: Indiana University Press, 1978, p134).

As this quote suggests, Kierkegaard's intention was always to move his readers towards religion or, more specifically, to move them towards Christianity. He was a Christian writer through and through, and a Lutheran Christian writer at that. The journey on which he seeks to draw his readers is in many ways parallel to the journey undertaken by the young Augustinian monk Martin Luther, whose life as a monk was shaped more and more by the idea 'That in Relation to God We Are Always in the Wrong' until he discovered – or, rather, was discovered by – God's grace, and had his whole way of understanding himself and his obligations transformed.

Kierkegaard's writings contain two different kinds of description of the transition to the religious. When he writes adopting the persona of an outsider, the demands of religion look harsh, even impossible and absurd, and it is clear that there can be no other response than to throw oneself upon the mercy of God. Those writings push

God's demands into the faces of complacent readers, insisting that they recognise how high the bar is that they ought to jump and how puny are the jumps they take. When he writes adopting the persona of an insider, someone who already has Christian faith, however, his tone is different: he writes not as someone who has heroically thrown himself anywhere but as one who has been taken hold of by God's captivating and welcoming grace. Kierkegaard certainly writes as someone who can and must recognise himself as a sinner still, but only at the same time as recognising himself as already a recipient of mercy – and as one called to a delighted and thankful response to that mercy. So he continues to stress the absolute, uncompromising, total demand that God makes on each person – demanding everything that one has and is, asking for total self-denial, suffering renunciation and the imitation of Christ on the way of the cross – but that demand makes a different kind of sense when held between God's grace and our gratitude than it does when seen from outside, from the viewpoint of the ethical or the aesthetic.

Kierkegaard can also fruitfully be compared to a later Lutheran theologian who kept up a very strong insistence upon God's free, merciful grace, but who at the same time railed against any idea of 'cheap grace', or any watering down of the cost of discipleship: Dietrich Bonhoeffer.

Truth as subjectivity

In order to understand Kierkegaard's attempt to 'deceive men into the religious', one might compare him with the biblical figure of Nathan in 2 Samuel 12. David, who had recently arranged for the death of Uriah, the husband of Bathsheba whom David wanted for himself, received a visit from the prophet Nathan. Nathan told him a story about a rich man who has stolen a poor man's lamb, and David, anger aroused, insisted that the rich man should die. 'Then Nathan said to David, "You are the man!"' and David was suddenly tipped into seeing himself in a new, deeply unflattering light.

Nathan might perhaps have been able to explain to David the error of his ways and might even have been able to secure David's agreement to an abstract description of his crime. But Nathan's indirect communication aims at something more: it aims at provoking a deep transformation in the way that David sees himself. Kierkegaard too is interested not in informing his readers, not even in informing them accurately and convincingly, but in provoking transformations in the deepest patterns of their perception of themselves and their world.

In this sense, he is pervasively interested in *subjectivity* – in truths that can become the truth *for* someone, *in* someone. For Kierkegaard, in fact, to speak about truth is to speak about a right orientation of someone's life in the world, before God. It is to speak about a right way of grasping the situation in which one finds oneself, and the ways in which one is called upon to act in that situation.

In one of the most famous entries in his journal, Kierkegaard puts it this way:

> What I really need is to get clear about *what I am to do*, not what I must know, except insofar as knowledge must precede every act. What matters is to find a purpose, to see what it really is that God wills that *I* shall do; the crucial thing is to find a truth which is truth *for me*, to find *the idea for which I am willing to live and die* ... [O]f what use would it be to me to be able to formulate the meaning of Christianity, to explain many specific points – if it had no deeper meaning *for me and for my life?* ... I certainly do not deny that I still accept an *imperative of knowledge*, and that through it men may be influenced, but *then it must be taken up alive in me*, and *this* is what I now recognize as the most important of all.
>
> *Journals and Papers* 5: *Autobiographical, Part One: 1829–1848*,
> ed. Howard V. Hong and Edna H. Hong,
> Bloomington: Indiana University Press, 1978, pp34–35.

Kierkegaard famously insisted that 'truth is subjectivity' (*Concluding Unscientific Postscript*, p189). This is sometimes taken to mean that Kierkegaard was some kind of relativist (such that one thing might be true for me, another true for you and nothing could be declared true for everyone) or idealist (such that there is no objective truth, only truth as it appears to us) or solipsist (such that all that is real is what is played out on the screen of my mind). In the light of the discussion in this section, what do you think Kierkegaard meant?

Practice in Christianity

Kierkegaard's attempt to provoke the subjective transformation of his readers is best seen in action, and we've chosen one short writing in which we can see Kierkegaard (or, rather, one of Kierkegaard's pseudonyms, Anti-Climacus) at work. Kierkegaard described *Practice in Christianity* as 'the most perfect and truest thing I have written' (*Practice in Christianity*, p287). It was intended as an uncompromising description of true Christian life, and of what a real church would be like – a description in which 'the requirement for being a Christian is forced up ... to a supreme ideality' (p7). It therefore works both as a call to the church of Kierkegaard's day and a condemnation of it for failing to hear or respond to that call. Kierkegaard explained that it had to be written by a pseudonym precisely because he too needed to hear the call and the condemnation; he could not write in his own name, as if describing a kind of Christian life that he had himself achieved.

We're going to look at the first of the book's three parts, which bears the subtitle '"Come here all you who labour and are burdened, and I will give you rest": For awakening and inward deepening'. Over the 60 pages that follow, Kierkegaard's pseudonym, Anti-Climacus, asks his readers what it means to hear and respond to Jesus' invitation. He also asks them to recognise the ways in which they hold the invitation at bay and neutralise its power.

The first note of the whole presentation is *grace*. For Anti-Climacus, that grace is seen in the gratuitous recklessness of the invitation: Christ invites *all* who labour and are burdened, without precondition and without distinction. It is also seen in the fact that this invitation is not shouted from a distance but is made by one who comes to those who need help, and offering himself completely to them. It is an invitation that comes to meet people, rather than one they have to go out and discover for themselves. Grace is also seen in the fact to hear the invitation, and so to meet the inviter, is already to find the good gift that the inviter promises – because the invitation is to come to *him*, and there to find rest. 'The helper is the help' (p15).

Elsewhere, Kierkegaard contrasts the roles played by Jesus and by Socrates. An encounter with Socrates could be the point of departure for one's learning, but that point of departure (the 'moment') would not itself be essential to the learning that takes place. The Socratic teacher can eventually vanish into the past, because the Socratic pupil is learning to uncover a general truth that has always been in her grasp (just as it is in principle within *everyone's* grasp): the encounter with Socrates does not deliver the truth to the pupil nor the pupil to truth, but simply catalyses a process of discovery. With Jesus, things are different, because in the encounter with the teacher the disciple (not the pupil) *is* delivered to the truth, and the truth to the disciple, because the truth is the disciple's relation to Jesus.

The second note of Anti-Climacus' presentation is *demand*. This gratuitous invitation Jesus offers is an invitation to join him in just the reckless self-abandonment that he displays in making the invitation. As such, it is bound to look from the outside like an invitation to suffering. Later on, Anti-Climacus will say that 'to become a Christian ... is, *humanly speaking*, an even greater torment, misery and pain than the greatest human torment, and in addition a crime in the eyes of one's contemporaries' (p63, our emphasis). It is an invitation to reckless self-abandonment for the sake of others.

Grace and demand go together, however. Jesus' invitation is so demanding precisely because it is so gracious. According to Anti-Climacus, Jesus makes by his life (in 'the silent and veracious eloquence of action', p15) an utterly free, utterly generous invitation to join him in a life of utterly free generosity. Furthermore, by being utterly free and utterly generous, this invitation overthrows any pretension the recipient may have that they deserve to be invited, or that they have been invited because they are in some way specially qualified (pp16–20). Nevertheless, though uncompromisingly demanding, the invitation remains completely gracious: Jesus promises to be with those who, in response to his invitation, recognise the demand made upon them, recognise their utter helplessness and turn to him for help – even if only with a sigh (p22).

In the whole of the remainder of this part of the book, Anti-Climacus' self-appointed task is to persuade his readers to recognise the situation they are in: that they are faced directly with this gracious demand and demanding grace, and that their most important task is to respond. In order to understand his strategy fully, it is useful to skip ahead temporarily, to the last few pages of this part of the book (pp62–68). In those pages, Anti-Climacus makes it clear that the response that this invitation demands of his readers is that they recognise that the whole shape of their existence is called into question or, as he puts it, that the demand made of them here is *absolute*. That is, if one has understood the nature of this demand properly, there will be no way of judging it relative to some deeper principle or higher aim. One cannot properly say: 'Given that I am committed to this other goal (my own happiness, perhaps, or the greatest happiness of the greatest number, or the good order of society, or the triumph of justice), I can see on reflection that it does make sense for me to accept this invitation from Jesus.' Such an acceptance would be *relative* to the higher goal, but Anti-Climacus insists that the demand here seeks to become the one by which all others are judged.

This demand is absolute because it is made by God, but it remains a demand made by God in and through the life of a lowly, humble, abused and crucified man in a particular time and place. That historical individual, living then and there in his own time and place, becomes insistently present now for those who truly hear that demand; they know that Jesus makes a direct appeal to them, and that he thereby becomes their contemporary. To recognise oneself as faced with this demand is to recognise that one stands in this situation of contemporaneity with Christ. 'Thus,' says Anti-Climacus, 'every human being is able to become contemporary only with the time in which he is living – and then with one more, with Christ's life upon earth' (p64).

In the sections of this part of the book that I have so far skipped over, Anti-Climacus tries to clear the way for his readers to hear the invitation of Christ and so find that he has won them into that contemporaneity. He presents a series of imaginative vignettes to help his readers imagine how they and their contemporaries might have thought of

Jesus had they lived in first-century Palestine – imagining themselves into one kind of contemporaneity with Christ, but as those who refuse the invitation (pp36–62). By this means, Anti-Climacus hopes to help them see that the ways they have of relativising the demands of Christ – by judging him by supposedly higher standards, or fitting him into a supposedly larger intellectual framework – are ways of refusing Christ's invitation and so refusing to be his contemporaries.

Anti-Climacus also, however, explains that the very ways in which his readers think of Christ as a *historical* figure are already inherently relativising (pp23–36). Normally, he acknowledges, we judge someone's importance by the influence that he or she has, and someone counts as historically important if and only if he or she makes a difference to subsequent historical periods that we can recognise as important. Anti-Climacus partly rejects this approach because Jesus' abasement (his weakness, apparent failure and lack of influence) is not a temporary diminishment of his importance, but is precisely the way in which he is important: his failure and lack of influence is the form in which God has chosen to present the absolute invitation.

Anti-Climacus also insists, however, that ordinary historical importance differs in kind (not just in degree) from Christ's absolute importance. It does not, after all, make any sense to think that if a certain amount of influence might prove Jesus a very great man, just a little more would prove him divine, as if divinity lay on the same spectrum as 'great', 'greater', 'very great' (p27). There is no way of getting from this relative scale to the judgement that Christ's importance is absolute. Kierkegaard explains that Jesus, if he is what the Gospels present him as being, would remain absolutely important even if he had had no influence on subsequent generations: that would be a judgement on *them*, not on him. Far from letting history be Jesus' judge, '[i]t is he who is the examiner; his life is the examination, and not for his generation alone, but for the human race' (p34).

Kierkegaard has in his sights here the confident and comfortable Christianity of the Danish Golden Age. As he saw it, the Christians of his day were deeply concerned with the spreading historical influence of Jesus – because they saw themselves as *part* of that spreading historical influence. One could know the truth of the Christian faith and the power of Jesus its founder by looking at the benign and all-pervasive sway that Christianity now exercised over the world. Look how *civilised* the world had become, and how that civilising power is spreading more and more within European society, and now beyond it to the wider world! From Kierkegaard's point of view, this is blasphemous. It makes the present generation the standard by which Christ is judged, by which *God* is judged. This is to get matters exactly the wrong way round: the contemporary believer does not stand at the far end of a process of benign cultural evolution from an influential former of lives and opinions. Rather, the true believer stands in contemporaneity with an absolute judge and saviour.

It is probably worth noting that Kierkegaard's understanding of Christ's contemporaneity does not mean quite the same thing as a more recent Christian might mean when talking about the need for a personal relationship with Jesus. Rather, Kierkegaard is talking about the need for a compelling personal experience of the absolute invitation and demand that Jesus of Nazareth, living out his life on the way of the cross, makes upon one: a call to join him on the way of the cross, in a life of grace-driven self-abandonment.

Kierkegaard is sometimes represented as a thinker who thought Christianity involved an irrational 'leap of faith' and we are now in a position to understand what such a claim means. Rationality – the accumulation of evidence, and the making of sober judgements proportioned to the weight of that evidence – cannot deliver faith, for Kierkegaard, because faith has to do with what is absolute.

The most that sober rationality can deliver is a qualified, relative assent; it cannot in Kierkegaard's view deliver the total reorientation that the absolute invitation of Christ requires, a reorientation that reshapes all the frameworks within which we make relative judgements. There is no way in which the claims of Christianity can be put beyond all reasonable doubt, no way in which rationality can be satisfied that enough evidence has been accumulated to justify a sensible decision to accede to Christ's demands. The demand that faith be rational – the demand of the Enlightenment – can only ever be a way of holding the absolute at arm's length and so of avoiding God's demand. True grace, by contrast, invites one to stake one's whole life on the invitation one has received, and if from the point of view of a person without faith this looks like a heroic or foolish leap into the dark, from the point of view of faith it is simply a grateful response to a hand held out in gracious invitation.

The phrase 'leap of faith', indicating an irrational decision to opt for faith despite the lack of secure evidence supporting that choice, is often attributed to Kierkegaard but he never uses the Danish equivalent of this phrase, nor is it an idea that sits fully comfortably in his theology. The phrase appears instead to derive from English translations of Albert Camus' 1942 philosophical essay, *The Myth of Sisyphus*.

Conclusion

Despite a lack of immediate influence in his own day, Kierkegaard has become an immensely influential figure since. (One wonders, given his analysis of the nature of historical significance, what he might have made of this fact.) Two strands of that influence are particularly noteworthy.

First, Kierkegaard's insistence upon 'truth as subjectivity' (discussed above) and on the strange, rationality-defying nature of transformations in one's deepest frameworks for judgement and decision, proved very attractive both to some later theologians and to some non-Christian philosophers of an 'existentialist' bent. When one finds in later writers a focus on the human individual faced with a life-orienting decision, suspended between possible ways of living and thinking without access to any supervening framework that could allow rational decision between the options, Kierkegaard is often in the background – even if (as we have seen) such heroic decision is not actually at the heart of Kierkegaard's own vision. For instance, Rudolf Bultmann (see Chapter 10), writes:

> [T]he Kingdom of God ... compels man to decision; he is determined thereby either in this direction or in that, as chosen or as rejected, in his entire present existence ... The coming of the Kingdom of God is therefore not really an event in the course of time, which is due to occur sometime and toward which man can either take a definite attitude or hold himself neutral. Before he takes any attitude he is already constrained to make his choice, and therefore he must understand that just this necessity of decision constitutes the essential part of his human nature ... If men are standing in the crisis of decision, and if precisely this crisis is the essential characteristic of their humanity, then every hour is the last hour ...
> *Jesus and the Word* (New York: Scribners, 1934), Chapter 2; available online at
> <www.religion-online.org/showchapter.asp?title=426&C=279>,
> accessed 6 July 2011.

There has been another important strand of Kierkegaard's influence as well, however. It is not hard to point at various instances before and after Kierkegaard's time of a perceived tension between the work of academic theology and the life of discipleship and devotion. In practice, of course, any such tension is hugely complex. However easy it may be, for instance, to set up Pietism and Protestant scholasticism as opposing poles of such a tension, the multiple overlaps and mutual implications of both sides get in the way of any such characterisation. Nevertheless, despite that complexity, one can still find many examples of the worry that there is something odd or inappropriate about subjecting the life of faith to the kinds of rational analysis beloved of intellectuals – a worry voiced by those standing outside the intellectual conversations, or by insiders when they turn away for a time from their intellectual pursuits. With Kierkegaard, however, we find just such a critique of the foolishness of trying to capture God's ways with the world in an intellectually coherent and graspable system – but this critique is itself articulated in ways that are intellectually sophisticated, conceptually dense and that require a philosophically alert patience to unravel. Rather than asking whether or not one should engage in sophisticated intellectual analysis of theological matters, Kierkegaard's work asks how one can pursue sophisticated intellectual analysis of God's invitation to new life in such a way as to acknowledge and display the unmasterable nature of one's subject matter. For many theologians of the twentieth century – perhaps especially the young Karl Barth (see Chapter 10) – something like that question has become perhaps *the* central question of modern theology.

Exercise

Spend some time finding online descriptions and discussions of Kierkegaard and his work – especially in online encyclopaedias and other reference sources. Now look carefully at how each of those sources portrays him.

What company does it put him in? (Is he placed among theologians? Among German idealist philosophers? Among more recent existentialist philosophers? Among postmodern philosophers? Among forerunners to Karl Barth?)

How much of his work is discussed? (Is it just the major, pseudonymous works, or do the edifying discourses that he published under his own name get a look in? How much importance is placed on *Practice in Christianity* and *Works of Love*? and how much on works like *Either/Or* that explore non-religious points of view?)

How much is Kierkegaard himself the focus and how much does the focus fall where he claimed he wanted it to fall: on the question of what it means to become a Christian?

If you look around long enough, you should find quite a variety of portrayals. What do you think it is about Kierkegaard's life and work (as described above) that makes such diverse portrayals possible? How do you think one might go about judging between these portrayals? From Kierkegaard's own point of view, do you think the 'truest' portrayal is the one that most accurately divines the intentions of the historical Kierkegaard?

Bibliography

Primary texts

The works of Kierkegaard have been published in a fine uniform English translation by Howard V. Hong and Edna H. Hong in the Princeton University Press series, *Kierkegaard's Writings*. There are 26 volumes in all, but you might begin with the following:

Either/Or, Kierkegaard's Writings vols 3–4, 1988.
Fear and Trembling, Kierkegaard's Writings vol 6, 1983.
Concluding Unscientific Postscript to Philosophical Fragments, Kierkegaard's Writings vols 12.1 and 12.2, 1992.
Works of Love, Kierkegaards's Writings vol 16, 1995.
Practice in Christianity, Kierkegaard's Writings vol 20, 1991.

Secondary texts

There are numerous one-volume introductions to Kierkegaard.

Julia Watkin, *Kierkegaard*, Outstanding Christian Thinkers (London: Continuum, 1997). Very respectable and widely used.

John D. Caputo, *How to Read Kierkegaard* (London: Granta, 2007). Provides a readable exploration of several key extracts from Kierkegaard and is a good route in to grappling with the texts for yourself.

Murray Rae, *Kierkegaard and Theology*, Philosophy and Theology (London: Continuum, 2010). Provides a readable account of Kierkegaard as a Christian theologian.

David Gouwens, *Kierkegaard as Religious Thinker* (Cambridge: Cambridge University Press, 1996). Pursues a similar line to Rae, but is a little more detailed and complex.

Given the complex relationship between Kierkegaard's life and work, it is also worth reading:

Joakim Garff, *Søren Kierkegaard: A Biography*, trans. Bruce H. Kirmmse (Princeton: Princeton University Press, 2000).

7 Friedrich Nietzsche

AIMS

By the end of this chapter, we hope that you will:

- understand what Nietzsche thought was wrong with Christianity

- understand his positive vision of an alternative to Christianity

- know what is involved in a genealogical critique

- grasp something of Nietzsche's significance for later Christian theology.

Introduction

Friedrich Nietzsche (1844–1900) was one of the most influential critics of Christianity – and of the whole influence of Christianity on Western culture – in the modern period. Writing in a context shaped by earlier critics of Christianity, like David Friedrich Strauss (see Chapter 10 'Reading the Bible') and Immanuel Kant, he came to believe that their criticisms did not go far enough – that they had cut down the plant without pulling up the roots.

It would therefore be easy, when discussing him in the context of an account of modern Christian theology, to present him primarily as a negative figure: one who denies, overthrows, undermines and attacks. To do that, however, would be to miss the fact that Nietzsche's critique of Christianity emerges from a positive conviction that there is a real alternative, a *better* alternative, to Christianity available: an alternative that is healthier, more life-affirming, more energetic and more powerful. To understand Nietzsche's influence on modern theology, we will need to understand both this positive vision and the strident critiques that it prompted Nietzsche to launch.

Figure 7.1 Friedrich Nietzsche

Nietzsche's development

Nietzsche grew up in a comfortable and supportive household, imbibing his parents' loyal Prussian royalism and deeply felt Lutheran piety. He had a precociously intense and articulate faith as a child, and was by all accounts shy, obedient and – in the phrase of the biographer Julian Young – 'a *passionate* social conformist' (Young, *Nietzsche: A Philosophical Biography*, p17).

> Young notes that, writing in a private notebook when he was 13 years old, Nietzsche recorded that he had 'firmly resolved within me to dedicate myself forever to [God's] service ... All he gives I will joyfully accept: happiness and unhappiness, poverty and wealth, and boldly look even death in the face ...' (Young, *Nietzsche*, p18, translating a text from *Nietzsche Werke: Kritische Gesamtausgabe*, eds. G. Colli and M. Montinari, Berlin: de Gruyter, 1967–2006, vol 1.1). There is an extent to which Nietzsche's mature philosophy, discussed below, can be seen as an attempt to recover such a joyful acceptance of all that life and death can bring, without the theological and metaphysical supports that had underpinned his youthful declaration.

Nietzsche attended Pforta, a top-rank secondary school that provided a formation in the loyalty, discipline and self-reliance that were supposed to be the hallmarks of a true Prussian, and in the classics, especially the Greek classics. As young Nietzsche's Christian faith began to disappear (evaporating in the heat of his wide and inquisitive reading), it is not too misleading to say that it was replaced by love for the world of the ancient Greeks – particularly the Homeric world and the world of the earliest Greek literature: Greece before Socrates and Plato. One might even say that he began to find in that world an alternative religion, more profoundly attractive than the Christianity he was leaving behind.

Nietzsche also emerged from Pforta as an amateur philosopher and cultural critic. He and some of his friends had formed a small society for friendship and discussion, and Nietzsche wrote pieces for this society on the ingredients required to constitute a 'people' (a *Volk*), on the history of religion, on the evolution of Christianity beyond supernatural beliefs into a pure ethic of love, on music as the heart of true religion and so on. Although his university studies focused on philology, and although the academic post he was awarded with remarkable rapidity once he graduated was in that subject (he was appointed to a professorship of classical philology in Basel in 1869), the philosophical note in his thinking slowly but surely became the dominant one.

Nietzsche, Wagner and Schopenhauer

For most of Nietzsche's time as a Basel professor, his thinking was dominated by three things: the philosophy of Arthur Schopenhauer (1788–1860), his devotion to the composer Richard Wagner (1813–1883) and his love of the ancient Greek world. Together, they provided him with the ingredients for a new, non-Christian vision of life – an alternative to Christianity that was, in its own way, profoundly religious.

Figure 7.2 Arthur Schopenhauer

Figure 7.3 Richard Wagner

Nietzsche's love of Greek antiquity was, as we have seen, nurtured during his time at Pforta, but it is most visible in his first book, *The Birth of Tragedy* (1872). He was intoxicated by what he saw as the vitality, the love of strength, the delight in human beauty of the ancient Greek world. He believed that this ethos, which bound the Greeks together as a recognisable people, was inculcated and sustained by their great artistic–religious festivals. On the one hand, in such festivals the people were given *myth*: a set of narratives that penetrated to the deepest levels of their consciousness and structured the way in which they perceived the world – in particular determining what they found valuable and what they found repulsive. In myth, the Greek people were given their world back again, with its grandeur and vitality heightened, and they were given heroes to celebrate who embodied and displayed the strength and beauty that were properly admirable.

Think of the way in which some Hollywood films turn battles into ballets – dazzlingly choreographed patterns of strength and agility, as the human participants are forced by circumstance to their utmost efforts and rendered strangely beautiful as everything extraneous about them is stripped away. Their actions are portrayed as having a kind of elemental purity, a raw grace – an arm throwing a spear becoming a demonstration of the force and accuracy of which arms are capable. Death, injury and loss are real, but they are secondary to the ballet, an unavoidable price but a price worth paying to be so directly alive while the battle lasts. This is the kind of myth-shaped vision that Nietzsche labels 'Apollonian' – a glory in vitality and in the beautiful shape, surface and movement of life – and it is a vision he finds embodied in the words and images of Greek festival art.

The Greeks' religious festivals had a second function, however, beyond this myth-bearing, value-forming Apollonianism and it is one that (at this stage in his work) was even more important for Nietzsche. The Greek festivals were not simply filled with words and images: they were also, perhaps above all, filled with music. Attending such a festival was, therefore, not simply a matter of being made an observer of Apollonian spectacles, but of being caught up in the music as participant. Nietzsche describes this as a *Dionysian* experience: the experience of being so involved in a musical performance that you feel the music as a force that is played out through you – so that you become an instrument on which that music is played. In such an experience, according to Nietzsche, the ancient Greeks were given a glimpse beyond their existence as discrete individuals, whose desires and wills and projects might conflict; they were enabled to see, to *feel*, that there was a wider reality surging through them – to feel themselves, momentarily, as patterns of dancing foam on a great surging wave of life that was playing out its energy in them and through them. They were lifted, by the music of the festival, out of the world of individuality and suffering, and shown something deeper.

In the philosophy of Schopenhauer, which he first encountered in 1865, Nietzsche thought he had found a way of articulating his emerging sense of this Dionysian dynamic. In *The World as Will and as Representation* (1818; second edition, 1844), Schopenhauer had taken up one of the typical tasks of philosophers standing in Kant's wake: an attempt to make sense of the relationship between phenomena (appearances) and noumena (unknowable things in themselves). Schopenhauer believed that Kant was right to insist upon such a divide, but he gave each side a rather different characterisation. The world of appearances – the world of surfaces captured by Apollonian portrayal, Nietzsche might say – is inevitably a world of clash and of suffering; it is a world inevitably but fatefully taken by the actively construing mind to be divided into distinct individual realities, each of which has its own specific projects and desires. The existence of such individual realities must either lead to the suffering caused by the frustration of their desires or the disillusioned boredom caused by their satisfaction.

The noumenal world beneath this phenomenal reality, however, is not entirely hidden from us: we touch upon it as we experience ourselves as ineradicably desiring, willing and preferring creatures. Schopenhauer regarded the noumenal world, the real world behind the veil of individuality and conflict, as consisting in a primal, insatiable, universal will – a will that, in the image used above, is like a wave throwing up the froth of appearances as it surges on.

Schopenhauer assigned music a central role in our orientation towards this primary reality. Music, precisely because it is not a form of art that represents individual phenomenal realities, does not lead us to deeper attention to the world of appearances. Rather, it enables us to glimpse, to *feel*, our connection to the wave of will that underlies and constitutes the world. By means of music, we experience a kind of recognition of the true nature of world, and an exposure of the world of illusion in which we live. With music's help, we discover that we must overcome our individuality, our nature as individual clashing wills, and lose ourselves in the underlying reality of the primal will. Music teaches us to long for oblivion, the only antidote to suffering.

In the musical ambition of Richard Wagner, Nietzsche found someone who was trying to create in the modern world a new version of the Greek religious–artistic festival – who was, in effect, trying to create a new religion, that drew upon both classical and Schopenhauerian roots. Wagner had begun with a rather Apollonian vision of the power of musical art, focused on its power to form a people or 'folk' by providing a powerful vehicle for myth. He, too, had then discovered Schopenhauer and had developed an increasingly Dionysian vision. His ambition was to create a great Germanic artistic festival in which the German people would both be given back a myth that had the power to renew them as a people, and be given a means of glimpsing the nature of the illusions under which they laboured, and of the deeper reality of the primal will, which they might touch in the ecstatic oblivion to which his music moved them. (At the end of *Tristan und Isolde* (1865), Isolde sinks on to Tristan's body, singing: 'In the surging swell, in the ringing sound, in the vast wave of the world's breath – to drown, to sink unconscious – supreme bliss!' An English translation of the libretto is available online at www.opera-guide.ch/opera.php?id=412&uilang=en.)

Nietzsche was delighted to be introduced to Wagner in 1868, and soon became his friend and disciple (with the emphasis more often on 'disciple' than 'friend'). He became, in effect, Wagner's pet philosopher and a philosophical evangelist for his work – an evangelist for the new religion that he believed Wagner was striving to create. He contemplated giving up his work as a professor in order to be able to devote himself wholeheartedly to raising money and expectations for Wagner's plan to build an opera house in Bayreuth, believing that here was the best chance in the modern world for the rediscovery of the vitality of ancient Greece, and the conversion of that world to Schopenhauerian understanding.

The Birth of Tragedy, in which Nietzsche set something of his non-Christian religious vision before the world, was not by any means the sober work of academic philology that was expected from a young professor. It was full of confident speculation about the nature of Greek art-shaped life, laced with enthusiastic intimations of the possibilities for the retrieval of such life in the present. It more or less killed off Nietzsche's philological reputation – and his subsequent writings, the series of *Untimely Meditations*, made no further attempt to disguise themselves as philology. Instead, it began his career as a public philosopher – albeit, at this stage, as one acting as a satellite to Wagner's ambition.

The next great shift in Nietzsche's thought occurred, however, as over the next few years his need to prove himself something other than Wagner's pet grew, as did his doubts about Wagner's art and philosophy. Beyond all the complex dynamics of his personal relationship to Wagner (and to Wagner's wife, Cosima), Nietzsche began increasingly to worry that the Wagnerian–Schopenhauerian philosophy still involved a set of intellectual commitments that devalued life in the world – that directed attention to a level of reality beneath or behind the world of appearance and taught a kind of indifference or hatred of that world. Such a philosophy cut directly against the vitality, the love of life and strength, that Nietzsche so valued in the ancient Greeks. The desire for oblivion, for the dissolving of individuality into the surge of the will underlying the world, was a way of saying 'no' to strength and struggle, and to *life*.

There were other factors, too, in Nietzsche's increasing distance from Wagner. He began to find Wagner's deeply ingrained **anti-Semitism** obnoxious, for instance, and after experience in 1870 as a medical orderly at the front during the Franco-Prussian war, he also came to be fiercely antagonistic to militarism, to the militaristic Prussian policies of Otto von Bismarck (1815–1898), and to the wider German Reich that Bismarck's policies inaugurated – and he distrusted the all-too-easy availability of Wagner's music as a supporting pillar for crude German **nationalism**.

Nietzsche's writings during his Wagnerian period show that he was certainly not free from casual anti-Semitism, and that he was perfectly willing to turn the dial beyond casual in order to echo the more virulent anti-Semitism of the Wagners. Once he had turned against Wagner, however, a marked rejection of anti-Semitism becomes a characteristic of his work. He seems to have been genuinely revolted by his sister's marriage to a vituperative and active anti-Semite, Bernhard Forster.

His mature view of Judaism was complex. He certainly saw Judaism as a part of the story of the great religious betrayal of pagan strength and vitality (see below). But on the whole, he presented Judaism as playing a simpler, more honest, less diseased part in the story than Christianity.

Nietzsche's influence on subsequent German history – the encouragement which his work was taken to give to Nazism, including to its militarism, its German nationalism and its anti-Semitism – was in part a great betrayal of his work aided and abetted by the control his sister won over his literary estate and his reputation after his final collapse. That betrayal was, nevertheless, able to draw upon strands in his own thought – both his idea of the need for people-forming religious festivals in praise of strength and his continued association of Judaism with weakness and with the story of resentment's triumph over strength.

Nietzsche attended the first Bayreuth Festival in 1876, and found it a bitter and shattering disappointment. This was not the re-birth of religion he had hoped for. Fleeing (temporarily, and not quite as dramatically as his later self-presentations would suggest), he began feverish work on the book that became *Human, All Too Human* (1878), in which a new, anti-Schopenhauerian and anti-Wagnerian version of his philosophy was given its initial airing. By the time of *The Case of Wagner* (1888), one of his last works, he could write: 'Is Wagner even a person? Isn't he really just a sickness? He makes everything he touches sick – he has made music sick' (in *The Anti-Christ, Ecce Homo, Twilight of the Idols, and Other Writings*, eds. Aaron Ridley and Judith Norman, Cambridge Texts in the History of Philosophy, eds. Karl Ameriks and Desmond M. Clarke, Cambridge: Cambridge University Press, 2005, p240).

Life after God

Nietzsche's health had been bad ever since his time at Pforta, and his work was regularly interrupted by a collection of unpleasant symptoms from headaches to vomiting. It was in part due to the further deterioration of his health and in part due to his continued shift away from philology that he retired from his Basel professorship in 1879. With the help of a generous pension he became a nomad, wandering around Germany, Switzerland, Italy and France from spa town to coastal resort to mountain retreat. He devoted himself henceforth entirely to philosophical writing and to an incessant and disastrous experimentation with his own brand of quack health regimes.

After *Human, All Too Human*, he went on to produce a series of works, including *The Gay Science* (1882), *Thus Spake Zarathustra* (1883–1885) and *The Twilight of the Idols* (1889). His philosophical position continued to develop as he produced these works, but it is possible to make out the lines of a fairly consistent shape to his thinking, particularly in the works from 1882 onwards.

Nietzsche had turned to Schopenhauer and to Wagner when his Christian faith had trickled away – but he had come to see by 1876 that in the battle between a properly life-affirming Greek religion and Christianity, both Wagner and Schopenhauer actually stood on the Christian side. They represented at most partial rejections of Christianity, disavowing it with one hand, while installing a variant of Christian metaphysics and a variant of Christian morality with the other. Nietzsche's quest now was to complete the task of rejection: to find a way of thinking and living that was no longer caught under Christianity's shadow, and that was fully free to embrace the Greek alternative. He sought to produce a new philosophy of life, without God, and without the metaphysics and warmed-over Christian morality in which faith lingers.

Metaphysics

'Metaphysics' here names the deepest, most pervasive and persistent structures of our picture of the world. It includes such grand items as the Kantian distinction between noumena and phenomena, but also many smaller scale items of our mental furniture. Nietzsche's main strategy for cleaning out the stables of metaphysical thought is to expose the process by which certain ideas came to be so universally accepted as to be taken for foundational truths, and to show that the success of such a process is in no way evidence for the truth of the ideas involved. That success simply shows us that the ideas in question were *useful*, that their acceptance and employment aided human survival or, better, that it aided the ability of those who held them to impose themselves on others and to propagate their way of thinking – to create a kingdom within which their patterns of thought held sway.

Nietzsche has in mind some of the most basic ideas we use. He examines, for instance, the idea that the world naturally divides up into discrete items, substances with properties – and insists that such dividing up of the world is precisely something that *we* do, in order to enact our projects, our interests. We are not teasing the world apart at its natural joints, but going at it with a cleaver – and while we may persuade ourselves that success is evidence that our views are unavoidable and natural, we are instead simply demonstrating our own vitality and prowess.

> There is something akin to Kant's 'turn to the subject' here. Things that we have taken to be basic structures of the world turn out instead to be structures of our way of seeing the world: space, time, cause and effect, and so on. But whereas for Kant these are the timeless structures of human rationality, for Nietzsche these are ideas with a history – and a messy political and social history of errors and power plays at that.

Another idea that Nietzsche critiques is the idea that there are classes of identical things. This is an idea that provides tremendous aid in our attempts to navigate and manipulate the world, but it involves a constant forgetting or ignoring of the multiple manifest differences between any two supposedly identical items. In order to grasp Nietzsche's point, one might think of the story of Funes the Memorious, told by Jorge Luis Borges:

> It was not only difficult for him to understand that the generic term dog embraced so many unlike specimens of differing sizes and different forms; he was disturbed by the fact that a dog at three-fourteen (seen in profile) should have the same name as the dog at three-fifteen (seen from the front). His own face in the mirror, his own hands, surprised him on every occasion ... To think is to forget a difference, to generalize, to abstract. In the overly replete world of Funes there were nothing but details, almost contiguous details.
>
> *Ficciones*, ed. Anthony Kerrigan,
> trans. Emecé Editores, New York: Grove Press, 1964, pp114–115.

Nietzsche's point is, roughly speaking, that Funes' way of seeing might be 'truer' than ours, but that the forgetting and misrepresenting of reality that Funes cannot manage turns out to be necessary to our survival. (Nietzsche makes similar claims about causality, and our tendency to arrange the world into neat chains of cause and effect, even though it would be truer to see not sequences of events but a complex and evolving continuum.)

Finally, Nietzsche also casts doubt on our need to see ourselves as free, in the sense that we regard our actions as somehow escaping from the world of cause and effect (or of the natural continuum that our language of cause and effect misrepresents). We claim for ourselves – think of Kant! – a free, noumenal reality behind the deterministic phenomenal world, in order to be able to build (very successful, but fundamentally untruthful) social structures that rely upon ideas of responsibility and guilt. (As we will see, Nietzsche went on to develop his own account of human freedom, but it was not a freedom *from* the continuities of the physical world.)

Nietzsche's method here is often described as a 'genealogical critique'. He does not set out to prove directly that the idea he is critiquing is false – by, say, *proving* that the idea of noumenal freedom is incoherent. Rather, he explains how such an idea arose, and how it gained support, and how it successfully spread, without needing to be true – indeed, how the question of its truth was irrelevant to that whole process. When such an explanation is combined with even quite flimsy indications of the *implausibility* of the idea or of the support that is normally adduced for it, the effect can be devastating. It is as if, during an interview with a politician about some policy that the politician claims is 'evidence-based', the interviewer were to say, 'Well, you're bound to say that, aren't you ...' – and then to reveal the personal financial gain the politician stands to make thanks to the policy in question.

Nietzsche believes, however, that a strange thing has happened. These and other metaphysical errors have helped give rise, bit by bit, to the very idea of truth, and to the idea that illusion can and should be critiqued. Those ideas could not have evolved except among fairly advanced civilisations, whose existence and state of advancement would not have been possible had not all these useful metaphysical errors held sway. But because that idea of truth now exists, and because the idea of the pursuit of truth over against illusion now exists and is powerful, we are faced with an interesting dilemma. Can the will to truth – the will to pull away the comforting blanket of illusion and to face up to the erroneous nature of these beliefs – be compatible with life, strength and success? If these illusions coddled us and thereby made flourishing life possible for us, will the exposure of their illusory nature not kill us?

Nietzsche's mature philosophy is, in some way, simply a wager – a wager that now, perhaps, life *can* finally be lived truthfully and be a more flourishing life as a result. Nietzsche does not insist that we pursue truth at any cost – at least, he does not make any such insistence unambiguously – but neither does he display any willingness to preserve old illusions just in case their absence should prove to be dangerous. He is willing to try the great experiment of seeking either to dispense with the old illusions altogether, or to live with them only in the full knowledge of their real character – as cunning human creations.

The alternative – in which we continue to peddle such ideas, and continue to peddle the notion that they are unavoidable and that we are simply following the orders issued to us by the real structure of the world – is, for Nietzsche, a failure to accept responsibility for our own actions and decisions. It is to see as passive obedience what is really our active and risky creativity. And it is a way of persuading ourselves that the world around us has a clear, stable, reliable order that demands our acquiescence, rather than being a surging, uncontrollable flux that we must actively surf – or, to use a more Nietzschean metaphor, with which we must actively dance. Nietzsche's fight against metaphysics is part of his fight for a new form of Greek religion: a celebration of daring, creativity, life and strength.

Nietzsche's insistence that we should accept responsibility for our activity does not contradict his negative comments about human freedom. He rejected the idea of human freedom as a freedom *from* the continuum of cause and effect that shapes the world. It is still possible, however, for people who are firmly *part* of that continuum of cause and effect to be active and influential parts of it, and it is possible for them to come – by some process of cause and effect – to a clearer understanding of the part they play. Nietzsche is hoping that his own writings (themselves the product of an active and influential person who has himself been produced by a whole history of earlier causes and effects) will be one of the causes that will bring it about that more people recognise the part that they play within this continuum.

Nietzsche's vision of the survival of successful ideas can sound rather Darwinian, as if it were simply a version of the 'survival of the fittest'. And it is certainly true that Nietzsche's language and ideas are deeply imbued with ideas about evolution drawn from contemporary biology. His vision of evolution (in the world of ideas, in human society, in the living world more generally) is not, however, truly Darwinian. He does not believe simply in random mutation and natural selection of particular variants driven by their differential capacity to survive and reproduce. Rather, Nietzsche's evolutionary metaphors are full of non-Darwinian evolutionary imagery which suggests that creatures have an inherent vitality, a desire to imprint their own individuality (a mixture of what they have inherited and what they have achieved with that inheritance) on the world around them, and to subordinate others to their reign. Evolution is, Nietzsche thinks, driven by such a 'will to power' (see Gregory Moore, *Nietzsche, Biology and Metaphor*, Cambridge: Cambridge University Press, 2002). In some of his late notebooks, Nietzsche toys with a grand metaphysical system in which *everything* (in the realms of physics and chemistry as much as in the realm of biology) is ultimately driven by the will to power. However, exciting though the sketches for that system have been for many later commentators, the attempt seems to have been abandoned (the ideas perhaps lacking the vitality they needed to impose themselves successfully) and Nietzsche never had to explain how such a grand unified metaphysics was compatible with his persistent anti-metaphysical stance.

Christianity

Nietzsche's critique of religion, especially of Christianity, begins in the same sort of way as his critique of metaphysics. He attempts to show how it caught hold, how it had *power*, how it propagated itself, even overcoming apparently more vital, vibrant forces, without that in any way supplying evidence of its truth. However, though he does sometimes indicate that its success must be acknowledged – and that therefore it must be granted to have a kind of vitality and strength – Nietzsche insists that Christianity's triumph has been a human disaster. Christianity has been, in fact, a curse.

> I want to write this eternal indictment of Christianity on every wall, wherever there are walls, – I have letters that can make even blind people see ... I call Christianity the one great curse, the one great innermost corruption, the one great instinct of revenge that does not consider any method to be poisonous, secret, subterranean, *petty* enough, – I call it the one immortal blot on humanity.
> *The Anti-Christ*, §62.

In the first place, Christianity is a curse because it fabricates another world and devalues the present world. It destroys, in Nietzsche's view, all positive focus on strength and vitality in this world, or acknowledges it only backhandedly, as a shadow of the *real* life of the world to come. Think of the end of C.S. Lewis's *The Last Battle*. With their hearts leaping, and 'a wild hope' rising within them, the children of the story learn that, in this world – which the great lion Aslan calls 'the Shadowlands' – they have *died*. Their joy stems from their realisation that:

> All their life in this world ... had only been the cover and the title page: now *at last* they were beginning Chapter One of the Great Story which no one on earth has read: which goes on forever: in which every chapter is better than the one before.
> C.S. Lewis, *The Last Battle* (London: Lion, 1980, p172).

That kind of thing, a Nietzschean critic might say, amounts to nothing less than a hatred of this world and a hatred of life – and it is only evidence of how deeply such diseased views have hold of us that we find it beautiful. It is a beauty only made way for by the violent obliteration of the world earlier in the book: we contemplate it only by turning our backs on the world.

In the second place, Nietzsche believes that Christianity inculcates another kind of hatred of strength. It is born of resentment or, because Nietzsche always uses the French word here, of *ressentiment*. It is a religion of the weak, who have found a way of triumphing by bringing others down to their level: teaching the strong and the noble to regard their strength and nobility as sinful pride and teaching them that humility, even to the point of self-emptying, is a virtue. It is a value system born of envy and of the conviction that if you can't beat the strong you can at least make them join you in weakness.

In the third place, Nietzsche believes that Christianity propagates a morality that says 'no' to our humanity and that demands that we avoid living to the full. It disavows strength and command while backing up its own strictures with a cowardly threat of divine retribution. It lives by spreading fear, by steeping us in guilt and then by asking us to accept in humble weakness its patent remedy for the condition it has itself induced.

In *The Anti-Christ* (the German title could also be translated *Anti-Christian*), Nietzsche paints a fascinating portrait of Jesus – portraying him as the antithesis of Nietzsche's own views, but as having a consistency and nobility that his followers, then and now, in their craven *ressentiment*, utterly lack. It is worth spending some time reading Nietzsche's pen-portrait of Jesus, because it throws Nietzsche's own philosophy into sharp relief.

Nietzsche sees that Christianity weakened and destroyed both Greece and Rome – and that the world thereby lost the celebration of life and strength that these ancient cultures both sustained in their different ways. It did so, in part, by inventing critiques of Greek and Roman virtue and using those critiques to expose the flaws in the supposedly noble examples of Greek and Roman virtue. Those techniques, however, can now be turned in a refined form against Christianity itself. The life-denying flaws in its own understanding of virtue can be exposed, and the way cleared for a new understanding of the nature of virtue, transformed root and branch – a 'revaluation of all values', as Nietzsche puts it (*The Anti-Christ*, §13).

Similarly, Christianity helped to generate the will to truth, by valuing honesty, supposedly regardless of its contribution to life – and now it can't rein that will in. So when that same will to truth undermines Christian metaphysics, Christianity only has itself to blame. Liberal Christians may hold on to watered-down versions of Christian truth-claims, but even they know in their hearts that the game is up and that Christianity is dying under the blows of its own weapons.

Nietzsche wants to finish the task: to discover what life can and should be once we have got rid not only of our addiction to God, but of all the metaphysical and moral nicotine patches we have been using to stave off the withdrawal symptoms. Or, as Nietzsche puts it:

> After Buddha was dead, they still showed his shadow in a cave for centuries – a tremendous, gruesome shadow. God is dead; but given the way people are, there may still for millennia be caves in which they show his shadow. – And we – we must defeat his shadow as well!
>
> *The Gay Science*, §III.108.

Nietzsche does not think that the citizens of the modern West, many of whom are so pleased with themselves for having outgrown belief in God, are at all aware of the magnitude of the task of rethinking that faces them if they want to be free of God's shadow as well. They have not begun to ask what it means to live without the idea that one's actions ought to be an obedient response to a fixed moral and metaphysical order in the world; what it means to live without the idea that humility and passivity are somehow holy; what it means to live without the idea that there is something distasteful about triumphant strength. In a famous passage, he describes a madman running round the marketplace with a lantern, proclaiming that 'God is dead!'

> *We have killed him* – you and I! We are all his murderers. But how did we do this? ... What were we doing when we unchained the earth from its sun? Where is it moving to now? Where are we moving to? Away from all suns? Are we not continually falling? ... What festivals of atonement, what holy games will we have to invent for ourselves? Is the magnitude of this deed not too great for us? Do we not ourselves have to become gods merely to appear worthy of it?
>
> *The Gay Science* §III.125.

The madman, looking at the silent incomprehension on the faces of his audience, eventually throws down his lantern. '"I come too early", he then said; "my time is not yet."'

Nietzsche's attack on the idea of God does not follow the same route as that of more recent writers like Richard Dawkins. He is not interested in the lack of evidence supporting the hypothesis that there is a God; he is not interested in the existence of alternative ways of explaining facts about the world that were previously held to be explicable only by reference to God; he is not interested in pursuing the 'problem of evil' and the difficulties it raises for belief in a being both good and omnipotent; he is not even interested in the idea that belief in God makes some individuals and social groups do bad things. Rather, he focuses on two things. In the first place, he is interested in explaining how the idea of God arose, by showing how it was *useful* – how it enabled certain people to gain the upper hand and spread their influence and ideas. This is a *genealogical* critique, in the sense defined above. In the second place, however, he is interested in the idea of God as the supreme example of a way of thinking that prevents people from taking full responsibility for their own decisions and actions. It makes life out to be a matter of following, of obedience and of passivity, rather than of leading, of active creativity and of strength.

A philosophy of affirmation

At the centre of the new set of values that Nietzsche hopes will emerge from under God's long shadow is a great affirmation of the world. Once all theological and metaphysical otherworldliness is done away with, the way is clear to recognise that there is no world but this and that we have no lives other than the ones we are leading now. As well as being an experiment in attempted truthfulness, then, Nietzsche's mature thought can be seen as an experiment in affirmation.

When walking beside a Swiss lake in the summer of 1881, a particular way of understanding the nature of such affirmation struck Nietzsche forcefully. One could count oneself fully as an affirmer of life only if one could face the prospect of one's life being repeated, moment for moment, again and again down through eternity, and not despair but rejoice. 'What doesn't kill me makes me stronger,' says Nietzsche (*Twilight of the Idols*, p157). I ought to be able to look at my life, everything that I have done and that has been done to me, recognise that it is that whole life that has made me what I am – and feel no envy, no resentment, no wish to be someone or something else, no desire to escape from the implications of my decisions and actions. Rather, I should be able to see my life and my world without delusion or evasion, and – as if I were a sculptor, perhaps – affirm them with a fierce delight as the material I have to work with, and from which I am making something extraordinary.

This affirmation of oneself is also an affirmation of the world. Nietzsche has abandoned any sense that human beings are metaphysically distinct from the world, possessed of a mysterious freedom from the processes by which the natural world proceeds and evolves. The affirmation that Nietzsche proclaims is an affirmation of the whole complex flux of the world of which he, and all individuals, are a part. In a way, this is a version of the Dionysianism of his Wagnerian period, but it does not now

> Were Nietzsche to rewrite Lewis's *The Last Battle*, the children would not reach the end of the story and discover that they have only turned the title page of the *real* book, the book beyond the book they know. They would reach the end of the story and, with a ringing cry of delight, would turn back to the first page to live it all over again.

involve a Schopenhauerian belief that one can discover some primal undifferentiated world *behind* this world, but rather involves an affirmation that one's individuality, one's distinctness or separation from other persons and objects, is only a secondary, partial and derivative fact about the world: one is simply part of the way in which the whole life of the world is proceeding and evolving, one of the forms it has thrown up in the constant surging cataract of its development.

A good deal of Nietzsche's description of the new world of values that he is exploring is framed not in terms of right and wrong, but in terms of health and disease. Affirmation is, he believes, simply healthier than denial or resentment: it allows life to flourish, to grow strongly and vibrantly, to imprint its pattern brightly and clearly on the world around it, rather than becoming sickly, weak and passive. And, to an extent, it is the route to happiness – although it is important to note that Nietzsche did not think one could pursue happiness directly. Happiness flows from having a task, a goal and the freedom to pursue it – and one only achieves happiness if one pursues one's task, rather than by aiming at happiness itself.

Here, 'freedom' does not name a mysterious metaphysical 'get out of causality free' card, but freedom *from* resentment and denial, and freedom *to* have and pursue a task. One is free if one has a central goal and can arrange all one's other goals and desires around it, making one's life a coherent and dedicated pursuit of that central goal. One is free to the extent that one can work at producing that coherence from the stuff of one's life, sculpting all the material that one's life has given one into a unified artwork. One is free, therefore, if one can accept and affirm all the stuff of one's life *as* the material for this artwork. One is free, finally, only if one can affirm the world.

Pursuit of coherence involves developing a clear-sighted understanding of the drives that really motivate our actions and then working to nourish some drives while weakening others – tending the garden of one's character. Nietzsche's vision of the life well lived is therefore shaped by a life-affirming, goal-driven asceticism: a deliberate and intelligent pursuit of the education of one's desires, in the service of one's mission.

Consider the character Omar Little in the US television serial *The Wire*. He is a stick-up man, taking money and drugs from dealers, and he lives in a world where moral codes – even the moral codes that have shaped life among the drug-dealers and their gangs – are breaking down. Yet Omar is one of the most fiercely moral characters in *The Wire*. He does not give in to despair; he chooses – and is aware that it is a choice, an act of self-definition – a code: 'A man must have a code', he says. And the code he chooses is not a selfish one but it is in part about living with a certain kind of elegance, a certain kind of love for life and a certain kind of wit. He moves like a dancer through his world and his code is an *aesthetic* as much as it is a *morality*. Omar is rigorous in his adherence to it, determined to make something of himself of which he can be proud and to avoid actions that would be beneath him, such as using his considerable strength to attack those who pose no real threat to him. He will not destroy what he admires, in himself or in the social world around him. And it is his adherence to this code that makes him a model for emulation in the world he inhabits. In Omar Little, then, we perhaps have a portrayal of a Nietzschean ethical hero.

What, though, *is* the goal that Nietzsche sets himself? It is not simply *self*-cultivation: he has a mission *to others*. After all, he regarded himself above all as an author, with a mission to write and publish – not simply as someone devoted to thinking deep thoughts on his own. He saw himself as that madman in the marketplace, proclaiming a new world of values – a new *society*.

Nietzsche may have given up on Wagner, but he never gave up on the 'Greek' vision that had shaped his hopes for Wagner: his belief that a new mythology, new 'festivals of atonement ... [and] holy games' were needed to reshape the people. But what kind of social transformation does Nietzsche want to usher in? He was certainly not an egalitarian or democratic thinker: the social vision he sets out is firmly hierarchical. He wanted a society gathered around clear exemplars of strength and vitality – exemplars set out in that society's myths and celebrated in their festivals, but also exemplars living in the society's midst. Nietzsche wants a class of aristocrats, in a sense – but this is not an aristocracy of blood, money or vulgar fame, but one defined by the decisive embodiment of the virtues recognised by this society, or the effective proclamation in word and deed of the new virtues this society is coming to recognise as its own. (One might say that Nietzsche envisages a nobility that holds both kingly and prophetic office.) This philosophical nobility will consist of 'free spirits' – people free of resentment, free of the shadow of God, free to pursue their task, free to affirm their lives and the world. It will be an aristocracy of yes-sayers.

Below this nobility, Nietzsche envisaged an educated class that would provide the administrators and functionaries who would in practice keep society running – but which would also provide the seedbed from which future free spirits might emerge (though only a tiny proportion of the members of this educated class will turn out to have the clarity, the insight and the intellectual *courage* to be such free spirits).

Finally, there are those whose work is simply to support the rest – manual labourers, of various kinds. Some of the time, it sounds like these labourers are simply slaves, with no function other than to serve the higher strata of the society and no real participation in the good of the society for themselves. At other times, Nietzsche's descriptions suggest that he envisages these labourers being made happy in the way appropriate to them, by pursuing the tasks fitted to their own gifts and strength. There are even hints early on in Nietzsche's work, although less so later on, of an account of the proper nobility of the crafts and of an ordered society in which everyone has his place and receives the honour due to that place.

One thing is perfectly clear about this society, however. It will be one in which violence is not repressed or denied (which would involve a repression or denial of vitality and strength and ambition), but is *sublimated* – into various kinds of non-violent contest, such as sporting events and competitions. Violent warfare, Nietzsche insists, is harmful, stupid and wasteful – he could remember all too well the appalling waste of strength and beauty that he saw dismembered on the Franco-Prussian front. Nietzsche wants a world marked by a Homeric celebration of strength and contest but one in which the contest is not carried on with swords, but with wit and intelligence and a daring willingness to rethink the inherited patterns of our thinking and acting, in pursuit of more flourishing life.

The end

Nietzsche's belief that the social transformation he sought required new 'religious' myths led him to write his own – *Also Sprach Zarathustra* (*Thus Spoke Zarathustra*), an attempt at a new set of scriptures, containing the story and sayings of the eponymous prophet. Nietzsche came more and more to see himself as the prophet of a new age, the 'free spirit' proclaiming the death of the old and the dawn of the new.

The composer Richard Strauss (1864–1949) composed in 1896 a tone poem inspired by Nietzsche's book. It was also called *Also Sprach Zarathustra*, though many people now know its opening fanfare best from its use at the beginning of Stanley Kubrick's film *2001: A Space Odyssey*.

Towards the end of 1888, that self-confidence and the affirmation of life that Nietzsche sought to sustain turned to a hectic euphoria and increasingly delusional megalo-mania. By the end of December, he had suffered a complete mental and physical collapse, from which he never recovered – though he lived until August 1900. He eventually fell under the care of his sister, Elizabeth, who lost no time in assuming control of his works and his reputation – with effects that, as noted above in the discussion of anti-Semitism, were sometimes deeply at variance with Nietzsche's own ideas.

Conclusion

Nietzsche's influence on modern Christian theology has been huge, but it is possible to identify three main directions in which that impact has run. First, there is the impact of Nietzsche's genealogical account of the rise of belief in God. A good deal of theology since Nietzsche's time has become much more sensitive to the idea that claims about God are (or can be) attempted exercises of power on the part of those who make the claims and that the surface logic of arguments about God's existence and nature might mask a deeper, political logic of bids for power or of resistance to such bids. Unearthing such power-plays under the surface of past and present claims about God has become a major component of late twentieth-century theology, as has argument about whether anything remains *beyond* power-play in such claims. The chapters on Feminism and on Liberating Theology later in this book (Chapters 14 and 15) pick up on some of these strands of response.

> The philosopher Paul Ricoeur (1913–2005) named Nietzsche as one of the 'Masters of Suspicion', alongside Marx and Freud. Each of them showed that there is more than meets the eye to religious claims: that beneath the apparent reasons offered for those claims lurk the *real* reasons why they are held and propagated – the economic interests of the class whose position is protected by religion, for Marx, or the deep, unconscious psychological needs and desires of the religious person, for Freud, or the machinations of the will to power, for Nietzsche.

Second, under the influence of Nietzsche and others, there have been various attempts to ask what difference it makes if claims about God are not presented as unavoidable conclusions resting upon indubitable foundations, but simply as part of the intellectual DNA of certain contingent ways of living in the world. Does that mean that questions about the *truth* of those claims are ruled out, and if not, what does it mean to claim truth for something that cannot be secured from all reasonable denial by appeal to the available evidence and the universal rules of human reasoning? Chapter 17 on postmodernism picks up on this 'non-foundationalist' strand of response – and Nietzsche is widely regarded as one of the prophets of the postmodern turn that we discuss there.

Third, Nietzsche's passionate critique of Christianity as life-denying has helped call forth responses from numerous Christian theologians, who have sought to demonstrate the ways in which Christianity is, or can be, profoundly affirmative about life, creativity and strength – even if not in quite the ways that Nietzsche himself might have wanted. To give just one example, the theology of the English theologian Timothy Gorringe could be read as one long extended and multi-faceted riposte to Nietzsche. In Gorringe's hands, the central note of Christian theology becomes God's unreserved 'yes' to the world in Jesus Christ, and the echoes which that 'yes' should find in Christians' free and open celebration of the possibilities of flourishing creaturely life (see Mike Higton, 'The Theology of Tim Gorringe' in Mike Higton, Jeremy Law and Christopher Rowland (eds), *Theology and Human Flourishing*, Eugene: Wipf and Stock, 2011, pp1–15). By way of the response of theologians such as Gorringe, one of Nietzsche's paradoxical forms of influence has been in the spread of such more thoroughgoing affirmative notes in modern Christian theology – such that it is now rather difficult to find theologians for whom the *primary* notes of a Christian theology of human life are self-denial and humility.

Exercise

Most of Nietzsche's works are aphoristic. They are collections of short sections – sometimes no more than a sentence, seldom longer than a paragraph or two. These aphorisms are not meant to lead you step by steady step through a logical progression into Nietzsche's ideas. Rather, they are meant to explode like fireworks – by the light of which Nietzsche hoped that the tiny minority among his readers who were ready to be free spirits would see the landscape of the new world of values to which he was calling them. When reading Nietzsche, therefore, it is more than ordinarily important to take your time and not to let your annoyance or excitement at the latest firework divert you from the task of serious understanding.

Try reading two extracts from *The Gay Science*, slowly and carefully: Book III, §§108–125; and Book V, §§343–347. The sections from Book V are longer and more connected; the sections from Book III shorter and more varied – but both can be a confusing read, if tackled head on. Once you have read all the way through both extracts fairly steadily, go back to Book III §125 – the famous story of the madman speaking about the death of God. Read it carefully and then see whether, in the light of all that you have read, you are able to make sense of it. It's not an argument, as such – but what is it? Jot down some notes explaining what you think Nietzsche was trying to persuade his readers to think or to do, how he was trying to reshape their imaginations, and how he was trying to make that persuasion effective.

Now look at §124. It's a very different aphorism in style and tone. What does that section add to the picture you've just sketched? What persuasive work is Nietzsche trying to do, and how does it relate to the persuasive work you've identified in §125? And what about §123, different again?

You can keep going, reading the other aphorisms in these extracts again, to see what, if anything they add – or where, if at all, they fit – into the picture of Nietzsche's persuasive work that you are producing. But are there aphorisms that don't fit? Are there aphorisms that even contradict the picture you're developing? Are there aphorisms that belong together in something like a connected argument?

This is the kind of work you need to do to understand Nietzsche properly: not simply starting at the beginning, reading through to the end and then trying to summarise the argument (as if there *were* a connected argument), but taking your time, playing with the aphorisms and trying to gauge their persuasive power.

Bibliography

Primary texts

The following texts provide a good initial selection:

Friedrich Nietzsche, *The Anti-Christ, Ecce Homo, Twilight of the Idols, and Other Writings*, eds. Aaron Ridley and Judith Norman, Cambridge: Cambridge University Press, 2005. We'd suggest starting with *Twilight of the Idols*; it is the closest thing to an overview, and sometimes shows Nietzsche at his witty and infuriating best.

Friedrich Nietzsche, *The Anti-Christ* – his most extended treatment of Christianity. Found in the volume listed above.

Friedrich Nietzsche, *The Gay Science*, ed, Bernard Williams, trans. Josefine Nauckhoff, Cambridge: Cambridge University Press, 2001 – good for a sense of Nietzsche's genealogical critique of metaphysics and religion.

Friedrich Nietzsche, *Thus Spoke Zarathustra*, eds. Adrian Del Caro and Robert B. Pippin, Cambridge: Cambridge University Press, 2006 – Nietzsche's attempt at a set of scriptures for his new world.

The editions in the Cambridge Texts in the History of Philosophy series, edited by Karl Ameriks and Desmond M. Clarke, are generally very good, and come with full introductions.

Secondary texts

Julian Young, *Nietzsche: A Philosophical Biography* (Cambridge: Cambridge University Press, 2010). Long and detailed, but readable and fascinating. If you have the time, a fantastic place to start. See also Young's *Nietzsche's Philosophy of Religion* (Cambridge: Cambridge University Press, 2006), a good companion piece to the biography, it shows how Nietzsche's work can be read as a pursuit of a Greek 'religious' ideal.

J.P. Stern, *Nietzsche* (London: Fontana, 1985). Fairly clear and with good focus on Nietzsche's relation to theology.

Lee Spinks, *Friedrich Nietzsche*, Routledge Critical Thinkers (London: Routledge, 2003). A useful and clear overview of Nietzsche's views on morality.

Bernard Magnus and Kathleen M. Higgins (eds), *The Cambridge Companion to Nietzsche* (Cambridge: Cambridge University Press, 1996). A useful collection of essays, including Jörg Salaquarda on Nietzsche's relation to the Judaeo–Christian tradition.

John Walker, 'Nietzsche, Christianity, and the legitimacy of tradition', in Keith Ansell-Pearson (ed.), *Nietzsche and Modern German Thought* (London: Routledge, 1991). An attempt to see how Nietzsche is responding to the theological heritage; worth reading alongside the Salaquarda piece in the *Cambridge Companion*.

8

Charles Hodge and Horace Bushnell

AIMS

By the end of this chapter, we hope that you will:

- understand Charles Hodge's approach to systematic theology

- understand how Horace Bushnell's theology differs from Hodge's

- appreciate the significance of that difference for later theology

- understand what it means to say that the distinction between liberal and conservative theology is not a timeless distinction.

Introduction

It is all too easy to assume that, in broad terms, the battle lines that divide the current theological landscape are as old as the hills. Even if the people who fight and the precise issues over which they disagree change over time, it might seem that something like the current division has always been around. It is all too easy, for instance, to assume that Christianity has nearly always been riven by a distinction between something a bit like that between *conservative* theology and *liberal* theology today. (As an example: I remember once hearing a talk in which it was argued that the clash between Jesus and the Pharisees in the gospels was really the same clash as that between evangelicals and liberals today.) Yet such distinctions actually have a history and the history is often not quite as long as we suppose. They emerged at a particular point in time, they have changed as time has passed and they will eventually give way to different distinctions. The landscape of theology alters, and it does not take geological timescales to do it.

In this chapter, we will look at the disagreement between two North American theologians whose lives spanned the first three quarters of the nineteenth century. We will find in their disagreement something like the distinction between conservative and liberal theology that has shaped so much Christian theology – especially English-language Christian theology – through the twentieth and into the twenty-first century. On one side stands Charles Hodge (1797–1878), who has been described by a recent biographer as the 'guardian of American orthodoxy' (the subtitle of Paul C. Gutjahr's 2011 biography of Hodge) and as a 'type of patron saint' for at least some strands of later conservative Christian theology in America (Gutjahr, *Charles Hodge*, p382). 'Countless American Christians,' Gutjahr says, 'still carry some portion of Princeton Seminary's cane of orthodoxy, many of [them] having no idea that it was Charles Hodge who passed it on to them' (p385). Horace Bushnell (1802–1876), on the other side, is 'deservedly remembered as the theological father of mainstream American liberal Protestantism', according to one of his biographers (Gary Dorrien, *The Making of American Liberal Theology*, 2001). We will examine the two men and the contrast between their approaches to theology and will see that they were not simply *representatives* of a perennial tension between conservative and liberal, but that their arguments (and those arguing in similar ways around them) helped to bring that tension into being and so change the theological landscape. It is a characteristically *modern* tension, and it is in part generated by differing responses to modernity.

Charles Hodge

Charles Hodge entered Princeton Seminary as a student in 1816, four years after its foundation; he became a professor there in 1822, and principal in 1851, and by the time of his death in 1878 had been there almost uninterruptedly for 62 years.

Figure 8.1 Charles Hodge

Hodge did take a two-year trip to Europe, from 1826 to 1828. As well as studying Hebrew, Syriac and Arabic in Paris, and undertaking theological studies in Halle, he met Friedrich Schleiermacher (see Chapter 4) in Berlin – but was not much impressed. He does not appear to have met Hegel (see Chapter 5) but he certainly encountered Hegel's ideas, with considerable displeasure.

Hodge was a devout Presbyterian through and through, and the foundation upon which all his later theological thinking and writing would be built was laid early, with his mothers' drilling of him in the Westminster Shorter Catechism (a summary of Calvinist teaching in question and answer form, produced by the Westminster Assembly in England in 1647). He was also trained early in the careful reading of Scripture and in thinking of Scripture as the primary guide for life and thought. When he was first appointed to a full teaching job in the Seminary, it was as a teacher of

Scripture: he was Professor of Oriental and Biblical Literature, before becoming Professor of Exegetical and Didactic Theology in 1840.

He was a prolific author from early in his time at the Seminary, but the crowning work of his career, and the most influential, did not appear until 1872–1873: the three-volume *Systematic Theology*. In many ways, the *Systematic Theology* is the best introduction to Hodge's theological work as a whole. Hodge thought of himself as a defender of true Christian theology – which for him meant Protestant theology and specifically Calvinist theology, as it had been codified by the English Puritans in the seventeenth century and transported to the North American colonies in the seventeenth and eighteenth centuries. As well as defending it against external critics, he was defending it against internal changes – most notably against the changes that some theologians felt were necessary if they were to make sense of the American experience of religious revivals, and against the changes that others were seeking to make in the light of their familiarity with European debates, such as those surrounding Kant, Schleiermacher and Hegel (see Chapters 3–5).

In the 1730s and 1740s, and again in the early decades of the nineteenth century, religious revivals – periods of intense religious activity in which church membership was significantly increased by new converts and returning backsliders – were a notable feature of North American life. Some Presbyterian churchmen, who had been trained in Calvinist theologies, came to believe that their theology needed articulating in different ways in order to do justice to these phenomena – especially in order to do more justice to the central role that human decision for Christ in response to the preaching of the Gospel seemed to play in the revival experience. Yale was the intellectual centre for such revival-minded Presbyterians; Princeton was the intellectual centre for those who resisted the change.

Hodge's *Systematic Theology* is detailed, clear and forthright; it presents its key teachings as the unavoidable conclusions of a sober and sensible study of the evidence; it resolutely avoids any impression of innovation or any impression of capitulation to contemporary intellectual fashions. In the words of Paul Gutjahr:

> Hodge wrote his *Systematic* with the unshakeable conviction that the true church and its teachings were utterly incapable of change. More importantly, he believed that these immutable teachings served as the core of Princeton Seminary's curriculum, and that his *Systematic* was simply the compendium of a line of theological thinking that had characterized the Seminary since its founding.
>
> Gutjahr, *Charles Hodge*, p350.

Hodge insists that 'all true people of God in every age and in every part of the Church ... agree as to the meaning of Scripture in all things necessary either in faith or practice' (Hodge, *Systematic Theology*, vol I, p188), and that his task as a theologian in gleaning, arranging and connecting the teachings of Scripture is therefore a matter of saying again, as clearly and fully as possible, what has already been said by all true Christian teachers.

Of course, not every Christian who has turned to the Bible has derived sound teaching from it. Hodge insists on the 'right of private judgment' (p188) in theology, but that private judgement will only be exercised aright if it approaches the Scriptures humbly, sensibly, and honestly. 'The words of Scripture are to be taken in their plain historical sense' (p187), and it must be recognised that, as God is the author of the whole of Scripture:

> God cannot in one place teach any thing which is inconsistent with what He teaches in another ... If a passage admits of different interpretations, that only can be the true one which agrees with what the Bible teaches elsewhere on the same subject.
>
> Hodge, *Systematic Theology*, vol I, p187.

If only Christians will approach the Scriptures in this way, reading the whole Bible with diligent care, trusting in the perspicuity of what they read, humbly allowing themselves to be trained in that reading by earlier generations of Christian teachers, but having the confidence then to test that teaching at all times against the Scriptures themselves, then they will not go astray – and they will find that the teachings of the Christian church (including the Westminster Catechism and those who have been true to it) are secure 'beyond all rational or innocent dispute' (p296).

One way in which the *Systematic Theology* does differ from much of Hodge's earlier theological work, however, is in its direct, prominent and sustained insistence that theology is best thought of as a science. Hodge insists that his method 'agrees in everything essential with the inductive method as applied to the natural sciences' (p9). That is, his method:

> assumes that the Bible contains all the facts or truths which form the contents of theology, just as the facts of nature are the contents of the natural sciences. It is also assumed that the relation of these Biblical facts to each other, the principles involved in them, the laws which determine them, are in the facts themselves, and are to be deduced from them, just as the laws of nature are deduced from the facts of nature.
>
> Hodge, *Systematic Theology*, vol I, p17.

As a science, theology 'must include something more than a mere knowledge of facts. It must embrace an exhibition of the internal relation of those facts, one to another, and each to all ...' (p1). It is in that sense that theology can properly be called 'Systematic': it arranges the facts delivered in Scripture into a harmonious whole and demonstrates how those facts connect and together form a mutually reinforcing system, secure and stable against attack. As we shall see, despite Hodge's conservative intensions, this insistence on the scientific and systematic nature of his work marks a new, and fundamentally modern, development in theology.

Horace Bushnell

Charles Hodge was a Princeton man through and through, but Horace Bushnell studied at Yale. His initial studies were in law rather than theology because, unlike Hodge who had come early to a strong and clear Christian faith, Bushnell was deeply uncertain about Christianity until late in his twenties. Eventually, in 1831, he had a kind of conversion experience but it was, at this stage, a conversion to faith in the good and to a 'dimly felt' hope in the God who is the source of good (according to Bushnell, as

Figure 8.2 Portrait of Reverend Horace Bushnell (1802–1876)

quoted in Mary Bushnell Cheney, *Life and Letters of Horace Bushnell*, New York: Scribners, 1903, p59). His Christian faith nevertheless gathered around that nucleus and he enrolled in Yale Divinity School before becoming a Congregationalist minister in Hartford, Connecticut, in 1833. He was to remain as a minister until ill-health forced his retirement in 1859, after which time he devoted himself to independent writing and preaching.

His initial conversion experience was followed by other transformative experiences, each of which further secured and deepened his faith. The most significant was probably that of 1848, in which Bushnell found himself drawn into a more intense realisation that to be a Christian meant being conformed to Christ by the living and active presence of Christ in one's life. In a sermon preached immediately after, entitled 'Christ the Form of the Soul', he explains that 'as all material objects have their beauty in their forms, so the soul has her beauty in the character, that lovely shape of goodness and truth in which she appears to men'.

> The great design of God in the incarnation of his Son is to form a divine life in you. It is to produce a Christ in the image of your soul, and to set you on the footing of a brother with the divine Word himself ... [U]pon this Christly character formed in you rests the fellowship and glory of the redeemed world. He will raise the human even to the divine, for it is only in the pure divine that God can have complacence and hold communion. To entertain such a thought seems a kind of daring, but faith is a daring exercise.
>
> Bushnell, *The Spirit in Man: Sermons and Selections*
> (New York: Scribners, 1903), pp38, 48–49.

Bushnell's mature theology has this growth of Christ in the soul, or growth of the soul into Christ, at its heart. As he understood it, that process involves a transformation in how one sees the world through which one moves. As the soul grows into its proper beauty, it becomes more able to recognise the beauty of other things and to see the objects and movements of the world not simply as brute facts but as words spoken by God, expressing God's character and displaying God's glory. God 'stands *expressed* every where, so that, turn whichsoever way we please, we behold the outlooking of His intelligence' (Bushnell, *God in Christ*, p30).

These theological ideas were supported and shaped by Bushnell's view of language. For the ordinary physical objects and movements in the world around us, we might well use plain literal names. But all other uses of language are to some degree or another metaphorical: we take words that describe those physical objects and movements, and use them to speak about our thoughts and feelings. Such a transfer is certainly possible and does enable us to speak truly about those thoughts and feelings; it is, nevertheless, also inherently *limited*: words perfectly well fitted to describe physical objects and movements are only partially adequate to the task of expressing mental matters: 'They are only hints, or images, held up before the mind of another, to put *him* on generating or reproducing the same thought' (*God in Christ*, p46). They are 'earthen vessels in which the truth is borne, yet always offering their mere pottery as being the truth itself' (p48) – and we get ourselves into all sorts of difficulties if we mistake that pottery for the truth itself. Instead, to capture any thought or feeling well, we need to set multiple metaphorical descriptions alongside one another so that each can qualify the others and each have its inadequacies displayed by its difference from the others.

If this is true of our attempts to speak of thoughts and feelings, how much truer, argues Bushnell, is it of our attempts to speak of God. We do not have literal words for God, but metaphors – words taken from physical objects and movements, and put to work to express, and to help motivate, the journey of our souls to their true Christlike nature, and to enable us to glimpse the mysterious one who draws us on that journey. Bushnell insists that it is a mistake to

> assume that there is a literal terminology in religion as well as a figurative ... and then it is only a part of the same mistake to accept words, not as signs or images, but as absolute measures and equivalents of truth; and so to run by themselves, by their argumentations, with a perfectly unsuspecting confidence, into whatsoever conclusions the *logical forms* of the words will carry them.
>
> Bushnell, God in Christ, p40.

In particular, he insisted that Scripture should be read 'not as a magazine of propositions and mere dialectic entities, but as inspiration and poetic forms of life; requiring, also, divine inbreathings and exaltations in us, that we may ascend into their meaning' (p93), and that

> the best and truest doctrine ... will be that which a soul, purified and cleared by love, discovers under manifold terms of analogy, when it turns itself to the receiving of God through simple contemplation, perusing the faces of those words and symbols by which he is expressed.
>
> Bushnell, *Christ in Theology* (Hartford: Brown and Parsons, 1851), pp39–40.

Bushnell does not, therefore, aspire to write a *Systematic Theology*, but to write and preach in such a way as to evoke and inspire a spiritual journey, and his approach to doctrine is not to decide between the various competing formulae on offer by careful examination of the Biblical evidence, but to place alongside one another multiple different ways of speaking about each doctrinal topic – God's triune nature, Christ's incarnation, the meaning of the cross – and to allow the clashes between those formulae to push us beyond a precise literal interpretation of any one of them.

Bushnell first set his view of language out fully in print in a 'Preliminary Dissertation on Language' placed at the beginning of his 1849 book, *God in Christ*. One of the reviewers of this book was Charles Hodge himself, writing in the journal he had founded, *The Biblical Repertory and Princeton Review* (vol 21.2 (1849), pp259–298). His verdict was blunt: 'we think the book a failure' (p260); Bushnell's arguments 'lack the power of consistency. They say and unsay' (p264). He 'supposes there can be no revelation from God to men, except to the imagination and the feelings, none to the reason' (p266), yet '[t]he whole healthful power of the things of God over the feelings depends upon their being true to the intellect':

> The revelations of God are addressed to the whole soul, to the reason, to the imagination, to the heart, and to the conscience. But unless they are true to the reason, they are as powerless as a phantasm.
>
> Hodge, *The Biblical Repertory and Princeton Review*, vol 21.2 (1849), p269.

Hodge regards as a clear abdication of intellectual responsibility Bushnell's willingness to set alongside one another doctrinal formulae long accepted as orthodox, formulae regarded as heretical and formulae culled from his own fertile imaginations and those of other contemporary writers, searching for the deeper ways in which all might be true (though only partially true) as metaphors.

> Dr Bushnell forgets that there are certain doctrines so settled by the faith of the church, that they are no longer open questions. They are finally adjudged and determined. If men set aside the Bible, and choose to speak or write as philosophers, then of course the way is open for them, to teach what they please. But for Christians, who acknowledge the scriptures as their rule of faith, there are doctrines which they are bound to take as settled beyond all rational or innocent dispute.
>
> Hodge, *The Biblical Repertory and Princeton Review*, vol 21.2 (1849), p296.

There is a strong echo of Schleiermacher in Bushnell's willingness to reinterpret doctrinal statements as expressions of a relation between Christ and the soul that does not lend itself to literal description. Bushnell has, accordingly, sometimes been called 'the American Schleiermacher' and Hodge clearly thought of him in that light: 'All this agrees with Schleiermacher to a tittle', he says in his review of *God in Christ* (p295). Bushnell, though deeply appreciative of Schleiermacher, might have preferred to be thought of as the disciple of another Romantic figure he cites often with approval: Samuel Taylor Coleridge, for whom an imagination informed by multiple symbols can lead one more deeply into the mystery of God than can bare reason.

Christian nurture

The two men had been involved in an earlier, less vituperative exchange, when Hodge had reviewed Bushnell's 1847 work, *Discourses on Christian Nurture*. Their dispute there, though less sharply expressed, helps clarify the differences between their theologies. Bushnell wrote his book as a polemic against a way of understanding the development and nurture of children that he thought destructive and false. A good deal of Christianity in New England at that time was very revival-minded, both in that it hoped and prayed for intense movements of renewal and conversion to sweep through the population and fill the churches, and in that it focused on the dramatic movement of the individual soul from a conviction of sin to a clear assurance of salvation and public profession of faith. For Christians with such a focus, it made less sense to think of children as being brought up *in* the Christian faith than it did to think of them as brought up so that they might one day experience conversion *to* the Christian faith – and, as Bushnell saw it, that seemed to mean bringing them up in consciousness that they were sinners, and that they must await the mysterious inrushing of God's converting Spirit to turn them from their sins. Bushnell sees this as 'a piety of conquest rather than of love' (Bushnell, *Views of Christian Nurture*, p8).

He, by contrast, presents a picture – tenderly drawn – of children nurtured from the beginning of their lives in love of the good and in delight in Christ.

> Christ himself, by that renewing Spirit who can sanctify from the womb, should be practically infused into the childish mind; in other words ... the house, having a domestic Spirit of grace dwelling in it, should become the church of childhood, the table and hearth a holy rite, and life an element of saving power.
>
> Bushnell, *Views of Christian Nurture*, p16.

There is nothing strange, he suggests, in the idea that a love of the good for its own sake should *begin* to take root in even a child's mind, and this is all the more likely – indeed, almost certain – if the child is surrounded by the love and pious example of his or her parents:

> The child is under parental authority too for the very purpose, it would seem, of having the otherwise abstract principle of all duty impersonated in his parents and thus brought home to his practical embrace.
>
> Bushnell, *Views of Christian Nurture*, p16.

Hodge found much in Bushnell's book to approve of and agreed that a much stronger focus was needed on Christian nurture, and a much stronger expectation of the good it could do for children and of the difference it could make to their subsequent adult lives. He agreed that too revival-minded a theology could go wrong in precisely the

Bushnell's account of Christian nurture was well received by many because it chimed with popular portrayals of the home as both a realm of tenderness, and a training ground in virtue. Think of the *Little House on the Prairie* books by Laura Ingalls Wilder, and their presentation of the loving moral guidance provided to Laura and the other girls by their Ma and Pa.

ways that Bushnell identified; and agreed in particular that a less individualistic account of Christian salvation and discipleship was needed. (Hodge's review appeared in the *Biblical Repertory and Princeton Review* vol 19.4 (1847), pp502–539). He nevertheless rejected what he saw as the book's 'naturalistic account of conversion or the effect of religious training' (p525). 'The whole tenor of his book is in favour of the idea that all true religion is gradual, habitual, acquired as habits are formed. Every thing must be like a natural process, nothing out of the regular sequence of cause and effect' (p533).

He was, to an extent, quite right – but Bushnell would have denied that his account was thereby 'naturalistic' in the sense that it left out or did inadequate justice to the *super*natural. Rather, for Bushnell, in the process of Christian nurture, as elsewhere in the Christian life, we see the supernatural working in and through the natural. Much later in his life, in a book called *Nature and the Supernatural*, Bushnell would write that while 'there is no hope for man, or human society, under sin, save in the supernatural interposition of God':

> the supernatural divine agency, required to produce an efficacious remedy for sin, is wholly compatible with nature; involving no breach of her laws, or disturbance of their systematic action.
>
> Bushnell, *Nature and the Supernatural*, p250.

For Bushnell, therefore, one may talk about the supernatural – God's gracious salvation of human beings – precisely by talking in a certain way about the natural – the ordinary processes by which human beings imbibe their virtues and their vices from their parents and their environment. The supernatural does not *reduce* to the natural (so 'God's grace' is not simply a rather high-flown name for what we would normally call 'moral education'), but we most clearly describe the supernatural by describing its effects in and through the natural, just as we might talk about a wind by talking about the way in which leaves and branches are swayed by it.

For Hodge, on the other hand, our theological descriptions of salvation cannot be translated even to this degree into descriptions of natural processes. Of course, plenty of natural processes are involved in the whole story of salvation – but there is something beyond all of them, and distinct from them, that can only properly be described in theological terms. When we say that sinners 'need to be quickened by that mighty power which wrought in Christ when it raised him from the dead' (Hodge, review of *Christian Nurture*, p536), we are talking as plainly as we can about a spiritual transaction or occurrence that can't be explained in naturalistic terms, or re-described by the portrayal of a natural process.

Hodge and Bushnell famously disagree about the latter's account of Christ's sacrifice and its effects. From Hodge's point of view, the choice is clear: either one has (like himself) a theology of salvation that begins with God's objective work on the cross on our behalf, or one has (like Bushnell) a theology that begins with the subjective effect of the cross on our lives. The former, objective view still leaves room for subjective elements to be included; the latter, subjective view leaves no real room for God's objective work.

From Bushnell's point of view, on the other hand, to describe the options in this way is already to have the relationship between natural and supernatural wrong. God's objective work and the internal processes by which nature develops – including the internal processes that constitute human subjectivity – can't be separated: God objectively works in and through the subjective.

Cosmic harmony

Another way of getting at the difference between Hodge and Bushnell is to note that they are each convinced of a deep and pervasive harmony uniting God and the world.

For Bushnell, we have already seen that there is such a harmony uniting the physical and the spiritual. He thinks that the transfer of words from their original uses to name physical things and arrangements to name mental processes and feelings is *possible*, because there is a strange resemblance, an analogy, between the mental world and the physical: 'There is a logos in the forms of things, by which they are prepared to serve as types or images of what is inmost in our souls' (*God in Christ*, p30). And it remains possible to speak of God, despite the inherent limitations of our language, precisely because the same resemblance or analogy that binds the physical and the mental also extends to God. Just as 'there is a vast analogy in things, which prepares them, as forms, to be signs or figures of thoughts' (*God in Christ*, p22), so it is possible for us to be given words that allow us to speak of God 'only on the ground of this vast, original and truly Sacred Analogy between things visible and invisible' (*Christ in Theology*, p39). The things of the world are means by which God has expressed Godself to us; as such, they are also fitted to be means by which we can express ourselves to each other. The world is not a world of isolated substances each with its own proper name, but of resemblances and echoes, of hints and glimpses, made for the communication of what is ultimately inexpressible.

For Hodge, on the other hand, the harmony that unites all things is most easily apprehended as a symphony of interconnected facts.

> It is impossible that one truth should contradict another. It is impossible, therefore, that God should reveal anything as true which contradicts any well authenticated truth, whether of intuition, experience, or previous revelation.
>
> Hodge, Systematic Theology, vol I, p51.

This confidence extends to any 'well-authenticated testimony of our senses' (p60). There can, in particular, be no contradiction between the claims we find plainly set out in the Bible and the claims about the natural world properly made by diligent and sober scientific inquiry. In principle, this means both that scientific inquiries should be interpreted in the light of the Bible, and that the Bible should be interpreted in the light of claims made on the basis of scientific enquiry – though, of course, Hodge does qualify this latter insistence quite carefully.

> The theologian ... acknowledges that the Scriptures must be interpreted in accordance with established facts. He has a right, however, to demand that those facts should be verified beyond the possibility of a doubt. Scientific men in one age or country affirm the truth of facts, which others deny or disprove ...

Furthermore:

> While acknowledging their obligation to admit undeniable facts, theologians are at liberty to receive or reject the theories deduced from those facts. Such theories are human speculations, and can have no higher authority than their own inherent probability.
>
> Hodge, Systematic Theology, vol I, p57.

The nature of the coherence that Hodge seeks is clear if we look at a particular example: his account of the creation of the world. He argues that the account in the first chapter of Genesis of creation in six days must be intended to be historical, because of its genre, its place at the beginning of the Bible's historical narrative, its citation as history in other places in Scripture and its importance to the whole scheme of God's ways with the world revealed in Scripture. If that is so, he is then faced with an absolute constraint upon his freedom to interpret the origin of the world: whatever happened, it must be the case that the account presented in Genesis 1 presents an appropriate factual description. What, though, of the apparent contradiction between the Genesis account of a six-day creation, and the findings of the science of geology regarding the enormous age of the Earth and the vastly extended timescale of its formation? Noting that the word 'day' is plainly used in Scripture to name various different timescales, Hodge says:

> It is of course admitted that, taking this account [in Genesis 1] by itself, it would be most natural to understand the word in its ordinary sense; but if that sense brings the Mosaic account into conflict with facts, and another sense avoids such conflict, then it is obligatory on us to adopt that other. Now it is urged that if the word 'day' be taken in the sense of 'an indefinite period of time', a sense which it undoubtedly has in other parts of Scripture, there is not only no discrepancy between the Mosaic account of the creation and the assumed facts of geology, but there is a most marvellous coincidence between them.
>
> Hodge, *Systematic Theology*, vol I, pp570–571.

Note that this interpretation is made possible by the undoubted fact that 'day' has multiple meanings in Scripture and that, once this latitude of possible interpretation has been seen, trust in the harmony between scriptural claims and true scientific discoveries *obliges* the interpreter to select the available interpretation that maximises that harmony.

Given this interest in the harmony between scientific discoveries and the fact-claims in the Biblical account of creation, it should be no surprise that Hodge's last book was a response to Darwin. *What is Darwinism?*, he asked – and he answered, 'atheism' (*What is Darwinism?*, p177). Hodge identified the key question in a way that influenced much subsequent debate (including, for instance, Benjamin Warfield – see Chapter 11): divine design versus the workings of a natural process blind to the future and to all sense of purpose. No diligent research into the possible meaning of the words of Scripture leaves room for a creation without deliberate, purposive intention driving its formation; no accommodation can therefore be reached, according to Hodge, with an account of that formation that does away with such intention altogether. Here more clearly than anywhere Hodge exercises the theologian's right, '[w]hile acknowledging their obligation to admit undeniable facts ... to receive or reject the *theories* deduced from those facts' (*Systematic Theology*, vol I, p57) – and he insists (in a way that will be recognisable to anyone familiar with more recent debates) that Darwinism is at best a theory, and probably better described as a mere hypothesis (*What is Darwinism?*, p74).

Conclusion

Even if the precise details are unfamiliar, the whole debate between Hodge and Bushnell is quite likely to seem recognisable to readers familiar with debates between conservative and liberal Christian theology in the generations since their time, especially in English-speaking contexts. That should not mislead us, however, into thinking that the conservative/liberal divide that Hodge and Bushnell represent is a timeless one. The reality is more complex than that.

For one thing, the disagreement between Hodge and Bushnell does not map easily onto divisions in American theology in the generation before them. If one had been attempting to map American theology in *that* generation, one might have distinguished the conservative theologians of Princeton from the more revival-minded theologians of Yale, and from the Unitarians of Harvard – and even if it is fairly clear where one would put Hodge on this map, it is not clear that Bushnell, or the kind of theology that he represents, would fit anywhere.

More importantly, there is nothing timeless about the association of conservative theology with a scientific approach, with a strong dose of common sense realism, or with an insistence upon the single, plain historical sense of the Scriptures; nor is there anything timeless about the association of the rejection of conservatism with an interest in metaphor, mystery and multiple meanings. In the generation immediately before Hodge and Bushnell, for instance, something rather like Hodge's scientific, literalist approach was common currency on all sides, and if one had to identify a spectrum from a lesser to a greater insistence upon 'scientific' approaches, it would probably have run away from the conservatives and towards the Unitarians. Whether or not that is true, it is certainly the case that, if one takes a much longer view, it is no uniform feature of Christian history to find orthodoxy associated with simple literalism and heterodoxy with mystery and multiple meanings.

Then there is the fact that the discipline of systematic theology, which Hodge defends so eloquently, is a relatively new discipline, at least in the form that Hodge gives it. Of course, there had been compendious presentations of theology before – such as Aquinas' *Systematic Theology*, Melanchthon's *Loci Communes*, Calvin's *Institutes* or, most pertinently for Hodge's own training, Francis Turretin's *Institutes* – but Hodge's *Systematic Theology* is a new variation on that existing tradition, and one that by inspiring a whole slew of imitators virtually created a genre. (Hodge's is the first substantial American systematic theology, though there had been some more loosely organised works such as Charles Finney's 1846 *Lectures on Systematic Theology*.) His biographer, Paul Gutjahr, says 'the appearance of Hodge's *Systematic* marked a pivotal change in how Americans pursued the genre', and that it initiated 'a new era of synthetic theological study in America' (Gutjahr, *Charles Hodge*, pp350, 352).

For our purposes, one of the most striking things about this new discipline is that it was, at least in part, generated in response to theologians like Bushnell. It was partly in response to them, and to the influential Schleiermacherian strands of European theology that they were seen to represent, that Hodge was pushed to make more of the 'scientific' quality of systematic theology than any of the compendia listed above: its nature as an arrangement of the propositions yielded by careful analysis of scripture into a coherent framework of causes and effects, laws and instances; the trust it places in the capacity of the humble and diligent enquirer to make sense of the materials at his disposal; its insistence upon clarity, simplicity and – as far as possible – an absence of technicality and jargon; its 'indomitable optimism' (Gutjahr, *Charles Hodge*, p352). Hodge's *Systematic Theology* is, in its way, as much a work of *modern* theology as any of Bushnell's.

More than a century after the deaths of Hodge and Bushnell, another American theologian, George Lindbeck, wrote a book called *The Nature of Doctrine: Religion and Theology in a Postliberal Age* (Louisville: Westminster John Knox, 1984). His aim was to describe and to justify a particular way of doing theology that he called 'postliberal' or 'cultural-linguistic'. The details of his proposal needn't detain us here but what is noteworthy is that, in a very influential move, he described this postliberal approach by distinguishing it from two existing dominant forms of modern theology, that he calls cognitive-propositional and experiential-expressive. Neither Hodge nor Bushnell appears in Lindbeck's index, but the theological landscape he describes – divided between the cognitive-propositionalists and the experiential-expressivists – is precisely the landscape bequeathed by Hodge and Bushnell.

Exercise

Because the broad landscape of liberal versus conservative may well be familiar to readers today, it is hard to avoid making assumptions on the basis of that familiarity about what Hodge and Bushnell must have thought – to assume, for instance, that Hodge probably somewhat resembled more recent conservative American Christians in his political and social views and that Bushnell probably resembled more recent liberals or mainline Protestants. Without doing any research, ask yourself – based on what you now know about their theology – what you guess each man might have thought about race and slavery, given that they both lived through the American Civil War, and can hardly have failed to have opinions on the issue.

Now see what you can find out about what they actually said and did. See, for example, David Torbett, *Theology and Slavery: Charles Hodge and Horace Bushnell* (Macon: Mercer, 2006) and Mark Noll, *The Civil War as a Theological Crisis* (Chapel Hill: University of North Carolina Press, 2006), as well as relevant sections in the other secondary literature listed below.

Bibliography

Primary texts: Hodge

Hodge's great *Systematic Theology* – all three volumes of it (New York: Scribner, 1873) – remains the best place to start. Though detailed and thorough, it is surprisingly readable – and available online at <www.ccel.org/ccel/hodge/theology1.html>. Three other works are worth turning to next.

Charles Hodge, *Commentary on the Epistle to the Romans* (Philadelphia: Grigg and Elliot, 1835). The book that established Hodge's reputation, a staunch Calvinist reading of Paul. A later edition (Philadelphia: Martien, 1864) is available online at <books.google.co.uk/books?id=Y_fu2XupxusC>.

Charles Hodge, *The Way of Life* (Philadelphia: American Sunday School Union, 1841). A simpler compendium of Hodge's theology, written for a more popular audience. Available online at <books.google.co.uk/books?id=zWAXAAAAYAAJ>.

Charles Hodge, *What is Darwinism?* (New York: Scribner, Armstrong, 1874). Crucial for understanding the direction that the creation/evolution debate took in American theology. Available online at <www.gutenberg.org/files/19192/19192-h/19192-h.htm>.

Primary texts: Bushnell

There is no equivalent amongst Bushnell's works to Hodge's *Systematic Theology*, but there is nevertheless no shortage of material to read. It is, if anything, even more readable than Hodge's work: Bushnell's prose flows in colourful arcs, and it is not hard to see why he was an immensely popular preacher and orator.

Views of Christian Nurture (Hartford: Hunt, 1847). The book that sets out Bushnell's view on the bringing up of Christian children. Available online at <www.archive.org/details/viewschristiann02bushgoog>.

God in Christ: Three Discourses (Hartford: Brown and Parsons, 1849). A set of lectures on Christology, prefaced by the all-important dissertation on language. I have used the third edition (Hartford: Wm. James Hamersley, 1867), available online at <www.archive.org/details/godinchristthre02bushgoog>.

Nature and the Supernatural as Together Constituting the One System of God (New York: Scribner, 1858). Bushnell's clearest explanation of how God and the world relate and form a harmonious unity. Available online at <www.archive.org/details/natureandsupern03bushgoog>.

The Vicarious Sacrifice Grounded in Principles of Universal Obligation (New York: Scribner, 1866). His controversial account of the work achieved by Christ on the cross. Available online at <www.archive.org/details/vicarioussacrif00bushgoog>.

Secondary texts

Paul C. Gutjahr, *Charles Hodge: Guardian of American Orthodoxy* (Oxford: Oxford University Press, 2011). A detailed but very readable biography.

John W. Stewart and James H. Moorhead, *Charles Hodge Revisited: A Critical Appraisal of His Life and Work* (Grand Rapids: Eerdmans, 2002) A good accompaniment to Gutjahr's biography.

Mark A. Noll (ed.), *The Princeton Theology 1812-1921: Scripture, Science and Theological Method from Archibald Alexander to Benjamin Warfield* (Grand Rapids: Baker, 2001) Helps put Hodge in his Princeton context.

Robert Bruce Mullin, *The Puritan As Yankee: A Life of Horace Bushnell* (Grand Rapids: Eerdmans, 2002). Provides a good account of Bushnell's life and theology, stressing its continuity with earlier American theology.

Robert L. Edwards, *Of Singular Genius, of Singular Grace: A Biography of Horace Bushnell* (Cleveland: Pilgrim, 1992). A good accompaniment to the Mullin book.

Gary Dorrien, *The Making of American Liberal Theology: Imagining Progressive Religion, 1805–1900* (Louisville: Westminster John Knox Press, 2001). Very useful for setting Bushnell in a broader context of developing liberal theology.

9

Other nineteenth-century voices

AIMS

The preceding chapters represent the strands of nineteenth-century religious thought that are most often taught and studied, at least in the West. In this chapter, we introduce a range of other figures and movements from the long nineteenth century. These are figures and movements that are less often seen as central to the story of modern theology, but that might, if we pay attention to them, disrupt some dominant assumptions about the key modern themes of freedom, reason, history, the knowledge of God and suspicion of religion. They have been selected both because they are important and worth studying in their own right, and because they represent perspectives that are particularly significant and particularly prone to be excluded from stories of modern theology that focus on the Western Protestant academic elite.

Mary Wollstonecraft and Josephine Butler

Mary Wollstonecraft (later Godwin, 1759–1797) is one of the many modern thinkers who is more talked about than read. She is well known as an early – perhaps the first – feminist writer. Her most famous work, *A Vindication of the Rights of Woman* (1792), written in the wake of the French Revolution, put forward a detailed and damning analysis of the position of women in society and called for a 'revolution in female manners'. Wollstonecraft wanted women to think and act differently – but she was sure that they could not do so until social expectations and educational and political systems were themselves radically different.

She appealed to the shared humanity of men and women. Men and women shared the gift of reason, the capacity to be virtuous and the ability to learn – and the natural right to develop all these capacities. Women, she believed, were deprived of their rights as human beings – not only through oppressive political systems but also through much more deep-seated prejudices and social customs. Women were, she wrote, 'treated as a kind of subordinate beings, and not as part of the human species'.

Figure 9.1 Mary Wollstonecraft

One of the biggest obstacles to women's advancement in reason, virtue and learning, as Wollstonecraft saw it, was the pressure they were under to make themselves sexually attractive. The solution was the transformation of women's education, to instil proper self-respect and habits of reasoning – and also wider social reform. Among other things, Wollstonecraft called for co-education, better sex education for girls, legal protection for married women and the entry of women into industry and the professions.

Where would Wollstonecraft fit into an account of modern theology? She is not particularly well known as a theologian but her work is full of references to religious ideas. Like Thomas Paine, she rooted her account of the rights of humanity in the relation of each person to God the Creator. God endows each person with the gift of reason and it is an offence to God for anyone, male or female, to neglect this gift or suppress it in others. Her writings are full of reflections on the 'wisdom' of God, seen in the ordering of nature and of the human person; the will of 'Providence' can be understood through reason and must be followed even at the expense of breaking with human customs. Unlike Paine, she appealed directly to Christian Scripture and tradition in advocating her 'revolution'. In particular, she used biblical texts to call both men and women away from excessive devotion to material goods and from the abuse of sexuality.

Wollstonecraft looks at first glance like an advocate of the eighteenth century's 'religion of reason'. Just because of her sex and the subject-matter of her writings, however, she does not fit so easily into that category. She could not ignore the importance of the 'passions' and how they affected everyone's reasoning. Indeed, she took great pleasure in pulling to pieces the irrationally prejudiced descriptions of women written by supposedly 'rational', modern men. Were these men really as free from emotion, custom and prejudice as they claimed to be? Wollstonecraft, while herself a powerful advocate of reason, implicitly and explicitly raised questions about anyone's claims to take a detached, objective, rational, unprejudiced view of humanity. She was realistic about the depth and extent of social conditioning and the ways it could distort people's reasoning.

Despite her many appeals to the universal gifts of the Creator, Wollstonecraft poured scorn on the idea that humanity could escape its history and return to a perfectly good 'state of nature'. The solution, and indeed the way to follow the will of God, was not to flee civilisation, but to develop a better civilisation in which the 'passions' would not disappear, but would help to advance human virtue and happiness. Like her feminist successors, she was interested in the possibility of historical change that went beyond political systems and extended to all aspects of life. Significant injustices against women took place in 'private', so reform – or indeed revolution – could not stop with the 'public' sphere. If we take Wollstonecraft's work seriously, many of the central dichotomies of the Enlightenment – public and private, reason and passion, nature and civilisation, universal and particular – begin to look very dubious. At the very least, her writings draw attention to the partial character of the nineteenth-century academy, the context where our 'classic' texts were produced and a context from which the reasoning and experiences of half the human race were almost entirely excluded.

Wollstonecraft's work did not immediately give rise to a 'feminist' movement but some of her ideas reappear in the thought of nineteenth-century campaigners for women's rights. As we shall see in Chapter 14, the feminists of the nineteenth century – now generally referred to as the 'first wave' of feminism – were often both deeply religious and theologically creative.

Wollstonecraft's background was in the rational and progressive atmosphere of eighteenth-century English 'Dissent'. The background of Josephine Butler (1828–1906) was the very different, but no less radical, atmosphere of nineteenth-century English evangelicalism. Butler became famous as a campaigner against the Contagious Diseases Acts and more generally against manifestations of the sexual double standard in Victorian Britain.

Figure 9.2 Josephine Butler

Contagious Diseases Acts: Laws to regulate prostitution, intended to prevent the spread of venereal diseases among the armed forces. They allowed the arrest, the forcible subjection to medical examination and, in some circumstances, the imprisonment, of any woman suspected of being a prostitute. Butler's basic objection to them was that they punished *women* (including many women who were not in fact prostitutes) for the consequences of *male* promiscuity – and that they institutionalised prostitution, and hence the sexual double standard.

Sexual double standard: Sexual promiscuity in men, especially unmarried men, was tolerated and indeed expected, whereas even the suspicion of premarital sexual involvement brought lifelong disgrace on a woman. The double standard created, in effect, two classes of women – 'good women', whom men married, and 'bad women', with whom men had sex before marriage. One of Butler's most radical moves was breaking down this division among women – as a 'respectable' married woman, she associated herself publicly with prostitutes.

Butler was a famous – and in her time notorious – orator and political organiser. Her writings make it clear that a primary motivation for her work was her religious beliefs as an evangelical Christian. Calling men and women to join her campaigns, she appealed to the individual conscience and to the real possibility of personal conversion. The Contagious Diseases Acts, as she saw them, were un-Christian because they were 'materialist' – meaning, in this context, that they were concerned only with the well-being of people's bodies, and that they were narrowly utilitarian (sacrificing a few people for the sake of some 'greater good'). Her calls for reform were based on the theological claim that individuals and societies could be transformed, practically and materially as well as spiritually, through the grace of God – and they engaged her in a theological argument with those who claimed that prostitution was an inevitable consequence of a fixed *human nature*. She also drew extensively on the biblical imperative for solidarity with the poorest and most marginal people in society. In several of her speeches and writings, she compared prostitutes with Christ.

Butler, and those who supported her, faced considerable opposition from the religious establishment; her husband, an Anglican priest, suffered considerable setbacks in his career because of his unequivocal support for her work. In turn, the religious establishment was a target of her criticisms. The Church, Butler argued, had allowed the sexual double standard to persist and had failed to call people to account for the consequences of their actions. Most of her support, however, also came from committed Christians of various denominations.

J. Ellice Hopkins (1836–1904) is a less well-known, but in her time even more controversial, campaigner on issues relating to the sexual double standard, prostitution and 'social purity'. A devout Anglo-Catholic and a powerful preacher and public speaker, she developed a strong theology of the body, based on an incarnational and sacramental theology. She claimed that Christian failures to proclaim the body, and sex, as created good and sanctified in Christ led to *more* sexual immorality. She was best known, and widely reviled, for her book *The Power of Womanhood* (1899), which included (among other things) advice for parents on sex education for boys and girls.

William Seymour and Azusa Street

For many Christians worldwide in the early twenty-first century, the decisive historical turning-point of 'modern' religion came at the beginning of the twentieth century. It came, not with the intellectual, social and political revolutions of the Enlightenment, but with a transformation of Christian experience and practice that spread from the southern USA to become a worldwide phenomenon. The 'Azusa Street' revival, beginning in 1906 and centred on the ministry of William Seymour, is for Pentecostal Christians the beginning of the new 'age of the Holy Spirit' in which they themselves have been caught up.

William Seymour (1870–1922) was a black preacher from Louisiana, the son of former slaves and largely self-taught. Attending Charles Fox Parham's classes at the Bible School in Houston, he heard and became convinced of the newly-developed doctrine of 'initial evidence' – that speaking in tongues was the evidence of baptism in the Holy Spirit, a blessing promised to all believers.

Speaking in tongues: Now usually refers to glossolalia (speaking in unintelligible 'language'). Parham and many of his students, though not Seymour, believed that the evidence of baptism in the Holy Spirit was xenolalia (speaking in real foreign languages that the individual has not learnt). See Acts 2:2–11 and 1 Corinthians 14:1–33.

Seymour was called as a preacher to a small church in Los Angeles and, when his teaching on the gift of 'tongues' caused a rift with that congregation, began to hold prayer meetings in the house of one of his supporters. It was here, in 1906, that the explosion of new manifestations of baptism in the Holy Spirit – especially speaking in

Figure 9.3 Leaders of the Azusa Street Mission, 1907

tongues – began. The 'Azusa Street' church was opened soon afterwards and became the centre of a city-wide, and then a much more widespread, religious revival.

When Seymour 'attended' Charles Parham's classes, he did so from outside the lecture room, listening at an open door – the closest he, as a black man, was allowed to come to the 'whites only' classes. If the theological teaching that inspired Azusa Street was racially segregated, the experience itself was anything but that. Contemporary (hostile) news reports emphasise the apparent 'chaos' of the Azusa Street meetings, as all expected structures – of worship and religious authority, but also of race relations and gender roles – fell apart. In Seymour's prayer meetings, black and white prayed together, with white congregants recognising the leadership of a black minister. Women prophesied and preached – and took the revival movement to other cities where they led prayer meetings and founded churches. Although the meetings were dominated by poor and working-class people, they also crossed class divides. The *Los Angeles Times* report of April 1906 reflects the shocked response – shaped by strong racial and gender stereotypes – of the social and religious establishment to this collapse of 'normal' structures and relationships:

WEIRD BABEL OF TONGUES. NEW SECT OF FANATICS IS BREAKING LOOSE ... Breathing strange utterances and mouthing a creed which it seems no sane mortal could understand, the newest religious sect has started in Los Angeles ... Colored people and a sprinkling of whites compose the congregation ... They claim to have the 'gift of tongues' and to be able to comprehend the babel ... 'You-oo-oo gou-loo-loo come under the bloo-oo-oo boo-loo', shouts an old colored 'mammy', in a frenzy of religious zeal. Swinging her arms wildly about her, she continues with the strangest harangue ever uttered ...

Seymour was clear that what was happening at Azusa Street was the beginning of a new age of salvation history – the renewal of the earliest Christian experiences of the gift of the Holy Spirit. It presaged the imminent return of Christ and demanded urgent action – worldwide evangelisation to spread the experience of 'baptism in the Holy Spirit' in preparation for the Second Coming. Seymour and others saw themselves as being filled with the Holy Spirit, who broke through the ordinary structures and capacities of the sinful human world. This work of the Spirit showed itself in transformed speech and transformed community. For the Azusa Street Christians, what they were experiencing was not chaos but rather a breaking through of heavenly order, which the world is incapable of recognising or accommodating – a foretaste of God's eschatological reordering of all things.

Focusing on Azusa Street brings some of the limitations of our story of 'modern theology' into sharp focus. The Azusa Street movement is in many ways an example of Christian life and thought refusing to accommodate to modernity's dominant criteria. It is not a coincidence that the people involved were mostly those who had not benefited from modernity's social and economic upheavals – the urban poor, the black community for whom modernity had meant slavery and segregation. Furthermore, the image of Seymour, a poor, self-educated black man, eavesdropping (albeit with permission) on a white man's theology lectures, draws attention to the exclusions that shaped the context of modern academic theology. For example, the Enlightenment's discourse of progress – which we have seen reflected, especially, in the work of Kant and Hegel – was also a discourse of racial superiority, of the advance of (white) Western Christian civilisation beyond the 'primitive' ways of earlier – and non-white, non-Western – humanity.

The events of Azusa Street, in turn, draw attention to sources of theology – of reasoning about God – that tend to be systematically neglected in academic study but are highly relevant in modernity. Among the most important of these is *oral* religion. The Enlightenment was partially driven by an explosion in literacy and in the printing and distribution of texts; and we can characterise many theological developments as shifts in *ways of reading* – especially, ways of reading the Bible. In Azusa Street and in many Pentecostal congregations worldwide, then and now, the emphasis is on *hearing* and *speaking* (and singing, praying, enacting) Christian faith. Studying the Azusa Street phenomenon through written texts, of any kind, feels like studying a 'secondary', not a 'primary', source. Seymour's creative theological contribution is not contained in writings.

How are the key themes we have identified in our account of modern theology reflected in the Azusa Street movement and its continuing influence? First, in relation to the Enlightenment's emphasis on *freedom*, we find in Pentecostalism an emphasis on *empowerment* – not, then, freedom *from* restrictions, but freedom *to* act and to bring about change. The most obvious form of 'freedom' celebrated here is God's freedom to act in human history but this is experienced as the miraculous empowerment of human beings. There *was* an experience of 'freedom from' at Azusa Street, interpreted as the results of God's powerful and empowering action. Liberation from segregation and mutual hatred was part of the Azusa Street experience and vision, as was liberation from the church structures that might constrain the manifestations of the Holy Spirit.

The Pentecostal movement is easy to categorise as anti-rational, falling squarely on the 'passion' side of the Enlightenment's dichotomy. The reports that emphasised the involvement of women, of black people and of people without formal education also emphasised how distant Azusa Street was from the dominant academic and intellectual culture. However, it would be wrong simply to portray the movement as irrational or unconcerned with reasoning. It is worth noticing that Charles Parham and his students developed a biblical *argument* for 'speaking in tongues' before they experienced it. In order not to be consigned (as the *Los Angeles Times* reporter would apparently have liked) to the margins of religious history, Pentecostal Christians had to reason *about* the phenomenon of which they were a part. There is, and was from the beginnings of the movement, a reasoned framework for interpreting and explaining the experiences of Pentecostal congregations. It is not a framework that makes sense in terms of *universal* features of the human condition. Rather, it is based on the Bible, which is assumed to provide both the most reliable and the most universally applicable framework for reasoning.

Knowledge of God, for Seymour and his congregation, was gained in the first instance through experiencing what God does. Rather than looking for a specific human 'faculty' or 'capacity' for knowing God, they spoke of the Holy Spirit's effects on the whole human being – body, mind, emotions, speech, actions. The language of 'evidences' in Pentecostal writings recalls the modern interest in 'proving' knowledge-claims. However, we should not take 'evidence' here as primarily a reference to proving disputed claims. The various miracles cited by Pentecostals are not just 'supporting evidence' supplied by God to prove something about God; they are the way in which God does God's work. Speaking in tongues, for example, is not only a proof (for others) that a person has received the baptism of the Holy Spirit, it is a gift that transforms the person. Nonetheless, there was from the early days of Pentecostalism an interest in describing and publicising the miracles that occurred, emphasising that they could not be explained 'naturally'.

In all this, one respect in which Pentecostals can seem very 'modern' is their focus on historical change. Azusa Street was and is read as a turning-point in history, the start of a new era. A recent account of the Pentecostal and charismatic movements since 1901 is entitled *The Century of the Holy Spirit* (Vinson Synan, *The Century of the Holy Spirit: 100 Years of Pentecostal and Charismatic Renewal*, Nashville: Thomas Nelson, 2001). Like so many moderns, Seymour and the members of his congregation believed they were living in a radically new age and that history was moving towards even greater events. For them, of course, the 'even greater' event was the imminent return of Christ. History was not a story of gradual progress but of a series of dramatic changes in which God was revealed in God's actions. Alongside this, we find in Pentecostal writings a very 'modern' dislike of tradition – an appeal to the purity of the Church in New Testament times, accompanied by the call to sweep away the results of centuries of corruption and restore the original purity.

'Suspicious' interpreters of religion – ever since the *Los Angeles Times* reports – have found various ways to denigrate and to explain away the Azusa Street events. One response to that suspicion was (and is) to draw attention to miracles as 'evidences' of the work of God. This implicitly appeals to a very modern public sphere, within which all rational people can meet to consider and debate claims on the basis of evidence available to all. Another response, however, was (and is) to reject the explanatory framework from which suspicious readings come. Why should the Bible, and its interpretation within the community, *not* be allowed to provide the definitive 'explanation' of what happened at Azusa Street? Why should we privilege the modern, Western, secular, white elite's frameworks of explanation? Here, Azusa Street points us forward to those theologies of the later twentieth century that sought to break down modern 'universals' – both for the sake of Christian 'particularity' and for the sake of the communities that modernity marginalised.

Johann Adam Möhler

Johann Adam Möhler (1796–1838) was born in what was then the Duchy of Württemberg, in the southwest of what is now Germany – though by the time he was in his early teens it had become a kingdom, as the political landscape was changed by Napoleon's armies. Möhler went to a Catholic seminary at Ellwangen, and then on to the University of Tübingen. He was ordained as a Catholic priest in 1819, but then returned to Tübingen as a tutor, at first in classical literature and history, and then in Church history.

As part of his preparation for his teaching work, he travelled in 1822 to other famous universities – including a visit to hear Schleiermacher lecture in Berlin. He later said: 'With all his deviations on particular points, Schleiermacher is, in my opinion, the only genuine disciple of the Reformers' (*Symbolik* I.285). As we shall see, on Möhler's lips this is a rather back-handed compliment.

Möhler was one of a group of Catholic thinkers – who are sometimes known as the Catholic Tübingen school – who had been trained in the new critical historical methods that were flourishing in German universities, and who brought those techniques to bear on questions of Church history. Möhler himself is most famous for two works that stand firmly within this movement: *Die Einheit in der Kirche* (*Unity in the Church*, 1825), in which he asks what it is that holds an historically developing Church together as a coherent reality, and *Symbolik* (1832), in which he brings his historical thinking to bear on the relationship between Catholicism and Protestantism.

To some extent, Möhler's work fits into the story we will be telling in Chapter 12, about the idea of the 'development of doctrine': the growing realisation among those informed by the newly-grown methods of academic historical inquiry that the official teaching of the Church had changed or developed over time. Faced with such a realisation as a result of his own historical inquiries, Möhler sought to account for the abiding constancy of the Church in the midst of all that development. In ideas not far different from those of the slightly younger John Henry Newman (whose work on this topic we will examine in detail in Chapter 12), Möhler described first of all the organic, spiritual unity into which the Holy Spirit had gathered Christ's faithful people and then the processes by which that people were required to become more explicit, and more formal, in their statements of their belief – developing a body of official teaching (in response to heretical movements and other challenges). He then described how that process, which gave a new distinctness and order to their existing belief, was accompanied by the development of institutional structures capable of sustaining it – especially the expanding role of bishops, who slowly but surely became guardians together of the Church's official teaching, and then the development of the role of the pope, who helped hold together the bishops and the whole Church that they represented. Thus the inner, spiritual unity of the faithful people is expressed in the outward unity of official teaching and institutional structure; and that outward unity helps secure and protect the unified inward life. It is a harmonious vision of doctrinal development put forward in full confidence that the Catholic Church had preserved unsullied the inward, spiritual unity of the original followers of Jesus.

As noted, similar ideas will occupy us in the discussion of doctrinal development and of modern theological approaches to tradition more generally in Chapter 12. It is also worth, however, pointing out a different aspect of Möhler's account, which emerges in his attempt to explain why it is that (as he sees it) the Protestant Churches *can't* claim to stand in the line of the continuous, harmonious development of the Christian Church, whilst the Catholic Church of his day can. The problem is, as he sees it, a deep-seated mistake about the nature of human freedom.

The title of Möhler's great work, *Symbolik*, is the name of the sub-discipline of theological study that he was pursuing: the study of Christian 'symbols' which, in a peculiar technical sense of the word, means the study of official statements of Christian teaching such as creeds and confessions. Given his views on the unity and continuity of the Church, he was unsurprisingly interested in these official teachings as the crystallisation of the deep patterns of thought and feeling of the Churches from which they emerged – as windows into the spirit of a community. One of his central claims was that Protestant versions of these windows simply worked in a different way from Catholic versions. To understand a Protestant creed or confession, he claimed, one needed to understand the theology of the personalities involved; one needed to delve into Luther's thought, or Calvin's, or Zwingli's. Those men (and others) were directly or indirectly the *authors* or *creators* of Protestant creeds: they regarded themselves as free to determine, in the light of their own examinations of the Bible and of tradition, what should and should not be confessed by the community.

What the Protestants had missed, Möhler thought, was the way in which the individual believer *becomes* an individual believer by being drawn into the pre-existing organic unity of the Christian community – by being conformed to its patterns of thought and feeling, and so fitted to the creeds and confessions that have been handed down with it, and to the ongoing labour of patient and incremental clarification which those creeds and confessions might still demand of us in the midst of the challenges that face us. Early in *Symbolik*, Möhler writes: 'The distinction between individual opinion and common doctrine presupposes a very strongly constituted community, based at once on history, on life, on tradition, and is only possible in the Catholic church' (*Symbolik* I.10).

Möhler argues that the primary differences of *content* between Catholic and Protestant creeds or confessions are closely related to this difference in form. The biggest differences – in the accounts of original sin, and in the accounts of God's justification and sanctification of sinners – are in the understanding of how individual human freedom relates to God's action – and to the Church.

> The principle of freedom Luther did not apprehend ... viewing in it an encroach-ment on the rights of the Divine Majesty, nay, the self-deification of man. To be free and to be God was, in his opinion, synonymous.
>
> Möhler *Symbolik*, p273.

By thinking of human freedom and divine freedom in opposition in this way, Protestants such as Luther cut themselves off from any account of the harmonious co-operation between human freedom and divine freedom – and so cut themselves off from any account of the harmonious co-operation between the free human intellect and the organic spiritual unity of God's Church. Only on the Catholic side of the divide is it possible to offer an account of the individual freely consenting to, and then freely co-operating with, the Spirit's work as the Spirit draws the individual into the organic, spiritual community of God's Church. Only on the Catholic side, then, is it possible to give an account of the harmonious unity between the free, questing, judgement-making intellect of the believer and the official teachings and institutional authority in which the God-given spiritual unity of the Church is expressed.

Möhler's account of Protestantism was controversial at the time (he eventually left Tübingen for Munich in 1835, in order to leave the controversy behind) and much of what he says about Protestant views of freedom would hardly be recognised by scholars of the Reformation today – Protestant or Catholic. Yet he did correctly identify the fact that changing understandings of human freedom, and of the relationship between human freedom and the authoritative teaching of the institutional Church, were deep currents underlying some of the surface movements of the Reformation. More to our point, he identified that those currents still shaped some of the deepest differences among modern theologians.

Debate between Protestants and Catholics about the relationship between human freedom and divine freedom in the process of salvation has continued to flicker since Möhler's time – much of it focusing on the nature of God's 'justification' of sinners. In the twentieth century, there were (at least) two important moments in the history of that debate. In the first place, the Catholic theologian Hans Küng wrote a book on the Protestant theologian Karl Barth's doctrine of justification, in which he (with some success) argued that Barth's thoroughly Protestant account was compatible with official Catholic teaching. More recently, the Catholic Church and the Lutheran World Federation have produced a 'Joint Declaration on the Doctrine of Justification', which claims a very substantial (though not perfect) agreement on the topic between the two Churches.

When, in Chapter 3, we looked at Kant, we saw that his account of Enlightenment was centred on a call to intellectual freedom: *Sapere aude!* (Dare to know!); we also saw how this freedom stood in opposition to the imposition of external authority for him. Möhler would see in this Kantian call a fundamental shift from earlier understandings of theological thinking – but he would not see it as the arrival of freedom after a period in which people lacked freedom. Rather, he would see it as the arrival of a new, mistaken form of *oppositional* freedom, ousting the older, *harmonious* freedom – freedom to be formed within a tradition and to speak freely as someone who has freely co-operated with the process by which she has been formed in that tradition. In some ways – though the comparison might have horrified him – he is somewhat closer to Hegel than he is to Kant (see the section on 'Religion and freedom' in Chapter 5).

Vladimir Soloviev

Vladimir Soloviev (1853–1900) – whose surname can also be transliterated as Solovyov or Solov'ëv – was born in Moscow to an academic family. After a teenage rejection of Christianity, he returned to faith and embarked upon a career as a theological and philosophical intellectual. He took a teaching job in Moscow University in 1876, but institutional academic life did not prove conducive, and a year later he moved to St Petersburg and the life of an independent writer and lecturer.

SOLOWJEFF.

Figure 9.4 Vladimir Soloviev

> While travelling abroad in his early twenties to broaden his studies, Soloviev
> visited London. He spent time in the Reading Room of the British Museum,
> researching Christian mysticism of various kinds, until he had a vision of the
> face of the lady 'Sophia', a personification of divine wisdom, who was to be a
> significant feature of his later work. It is entirely possible that a rather more
> famous modern thinker, and another habitué of the Reading Room, was there at
> the same time: Karl Marx (1818–1883).

Soloviev was a thinker who liked grand sweeps and syntheses; he was deeply concerned
with finding the hidden unity between apparently divided realities. One of the unities
that he sought lay between philosophy and theology. He was an avid reader of German
philosophy, and drew deeply on Kant (see Chapter 3) and on Hegel (see Chapter 5),
among others. But he was convinced that such philosophy was (often without knowing
it) beginning to approximate more and more closely to the theology of the Eastern
Church – the theology of the Greek and Russian Orthodox tradition.

More deeply, however, Soloviev was concerned with the unity of *people*, and the
unity between people and God. The world in which we live is, he said, a fallen world
and what it has fallen away from is unity. It is characterised by all kinds of
fragmentation, including political and cultural fragmentation. Yet human beings live
in this fragmented world as seekers of the lost unity; they have some kind of grasp of,
some kind of sense and taste for, the whole of which they are a part – most deeply in
their religious experience.

Orthodox theology, as Soloviev read it, spoke of the process by which God was
drawing all things back into unity – and, above all, of the incarnation as the motor of
that process. The incarnation is the reestablishment of a unity between God and
humanity, and the vanguard of a humanity drawn back into unity with itself and with
God. In fact, the incarnation establishes the process by which human beings are drawn
into a living unity which *is* the life of God in the world: a reality Soloviev called
'Godmanhood'. This unity does not, however, involve the overcoming of the free
individuality of those who are drawn into it, but rather the creation of a synthesis that
emerges organically from the interactions of their free activities and which forms
them for the fuller exercise of that freedom.

Soloviev used the Russian term *sobornost* – catholicity – to refer to this lively, free
unity. But he also used the term 'Sophia' – (divine) wisdom – and described the process
of unification as the life of God's active wisdom taking place in the world, drawing
individuals into itself. Sophia is both the life of God's active wisdom in the world, and the
corporate life of those people who have been drawn into *sobornost* together – and the life
of the Church is its harbinger. 'The higher, free unity of the Church', Soloviev writes, is

based not on tradition and custom *alone*, and also not on abstract, rational conviction, but on moral, spiritual deed. The Universal Church appears to us not as a dead idol, and not as an animated, but unconscious body, but as a being that is self-conscious, morally free, and active in its own realization. It appears as God's true friend, as a creation that is united with the Divine fully and completely, that fully makes space for God in itself. In other words, it appears as *Sophia, the Wisdom of God*, to whom our ancestors, in a surprising prophetic impulse, built altars and cathedrals, themselves not knowing who she is.

From Soloviev's *The History and Future of Theocracy*, quoted in *Divine Sophia: The Wisdom Writings of Vladimir Solvyov*, ed. Judith Deutsch Kornblatt (Ithaca: Cornell University Press, 2009), p165.

The echoes of Hegel are clear (and you should compare this account of Soloviev with the section on 'Religion and freedom' in Chapter 5) – but Soloviev has given it a distinctive theological spin. He is drawing on Orthodox theological ideas about *theosis* – that is, theological accounts of salvation that see it as a matter of being drawn to share in the life of God, or becoming transparent to the glory of God. In the process of *theosis*, believers become by God's gracious assistance what Jesus Christ was and is by nature: their human lives are so caught up in the flow of God's life that they become what God is doing in the world. For Soloviev, this process of *theosis* is not a matter of individuals being drawn towards God by being drawn away from the world around them; it is not a matter of them being abstracted from their contexts. Rather, it is something that happens as they are drawn, as people living in history, into new configurations of social life together. *Theosis* is the forming of a corporate life on earth which *is* what God's wisdom is doing: the life of Sophia.

This unity to which human beings are being drawn is certainly pointed to by philosophy, but in order to grasp it concretely (for it to take hold of one's imagination and shape one's life in practice) one needs the real glimpse of it and taste for it that Christianity provides: philosophy on its own is not enough. Soloviev allowed himself considerable latitude as he sought to bring philosophy and theology together in this way, interpreting each so as to bring it into unity with the other – and his theological writings involve headily speculative reworkings of the doctrines of the Incarnation, the Holy Spirit and the Trinity – but he is insistent that his synthesis is as much religious as it is philosophical.

Soloviev's work was also, however, deeply political. He believed that Russia was well placed – indeed, divinely commissioned – to bring this unity of Godmanhood to fruition in human affairs. Russia stood between the inhuman God of the East (Soloviev's characterisation of Islam) and the Godless humanity of the West (his characterisation of post-Englightenment Europe). Similarly, Orthodox Christianity could stand between the authoritarianism of Catholicism and the individualism of Protestantism.

Russia, with its Orthodox Church, was – or could be – the place of synthesis, where the partial visions of East and West and of Catholicism and Protestantism would be drawn into a fuller unity, both divine and human. Soloviev was therefore full of a patriotic belief that something different, something glorious, was possible among the Russian people that was not possible elsewhere – something that would be Russia's great gift to the world.

Soloviev was a close friend of the great Russian novelist Fyodor Dostoevsky, and may have been a model for either of the two Brothers Karamazov in Dostoevsky's novel. Echoes of his thinking can be found elsewhere in Dostoevsky as well, as in this extract from a speech that Dostoevsky delivered in 1880, at the unveiling of a monument to the poet Pushkin in Moscow:

And in course of time I believe that we – not we, of course, but our children to come – will all without exception understand that to be a true Russian does indeed mean to aspire finally to reconcile the contradictions of Europe, to show the end of European yearning in our Russian soul, omni-human and all-uniting, to include within our soul by brotherly love all our brethren, and at last, it may be, to pronounce the final Word of the great general harmony, of the final brotherly communion of all nations in accordance with the law of the gospel of Christ! I know, I know too well, that my words may appear ecstatic, exaggerated and fantastic. Let them be so, I do not repent having uttered them.

Fyodor Dostoevsky, *Pages from the Journal of an Author*, trans. Samuel Solomonovitch Koteliansky and John Middleton Murry (Boston: John W. Luce, 1916), pp47–68: 67; available online at <www.archive.org/stream/pagesfromjourna00murrgoog#page/n83/mode/2up>, accessed 13 October 2011.

Soloviev could describe the social outworking of his vision as a matter of organically evolving theocracy – the rule or reign of God emerging incrementally and naturally in the midst of human affairs. In his earlier works, his descriptions of this evolving theocracy have strong top-down elements, where the unity is in part secured by the hierarchical authority of the state and the Church (and, unusually for an Orthodox thinker, he argued at this stage that a reunion of the Church under a reformed papal rule was needed.) In his later work, however, the bottom-up elements come to dominate, and the vision of unity under hierarchical authority disappears in favour of a greater insistence on the organic, democratic emergence of unity from among the people.

Soloviev exerted a significant influence on the development of Orthodox theology in the twentieth century (see the section on 'Engagement with tradition' in Chapter 12). Many were captivated by his vision of a divinely instituted and sustained human unity, in which the free individuality of the participants is fulfilled rather than overcome and in which philosophy and theology are united – but a good deal of argument was triggered between those who broadly followed Soloviev down this path and those who thought his free reinterpretation of Orthodox doctrine had gone too far.

Brahmabandhab Upadhyay

Brahmabandhab Upadhyay (1861–1907) is the name chosen later in life by the man who was born near Calcutta in 1861 with the name Bhabanicaran Bandyopadhyay. The context into which he was born and in which he lived most of his life is a long way – geographically, culturally and religiously – from the ones we have been exploring so far in this book: India (or, more specifically, Bengal) under British colonial rule. Until shortly before Upadhyay's birth, Bengal had been ruled by the strange commercial–military–administrative British institution known as the East India Company, which had wrested power from the region's Muslim rulers in the mid-eighteenth century. After an uprising in 1857 against British forces known as either the 'First War of Independence' or as the 'Indian Mutiny', Company management of Bengal was replaced by the direct rule of the British crown.

Bengal's population was a mixture of Hindu and Muslim, but (in broad terms) the two groups reacted differently to British rule. For the Hindu population, British rule was simply a replacement for Muslim rule, rather than a replacement of Hindu self-rule, and there seems to have been a fairly widespread pragmatism in parts of the Hindu population: they had learnt to seek what advancement, protection and autonomy they could under one set of rulers who were not of their own cultural and religious background, and they would now do so again. For high-caste Hindus – Brahmins – that often meant a readiness to move wherever in British India there were subordinate administrative roles available to them, and learning English in order to be able to take up those posts.

The British had decided to insist upon English as the language of administration in India, and therefore as the language of advancement – in line with their perception of their mission to bring (Western, Christian, English-speaking) civilisation to a Hindu population whose language, culture and religion many of them regarded as inherently inferior – or at least as having declined into stark inferiority from some purer, more civilised and now long-gone original Hinduism.

There were unanticipated consequences to British endeavours in this area. Without quite realising it, the British helped to produce a well-educated Hindu elite, who were used to migrating from place to place within British India, who could see the disparate Indian territories being united by roads and other forms of infrastructure, and who had been exposed to Western political ideas and ideals. In so doing, the British helped inadvertently to create an emergent sense of united *Indian* identity and a desire for Indian self-rule. During the time that Upadhyay was growing up, Indian nationalism was beginning to become a significant political force.

At the same time, there was another movement amongst Hindus – especially Brahmins – that gathered pace during Upadhyay's early years. Various Hindu teachers and thinkers sought to purify popular Hinduism, and move in the direction of a simpler, more philosophical and more unified religious and cultural life. In part, this was a movement that grew directly from currents within the Hinduism of the day; in part, however, it seems to have been a result of Hindus in the situation of colonialism beginning to see themselves through the colonial power's eyes – and so to see popular Hinduism as a decadent, fragmented and superstitious decline from an idealised earlier purity.

Upadhyay was therefore surrounded by representatives of very different responses to British rule, and to the Christianity of the Empire, as he grew up. Some of his fellow high-caste Hindus converted to Christianity and turned their back (to a greater or lesser degree) on their Hindu past. Some were happy to benefit from British education but rejected an orthodox Christianity that looked to them less noble than the pure Hinduism they were seeking to regenerate. And some were determined opponents of British rule and sought to retrieve a thoroughly Hindu sense of identity for themselves and their compatriots.

It is in this context that Upadhyay was formed, and to it that he made his complex contribution – and something of all these strands can be seen in his own life and thought. He was born into a Kulin Brahmin household – the purest form of the highest caste in Bengali Hinduism – but into a family that by the time of Upadhyay's birth had been shaped by the movement to purify and simplify Hinduism (Upadhyay was brought up to be well- and deeply-read in classic Hindu literature), and by Western education.

From early on, Upadhyay seems to have been pulled in directions that are not easy to reconcile. He was captivated by the idea of independence from British rule – but he also became fascinated by the figure of Jesus Christ, who loomed so large in British religion. Eventually, the latter fascination blossomed into something more: he came to believe in Jesus' divinity and then in his resurrection – and in 1890 he converted to Christianity, becoming a Roman Catholic in 1891.

If, in the early years after his conversion to Christianity, Upadhyay turned away from his Hindu heritage, that soon changed. He became convinced that the ideas of Christianity could be thought through in a Hindu way, in the sense that existing Hindu ideas could be shown to be compatible with Christianity, to be capable of making sense of Christian ideas to a Hindu thinker, and even to lead towards Christianity as their fulfilment. The form of Hindu thought to which he looked most directly was Advaita Vedanta – an influential philosophical school of Hindu thought and practice, based on a reading of the Vedanta (a key subset of the Hindu scriptures). To an extent, at least at first, his attempts to present Christianity in Advaita terms could simply be seen as an apologetic or evangelistic strategy on Upadhyay's part: he sought to demonstrate how his fellow-Hindus could understand Christianity in their own terms, and could see its continuity with their existing patterns of practice and understanding. It soon went beyond that, however. Upadhyay was convinced that Hindu thought was deeply compatible with the neo-Thomist theology (see Chapter 12) in which the Catholicism of his day was steeped. He thought that much of what was said in neo-Thomist philosophy was already said in Advaita, and that the crowning theological truths which completed neo-Thomist theology could also crown the thinking of Advaita as well – and bring Hindu thought to completion.

In Chapter 16, various different attitudes to the relationship between religions are set out. Read the section on 'Theology of religions: defining the issues in the contemporary world' now, and see where (if anywhere) you think Upadhyay stands on the typology of different attitudes described there. What kind of relationship between Hinduism and Christianity is suggested by his claims about Advaita and Catholic theology?

Upadhay's attitude to the relationship between Hindu philosophy and Christian theology is only one part, however, of the relationship between Hinduism and Christianity for him. He came to believe that referring to Christianity and Hinduism as two differing 'religions', or two different theological systems, led inevitably to a misunderstanding of their relationship. If Christianity was a religion, Hinduism was something more like a culture – and just as Christianity had existed in relation to multiple cultural forms, from the Middle East to Rome to Northern Europe and elsewhere, so it could now exist in relation to Hindu culture. In this sense, therefore, and very firmly, Upadhyay began to think of himself, and present himself, as a 'Hindu Christian'. 'The religion of Christ is fixed', he wrote:

> But its influence, so far as society, politics, literature, science and art are concerned, varies with racial differences ... No mistake could be more fatal to progress than to make the Indian Christian community conform to European social ideals because Europeans happen to be prominent in the Christian world. So long as the Christians of India do not practice their faith on the platform of

Hindu life and living, and Hindu thought and thinking, and elevate the national genius to the supernatural plane, they will never thrive.

Quoted in Julius Lipner, *Brahmabandhab Upadhyay*, p256.

Upadhyay's commitment to Hindu culture was shown in his (ultimately fruitless) attempts, begun soon after becoming a Catholic, to persuade the Catholic hierarchy that an institution should be set up to train up Indian teachers of Christianity.

The proposed institution should be conducted on strictly Hindu lines. *There should not be the least trace of Europeanism in the mode of life and living of the Hindu Catholic monks.* The parivrajakas (itinerants) should be well versed in the Vedanta philosophy as well as in the philosophy of St. Thomas.

Quoted in Julius Lipner, *Brahmabandhab Upadhyay*, p210, emphasis added.

Although this particular proposal came to nothing, it does indicate the direction in which Upadhyay's own thinking and practice was going. He wanted 'not the least trace of Europeanism' (Lipner, p210) to show in his own mode of life and living, and he returned increasingly to Hindu practice – to the dismay of some Christian friends, colleagues, and observers.

Upadhyay remained committed to aspects of Hindu culture that both Western observers and some Indian reformers had deprecated, most especially the caste system. The Hindu culture that he sought to inhabit as a Christian was both conservative and high-caste – and his theology and practice are not in any direct way forerunners of the more recent phenomenon of Dalit Christianity – the Christianity of the out-caste or untouchables of the caste system.

When he died, Upadhyay was given a full Hindu funeral and debates began that have still not entirely died away about whether he died a Hindu or a Catholic. Some on both the Hindu and the Christian sides were not sure whether it was possible to maintain the distinction between religion and culture that was so important to him. Didn't continued Christian religious commitment involve some kind of abandonment or turning away from Hinduism? Didn't commitment to Hindu practice involve some kind of weakening or betrayal of Christian religious commitment? It seems clear that Upadhyay himself would have insisted that he died an Indian – he had continued to the end to believe in the right of India to self-rule – and that he died a Hindu–Christian, and that the proof of the possibility of such a combination (if proof there could be) lay primarily in the living of it.

Bibliography

Mary Wollstonecraft

Mary Wollstonecraft, *A Vindication of the Rights of Men; with A Vindication of the Rights of Woman*, ed. Sylvana Tomaselli (Cambridge: Cambridge University Press, 1995). Good critical edition with detailed biographical and contextual information. Includes Wollstonecraft's response to Edmund Burke's *Reflections on the Revolution in France*, which predates Tom Paine's more famous *Rights of Man*.

Claudia L. Johnson (ed.), *The Cambridge Companion to Mary Wollstonecraft* (Cambridge: Cambridge University Press, 2002). See especially Chapter 7 by Barbara Taylor on Wollstonecraft's religious thought.

Arlene Ingham, *Woman and Spirituality in the Thought of More, Wollstonecraft, Stanton and Eddy* (New York: Palgrave Macmillan, 2010).

Barbara Taylor, *Mary Wollstonecraft and the Feminist Imagination* (Cambridge: Cambridge University Press, 2003), especially Chapter 3.

Josephine Butler

Josephine Butler, *Personal Reminiscences of a Great Crusade*, originally published 1898 (Warrington: Portrayer, 2002). Butler's account of the campaign against the Contagious Diseases Acts, giving useful insights into how she understood the relationship between religion, political activism and feminism.

Many of Butler's speeches and pamphlets are available online but not in print. A good example of her explanation of the sexual double standard is in 'Social Purity', an address to students at the University of Cambridge in 1879. This and other works are available via the Victorian Women Writers' Project at Indiana University, <http://webapp1.dlib.indiana.edu/vwwp/welcome.do>, accessed 31 October 2011.

Ann Loades, *Feminist Theology: Voices from the Past* (Cambridge: Polity, 2001). See chapter on Josephine Butler.

Julie Melnyk, *Women's Theology in Nineteenth-century Britain: Transfiguring the Faith of their Fathers* (London: Garland, 1998). See pp151ff on Josephine Butler and 165ff on Ellice Hopkins.

Lesley Hall, 'Hauling Down the Double Standard: Feminism, Social Purity and Sexual Science in Late Nineteenth-Century Britain', *Gender and History* 16/1 (April 2004), pp36–56.

Melissa Raphael, 'J. Ellice Hopkins: The Construction of a Recent Spiritual Feminist Foremother', *Feminist Theology* 5 (1996), pp73–95. Interesting theological discussion of Hopkins that includes general discussion of the social purity movements in relation to religion and feminism.

William Seymour and Azusa Street

Vinson Synan, *The Century of the Holy Spirit: 100 Years of Pentecostal and Charismatic Renewal, 1901–2001* (Nashville: Thomas Nelson, 2001). See especially Chapter 3.

Walter J. Hollenweger, *Pentecostalism: Origins and Developments Worldwide* (Peabody: Hendrickson, 1997).
Allan Anderson, *Spreading Fires: The Missionary Nature of Early Pentecostalism* (London: SCM, 2007).

Johann Adam Möhler

Johann Adam Möhler, *Symbolism: or, Exposition of the doctrinal differences between Catholics and Protestants, as evidenced by their symbolical writings*, translation of Möhler's *Symbolik* by James Burton Robertson, 2 volumes (London: Charles Dolman, 1843). This (very readable) translation of Möhler's major work is available free on Google Books.
Derek Michaud and Rady Roldán-Figueroa, 'Johann Adam Möhler (1796–1838)' in *The Boston Collaborative Encyclopedia of Western Theology*, 2000; available online at <people.bu.edu/wwildman/bce/moeler.htm> – incomplete, but not a bad place to start.
Philip J. Rosato, 'Between Christocentrism and Pneumatocentrism: An Interpretation of Johann Adam Möhler's Ecclesiology', *Heythrop Journal* 19 (1978), pp46–70. A more detailed investigation.
Hans Küng, *Justification: The Doctrine of Karl Barth and a Catholic Reflection* (New York: Thomas Nelson, 1964).
Joint Declaration on the Doctrine of Justification by the Catholic Church and the Lutheran World Federation, 1999. Available online at <http://www.vatican.va/roman_curia/pontifical_councils/chrstuni/documents/rc_pc_chrstuni_doc_31101999_cath-luth-joint-declaration_en.html>, accessed 12 October 2011.

Vladimir Soloviev

Vladimir Solovyov, *Lectures on Divine Humanity*, ed. Boris Jakim (Hudson: Lindisfarne Press, 1995).
Vladimir Solovyov, *Divine Sophia: The Wisdom Writings of Vladimir Solvyov*, ed. Judith Deutsch Kornblatt (Ithaca: Cornell University Press, 2009).
Paul Valliere, *Modern Russian Theology – Bukharev, Soloviev, Bulgakov: Orthodox Theology in a New Key* (Edinburgh: T&T Clark, 2000). A good overview of Soliviev's work.
Judith Deutsch Kornblatt and Richard F. Gustafson (eds), *Russian Religious Thought* (Madison: University of Wisconsin Press, 1996). Contains three chapters on Soloviev's theology.
Greg Gaut, 'Christian Politics: Vladimir Solvyov's Social Gospel Theology', *Modern Greek Studies Yearbook* 10/11 (1994/1995), reproduced by The Transnational Vladimir Solovyov Society at <www.valley.net/~transnat/gautfp.html>, accessed 13 October 2011. Good on the social and political aspects of Soloviev's thinking.

Brahmabandhab Upadhyay

Brahmabandhab Upadhyay, *The Writings of Brahmabandhab Upadhyay*, ed. by Julius Lipner and George Gispert-Sauch, 2 volumes (Bangalore: United Theological College, 1991 and 2001). The main source of English translations of Upadhyay's work.

Julius Lipner, *Brahmabandhab Upadhyay: The Life and Thought of a Revolutionary* (New Delhi: Oxford University Press, 2001). A very readable, and comprehensive, account of Upadhyay's life and work.

Madhusudhan Rao, 'Brahmabandhab Upadhyay and the Failure of Hindu Christianity', *International Journal of Frontier Missions* 18.4 (2001); available online at <www.bhaktivani. com/volume2/number4/brahmabandhab.html>, accessed 14 October 2011. An example of a reading of Upadhyay's life and achievements that comes to the conclusion that Hinduism and Christianity are not compatible in the way he hoped.

Section B

Key Themes

The chapters in this section are focused on key themes and issues that emerge for theology in, or as a result of, the long nineteenth century, and that continue to shape theological thought up to the present day. We aim, in this section, to equip you to think about these issues now, by understanding how we got here – what threads of modern theological, and other intellectual, history are woven into contemporary discussions of these themes.

One of the basic claims of this book is that the long nineteenth century set directions for theological thought that are still highly significant, and that it is important to study nineteenth-century thought to understand the present. In each chapter in this section, we attempt to demonstrate that. However, as you will see, we are not arguing that nothing new has happened in theology since 1914. On the contrary, many of the theological issues and movements discussed in this section – for example, liberation theology and postmodernism – are clearly products of the twentieth (and the twenty-first) century. Having said that, we do still want to suggest that you cannot tell the story of these movements accurately without looking further back in history – looking, in particular, at the transformation of theology in modernity.

Each of our chapters takes as its focus one or more key 'moments' or figures in theology. These moments and figures are important, and worthy of study, in themselves – but we want to interpret them as representative or indicative of wider trends. Once again, our chapters are not a substitute for reading the primary texts – but when we are dealing with living theological issues and movements, the range of possible primary texts is much wider, and is still growing. You should gain, from these chapters, some historical and conceptual tools that you can use for your own critical analysis of the large body of primary texts.

10 Reading the Bible

AIMS

By the end of this chapter, we hope that you will:

- understand the impact of historical criticism on the study of the Bible

- know what is meant by 'the eclipse of Biblical narrative'

- understand some of the differences between the approaches to the Bible of Adolf von Harnack, Karl Barth and Rudolf Bultmann

- be aware of the existence of a wider variety of approaches to the Bible in modern theology.

Introduction

The developments and disagreements of modern theology have very often involved arguments about the right way to read the Bible. We're going to begin this chapter with one fairly simple and common way of describing changing approaches to the Bible in the modern period: as the rise of something called historical criticism, and of the reactions that historical criticism provoked. That is not the only description available, however, and later in the chapter we will supplement it with another: the description of what has been called the 'eclipse of biblical narrative' – a description that, roughly speaking, focuses on the difference between reading biblical passages for the story that they tell and reading them as evidence for use in historical investigation. To describe modern approaches to the Bible this second way will make it more difficult to arrange modern theological readings of the Bible on a simple spectrum from radical to conservative, or liberal to evangelical.

We will move on to a trio of modern Protestant writers who argued with each other about the proper use of the Bible in theology: Adolf von Harnack, Karl Barth and Rudolf Bultmann. We will trace in some detail their disagreements about the purpose of historical criticism, about the ways in which the Christian gospel is witnessed to or proclaimed in biblical texts and about the methods one should use in approaching those texts in search of the gospel – while also paying attention to the determination of each of the three to be obedient to the gospel message that the Bible conveys.

The chapter will finish with some briefer notes about the wide variety of approaches to the Bible that can be found in contemporary Christian theology – including some pointers to other chapters of this book (such as those on liberation theology and feminist theology) in which changes in biblical interpretation are described.

The rise of historical criticism

One standard way of describing the development of new approaches to the Bible in modern theology – in which there is a good deal of truth – is in terms of the rise of historical criticism. There are two aspects to that description. On the one hand, this description of modern approaches to the Bible focuses on the *methods* that modern thinkers began to use to analyse the Bible: new scholarly techniques that allowed biblical texts to be used as evidence for the reconstruction of the historical events that lie behind them – whether that means the events that the texts purport to describe or other events that shaped the emergence of the texts and their evolution into the form in which we now have them. On the other hand, this description of modern approaches to the Bible focuses on the *conclusions* to which those new methods led and the slow shift they helped bring about from a situation in which the Bible was believed to be a trustworthy account of the history of God's dealings with the world to a situation in which all sorts of doubts about the Bible's historical reliability had become widespread.

These developments should not be described as if they were a smooth journey along a one-way street, of course. Even if there is some plausibility in describing nineteenth-century scholarly approaches to the Bible in terms of an ever-increasing dominance of historical criticism and an ever-decreasing trust in the Bible's historical reliability, any description of twentieth-century developments would have to include uneven, partial and controversial movements in the other direction. Nevertheless, a description of the rise of historical criticism is certainly one important component in any description of changing approaches to the Bible in modern theology.

Those changes have roots well before the modern period, however. A full account of them might begin with the emergence in the Renaissance of the basic tools of historical criticism – even though, at this point, these techniques were developed in relation to texts other than the Bible.

An example often cited is Lorenzo Valla's 1440 demonstration that a document known as the 'Donation of Constantine' was a forgery. This document purported to be a fourth-century grant of various territorial privileges from the Emperor Constantine to Pope Sylvester. Doubts about its authenticity and about the propriety of using it in debates about papal privileges had already arisen by the fifteenth century, but Valla provided a *demonstration* that the doubts were justified. In effect, he subjected the text to a lawyer's examination, using legal forms of argument to build a case against the text's authenticity. He drew attention to various features of the text's language as compared to other fourth-century documents and examined its consistency with other evidence about the relations between emperor and Church in the fourth century, and argued that this text *had* to have been written some centuries later. Valla's *Discourse on the Forgery of the Alleged Donation of Constantine* is available online at <history.hanover.edu/texts/vallatc.html>.

The account of the emergence of historical criticism could continue with the Reformation – both with the rise to greater prominence of the idea that all Christian people should be able to read and learn from the Bible for themselves, and with Protestant questioning of many of the existing interpretations of the Bible endorsed by the Church of Rome. The idea was abroad of Christian readers of the Scriptures digging back behind the accretions of later interpretation to find the Bible's *original* message.

The sixteenth-century reformer William Tyndale (c.1494–1536) is reported to have had an argument, while he was translating the Bible into English, with a supporter of the Pope. John Foxe, writing about the incident, tells us that Tyndale heard his opponent make some comment that seemed to elevate the Pope's authority over that of Scripture.

> [H]earyng this, full of godly zeale and not bearyng that blasphemous saying, [Tyndale] replyed agayne and sayd: I defie the Pope and all hys lawes: and further added that if God spared hym life, ere many yeares he would cause a boy that driveth the plough to know more of the Scripture, then he [the Pope] did.
>
> John Foxe, *Actes and Monuments*, 1570, Book 8, p1264;
> available online at www.johnfoxe.org.

In 1579 Matthew Hamont – admittedly a plough maker rather than a plough driver – was burned at the stake in Norwich for (at least according to his accusers) proclaiming that, in his judgement, the Scriptures were 'a fable' (Alexander Gordon, 'Hamont, Matthew (d. 1579)', rev. Stephen Wright in *The Oxford Dictionary of National Biography*, Oxford: Oxford University Press, 2004). Although he would have been horrified at the suggestion, it seems possible that Tyndale's translation helped make Hamont's sceptical judgement possible, both by providing the materials for Hamont to read, and by helping create the atmosphere in which Hamont felt authorised to make sense of those materials for himself.

The account of the emergence of historical criticism might continue into the eighteenth century, by drawing attention to various radicals and free-thinkers (Deists, for example) who took advantage of the accessibility of the Bible to subject it to sceptical investigation – whether it be to claim that the miracles described in the Bible didn't really happen, or to identify what they held to be the original pure and unmysterious message of Jesus behind the veils erected by his uncomprehending or dishonest followers.

Thomas Woolston (1668–1733) studied theology at Cambridge, and became a fellow of Sidney Sussex College there until his increasingly unorthodox views lost him the position. In an infamous *Discourse on the Miracles of Our Saviour*, he sought to demonstrate from an examination of the details of each story, from a knowledge of the of the original meaning of the Greek and from an appeal to common sense, that the stories of Jesus' miracles were, taken literally, 'full of Absurdities, Improbabilities, and Incredibilities' – and that they should rather be understood to be parables or figures designed to convey to us a spiritual meaning. (Thomas Woolston, *A Discourse on the Miracles of Our Saviour*, 2nd edition, London, 1727, p57. For discussion of a later and more influential example of this sort of argument, see the material on H.S. Reimarus in Chapter 2.)

Although these early developments are important, it was in the early part of the period covered by our book that the raising of questions about the historical reliability of biblical stories entered the mainstream. That is, it moved from the realm of individual authors writing from the fringes of academic and ecclesial life, and became the substance of conversations that are taking place firmly within the walls of the churches and the universities – conversations that slowly but surely drew in nearly everyone in those contexts who had a professional interest in the Bible. Some argued that the answer to these historical-critical questions should be a firm affirmation of the Bible's reliability; others argued the opposite – but all were caught up in the debate.

One central strand of this story focuses on the 'quest for the historical Jesus' – the attempt, using the gospel texts as evidence, to construct a picture of what the historical figure Jesus of Nazareth actually said and did, and what happened to him. It is by no means a story of uniformly decreasing confidence in the reliability of the Gospels or in the ability of historical investigation to produce a detailed portrait of Jesus' activity and message. See the Bibliography at the end of the chapter for some suggested guides to the debate.

At the same time as they moved into the mainstream (and partly as a result of that move), these debates about the historical reliability of the Bible began to draw upon an increasingly sophisticated and concerted set of historical-critical techniques, as scholars used ever more refined ways of scrutinising the texts for evidence of the historical contexts from which they came or to which they referred. In Germany in particular, these developments coincided with the emergence of history as a modern academic discipline – maintained in professional seminars and journals, with a strong sense of the scholarly diligence and neutrality required to be a member of the academic guild, and the existence of a system of lengthy apprenticeship designed to school new interpreters in those characteristics. The controversy in Christian circles surrounding historical criticism was in part a result of the application of these newly developed historical techniques, invented in relation to other stretches of historical subject matter, to the 'sacred' history of the Bible. In part, however, the historical criticism of the Bible was itself a laboratory in which these historical techniques were honed and developed in new and complex ways – with the passionate debates generated by the historical investigation of biblical material driving scholars to find new ways of interrogating their materials and supporting their conclusions. And though the universities remained, for much of the period covered by this book, the contexts in which Christian clergy were trained, there was a strong sense that the Bible was no longer simply the church's book, subject to study within the church and for church purposes: it was also the university's book, subject to study by historians, and the sense grew that *all* those who sought to study this book responsibly and with intellectual integrity needed to do so in the light of the findings of those academic historians.

This move of historical-critical questions into the mainstream took place later in England than it did in Germany. To get a sense of the passions that this move aroused in England, you could look into the story of the writing and the reception of the book *Essays and Reviews* in 1860, and especially of Benjamin Jowett's essay, 'On the Interpretation of Scripture'. (The first edition is available on Google Books at <books.google.com/books?id=FjY1AQAAIAAJ>.) The best guide to the debate is probably still Ieuan Ellis's, *Seven against Christ: A Study of 'Essays and Reviews'* (Leiden: Brill, 1980).

The eclipse of biblical narrative

To stop with this first description of the rise of historical criticism would be to risk painting an incomplete picture. Another way of describing changing attitudes to the Bible in modern theology was put forward by the American theologian Hans Frei (1922–1988) – about whom we will hear more in Chapter 17.

In a book called *The Eclipse of Biblical Narrative* (New Haven: Yale University Press, 1974), Frei focused his attention on what he called 'history-like' narratives in the Bible – i.e., those portions of the Bible that tell the kinds of story that, to our eyes, could well be historical or about which one might appropriately ask the same kinds of questions one might of other historical texts. For instance, the parable of the sower in Mark 4:3–9, Matthew 13:1–23 and Luke 8:1–15 describes a farmer sowing seed on different kinds of land. This parable is *not* normally taken to be a history-like narrative: the question of whether the events it depicts really happened is unlikely to arise for most readers and it would not occur to them to wonder what the sower was thinking, or how much he was getting paid, or whether he was new to the job, or what colour his hair was. We would, however, use the term 'history-like' for a story that depicts plausible characters interacting in a specific social setting, with the story driven forward by the interactions between the characters and between them and the circumstances in which they find themselves. So the story of *Jesus' telling* of the parable just mentioned – and of his disciples' confusion, and of Jesus' subsequent explanation – *is* history-like. It makes sense to ask why the disciples were confused and how this story fits in to the broader story of their relations with Jesus, and it makes sense to ask whether the story depicts events that really happened, whatever the answer to that question might be. Even a reader who was convinced that the events depicted did *not* really happen could still recognise the story as history-*like*.

Frei argued that pre-modern readers of certain key 'history-like' narratives in the Bible – most especially the narratives of the Gospels – normally assumed that such narratives portrayed real historical events. It was true, he acknowledged, that there were exceptions and that sometimes even readers who assumed the historical character of the Gospels passed quickly on to other (for example, allegorical) kinds of interpretation, barely letting their eyes rest on this historical reading. Frei nevertheless claimed that up through the Reformation this assumption was the unexamined norm and that history-like texts were seen as making accessible to readers a real historical world of characters and circumstances that was both their own world and the world of God's historical activity.

One of the terms that could be used to describe this kind of reading of history-like texts is 'literal reading' – but this is not likely to clarify the issue much since the definition of 'literal' is itself complex and contested. In informal discussion, people might say that someone 'reads the Bible literally', and mean by this that the person believes that everything the Bible describes really happened and happened in exactly the way the Bible says (down to the last detail). They might also mean that this person rather flat-footedly refuses to acknowledge that various passages are poetic or metaphorical and insists on taking them as straightforward reporting of real events. In academic discussions, however, the term 'literal' is used in more complex ways. For some, the literal sense of a text is the sense that it would have had for the community for whom it was originally written or perhaps for the author who wrote it. That seems like a common-sense definition – although it does have the disadvantage that it makes the literal sense something that one can't simply read off from the text itself, without some knowledge of the ways in which texts like this were used in their historical contexts. Some other definitions of 'literal sense' seek to focus more directly on the text itself and so might refer to the text as construed by the ordinary rules of grammar, syntax and vocabulary. Of course, if the reference is to the rules of grammar, syntax and vocabulary operative in the text's original historical context, this is actually another way of talking about the most obvious sense that the text would have had for an audience in that context – but for some definitions of 'literal sense', the focus is more on the 'common sense' rules of grammar, syntax and vocabulary that might be understood by any reasonable reader. Frei's discussion of the reading of history-like texts for the story that they tell is another attempt to get at what the literal sense (at least of certain narrative texts) might be: the literal meaning of a history-like narrative is precisely the history-like story that it tells.

By making the past accessible in written form, such texts enabled the history of God's ways with the world to be *read* with something rather like a literary sensitivity to rhetoric and plot, including the shapes, patterns and interconnections of the narrative. For people who read the text in this way, patterns found in the text were also taken to be patterns in the world that the text depicted. So if a story in the New Testament was told in such a way as to echo or resemble a story in the Old, that was read not simply as a fact about the text – an aspect of the artistry with which the text had been put together – but at the same time as a fact about the world: it revealed a pattern to God's ways with the world. So, for instance, if the story of Jesus is told in such a way as to bring out certain resemblances with the story of Jonah, that would be assumed to mean that Jonah's life had been shaped by God as a kind of living prophecy of Jesus.

With the rise of historical criticism, the assumption that history-like narratives portrayed real historical events began to be problematic for many readers. Under the influence of historical criticism there were increasing numbers of nineteenth-century readers who, when faced with a history-like passage in the Bible, would now ask whether what *really* happened matched the description. There was now a gap between the text and history. In its bluntest form, this new mindset said that the Bible's history-like materials could be converted into a set of historical propositions, and that the strength of one's assent to each of these propositions should be proportional to the weight of the historical evidence supporting it. And even though there were many for whom the result of weighing the evidence was a strong affirmation that the text was indeed a fully reliable guide to historical events, their approach to the text was now shaped by the fact that the question of the text's historical reliability existed and demanded an answer from them. So, according to Frei, it ceased to be the case, even for many conservative readers, that the real world of God's action could be faithfully explored simply by a grammatical and literary exploration of the patterns of the history-like text. Rather, to understand that world, one now had to trace the relations and implications of the facts to which the evidence of the text pointed. Sensitivity to rhetoric and plot, to textual resemblances and echoes, to all the literary shapes and connections of the depiction was still perhaps important as a way of understanding the artistry and imagination of the author, but it didn't have much to do with understanding the historical facts that the author had depicted. Indeed, from this new perspective too great a focus on the artistry or literary qualities of the text might even seem to undermine one's attempts to take its factual historicity seriously.

Of course, there were other nineteenth-century readers, influenced by Romanticism (see Chapter 4), who leapt the other way on this question. When text and historical referent began to drift apart, they stuck with literary sensitivity to the text, and its revelation of the artistry and imagination of its authors and turned their attention away from the historical world of character and circumstance that the text appeared to depict. In its most powerful form, this involved paying attention to the spirit or *Geist* of the text: the pervasive, developing way of seeing the world (or being in the world) discernible in the literary forms employed by succeeding generations of biblical authors. Such readers treated the history-like narratives in something like the same way that they might have treated poetry or folklore – as revealing the shape of the authors' imaginative worldview. For them the real meaning of the biblical texts is found by the empathetic reconstitution of that *Geist*.

What was lost in *both* of these approaches was, according to Frei, the ability to read history-like stories *as* stories: literary depictions of the interactions of characters and circumstances that could be understood only by paying attention to rhetoric and plot, textual resemblances and echoes, literary shapes and interconnections.

Frei noted that for many pre-modern Christians *figural* reading (in which an earlier episode in the Bible is read as a kind of living echo of a later episode, as when Moses is read as a 'figure' or 'type' of Christ) cohered naturally with the history-like reading of biblical stories. In fact, figural reading could often be the dominant form of reading such stories, because it was a technique that enabled connections to be found between disparate parts of the Bible (especially between the Old and New Testaments) on the one hand, *and* between episodes in the Bible and characters and events in the world of the reader on the other. In the modern period, however, at least until the end of the nineteenth century, Frei noticed an increasing uneasiness about such figural reading: it was relegated to a secondary position, quite separate from historical reading, or became part of an apologetic strategy designed to bolster claims about the Bible's miraculous origin by pointing to the remarkable accuracy of Old Testament prophecies of Christ.

One of the interesting features of approaches to the Bible in the last few decades has been a return to prominence of figural reading and other forms of 'spiritual reading', and the retrieval of more of the patristic and medieval heritage in which such reading plays a strong role. (See Chapter 12 for more on this.)

If the story of the rise of historical criticism prompts us to arrange modern readers of the Bible on a spectrum from those more sceptical about the Bible's historical reliability to those less sceptical, Frei's analysis suggests that we can combine that with an arrangement against a different axis: from those most inclined to take scriptural texts as evidence for the reconstruction of the historical events that lie behind them to those most inclined to read the scriptural texts simply as texts – reading to understand the pattern of the stories told. The combination of both axes would give us a map of modern approaches to the Bible's history-like texts like this:

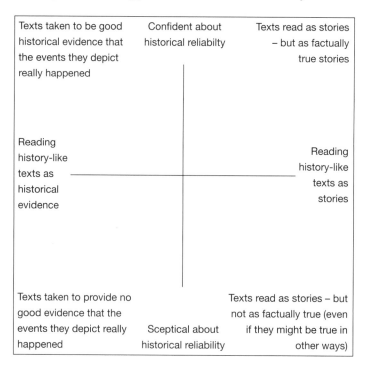

Figure 10.1 Map of modern approaches to the Bible's history-like texts

One of Frei's points is that quite a bit of what we might think of as 'conservative' biblical interpretation in the modern period is interpretation that takes history-like texts to be reliable evidence for a set of historical facts and that regards itself as called to understand the connections and implications of those facts. Yet such reading (in the top left of the diagram above) is just as fundamentally modern as is the kind of reading that is sceptical about the historical reliability of the texts (positions in the bottom of the diagram). Only the upper right corner resembles pre-modern reading of history-like texts – and even in this corner, any modern reader will be aware that the other ways of approaching the Bible exist and so will not be able to read with the innocence of a pre-modern reader.

> Look back to Chapter 8 on Charles Hodge and Horace Bushnell, and note what was said there about the fundamentally modern nature of Hodge's approach to systematic theology. In a similar way, in the light of the remarks we have just been making, we could say that Hodge's approach to the Bible was no less modern than Bushnell's.

Conservative readers of Scripture in the modern period have continued to insist on the complete trustworthiness and truthfulness of the Bible – and have, quite rightly, also insisted that a commitment to such complete trustworthiness and truthfulness had been a major feature of most pre-modern Christianity. But some of the ways in which that trustworthiness and truthfulness were articulated and insisted upon were new. So, although there was (and is) a considerable variety of opinion within conservative circles, the insistence that the text was a trustworthy guide to the history of God's dealings with the world sometimes became the insistence that the Bible provided reliable historical reporting that could stand up in the court of historical criticism, or the insistence that the Bible provided information about the formation and disposition of the world that could stand up in the court of natural scientific inquiry (see Chapter 11). Both of these ways of thinking about the Bible's trustworthiness and reliability were new and they had a significant impact on the ways in which the Bible was read.

> Hodge and the generation of conservative scholars that followed him helped propagate the use of the term 'inerrancy' to describe the Bible's trustworthiness and truthfulness and to define it in response to what they saw as the erosion of confidence in that complete trustworthiness. There has, subsequently, been much debate about inerrancy. Is it only the texts as they were originally written,

and not the texts as we have them now, that are inerrant? In what domains of knowledge is the text inerrant? Are there any limits to inerrancy? Such debate has been a common feature of evangelicalism in the late nineteenth and twentieth centuries, particularly in North America – and this is one of those debates that can be traced in some detail on the internet. You might start with the 1978 Chicago Statement on Biblical Inerrancy (available at <www.bible-researcher. com/chicago1.html>), which is probably the best-known attempt to define the doctrine, but you do not have to look hard to find all sorts of arguments for and against that definition and about various proposed alternatives – much of the debate internal to conservative or evangelical circles.

Harnack, Barth and Bultmann

In order to explore the complex territory that is opened up by all these modern developments, we are now going to look at three great modern readers of scripture: Adolf von Harnack, Karl Barth and Rudolf Bultmann. Although they lived and worked in very similar contexts, they developed ideas about the Bible that took them in very different directions.

Adolf von Harnack (1851–1930) was a Lutheran theologian, a New Testament scholar and a historian. He was one of the greatest of modern Church historians and a man utterly at home in German universities shaped by the traditions of thinking that flowed from Kant, Schleiermacher and Hegel (see Chapters 3–5).

Karl Barth (1886–1968) was a Reformed theologian and studied for a time under Harnack, whom he much admired. But around the time of the First World War, Barth came to break with the kind of liberal theology he had learnt from Harnack. He went on to become one of the most powerful voices in twentieth-century theology.

Rudolf Bultmann (1884–1976) was a Lutheran theologian and a hugely influential New Testament scholar, who was also at one point taught by Harnack. He and Barth became friends and for a time it seemed as if their developing theological views were moving in the same direction as they distanced themselves from the thinking of their teachers – but only for a time, as we shall see.

Adolf von Harnack

Adolf von Harnack stood very firmly on the left-hand side of the diagram given above, because he was utterly committed to historical criticism as the method best suited to making sense of the Bible. On the one hand, he believed that the methods of historical criticism were *needed*. The Bible contains a wide variety of materials, gathered over a

Figure 10.2 Adolf von Harnack

long period of time; even the New Testament includes layers of material from many stages in the development of the early Church. If our decisions about what is central amid this diversity are not to be based upon irrational subjective preference, he argued, they need to be based on a method that can discover the original and pure message of the gospel behind all the later developments – the seed from which all the later developments have grown. Rigorous, critical and diligent historical criticism is just such a method.

On the other hand, Harnack believed that the methods of historical criticism are *capable* of delivering what we need. If a revelation from God has indeed taken place, then something has happened in history, and it has happened for the sake of knowledge by human beings. For Harnack, we can only properly know what we can make sense of – that is, what can become intelligible for us. The methods of critical academic investigation are simply the most rigorous techniques available to us for making sense of intelligible realities, and historical criticism is the method of critical academic investigation suited to making sense of intelligible happenings in history. Historical criticism is therefore inherently adequate to the task of unearthing the kernel of the gospel, of God's revelation, within the materials of the Bible. Hence, at the very start of his lectures on the essence of Christianity, Harnack can say:

> What is Christianity? It is solely in its historical sense that we shall try to answer this question here; that is to say, we shall employ the methods of historical science, and the experience of life gained by studying the actual course of history.
>
> Harnack, What is Christianity?, p6.

And, a little later, he says that the historian's 'business and highest duty is to determine what is of permanent value' in the Christian religion (p13).

For Harnack, the centre that historical criticism finds is Jesus' preaching about love of God and love of neighbour. Identifying this as the heart of the gospel enables Harnack to tie together what he says about the Bible and about historical criticism in a particularly comprehensive way. Jesus' call to love God and to love thy neighbour does not simply repeat to us in a compelling form something that our reason could already have told us unaided, but it is nevertheless in deep continuity with the best human morality, the most cultured human understanding. It confirms and deepens that morality and understanding.

> Jesus combined religion and morality, and in this sense religion may be called the soul of morality, and morality the body of religion. We can thus understand how it was that Jesus could place the love of God and the love of one's neighbour side by side; the love of one's neighbour is the only practical proof on earth of that love of God which is strong in humility.
>
> Harnack, What is Christianity?, p73.

Of course, historical criticism is itself one of the methods used by cultured and moral human beings: it is one of the ways in which such human beings seek to be responsible and truthful knowers. Therefore, the message of the gospel uncovered by historical criticism, by confirming the best of human culture and morality, consecrates the very ground on which the historical critic stands.

Karl Barth

In 1923, Harnack wrote an open letter to the journal *Die Christliche Welt*, containing 'Fifteen Questions to the Despisers of Scientific Theology' – that is, 15 questions to a group of young theologians, including his former student Karl Barth, who seemed to have completely rejected the approach to the Bible that Harnack championed. (The English word 'scientific' in the title of the letter translates the German word *wissenschaftlich*, which here means something like 'rigorous and scholarly academic enquiry' and includes academic historical criticism as well as sciences such as physics, chemistry and biology.) The text of Harnack's letter, of Barth's replies, of follow-ups from both of them and of a final coda from Harnack, can be found in H. Martin

Figure 10.3 Karl Barth

Rumscheidt, *Revelation and Theology: An Analysis of the Barth-Harnack Correspondence of 1923* (Cambridge: Cambridge University Press, 1972, pp29–53). For a useful paraphrase, see George Hunsinger, 'The Harnack/Barth Correspondence: A Paraphrase with Comments', *The Thomist* 50.4 (1986), pp599–622.

Each of Harnack's questions asks – often in rather obscure language – whether some feature of this new, unscientific theology (as he saw it) can really be true, or whether we still in fact need the kind of scientific theology:

> Does one not rather need here historical knowledge and critical reflection? ... Do we not need, for an understanding of the Bible, next to an inner openness, historical knowledge and critical reflection? ... How can there be such preaching [of the gospel] without historical knowledge and critical reflection? ... [H]ow is education possible without historical knowledge and the highest valuation of morality? ... [H]ow can one erect barriers between the experience of God and the good, the true and the beautiful, instead of relating them with the experience of God by means of historical knowledge and critical reflection? ... How dare one introduce all kinds of paradoxes and whims here?
>
> In Rumscheidt, *Revelation and Theology*, pp29–31.

We can begin to understand Barth's rejection of Harnack's position if we think back to what we learnt about Kierkegaard (see Chapter 6). Kierkegaard had claimed that historical investigation is incapable of bringing us face to face with the *absolute* demand that God makes on us. By its very nature, historical criticism is a set of techniques that are capable of delivering probable judgements about happenings that fit within the historical landscape; any particular historical investigation places its subject matter *relative* to other historical events and movements; it renders the unusual explicable and shows how the apparently unique in history is the product of the same recognisable forces that are at work elsewhere.

For Barth, God is not a reality that can be placed relative to other realities, and God's work cannot be made intelligible in the light of forces that are at work elsewhere in history. If revelation has taken place – if, that is, *God* has truly spoken in history – then historical critical investigation of the kind that Harnack champions will necessarily be incapable of identifying it, acknowledging it and respecting its nature. The *properly* responsible and critical approach will, instead, be to find some method of talk about and response to this revelation that does *not* try to fit it into the box of our existing understanding.

If, for instance, revelation does teach us that God is love and that we are called to love God and to love our neighbour, this is not a message that stands in simple continuity with the best of human morality and culture. It is, properly understood, an utterly radical, utterly demanding message that overthrows all our existing ways of thinking and acting, and it is a lesson that we need to be taught and to go on being taught – dying to our existing life, in trust that God will raise us.

> Do we *love* our neighbour? Are we capable of it? And if we do *not* love *him*, what about our love of *God*? What shows more plainly than this ... that God does not give life unless he takes it first?
>
> In Rumscheidt, *Revelation and Theology*, p33.

After all, if we think this message is in continuity with the best of human morality and culture, we might end up thinking that the love that God teaches us is allied to the kind of patriotism with which Harnack supported the Kaiser's war aims in 1914.

When the First World War broke out, Harnack (like many others) was stirred by the feeling that Germany was fighting for the sake of all that was highest and finest and noblest in their culture, and the experience of being at war heightened his and others' awareness of the importance and value of that culture. Harnack therefore believed that this must be a war that he as a theologian should support

– in effect, a *holy* war – because Christ was on the side of the very culture that the war was defending and deepening. So, in October 1914, Harnack was a signatory to a public letter from 93 German intellectuals supporting the German war aims. 'Have faith in us!' the letter proclaimed. 'Believe, that we shall carry on this war to the end as a civilized nation, to whom the legacy of a Goethe, a Beethoven, and a Kant, is just as sacred as its own hearths and homes' ('Manifesto of the Ninety-Three German Intellectuals', available online at <wwi.lib.byu.edu/index. php/Manifesto_of_the_Ninety-Three_German_Intellectuals>).

   Barth was appalled when he saw this letter. He thought Harnack and the other theologian signatories had disastrously confused faith in Christ with confidence in human culture, and so had ended up trying to enlist Christ's support for a war that was nothing to do with Christ – a war that was, in fact, antithetical to Christ.

Barth insisted again and again that the form that God's communication of love to the world took – the communication of what the true life of faith looks like in this world, the foothold it can have among the ways of the world – was the Jesus who was completely rejected by the world around him, and crucified by it.

> The faith awakened by God will never be able to avoid completely the need for a more or less radical protest against this world as surely as it is a hope for the promised but invisible gift. A theology, should it lose the understanding of the basic distance which faith posits between itself and this *world*, would in the same measure have to lose sight of the knowledge of God the *Creator*. For the "utter contrast" of God and the world, the *cross*, is the only way in which we as *human beings* can consider the original and final *unity* of Creator and creature.
>
> In Rumscheidt, *Revelation and Theology*, p32.

Harnack's 'Fifteen Questions' refer in passing to Kant (and to Goethe). Does Barth's theology, he asks, provide him with any way of distinguishing between Kant's philosophy and barbarism? That is, he wants to know whether Barth is able to recognise in Kant's religious philosophy – Kant's identification, perhaps, of morality as the true meaning of religion – as a sublime human achievement that is *close* to Christian faith, even if Christian faith goes beyond it. Kant's identification of the essence of Christianity is, after all, not a million miles from Harnack's. Barth replies:

> 'Real statements about God' are made ... only where one is aware of being confronted by *revelation* and therefore of being placed under judgement instead of believing oneself to be on a pinnacle of culture and religion. Even Goethe's and Kant's statements about this subject stand under this judgment, together with all others.
>
> In Rumscheidt, *Revelation and Theology*, p33, translation slightly altered.

God's word in history, spoken in Jesus Christ, is for Barth the utterly radical, utterly demanding message that overthrows all our existing ways of thinking and acting; and it does not teach a lesson that human beings are capable of grasping in such a way that they could turn away from the one who has taught it to them in order to rely instead upon the understanding of it that they now have. Any human grasp of God's word is always, necessarily, inadequate; any knowledge of it that we gain is only, as it were, a fading impress of the word itself, and must constantly be renewed by that word. In fact, there is no set of techniques that can securely deliver our initial hearing of the word, nor the constant renewal of that hearing – because all techniques that we have for the secure delivery of understanding suffer from the same problem as historical criticism: they are capable only of delivering understanding of the kind of reality we can grasp for ourselves.

For Barth, therefore, rather than approaching the Bible with some set of critical techniques of the kind that we might bring to any historical text, believing that this will yield the appropriate material for a responsible and mature faith, we should read the Bible from *within* faith. And if we ask where that faith will come from, Barth will only say that God awakens it by speaking his word to the world. To say that the Bible should be read from within faith is to say that it should be read with the trust that God *has* spoken, that the Bible truly witnesses to that speaking and that by means of the Bible God's Spirit goes on giving the kind of knowledge of God that creatures can have.

If one reads the Bible as handing over a secure understanding of God's word – in the way, perhaps, that a theology textbook like this might conceivably hand over to its readers a secure understanding of the development of modern Christian theology – one will misread it. The Bible functions as God's word only if it becomes the means by which readers are brought again and again, in prayerful trust, to listen for God's word to them, ready once again for their supposedly secure understanding to be challenged and remade by that word.

> Humility, yearning and supplication, will always be the first and also the last thing *for us*. The way from the old to the new world is *not* a stairway, *not* a development in any sense whatsoever; it is a being born anew. If the knowledge that 'God is

love' is the *highest* and *final knowledge about God*, how can one consistently pretend to be in possession of it? ... Is not *our* faith also always unfaith? Or should we believe in our *faith*? Does not faith live by being faith in God's *promise*? Are we saved in a way other than in *hope*?

In Rumscheidt, Revelation and Theology, p34.

There are two further points to make about Barth's understanding of the Bible. The first point is that to speak of God's word spoken in history is, first and foremost, to speak of Jesus of Nazareth. To say that the Bible functions as God's word to us is to say that the Bible is given to us to bring us face to face, again and again, with Jesus. That cannot be simply with the construct 'the Jesus of history', however: the Jesus reconstructed by historical criticism will inevitably be a Jesus made graspable and intelligible – a Jesus who is *not* God's absolute word. The Bible functions as God's word to us precisely by witnessing to Jesus of Nazareth *as* God's absolute word – that is, by enabling us to look to Jesus in a way that historical criticism cannot.

> In the early years after his break with the liberal theology of Harnack and his other teachers, Barth was insistently focused on the negative side of this message: the denial that our grasp in faith of God's revelation is more than a fading impress of God's revelation, and the description of the ways in which human thinking and acting are overthrown by that revelation. This is clearest in Barth's most famous early work: his commentary on Paul's epistle to the Romans – particularly the thoroughly rewritten second edition of 1921 (trans. Edwyn C. Hoskyns, London: Oxford University Press, 1933). Over time, and without fundamentally changing the shape of his account of faith and revelation, Barth came to focus more insistently on the positive side: the claim that faith, even though utterly inadequate, could by the grace of God point beyond itself to the revelatory Word of God, insofar as it was obedient to that Word. His *magnum opus*, the massive, multi-volume *Church Dogmatics* (trans. Geoffrey Bromiley *et al.*, Edinburgh: T&T Clark, 1936–1975) sets out in great detail an account of Christian teaching about God's work in Jesus – a complete, interconnected arrangement of Christian doctrine – intended to practise and exhibit such obedience, and in so doing to point away from itself to its source.

The second point to make is that Barth does not, nevertheless, simply reject historical criticism. Barth's first move – a move that puts him firmly on the right-hand side of the diagram above – is to read the biblical witness to Jesus of Nazareth as God's word, and to read that witness in its own terms. But he can ask, as a second move, what role the techniques of historical criticism might play if this biblical witness is indeed truthful witness. Of course, if this witness is true and Jesus of Nazareth is God's word, historical criticism will certainly be incapable of confirming that for itself. If the witness is true, however, and God's word in Jesus of Nazareth has awoken witnesses to itself in history, there is no reason to think that historical criticism cannot help confirm *that* these witnesses (the writers of the Gospels, Paul and the rest) have spoken, and *how* they have spoken, as long as it does not try to claim competence over *the reality about which they have spoken*. In that sense, Barth does not deny at all that the Bible is a historical book, and quite properly the subject of thoroughgoing critical historical analysis. 'The task of theology is at one with the task of preaching. It consists in the reception and transmission of the Word of the Christ. Why should "historical knowledge and critical reflection" not be of preparatory service in this?' (In Rumscheidt, *Revelation and Theology*, p32).

Rudolf Bultmann

Barth's friend Rudolf Bultmann was just as convinced as Barth that Harnack's identification of the gospel was misconceived – and that Harnack's methods had led him to render revelation graspable and sensible in a way that neutralised its power. His understanding of what was needed instead, however, was rather different.

Precisely because God is God – absolute, impossible to fit into any scheme of understanding developed by our reason prior to taking God into account – to hear God's word is to hear a call to a total reorientation of our ways of seeing the world and our ways of understanding our place in it. Just like Barth, Bultmann emphasised that this could not be a one-off reorientation leaving us with a secure grasp of the Christian way of thinking; it needed to be an ongoing encounter.

> No one has ever heard [God's word] enough. One does not come to know this in the same way that one grasps an enlightening thought, nor so that one knows it once and for all. God's word is not a general truth that can be stored in the treasure-house of human spiritual life. It remains the sovereign word, which we shall never master and which can only be believed as an ever-living miracle, spoken by God and constantly renewed. How should he who has heard it once not listen and hope, strive and pray, that he may hear it again?
> Bultmann, 'How Does God Speak through the Bible?' in
> *Existence and Faith: Shorter Writings of Rudolf Bultmann*, trans. Schubert M. Ogden,
> London: Hodder and Stoughton, 1961, pp166–170.

Anything that we can hold at arm's length and make sense of – before or after we have been awoken to faith – is not God. To speak about God is always to speak about a total reorientation of all our ways of thinking and acting that undercuts our attempts to control or manage our way through the world and that requires us to live in trusting dependence upon the love of God.

For Barth, the focus – particularly as his work developed through the 1920s and 1930s – fell *first* on the word of God spoken in history in Jesus Christ, and only *second* on the ways in which Christians are caught into relation to that word and made witnesses to it. The subject matter that theology explores as it obediently and trustingly reads the Bible is first of all Jesus Christ as pointed to by the witnesses – and it is on Jesus that Barth wants readers' attention fixed. The subject matter is only secondarily the faith of those witnesses, which provides what I called above a fading impress of the word spoken to the world in Jesus Christ.

For Bultmann, however, to speak about either God's word or the faith that responds to that word, one must speak about them simultaneously: the only proper way of talking about revelation is by talking about the faith that it awakens; the only proper way of talking about faith is as faith awoken by revelation. This means that for Bultmann the subject matter that theology explores as it obediently and trustingly reads the Bible is always the transformation of human ways of seeing and acting in relation to God: the transformation we see taking place in the disciples in their encounter with Jesus, and the same transformation becoming real for us as we encounter their testimony. In fact, to talk about 'subject matter' in this way might be misleading: Bultmann is not primarily interested in *finding out about* this, as an academic exercise, but in this transformation actually taking place in the reader's encounter with the Bible.

Another striking difference between Bultmann's theology and Barth's derives from Bultmann's conviction that there was a form of philosophy that was capable of talking about total reorientations of human consciousness and will – and so capable of talking about the kind of subject matter Bultmann believed to be central to the Bible. It was not that the existentialist philosophy of his colleague Martin Heidegger said everything that Bultmann thought the gospel said, but that it provided a useful and appropriate set of tools for explaining what *kind* of subject matter the gospel was, and for explaining the demand of the gospel to a modern audience.

Bultmann was convinced that a total reorientation of consciousness and will in relation to God was the sole real subject matter of the gospel, and of the Bible as a document addressed to faith. Yet the Bible did not present that total reorientation of consciousness directly. It presented it by means of stories about miracles, stories about resurrection, stories about comings and goings between heaven, earth and hell. It did so, however, only because these were the best tools available for the witnesses to Jesus to communicate the kind of transformation that encounter with Jesus had worked upon them. The story of the transfiguration, for instance, is not really about an inexplicable event literally happening to Jesus of Nazareth in front of a select group of his disciples, but is a way of expressing pictorially and dramatically a transformation in the disciples' understanding of God's relation to Jesus and to themselves. Readers of the Bible therefore need to be able to translate between the pictorial and dramatic language that the witnesses use – the *mythological* language, as Bultmann would say – and the real subject matter about which those witnesses were struggling to talk. To get at the real subject matter, readers need to be able to *demythologise* what they read: to translate from mythological into existential terms. The subject matter of the Gospels is not, for Bultmann, a set of claims about things that Jesus did, nor about things that happened to him; it is the total reorientation of our consciousness and wills in relation to God that encounter with the witness to Jesus prompts.

Bultmann defined myth in the following way:

> Mythology expresses a certain understanding of human existence. It believes that the world and human life have their ground and their limits in a power which is beyond all that we can calculate or control. Mythology speaks about this power inadequately and insufficiently because it speaks about it as if it were a worldly power. It speaks of gods who represent the power beyond the visible, comprehensible world. It speaks of gods as if they were men and of their actions as human actions, although it conceives of the gods as endowed with superhuman power and of their actions as incalculable, as capable of breaking the normal, ordinary order of events. It may be said that myths give to the transcendent reality an immanent, this-worldly objectivity. Myths give worldly objectivity to that which is unworldly.
>
> Bultmann, *Jesus Christ and Mythology*, p19.

Demythologisation is not intended to explain away such mythological expressions, but to do justice to them.

> What follows from all this? Shall we retain the ethical preaching of Jesus and abandon his eschatological preaching? Shall we reduce his preaching of the Kingdom of God to the so-called social gospel? Or is there [another] possibility? We must ask whether the eschatological preaching and the mythological sayings as a whole contain a still deeper meaning which is concealed under the cover of mythology. If that is so, let us abandon the mythological conceptions precisely

because we want to retain their deeper meaning. This method of interpretation of the New Testament which tries to recover the deeper meaning behind the mythological conceptions I call *de-mythologizing* – an unsatisfactory word, to be sure. Its aim is not to eliminate the mythological statements but to interpret them.

Bultmann, *Jesus Christ and Mythology*, p18.

Rudolf Bultmann was one of the greatest historical critics of the New Testament in the twentieth century. The centre of his historical-critical endeavour was twofold: to identify the forms of witness that the earlier followers of Jesus gave to what had happened to them, and to translate that witness from the mythological form in which they had given it into existential terms. Bultmann was therefore not particularly interested in the quest for the historical Jesus; identifying which factual claims about Jesus were reliable and which were not was not central to his programme, and he was in fact quite sceptical about how much we could know about Jesus. Rather, Bultmann was supremely interested in using historical-critical techniques to identify the development and diversity of forms of early Christian faith in the God of Jesus Christ, and the ways in which those forms of faith had been expressed.

Conclusion

Each of the three men discussed in the second half of this chapter was hugely influential on the development of modern theology in the twentieth century. Harnack was probably least so, at least in a direct way, though there continued to be many (liberal and conservative) for whom the proper approach to the Bible was to use the tools of historical criticism to identify the original teaching of Jesus, and then to hold to that original teaching as the heart of the gospel.

Barth was influential on many, conservative and liberal alike, for whom interpretation of the Bible meant seeking to articulate as clearly as possible, in theological terms minted for the purpose, the central claims made by the biblical witnesses about God's work in the world in Jesus Christ, as well as the claims about the nature of God and the world which flowed from them. For these readers, the use of historical criticism and other non-theological methods of interpretation was a secondary matter, perhaps quite appropriate and even necessary, but only insofar as the more basic theological claims indicated that there was a role for it.

Bultmann was also influential on conservatives and liberals for whom the focus of biblical interpretation was uncovering the capacity of scriptural texts to transform the self-understanding (along with the world-understanding) of their readers. For those influenced by Bultmann, reading the Bible should provoke Aha! moments of changed imagination, in much the way that Jesus' parables were intended to instigate a revolution in the minds of his hearers. Bultmann was influential on many for whom modern existentialist philosophy could provide a way of talking about this kind of transformation and could help guide the interpretation of biblical texts in the direction of such transformation.

The approaches exemplified by Harnack, Barth and Bultmann are not by any means the only forms of biblical reading that have shaped modern theology. In addition to the conservative or evangelical approaches to the Bible described earlier in the chapter, you should see the other chapters in this part of the book – especially the extensive material on the Bible in the chapters on feminist theology (Chapter 14) and on liberation theology (Chapter 15) – for other important major tendencies in twentieth-century biblical interpretation. As we said at the start of the chapter, the developments and disagreements of modern theology have, to a very significant degree, involved developments and disagreements concerning the right ways to read the Bible and about what those ways of reading yield – and the variety of approaches to the Bible in modern theology is as wide as the variety of modern theology itself.

Bibliography

General works

Robert M. Grant with David Tracy, *A Short History of the Interpretation of the Bible*, 2nd edition (Philadelphia: Fortress Press, 1984). Provides a good, brief overview of pre-modern and modern developments.

Justin Holcombe, *Christian Theologies of Scripture: A Comparative Introduction* (New York: New York University Press, 2006). Provides chapters on Schleiermacher, Barth and Frei (among others) as well as on the approaches to the Bible of various contemporary theological movements.

Stephen Neill and Tom Wright, *The Interpretation of the New Testament, 1861–1986* (Oxford: Oxford University Press, 1985). A readable history of the rise of historical criticism.

The quest of the historical Jesus

The story of this quest (or quests – it is common to identify three distinct periods of questing over the nineteenth and twentieth centuries) can be found in numerous places, including:

Albert Schweitzer, *The Quest of the Historical Jesus: A Critical Study of its Progress from Reimarus to Wrede*, trans. W. Montgomery (London: Black, 1910). Available online at <www.earlychristianwritings.com/schweitzer/> – a classic work that is the origin for all talk of 'quests' for the historical Jesus.

Charlotte Allen, *The Human Christ: The Search for the Historical Jesus* (Oxford: Lion, 1998).

Mark Allan Powell, *Jesus as a Figure in History: How Modern Historians View the Man from Galilee* (Louisville: WJKP, 1998).

James M. Robinson, *A New Quest of the Historical Jesus* (London: SCM, 1959).

Ben Witherington III, *The Jesus Quest: The Third Search for the Jew of Nazareth* (Downer's Grove: IVP, 1995).

Harnack, Barth and Bultmann

Adolf von Harnack, *What is Christianity? Sixteen Lectures Delivered in the University of Berlin during the Winter-Term 1899-1900*, trans. Thomas Bailey Saunders, 2nd edition (London: Williams and Norgate, 1901). Provides a very accessible guide to Harnack's theology.

Martin Rumscheidt (ed.), *Adolf von Harnack: Liberal Theology at Its Height* (London: Collins, 1989). Selected writings, including lots of short extracts from a wide range of Harnack's works.

Karl Barth, 'The Preface to the First Edition' and 'The Preface to the Second Edition' in *The Epistle to the Romans*, trans. Edwyn C. Hoskyns (Oxford: Oxford University Press, 1933), pp1–15. Barth explains the approach to the Bible that he took in the commentary.

Joseph L. Mangina, *Karl Barth: Theologian of Christian Witness* (Aldershot: Ashgate, 2004). A good general introduction.

Rudolf Bultmann, *Jesus Christ and Mythology* (New York: Scribner, 1958). Probably the best place to start for understanding Bultmann's thought – and not a difficult read.

Roger Johnson (ed.), *Rudolf Bultmann: Interpreting Faith for the Modern Era* (London: Collins, 1987). Selected writings, includes lots of extracts.

Benjamin Myers, 'Faith as Self-Understanding: Towards a Post-Barthian Appreciation of Rudolf Bultmann', *International Journal of Systematic Theology* 10.1 (2008), pp21–35. A good brief guide to some of the main themes in Bultmann's work.

11 Religion and science

AIMS

By the end of this chapter, we hope that you will:

- know about, and have thought about the implications of, the complex historical origins of contemporary debates about 'religion and science'

- know about some examples of the interaction of scientific and religious thought in the nineteenth and twentieth centuries.

A major focus of this chapter is the work of Charles Darwin, and its implications for the relationship between religion and science. Before you begin, we suggest that you make sure you have a basic knowledge of what Darwin argued in his major works *On the Origin of Species* and *The Descent of Man*, and of what is meant by 'evolutionary theory'. There are useful sources of basic information about Darwin and evolutionary theory at <www.aboutdarwin.com> and <www.nhm.ac.uk/nature-online/evolution>. Darwin's works themselves are extremely readable and available in several good modern editions.

Introduction: a famous debate

In 1860, in the Lecture Room of the Oxford University Museum, the British Association for the Advancement of Science met to discuss a paper on the views of Charles Darwin. Darwin himself was not present. We have no complete contemporary account of the meeting. Despite this, it has gone down in history as the moment when (as the son of one of the participants put it) there emerged an 'open clash between Science and the Church'.

The side of the Church in this 'open clash' – if that is what it was – was taken by Samuel Wilberforce, Bishop of Oxford, well known for his skill in public speaking and debate, who had recently published an article against evolutionary theory. On the side of science was Thomas Henry Huxley, a marine biologist and popular science writer, who had already made a name for himself as a powerful exponent and defender of Darwin's views. Wilberforce's presence at the meeting was publicised in advance, and a crowd of academics, students, clergy and members of the public came to hear what they expected would be a lively debate.

The paper that was read introduced the topic of Darwin's book *On the Origin of Species* and Darwin's theory of evolution. Once the introduction was finished, the meeting was opened to debate and Samuel Wilberforce soon took the floor. According to one of the most famous accounts of the meeting, he spoke

> for full half an hour with inimitable spirit, emptiness and unfairness ... he assured us that there was nothing in the idea of evolution ... Then, turning to [Huxley] ... he begged to know, was it through his grandfather or his grandmother that he claimed descent from a monkey?

It was, Huxley's son later wrote, 'the fatal mistake of his speech'. Huxley, an enthusiastic and aggressive controversialist, seized the opportunity that Wilberforce's descent into personal insults gave him. As one of the undergraduates present recalled it, Huxley rose immediately after the Bishop's speech and said:

> I asserted – and I repeat – that a man has no reason to be ashamed of having an ape for his grandfather. If there were an ancestor whom I should feel shame in recalling it would rather be a man – a man of restless and versatile intellect – who, not content with an equivocal success in his own sphere of activity, plunges into scientific questions with which he has no real acquaintance, only to obscure them by an aimless rhetoric, and distract the attention of his hearers from the real point at issue by eloquent digressions and skilled appeals to religious prejudice.
>
> Account by Leopold Henry Huxley using notes from John Richard Green, reprinted in Tess Cosslett (ed.), *Science and Religion in the Nineteenth Century* (Cambridge: Cambridge University Press, 1984) p152.

The exact words of Huxley's response are lost, but he afterwards concurred with the substance of Green's account. The debate was widely reported at the time and even more widely discussed in the decades that followed. For a very detailed further study of the incident, see Ian Hesketh, *Of Apes and Ancestors: Evolution, Christianity and the Oxford Debate* (Toronto: University of Toronto Press, 2009).

Nineteenth-century science versus religion?

It is easy to see how the Oxford incident, and especially Huxley's words, could be reported ever afterwards as the beginning of a conflict between science and religion, focused on evolutionary theory. Huxley's response pits ignorance, prejudice and deliberate concealment of the truth – in the person of Wilberforce the bishop – against scientific honesty and the obvious plausibility of the theory of evolution. The Bishop of Oxford, in Huxley's view, can make no contribution to 'scientific questions'; he can only 'distract' people from them into less important matters.

Both Huxley's comment and the way it was later reported helped to establish a separation and enmity between 'science' and 'religion' in the popular imagination. If we look more closely at the Oxford meeting of 1860, however, it proves rather hard to draw the battle lines between 'science' and 'religion', or to place any of the protagonists on one side or the other.

Wilberforce was Bishop of Oxford; he was also a keen ornithologist, with an interest in geology, and the holder of a first-class degree in mathematics. He had gained most of his knowledge of Darwin's theories, and the arguments against them, from discussions with Richard Owen, the curator of the British Museum's natural history exhibits and probably the most famous biologist of the day. Owen never publicly accepted Darwin's theories of the evolutionary origin of species, although he did accept certain related claims (such as the fact that species could change over time). At the time of the Oxford debate there was already a professional feud between Owen and Huxley regarding the anatomical similarities and differences between human beings and apes. Huxley's attack on Wilberforce can be reread as a proxy attack on Owen, who had coached Wilberforce for the debate and who was present in the room. Already the debate begins to look less like a clash between science and religion and more like a clash within science, in which many of the participants were religious thinkers.

Wilberforce, as a clergyman with scientific interests and some scientific training, was not an oddity in the mid-nineteenth century. In 1860 there were still very few professional scientists; Huxley was unusual in being able to earn his living through scientific research and writing (Darwin himself lived on inherited wealth). Much research in biology, up to this point, had been done by clergymen such as Wilberforce – inspired in their work by the conviction that they were learning more about God's work in creation.

George Eliot gives a sympathetic portrayal of a 'clergyman-naturalist' in Mr Farebrother in *Middlemarch* – setting her narrative a few decades before Wilberforce and Darwin. Dr Lydgate, in the same novel, represents another, more 'professional', approach to science – but notice how few opportunities he has to pursue research and how much suspicion his efforts attract.

A more complex real-life figure in this vein is Professor John Henslow, who presided at the Oxford meeting. He was Darwin's teacher, mentor and close friend, who had received scientific correspondence from him during the *Beagle* voyage – and was also an Anglican priest. In his later years, he worked with farmers in his parish on developing a range of 'scientific' agricultural methods.

Of the clergy in the audience at the Oxford meeting, many would have had enough knowledge of natural history to understand Darwin's theories and, in several cases, to accept them. Huxley's son, in his account of the meeting, reports that a priest 'led ... the cheers for the Darwinians' in the face of other 'clergy ... who shouted lustily for the Bishop'. So now the debate also appears as an argument within Christianity, not about the place of 'science' in general, but about how to react to one particular scientific theory.

Darwin's religion

There is considerable controversy around Darwin's own religious beliefs. He studied at Cambridge and originally intended to take Anglican orders. In his youth and early adulthood, Darwin held (what were then) conventional Christian beliefs – including the belief that nature reflected the good purposes of God, who was its designer (see the discussion of Paley, below). His doubts about these beliefs appear to have begun in the 1830s, in the context of his scientific studies and in particular, of his growing awareness of the scale of natural waste and suffering. The early and painful death of his daughter Annie appears to have precipitated a decisive crisis of faith in the 1850s. After this, he was never again prepared to affirm Christian belief.

Later in life, pressed repeatedly to state his views on religious questions, he specifically denied various Christian doctrines. He also denied at least once that he was an 'atheist', and described himself at least once as an 'agnostic' – a term coined by his friend and defender Huxley, to denote a person who denies that the existence of God can be either proved or disproved. For the most part, he tried to steer clear of religious controversy and was wary of committing himself publicly to views on religion. Stories circulated after his death that he returned to Christianity on his deathbed are now discredited.

Figure 11.1 Charles Darwin pictured in a Punch cartoon entitled 'Man is But a Worm',
published in 1882

What is science anyway?

The word 'science' comes from the Latin *scientia*, which simply means 'knowledge' – and can refer either to what we know or how we know things.

'Science' has a similar range of meanings today, within a smaller sphere. When you 'learn science' in school, you learn information ('scientific facts') and you also learn the methods by which this information can be acquired and tested.

Debates about 'science and religion' sometimes focus on *content* (what are the religious implications of the evolutionary account of human origins?) and sometimes on *method* (how does the 'scientific method' relate to other means of acquiring knowledge and understanding of the world?).

Why worry about Darwin?

There are probably four main ways in which Darwin's theory of evolution could represent a challenge to, or be thought of as incompatible with, Christian belief.

1) Challenging the *factual accuracy* of the book of Genesis.
2) Reinforcing or assuming a *materialistic account* of humanity and the world by providing a narrative of the world and of human beings that has no 'role' for God or the soul.
3) Providing a different *narrative 'shape'* for the world's history. Christian tradition has told a story of (good) creation, fall and eventual redemption. The evolutionary narrative does not obviously have a 'fall' – and its hope of 'redemption' is ambivalent.
4) Questioning the *anthropocentrism* of Christian thought, by placing human beings alongside the 'other animals' and denying them the unique status that they are generally given in Christian tradition.
5) Linking (3) and (4) – making suffering and violence essential to the process by which the creation of humans and other animals, as the particular beings they are, takes place.

Arguably, the first of these in itself is of relatively minor importance within Christian theological tradition – although, as we shall see, it has assumed great importance in science-religion 'debates'. We discuss why this might be in our section on 'biblical science'.

The second is the most important for wider debates about 'science and religion'. It invites us to ask, for example, whether the truth of a materialistic worldview can be *demonstrated* scientifically, or whether it is a (possible) *assumption* that science itself cannot justify. It also invites us to ask whether scientific and religious questions are fundamentally of different kinds – or whether there are any questions to which both 'science' and 'religion' provide answers. These are questions about scientific method, and 'science' in general. Our next section looks at how they arise in modernity.

The third, fourth and fifth suggest that evolutionary theory (and perhaps other scientific theories) could lead theologians to rethink what they say – not just to account for some additional 'facts', but to engage with different visions of the world and humanity. These are questions about scientific content and the findings of particular sciences. Our final section looks at some of the ways in which theologians have engaged with scientific accounts of the world and humanity.

Modernity and the science/religion split

Huxley's response to Wilberforce seems to take for granted that scientific and religious questions can be separated. As we saw in the Introduction, the development of scientific method and the extension of scientific research was a key feature of modernity. But why did this development lead to the separation – at least in many people's perception – of scientific and religious knowledge?

It is easy to see how some of the trends we have identified in modern religious thought might pull religious questions away from scientific questions. We have seen the effects of the 'turn to the subject' in theology. Many of the key thinkers we have studied locate knowledge of God in the human subject, and some explicitly deny that knowledge about God can be gained from the study of the natural world. Consider, for example, Kant's rejection of the cosmological argument. We could argue that Kant's way of doing theology set the scene for a split between science (dealing with the world and nature) and theology (dealing with the human subject, freedom and morality).

> Philip Clayton, in his essay on 'Theology and the Physical Sciences' (David F. Ford with Rachel Muers (eds), *The Modern Theologians*, 3rd edition (Oxford: Blackwell, 2004) pp342–356) argues that 'the modern turn to the human subject ... artificially reduced the scope of theological reflection' and made productive theological engagement with the natural sciences much harder (p342).

It is certainly worth bearing the 'turn to the subject' in mind when we think about the major 'science and religion' controversies of the nineteenth and twentieth centuries – which have focused on scientific developments that affect our understanding of what *human beings* are. (Note that the spark for the confrontation between Huxley and Wilberforce was, in the end, not the interpretation of Genesis but the question of human dignity – was your grandmother an ape?) However, we have already seen that in the first half of the nineteenth century, at least in Britain, it was far from obvious that science and religion were answering different questions or that religion had nothing to do with understanding the natural world. The clergyman-naturalist could draw on the hugely influential work of William Paley (1743–1805), who eloquently presented the natural world, in all its complexity and beauty, as a testimony to the goodness and power of the God who designed and created it.

> Paley is most often cited for his 'watch analogy', advanced in his *Natural Theology* (London: Faulder, 1802) – the argument that the order and complexity of the universe can be compared, on a much larger scale, to the order and complexity of a machine such as a watch. If we found and studied a watch, noting its order and complexity, we would infer that it must have been designed by an intelligent being; and the same inference can be made about the universe as a whole.
>
> A parallel argument is presented – and critiqued – in David Hume's *Dialogues Concerning Natural Religion* (Edinburgh, 1779).

The gradual discovery, in the mid-nineteenth century, of evidence for the extinction of species – a process of discovery that began well before Darwin – would not have caused so much concern among those Christians who heard about it, had it not been for the popularity of Paley's natural theology. What could this theology say about fossils? Where had these extinct species fitted into God's well-ordered 'machine' and why had they been allowed to disappear? The whole idea of a *history* of nature, even before Darwin, challenged an established way of thinking about 'science and religion' – and about the world as a whole and humanity's place in it. The first significant controversy of this kind in England surrounded the (anonymous) publication of Robert Chambers' *Vestiges of the Natural History of Creation* (London: John Churchill, 1844).

Note that what was at issue here was not (only or mainly) the accuracy of the book of Genesis, but rather a theological worldview – a story of the world, to use the terms we gave above. The story of a stable natural order created and maintained by a divine designer was becoming hard to maintain. This did not only make the work of the Christian botanist or zoologist more complicated; it had major social and moral implications. Was it possible any more to see God as authorising and upholding a stable social order, or a stable set of moral values?

When Cecil Alexander wrote the hymn 'All Things Bright and Beautiful' in 1848, she gave voice to a powerful (and already threatened) vision of divinely-created order – in the social as well as the natural world.

> Each little flower that opens,
> Each little bird that sings,
> [God] made their glowing colours,
> He made their tiny wings ...
> The rich man in his castle,
> The beggar at his gate,
> God made them high or lowly,
> And ordered their estate ...

In the rest of this chapter, we examine some more recent examples of encounters – positive and negative – between scientific and religious thought. In each case, we will see that a straightforward separation of 'science' and 'religion' is very difficult to maintain, but so is the assumption that they deal with the same questions or can be forced into each other's service.

Biblical science?

Late twentieth- and early twenty-first-century discussions of the 'science and religion' debate have tended to focus on conservative, and particularly fundamentalist, Protestantism as the main source of religious opposition to evolutionary science. This focus has much to do with the legacy of the famous 'Scopes Monkey Trial' of 1925 in Dayton, Tennessee. The biology teacher John Scopes, responding to a call by the American Civil Liberties Union (ACLU), stood trial in a test case. The ACLU set up the case to challenge a recently-enacted state law that forbade the teaching of 'any theory that denies the story of the Divine Creation of man as taught in the Bible'. William Jennings Bryan, a leader of the **fundamentalist** movement and a prominent Democratic politician, who had worked for the introduction of the anti-evolution law, was among the prosecution lawyers; Clarence Darrow led the defence team. In the trial's most famous incident, Darrow called Bryan himself as a witness and questioned him on the literal interpretation of the Bible, seeking to expose the illogicalities in his claims about the Bible's historical accuracy. In the event, Scopes was found guilty, but after an appeal the case was eventually dismissed by the state's Supreme Court.

Figure 11.2 Defence attorney Clarence Darrow leans against a table during the 'Scopes Monkey Trial'. John Scopes is seated to Darrow's right with his arms folded

Comparing this incident with the Oxford meeting of 1860, we can see that the 'clash between science and religion' (again, if such it is) took a very different form, because of the involvement of a self-declared fundamentalist, committed to the historical – and 'scientific' – accuracy of the Bible and basing his case against evolution on that wider claim about the Bible. Although – as at the Oxford meeting – there was some discussion of the scientific arguments for belief in evolution, with some zoologists being called to give evidence, the real focus, unlike in Oxford, was on the 'truth' or otherwise of the Bible.

In the USA and increasingly in Europe, the teaching of evolutionary theory in schools – as scientific fact, see above – remains an area of controversy. The discussion often assumes a clear separation between 'science' and 'religion', as two separate areas of the curriculum – and then focuses on what topics and theories properly belong under each heading. (For example: should any account of the origins of species other than evolution be taught *as science* – or only as religion?)

But it was not always obvious to Christians that a very high view of the literal accuracy of the Bible, as a guide to the history and prehistory of the world, was incompatible with evolutionary theory. Although Charles Hodge (see Chapter 8) famously ended his treatise *What is Darwinism?* with the conclusion 'Darwinism ... is atheism', not all his followers shared his view. Most notably, Benjamin B. Warfield, the originator (with A.A. Hodge) of the key fundamentalist doctrine of the Bible's inerrancy through 'plenary verbal inspiration', saw no incompatibility between the Bible and Darwin's theories. Warfield also wrote a spiritual biography of Darwin, tracing Darwin's abandonment of Christianity and his movement towards agnosticism.

Warfield's willingness to accept evolutionary theory is less surprising if we consider his overall approach to the Bible. He and his fellow Princeton theologians were committed to judging the Bible as an accurate and reliable source of *information*, data, about the world and its history. Biblical interpretation, for them, was basically a scientific process. They had the data – first and foremost the biblical data but also any other data about the world and its history that might be obtained by other means – and their task was to formulate theories that would explain the data, as adequately as possible. Warfield, then, assumed that one of his tasks, as an interpreter of the Bible, was to reconcile it with the best scientific evidence available.

Note, however, that all Warfield was prepared to say about evolution was that it did not *conflict* with the Bible (and hence with Christian belief); it was theologically neutral. In keeping with what he took to be a good scientific approach, he recognised that others might find different ways of bringing together the Bible and the available natural evidence. His main mechanism for reconciling evolution and a strong view of biblical inerrancy was a belief that God works *in and through* the processes of nature. For him, biblical claims that God caused something to happen do not exclude the possibility that it happened by 'natural' means. Indeed, his understanding of how the Bible itself came to be written gave him a model for how to reconcile evolution and divine creation; the Bible is, for Warfield, entirely the work of human authors and *also* entirely – in all its details – the work of God.

So, we see that the strand in the Christian tradition from which the most well-publicised religious opposition to evolutionary science has come – fundamentalism, and conservative evangelicalism more generally – is also from its outset committed to *scientific methods*. This strand of Christianity takes an unusually 'scientific' view of the task of biblical interpretation, at least where texts about creation are concerned. The Bible provides a body of reliable data, to be placed alongside the data that our senses receive as we examine the natural world. All this data together enables the formulation of accounts of the emergence of the world we see around us (what really took place? what caused what, when, and how?), and those accounts are to be judged by their adequacy to the data.

Note that, for this approach, the biblical data is not simply a heap of raw observations; it is taken to have been selected, organised, interpreted and presented by someone who knows the whole truth, so we can expect it to be the most relevant data for our reconstructions. The natural data, on the other hand, frequently comes to us distorted by fallible (and often godless) scientists, who have their own prejudices and presuppositions – so what is ordinarily called 'scientific' data needs to be treated with great caution. 'Creation science', or **'creationism'**, arises from this approach – claiming to offer alternative, scientific accounts of the origins of the world and of species that conflict neither with the Bible nor with the other available evidence. As Harriet Harris puts it, Christian anti-evolutionists sometimes treat 'religion as science', using scientific methods in the interpretation of the Bible and interpreting scientific data within religious frameworks, and sometimes treat 'science as religion', emphasising the extent to which science is based on unprovable beliefs (Harriet Harris, *Fundamentalism and Evangelicals*, Oxford: Oxford University Press, 1998).

Religion, science and the 'new atheism'

Richard Dawkins' early-twenty-first-century bestseller *The God Delusion* (Oxford: Bantam, 2006) owes much, both to Huxley's attack on Wilberforce and the 'tradition' to which it gave rise, and to other scientific challenges to religion in the nineteenth century (notably that of Freud – see below). The core of Dawkins' argument for the falsity of religious belief, however, relies on a characterisation of religion as – in effect – bad, failed or mistaken science. Dawkins suggests that the only *justification* of religious belief worth taking seriously would be that the existence of God provided a good explanation for general features of the world that would otherwise be inexplicable. Religious belief, in other words, stands or falls by its *explanatory* power; the existence of God is like a scientific hypothesis.

We would suggest that the most interesting dialogues between scholars of religion (including theologians) and proponents of the 'new atheism' are likely to begin from a historically-informed discussion of how the whole 'science and religion' debate came to be set up in terms of competing explanatory hypotheses – and whether this is the best way to characterise or evaluate religion.

Scientific suspicion: Freud and the future of an illusion

At least in the twentieth century, then, the 'evolution debates' have tended to focus on one strand in Christian tradition and a few aspects of religion – conservative evangelicalism and, within that, attitudes to the Bible. Looking at the nineteenth and twentieth centuries more widely, however, we find 'scientific' challenges to religion that potentially affect a wider range of religious claims and stances. In this section, we look at one of the most influential examples of such a challenge.

Sigmund Freud (1856–1939) was ranked by Paul Ricoeur alongside Nietzsche, Marx and Feuerbach as one of the 'masters of suspicion'; Freud himself saw his work on religion as following on closely from Nietzsche's. Like Nietzsche, he found the sources of religion in human weakness and saw its persistence as a sign of humanity's distorted desire to remain weak and enslaved.

Where Freud differed from Nietzsche was in his claim that his suspicious account of religion was based on *science*. Psychoanalysis, the approach to studying the human mind that Freud developed and practised, was a science. It could be used to develop a scientific account – based on evidence, using known theories and (at least in principle) testable and falsifiable – of why people are religious and how religion affects them. We could contrast this with Nietzsche's attitude to 'science', which he placed alongside Christianity and Platonism, as another quest for the 'real world' that is in fact an attempt to run away from reality.

Freud published several distinct but interrelated psychoanalytic accounts of the origins of religion. *Moses and Monotheism* (1939) and *Totem and Taboo* (1913) both, in different ways, locate the origin of religion in guilt – the desires that people learn to suppress, the sense of prohibition and guilt that they internalise. *The Future of an Illusion* (1927) is a more general, 'popular' work on religion. Its central idea is that religious belief is wish-fulfilment (illusion); people are inevitably led to believe that things *really are* as they would *like them to be*. Religious belief arises from people's wishes for order, meaning and comfort in a chaotic, meaningless and cruel world; the wishes give rise to the conviction of truth.

Figure 11.3 Sigmund Freud

Unlike some of his later followers (see our comments on Richard Dawkins, above), Freud does not label religion a *delusion*. Calling something a delusion implies that we *know* it is untrue. Freud is careful to state that his analysis of religion as illusion proves nothing about its truth. As he suggests, using a rather dated example: a middle-class girl dreams of escaping her humdrum lot and starts to believe that she will marry a prince one day. Now, of course, this *may* turn out to be true ('commoners' do sometimes marry princes) but, irrespective of its truth, the girl's belief is still an illusion, because it arises from her wish and not from evidence. Likewise, it *might* turn out to be true that God exists, and is as religious people have thought God to be – but this would, Freud comments dryly, be a remarkable coincidence.

Note the challenges that this 'suspicious' reading raises for attempts to locate the knowledge of God in morality, or indeed in any kind of subjective experience or feeling. Freud's mode of suspicion – as he takes it up and develops it from Nietzsche – is particularly challenging to those theologies that base themselves on the human subject as the source of knowledge of God. Just as Darwinism provides a story of how the human *species* (together with all other species) came to be as it is, Freud claims to provide a story of how the human *subject,* religious feelings and all, came to be as it is. And, like Darwin's story of the origin of species, Freud's story of the origin of the religious subject has no need for God. Freud claimed to find a scientific explanation for the existence and persistence of religion, and hence to demolish any attempt to argue *from religion to God*.

There is an irony in what Freud does here – an irony that was not lost on him. He takes apart the human subject, unveiling its irrationalities and self-deceptions; but in doing that he also calls into question the free, rational subject of the Enlightenment, the subject who could reshape life on the basis of reasoned and scientific arguments – such as Freud's. If he undermines the subject of modern theology, he also undermines the subject of modern science. So, he begins *Future of an Illusion* with an account of why human beings, in their great and unavoidable irrationality, need religious illusion in order to avoid collapsing into individual and social chaos; and he ends it expressing the hope that his work will help to bring about the end of religious illusion. The tension is hard to overcome.

Again, compare this with Nietzsche – who is much harder to accuse of this kind of internal tension or contradiction, because he rejects the scientific worldview (and the vision of the human being that goes with it) along with the religious worldview.

There have been several further scientific theories of religion that propose accounts of the 'natural' – psychological, neurological or biological– origins of religious belief.

In studying and evaluating them, it is worth asking with what definition of 'religion' they are working – and what, exactly, any of them are saying about *God*. Several later writers have combined 'arguments against God' with 'suspicion of religion' but the two are, in fact, logically independent.

Changing the story: a few examples

We noted earlier that at least some of the challenges that Darwinian theory posed to Christian thought might appropriately produce *theological* responses – attempts to rethink Christian claims and narratives in the light of these new developments. The same could be said of other major scientific developments in the nineteenth and twentieth centuries. In other words, 'religion and science' is not just the name of a debate – it is also a source of new religious thought.

> There is a very extensive literature on contemporary issues in religion and science, which we have not attempted to cover in detail here – see the Bibliography for examples. The introductory chapters by Clayton and Deane-Drummond are particularly good starting-points, as is the collection edited by Southgate.

To return to our central example – in the case of Darwin's theories, the process of rethinking Christian thought began very early. There were prominent Christian thinkers in Britain who welcomed Darwin's work. Among them was the prominent Christian Socialist Charles Kingsley (now perhaps best known as the author of *The Water Babies*). The defences of Darwin mounted by Kingsley and those who agreed with him were twofold – first, they claimed that the doctrine of creation was unaffected by Darwinian theory; and, second, they claimed that Darwinian theory enabled Christians to tell a *better* story of creation, one more true to basic biblical and traditional insights about the nature of God and the world.

> Charles Kingsley corresponded with Darwin both about scientific questions and about the public reception of Darwinian theory. In one of his letters, which Darwin quoted in the introduction to the second edition of *On the Origin of Species*, Kingsley expressed his conviction that 'it is just as noble a conception of the Deity to believe that He created a few original forms capable of self-development into other and needful forms, as to believe that He required a fresh act of

creation to supply the voids caused by the action of His laws'. In other words, for Kingsley, a God who created *through* evolution made as much sense, or more sense, as a God who created each species individually.

Kingsley's correspondence with Darwin is available through the Darwin Correspondence Project: <www.darwinproject.ac.uk>.

The debate over *On the Origin of Species*, published in 1859, was nearly eclipsed by the debate over *Essays and Reviews*, published in 1860. This collection of essays by prominent Anglican clergy and scholars featured one of the first public expositions of theology 'after Darwin'. In his essay, Baden Powell described *On the Origin of Species* as a 'masterly volume', and argued that God as the supreme lawgiver must create, or allow the world to develop, through law-governed processes – such as evolution.

Another of the contributors to *Essays and Reviews*, Frederick Temple, who later became Archbishop of Canterbury, argued for the compatibility of Christianity and evolutionary theory in an influential series of public lectures in the 1880s. Temple suggested that Darwinian theory could allow us to perceive 'purpose' in natural processes of change, which otherwise might seem random and directionless; but he devoted more time to arguing that the Genesis texts and Darwinian theory were produced for completely different purposes, to answer different questions and to serve different human needs.

See Frederick Temple, *The Relations between Religion and Science* (1884), available online through the Gutenberg Project: <www.gutenberg.org/files/17194/17194-h/17194-h.htm>.

One of the best-known defenders of Darwinism in America was the botanist and evangelical Christian Asa Gray. For Gray, as for the Christian Socialists, Darwin's theory was not only compatible with Christianity – it could, rightly interpreted, positively support Christian faith. Gray devoted considerable energy to refuting the challenges to Darwinism by Charles Hodge and others – to demonstrating that Darwinism was not 'atheism', and that it made as much sense to regard a whole evolutionary process as the work of God, as to posit God's agency in an initial creation of fixed species.

Gray also particularly welcomed Darwin's demonstration that humanity constituted a *single species*. In the 1860s, in the middle of controversies over slavery, this gave further support to the abolitionists' cause in the face of various attempts to demonstrate, sometimes on biblical grounds, that Africans and whites were different species and that to accord full 'human' rights and status to Africans was therefore unjustified.

See Asa Gray, 'Natural Selection Not Inconsistent with Natural Theology', *Atlantic Monthly* 1860 (reprinted 1861) – available online at <www.darwinproject.ac.uk/gray-essay-natural-selection-natural-theology>.

For more on Darwin and abolitionism, see James Moore and Adrian Desmond, 'Introduction' to Darwin, *The Descent of Man*, Penguin Classics edition (London: Penguin, 2004).

A key area of disagreement between Gray and Darwin himself was over the question of suffering in the evolutionary process. As we have noted, for Darwin, and for many who read his work, the fact that suffering was integral to evolution placed in question the existence of a benevolent creator. Gray, on the other hand, argued that the waste and suffering undoubtedly found in nature might, on a Darwinian view, have a *purpose* – it might form part of the process whereby the species we now know, including humanity, come into being. Thus, for Gray, evolutionary theory offered a new way to make sense of suffering.

The idea that evolutionary theory might contribute to **theodicy** (see Chapter 13) – or alternatively, that evolutionary theory poses new and very difficult problems for theodicy – has had a long subsequent history. Pierre Teilhard de Chardin (1881–1955), a Jesuit priest and a leading palaeontologist, developed a far-reaching synthesis of evolutionary thought and Christian theology in his work *The Divine Milieu*. Teilhard extended the principle of evolution to cover developments in human life and society, and argued that the end-point of the process was the unity of nature with the divine, centred on humanity through the Incarnation. In this vision, suffering within the 'evolutionary' process – *including* the suffering that human beings cause to one another – all serves to advance the cosmic process of evolution that ends with the unity of all things in God.

While aspects of Teilhard's vision have been taken up in later theology, his optimism about the meaningfulness of suffering – and the 'progress' of human history – has found relatively few supporters and has been subject to sharp ethical critique. More prominent in recent years have been theological treatments of suffering in the evolutionary process as a *problem*. How can a good God demand suffering as part of how things come to be as they are – including, as part of how *humanity* comes to be as it is? What does it mean that the incarnation of God in a human being relies, in some sense, on millennia of development-through-suffering?

One example of Christian theology's attempts to engage with the 'evolutionary theodicy' question is the work of Christopher Southgate – see his *The Groaning of Creation: God, Evolution and the Problem of Evil* (Louisville: WJK, 2007). See also the helpful overview of these issues in Celia Deane-Drummond, 'Theology and the Biological Sciences' in David F. Ford with Rachel Muers (eds), *The Modern Theologians* (Oxford: Blackwell, 2004).

Asa Gray's defences of Darwinism focused mostly, not on the issue of suffering but on the issue of divine causality. Darwinism's (supposed) 'materialism' – the tendency to explain everything in terms of material and natural causes – was, as we noted above, one of the major objections to it in the nineteenth century. Materialism in accounts of human life and origins was particularly likely to be controversial because of the great importance attached to the soul and its immortality, in nineteenth-century discussions of Christianity across the social and doctrinal spectrum. However, the debate about Darwin's 'materialism' could equally be seen as an example of a wider and more general debate about how to understand God's action in a world of material and natural causes.

This is not only a contemporary problem, and not even essentially a 'modern' problem. The nature of divine causality has been debated for much of Christian history.

Thomas Aquinas' account of primary and secondary causality – in which God is the *primary cause* of every particular created thing and action, whatever *secondary causes* act within the world to bring it about – provides the basis for numerous theological engagements with the question today.

Some contrasting examples of recent theological engagements with the issue of divine causality can illustrate how science might – or might not – be relevant to these debates.

Austin Farrer (1904–1968) was a British Anglican theologian, many of whose best-known writings focus on issues of divine action and of the relationship between scientific reason and religious faith. Farrer's consistent claim is that 'science' and 'faith' describe the *same* world and the same events – and both tell truths about this world and these events. We should not assume (as some trends in modern theology might encourage us to do) that religious language is only 'about' the human subject or morality. From a Christian point of view, Farrer argues, it has to be asserted both that events within the world have natural and material causes *and* that God causes them – and the 'joint' that links these two forms of causality, the 'means' by which God causes natural events, is inaccessible either to the scientific or the religious way of reasoning about the world.

Farrer was already saying more than many twentieth-century thinkers have been prepared to say – and bringing theology closer to scientific 'territory' – when he argued that theology was not just 'another way of speaking' about a world that science described fully (comparable, say, to poetic 'ways of speaking') but a way of saying something *true* about that world.

Farrer's work was in part a response to Rudolf Bultmann's enormously influential programme of *demythologising* Christian texts. For Bultmann, famously or notoriously, modern attitudes to science and technology force a radical rereading of biblical texts: 'it is impossible to use electric light and the wireless and to avail ourselves of modern medical and surgical discoveries, and at the same time to believe in the New Testament world of spirits and miracles' (Rudolf Bultmann, 'New Testament and Mythology', republished in Hans Werner Bartsch (ed.), *Kerygma and Myth* (London: SPCK, 1953), pp1–44, here p5).

Bultmann's solution was to reread Christian claims about God acting in the world as *mythological* – as ways of conveying a deeper truth, and of bringing people into a transformative encounter with God. They do not, properly interpreted, tell us *anything* about the natural world, let alone provide scientific data or hypotheses. They express, and bring about, a particular orientation of human life. For Bultmann, to treat these Christian stories of God's action in a 'scientific' way would be a bit like treating a love poem:

> My love is like the red, red rose
> That's newly sprung in June

as the starting-point for a new system of botanical classification.

Farrer, as we have seen, did not want to go as far as Bultmann did in separating theology and scientific discourse.

Nonetheless, for Farrer and those who follow his approach, while there is an important general conversation to be had about the nature of causality, there are no *specific* scientific claims that make it easier or harder to speak about divine causality. The problem is at the level, not of science but of the philosophy of science.

Other thinkers in the twentieth century, however, have taken developments in modern physics (in particular) as offering new ways to think about the relationships between divine action, natural causality and human free will. Quantum mechanics – on the dominant 'Copenhagen' interpretation – makes it impossible (not just accidentally impossible, but *inherently* impossible) to give a comprehensive, closed account of the natural world and the relationships within it. The best and fullest scientific descriptions of the world, in other words, will include *uncertainty*; the set of physical causes and effects that makes up the world simply cannot be fully described and predicted (and that is not because we happen not to know enough but because of how the world is). Claims both about the present state of a physical system, and about what will happen next, are claims about *probabilities*. This is not the only way of understanding the wider significance of quantum mechanics, but it is one with obvious attractions for theology. The 'laws' of natural and material causality might, on this view, be *inherently* open to God's action – in a way that scientific developments could at least point towards.

Should conversations around 'religion and science' in the twenty-first century focus on specific scientific claims or developments, or are the important discussions all at the level of philosophical theology and the philosophy of science? We would suggest that there sometimes *are* genuinely new problems, or genuinely new angles on old problems, generated from scientific developments. However, it is worth being cautious when making or assessing the claim that some specific development in 'modern science' has *radically* changed theology or made some previously-held belief impossible. Often, when we assess such claims more closely, we find that either we are talking about a shift in philosophical assumptions rather than in scientific knowledge, or the 'new' theological problem in fact has a long history. What is certain is that scientific approaches to (for example) knowledge, belief and evidence affect how theological texts are themselves read and assessed.

Bibliography

Primary texts relating to Darwin and nineteenth-century controversies

Charles Darwin, *On the Origin of Species* (orig. pub. 1859), Jim Endersby (ed.) (Cambridge: Cambridge University Press, 2009).

Charles Darwin, *The Descent of Man, and Selection in Relation to Sex* (orig. pub. 1871), James Moore and Adrian Desmond (eds) (London: Penguin, 2004).

Correspondence available online via the Darwin Correspondence Project: <www.darwinproject. ac.uk>.

Tess Cosslet (ed.), *Science and Religion in the Nineteenth Century* (Cambridge: Cambridge University Press, 1984). Very useful collection of annotated primary texts.

Victor Shea and William Whitla (eds), *Essays and Reviews: The 1860 Text and its Reading* (Charlottesville: University of Virginia Press, 2000).

Secondary reading on the nineteenth-century debates and their aftermath

P.J. Bowler, *Monkey Trials and Gorilla Sermons: Evolution and Christianity from Darwin to Intelligent Design* (Cambridge, MA: Harvard University Press, 2009).

James R. Moore *The Post-Darwinian Controversies: A Study of the Protestant Struggle to Come to Terms with Darwin in Great Britain and America, 1870–1900* (Cambridge: Cambridge University Press, 1979).

Nigel Cameron, *Biblical Higher Criticism and the Defence of Infallibilism in Nineteenth-century Britain* (Lewiston: Edwin Mellen Press, 1987). See Appendix 1 on interpretation of Genesis after Darwin.

Peter Addinall, *Philosophy and Biblical Interpretation: A Study in Nineteenth-centuy Conflict* (Cambridge: Cambridge University Press,1991). See especially Chapters 1 and 8. Despite the title, this is mainly a work on science and religion.

Richard J. Helmstadter and Bernard Lightman (eds), *Victorian Faith in Crisis: Essays on Continuity and Change in Nineteenth-century Religious Belief* (Basingstoke: Macmillan, 1990). See especially essays by Frank Turner, James Moore, George Levine – and note that Moore and Levine disagree on the form of the post-Darwinian controversies.

Ian Hesketh, *Of Apes and Ancestors: Evolution, Christianity and the Oxford Debate* (Toronto: University of Toronto Press, 2009).

Freud (primary and secondary reading)

Sigmund Freud, *The Future of an Illusion*, trans. W.D. Robson-Scott (London: Hogarth Press, 1928; revised edition, 1962).

Sigmund Freud, *Moses and Monotheism*, trans. Katherine Jones (London: Hogarth Press, 1940).

Sigmund Freud, *Totem and Taboo: Some Points of Agreement between the Mental Lives of Savages and Neurotics*, trans. James Strachey (London: Routledge, 2001).

Michael Palmer, *Freud and Jung on Religion* (London: Routledge, 1997).

R.S. Lee, *Freud and Christianity* (London: Penguin, 1967).

Douglas Shaw, *The Dissuaders: Three Explanations of Religion* (London: SCM, 1978).

More recent work: Theology and science overviews

Philip Clayton, 'Theology and the Physical Sciences', in David Ford with Rachel Muers (eds), *The Modern Theologians*, 3rd edition (Oxford: Blackwell, 2004).

Celia Deane-Drummond, 'Theology and the Biological Sciences', in David Ford with Rachel Muers (eds), *The Modern Theologians*, 3rd edition (Oxford: Blackwell, 2004).

Christopher Southgate, *The Groaning of Creation: God, Evolution and the Problem of Evil* (Louisville: WJK, 2007).

Christopher Southgate (ed.), *God, Humanity and the Cosmos: A Companion to the Science-Religion Debate* (London: T&T Clark, 2005).

R.J. Berry and Michael Northcott (eds), *Theology after Darwin* (London; Paternoster, 2009). Includes essay by Amy Laura Hall on Charles Kingsley's 'Christian Darwinism'.

Primary texts referred to in final section

Austin Farrer, *A Science of God* (orig. pub. 1966) (London: SPCK, 2009).
Teilhard de Chardin, *The Divine Milieu*, trans. Sion Cowell, ed. Thomas King (Eastbourne: Sussex Academic Press, 2003).

12

Reclaiming
Christian tradition

AIMS

By the end of this chapter, we hope that you will:

- understand some of the implications of the rise of historical consciousness for modern theology

- be familiar with some accounts of the development of doctrine

- grasp something of the role that engagement with texts from the Christian tradition played in twentieth-century theology

- understand in particular some of the debates about engagement with tradition that have shaped recent Catholic theology.

Introduction

The very term 'modern theology' suggests theology that has in some way broken with the past or is, at the very least, conscious of its difference from the theology of the past. Yet the relationship between modern theology and the patterns of Christian thought and practice that characterised earlier generations of the church has been understood in very different ways by modern theologians. In this chapter, we will be looking at a number of different ideas about the relation between present theology and the past that were influential in the nineteenth and twentieth centuries. We will begin by examining the growth and impact in the nineteenth century of the idea that the history of Christian theology has been one of constant change – and various attempts that were made to identify what might have remained constant through all that change. That investigation will take us back to some figures we have already examined – such as Kant, Schleiermacher and Hodge – but also on to new figures, most notably John Henry Newman. The chapter will then move on to look at some of the ways in which these questions were answered in the twentieth century, particularly in Catholic theology – and will find that any attempt to portray modern theology as caught in a straightforward tension between faithfulness to the past and openness to the future is far too simplistic.

Historical consciousness

Chapter 10, on the Bible, has already described some aspects of the rise of historical consciousness and its impact on modern theology. That rise affected more than simply theologians' attitudes to the Bible, however. It affected their attitudes to everything that had happened in Christianity since the Bible as well. Nineteenth- and twentieth-century theology was deeply shaped by the growing realisation that all the institutions, all the patterns of worship, all the ideas, all the ways of seeing and feeling that constituted the Christianity of the present had a history. They had changed over time, in complex and sometimes uncomfortable ways, and it was not an easy matter to say whether anything about them had remained constant amid all that change.

> Recall the discussion of Nietzsche and his genealogical method in Chapter 7. Nietzsche was deeply invested in the idea that ideas have a history – and that their history has often taken the form of a power-struggle.

The seeds of this growing historical consciousness were planted well before the period this book covers – after all 'historical consciousness' is itself a set of ideas and attitudes that have a long and complex history. Particularly significant for our purposes were polemical debates between Protestants and Catholics in the period after the Reformation – debates that were still going strong in the nineteenth century. It was important to many Protestants to be able to show that Catholic Christianity was a corruption of the original purity of New Testament Christianity or the Christianity of the early centuries of the Church. Protestants needed both to be able to tell the story of that corruption – a development of doctrine and practice away from purity – and to be able to claim that the Protestant reforms had returned Christianity to its roots. On the other hand, it was important to many Catholics to show both that Protestantism was a deviation from the Christianity of the past thousand years and more, and that the Protestant Churches were themselves changeable and inconstant. The unintended result was that a huge amount of energy was devoted to the examination of Christian history with an eye to the discovery of continuities and discontinuities, with every claim about continuity needing to establish itself against polemical claims about discontinuity.

Unsurprisingly, given the polemical investments just described, the idea that the institutions and ideas of the Christian religion have been subject to constant change took hold more quickly on the Protestant side of the debate than on the Catholic – but the idea of digging down to original purity behind later corruptions, once set loose, proved to be difficult to contain. As we have seen in Chapter 10, critics of mainstream Protestant Christianity in the eighteenth century, and many voices within that mainstream in the nineteenth, pushed the quest for original purity all the way back, not just *to* the Bible, but *within* the Bible. They searched for the original purity of Jesus' message behind the misrepresentations and corruptions produced even by those early followers who wrote the biblical texts.

In this way, modern theological thinking about the past among Protestants was often shaped by a quest for purity in which change was seen as decay, and what was earlier was, almost by definition, purer. From this perspective, to move forward – reforming the Church, its practice and doctrine, purifying it from corruptions and distortions – it was first necessary to look backward. Think, for instance, of Adolf von Harnack (see Chapter 10), arguing that Jesus' original message about love of God and neighbour is the pure core of Christianity, often hidden behind layer upon layer of later developments, but still visible to those with the eyes to see. In such hands, historical criticism is a tool with which to purify the Church.

The search for original purity, however, is only one form of a more general response to the rise of the idea of mutability in Christian teaching. Many modern theologians and philosophers have responded by claiming that there remains something stable, unchanging or invariant throughout all the change. We have already seen various different ways in which such a claim might be made. We have, for instance, seen that Immanuel Kant, in *The Conflict of the Faculties* (Chapter 3), distinguished between the 'vehicle' of religious tradition (the mutable external trappings) and the 'core' (the pure and constant religion of reason that, at their best, those external trappings helped to teach to less philosophically-minded audiences). We have also seen that Charles Hodge (Chapter 8) was convinced that 'all true people of God *in every age* and *in every part* of the Church ... agree as to the meaning of Scripture in all things necessary either in faith or practice' (*Systematic Theology*, New York: Scribner, 1873, vol 1, p188). Hodge's systematic theology can be seen as an attempt to set out the teachings that have remained constant for properly orthodox Christians in the midst of all historical changes.

We have also seen that for Friedrich Schleiermacher (Chapter 4), the constant factor behind the changes and developments of Christian history is a deep-seated, pervasive 'feeling' that provides Christianity's particular way of experiencing relation to God (though you may recall how complex a notion 'feeling' is for him). For Schleiermacher, the institutions, words and patterns of life that characterise Christianity in any given time and place are an expression of that 'feeling' – and those institutions, words and patterns of life are only understood properly when they are understood together as an attempt to express and preserve that feeling. Stephen Sykes, analysing Schleiermacher's view of what it is that is constant in the changing life of Christianity, writes:

> For him, the identity of Christianity does not consist in a specifiable quantum of propositions handed down invariably in a particular community from generation to generation [cf. Hodge]; nor can it simply be constructed out of a reading of certain infallible texts. It consists, rather, in the perception and maintenance of a particular mode of faith (*Glaubensweise*) which permeates the whole, and causes the whole to cohere as a whole.
>
> Sykes, *The Identity of Christianity*, p86.

Schleiermacher's thinking about the mutability of Christianity in history was in some ways characteristic of the Romantic movement (see Chapter 4). One of the characteristic emphases of Romanticism was on identifying the spirit (or *Geist*) of a particular people and time, the basic shape of imagination and thought that gave the artistic output of that time and place its recognisable flavour and coherence. Spirit was thought of as something living, growing and evolving – something organic, to which change and development were neither foreign nor necessarily injurious.

Although Romanticism often did venerate the early – the primitive, original, youthful spirit of peoples now grown old and too sophisticated – it was also open to the idea of the development of *Geist* as growth or maturation. Hegel's account of the development of *Geist* (see Chapter 5) was one of the most thoroughgoing accounts of such maturation and it was deeply shaped by this Romantic pattern of thought. Here, change need not mean decay and corruption, nor need it be interpreted as the purely secondary expression of what was primary and constant. Change could instead be seen as the growing to maturity of early seeds. But how was one to tell the difference between appropriate organic growth and corruption?

Johann Gottfried Herder (1744–1803) was a German poet, philosopher and theologian. He was fascinated by the idea that the study of history need not simply be a study of events and external political changes, but could be a study of *inner* history: a study of changing patterns of imagination, moral sense and feeling. He was convinced that there were deep differences between the inner quality of different times and places, but that a story of organic development could sometimes be told about the changing spirit of a people over time. Herder's thinking on this point was deeply influential on later German thinkers.

Newman on development

Possibly the figure most closely associated with the idea of development of doctrine (i.e., the development of the Church's teachings) is a figure from a very different intellectual tradition from that of Kant, Schleiermacher and Hegel. John Henry Newman (1801–1890) was an Oxford don and Anglican priest who became one of the leading lights in the Oxford Movement, which was dedicated to fighting against changes in the Church that the members of the movement perceived as weakening its Christian distinctiveness and authority. Newman and others associated with the Oxford Movement had a strong sense of Anglicanism's continuity with the medieval and patristic heritage of the Church, and of its difference from forms of Protestantism that had broken with that heritage. They were convinced that renewal of the Church's distinctiveness and authority would come in part by a reconnection to medieval and patristic patterns of liturgy and devotion that had been lost or watered down since the Reformation.

The question of continuity and change in Christian history concerned Newman deeply. In the course of his academic work and as part of his involvement in the Oxford Movement, he had studied the history of Christianity (especially the patristic period) very closely. He had become convinced that there was indeed a development in the teaching and practice of the Church, and that even doctrines now regarded as central and secure had emerged slowly in the course of a long period of doctrinal development. His research did not lead him to agree with those who argued that it was only the process of formal public definition that had taken place over a long period, but that the doctrines themselves had always been taught to and believed by

Figure 12.1 John Henry Newman

the faithful. Nor did it lead him to believe that the process was simply one of logical unpacking – the identification by later generations of teachings logically entailed by teachings already securely held by earlier generations and so already implicit in their beliefs. And yet he was not remotely attracted by the radical Protestant solution of declaring that all development was corruption, and that only the original practice and belief of the Church, prior to all development, was faithful.

Newman instead came to believe that the truths originally revealed to the Church were not simple propositions that needed only to be understood clearly in order to be grasped completely. They were deep mysteries, which yielded slowly to prayerful pondering. In Luke 2:19, Mary, on being told by the shepherds what the angels had said about her son, 'treasured all these words and pondered them in her heart' – and Newman believed that, in the same way, the Church treasured the teachings it was given and pondered them in its heart over centuries. In particular, the Church pondered how the various things that had been revealed to it cohered, how they added up into a unified picture of God and God's dealings with the world. This process of pondering involved the Church allowing its understanding of each of its teachings to be qualified and adjusted by its relation to all of the others, as each teaching steadied the Church's understanding of all the others to which it connected. The mystery of each teaching was plumbed more fully as it was drawn into closer relation to all the others.

According to Newman, this process of doctrinal development was slow and organic, and it was not always easy to tell whether any particular development was a genuine insight into the truth or a deviation from it. Newman believed, however, that over time it is possible to see whether any particular development becomes deeply embedded in the life of the Church, whether it enables the Church to hold more securely to all the other teachings it has inherited, whether it enables the Church to live faithfully to those teachings amid all the challenges it faces, and whether it allows the Church to do justice to whatever it finds that is good and valuable in the world around it.

> Newman sets out seven criteria (or 'notes') meant to enable us to distinguish between true and false developments: (1) preservation of type; (2) continuity of principles; (3) power of assimilation; (4) logical sequence; (5) anticipation of its future; (6) conservative action upon its past; and (7) chronic vigour. The chapter in which he sets out these notes can be found online at <www.newmanreader.org/works/development/chapter5.html>. Read it through carefully. Do these notes, as Newman hoped, provide a basis for fair judgement, enabling us 'to discriminate healthy developments of an idea from its state of corruption and decay'?

Newman set out his views in 1845 in his *Essay on the Development of Christian Doctrine*. Shortly thereafter he left the Anglican Church and was received into the Catholic Church, which he had come to believe exhibited a pattern of doctrinal development more faithful to the heritage of the apostles. Yet he did not fundamentally alter his view on the subject of development once he was a Catholic, and that made him something of a controversial figure in his new Church, as the idea of development was very much less well established in the Catholic circles than it was amongst Protestants. Many of Newman's new Catholic colleagues wondered whether he had done sufficient justice to their sense that their Church, unlike the Churches of their Protestant rivals, was protecting the full deposit of revealed doctrine against corruption.

Part of the journey that Newman took from Anglicanism to Catholicism, however, was his growing belief that the process of doctrinal development – slow, organic, ongoing – needed to be accompanied by an authority capable of regulating it. He saw the need for an authority that could, on the one hand, spot developments that were undermining the faith as a whole and condemn them, and, on the other, recognise developments that had proved themselves indispensable and give them formal definition and permanent authority. The Church, in other words, needed to have a teaching office that could be relied upon to get these things right, and that was fully trustworthy. In this way, the development of Newman's understanding of the organic growth of doctrine went hand in hand with the development of his understanding of the need for an infallible teaching office – a pope – in the Church. If God had given the kind of revelation that required slow pondering over time, and that lent itself to organic growth rather than to simple logical explication, then God must also have given the means by which that organic growth could be pruned and secured for the sake of the Church's long-term health.

On 18 July 1870, at the fourth session of the First Vatican Council – the first worldwide (or 'ecumenical') council of the Catholic Church to be held since the Council of Trent in the sixteenth century – the following pronouncement was made on papal infallibility:

1. That apostolic primacy which the Roman pontiff possesses as successor of Peter, the prince of the apostles, includes also the supreme power of teaching ...

3. To satisfy this pastoral office, our predecessors strove unwearyingly that the saving teaching of Christ should be spread among all the peoples of the world; and with equal care they made sure that it should be kept pure and uncontaminated wherever it was received ...

5. The Roman pontiffs ... as the circumstances of the time or the state of affairs suggested, sometimes by summoning ecumenical councils or consulting the opinion of the churches scattered throughout the world, sometimes by special synods, sometimes by taking advantage of other useful means afforded by divine providence, defined as doctrines to be held those things which, by God's help, they knew to be in keeping with sacred scripture and the apostolic traditions.

6. For the holy Spirit was promised to the successors of Peter not so that they might, by his revelation, make known some new doctrine, but that, by his assistance, they might religiously guard and faithfully expound the revelation or deposit of faith transmitted by the apostles ...

9. Therefore ... we teach and define as a divinely revealed dogma that when the Roman pontiff speaks *ex cathedra*, that is, when, in the exercise of his office as shepherd and teacher of all Christians, in virtue of his supreme apostolic authority, he defines a doctrine concerning faith or morals to be held by the whole church, he possesses, by the divine assistance promised to him in blessed Peter, that infallibility which the divine Redeemer willed his church to enjoy in defining doctrine concerning faith or morals.

> Therefore, such definitions of the Roman pontiff are of themselves, and not by the consent of the church, irreformable. So then, should anyone, which God forbid, have the temerity to reject this definition of ours: let him be anathema.
>
> Translated in Norman Tanner, *Decrees of the Ecumenical Councils: From Nicaea I to Vatican II* (Washington: Georgetown, 1990), vol 2, pp815–816.

Twentieth-century Catholicism

Newman's ideas about development proved very influential, both within and beyond the Catholic Church; but they also remained controversial. The images of organic development and of the long and productive pondering of a multi-faceted mystery, were powerful ones, but it was not clear whether Newman had given a plausible account of the difference between a faithful and an unfaithful development. Controversy flared around exactly this question in the decades after Newman's death, as well as around a related question: what can and what cannot be reformed about the Church, if the Church is to remain faithful to its heritage? Newman's insistence on development was taken up – and itself developed – by a range of Catholic intellectuals who came to be called 'Modernists'.

> One of the most significant of these intellectuals was Alfred Loisy (1857–1940), a French Catholic theologian. Influenced by Newman, but also writing in opposition to Harnack's view of Catholic developments as corruptions, Loisy put forward an account of development that was more clearly directed towards enabling reform in the present. He articulated this view most notably in his 1902 work, *The Gospel and the Church*. He was excommunicated in 1908.

Pope Pius X published the encyclical *Pascendi Dominici Gregis* in 1907, condemning 'the doctrines of the Modernists' – including the idea that 'Dogma is not only able, but ought to evolve and to be changed', or, more specifically, the idea that dogmas are the partial and inadequate external expressions of inward religious truths and might need to be reformulated or revised in response to the changing patterns of external history in order to inculcate the same inward truth.

A Belgian Cardinal, Désiré Joseph Mercier, wrote a pastoral letter explaining the meaning of the pope's encyclical to his diocese. His encyclical prompted a response from one of the writers he had named as a Modernist: George Tyrrell (1861–1909), who had been expelled from the Jesuit order in 1906 for his views. Tyrrell's *Medievalism: A Reply to Cardinal Mercer*, is one of the key texts of Catholic Modernism. In it he writes:

> 'Modernist' ... means the acknowledgment on the part of religion ... of the need of effecting a synthesis, not between the old and new indiscriminately, but between what, after due criticism, is found to be valid in the old and in the new. Its opposite is Medievalism, which, as a fact, is only the synthesis effected between the Christian faith and the culture of the late Middle Ages, but which erroneously supposes itself to be of apostolic antiquity.
>
> Tyrrell, *Medievalism: A Reply to Cardinal Mercer*, pp143–144.

He continues:

> The modernist is a Catholic with a difference. What is this difference? The difference is that whereas the Medievalist regards the expression of Catholicism, formed by the synthesis between faith and the general culture of the thirteenth century, as primitive and as practically final and exhaustive, the Modernist denies the possibility of such finality and holds that the task is unending just because the process of culture is unending.
>
> Tyrrell, *Medievalism: A Reply to Cardinal Mercer*, pp146–147.

In 1910, Pope Pius created an oath 'to be sworn to by all clergy, pastors, confessors, preachers, religious superiors, and professors in philosophical-theological seminaries'. It included the following clause:

> I sincerely hold that the doctrine of faith was handed down to us from the apostles through the orthodox Fathers in exactly the same meaning and always in the same purport. Therefore, I entirely reject the heretical misrepresentation that dogmas evolve and change from one meaning to another different from the one which the Church held previously. I also condemn every error according to which, in place of the divine deposit which has been given to the spouse of Christ to be carefully guarded by her, there is put a philosophical figment or product of a human conscience that has gradually been developed by human effort and will continue to develop indefinitely.
>
> 'The Oath Against Modernism', available at
> <www.papalencyclicals.net/Pius10/p10moath.htm>.

The oath remained a requirement for Catholic clergy and teachers until 1967 – though it is fair to say that, during that time (and even when it was published) it did not represent the full breadth or liveliness of Catholic thinking on these topics. Nevertheless, the dominant atmosphere in Catholic theology in the early decades of the twentieth century, influenced by the teaching of Vatican I and expressed in documents such as this oath, was one of adherence to a firmly fixed tradition of teaching, in which later official clarification and explication simply guarded against errors in the interpretation of earlier materials – errors that might be generated as the result of a partial or one-sided grasp of the deposit of revelation or an inappropriate adherence to impious philosophies.

During this period, mainstream Catholic teaching was dominated by 'neo-scholasticism' – a training in philosophy and theology centred on textbooks containing a carefully refined version of the teachings of the great medieval theologian Thomas Aquinas (1225–1274). The tenor of this neo-scholasticism can be judged by the fact that it was possible for the French theologian, Marie-Dominique Chenu (1895–1990), to be dismissed from teaching in a Dominican seminary in the 1940s for teaching that Aquinas should properly be understood in his own cultural-historical context, rather than as the source of a system that – with suitable later clarifications and explications – could now be considered timelessly valid (see Fergus Kerr, *Twentieth Century Catholic Theologians*, Chapter 2). Such attitudes perhaps also explain the shape taken by the most prominent movement of reaction *against* neo-scholasticism. Rather than taking 'modernism' as its watchword, it promoted the idea of a 'return to the sources': *ressourcement*. Thinkers associated with *ressourcement* believed that renewal and reform for Catholic theology would come not by severing ties with the past, but by a deeper and richer engagement with it – engagement with figures from the past in their own terms rather than as names attached to a unified and timeless synthesis.

Ressourcement was one of the watchwords of a movement in Catholic thought that has become known as *Nouvelle Théologie*, with which numerous prominent Catholic theologians of the mid- to late twentieth century are associated. We will focus on just two: Henri de Lubac, who could be regarded as the central figure of the movement, and Hans Urs von Balthasar, who was rather less central but whose work has proved to be very influential on Catholic and Protestant theologians alike in recent decades.

Henri de Lubac

Henri de Lubac (1896–1991) was a Jesuit theologian. While he was receiving the accepted neo-scholastic training, he began supplementing his studies with his own reading of patristic and medieval texts – a practice that he was to continue for decades. He became remarkably well read in the Christian tradition and, when he came to put forward his own theological views and ideas about the necessary reform of the Catholic Church, it was in large part by means of a detailed engagement with and reproduction of those patristic and medieval voices. He also did a great deal to make those sources available to others. With his friends Jean Daniélou and Claude Mondésert, he founded in 1942 the *Sources Chrétiennes* series, which published patristic and medieval texts in their original languages with an accompanying French translation.

In 1938, de Lubac wrote a book called *Catholicism: The Social Aspects of Dogma*, which many of those associated with the *Nouvelle Théologie* movement regarded as something like an alternative to the neo-scholastic textbooks on which they had been brought up. With a characteristic accompaniment of medieval and patristic extracts, de Lubac sought to show how Catholic teaching, invigorated by re-engagement with earlier tradition, allowed modern believers to navigate between the temptations both of individualism and of excessive corporatism.

> One of de Lubac's most influential works was his four-volume study *Medieval Exegesis* (1959–1963). It is one of the books that has fuelled the return to 'spiritual exegesis' among Christian theologians mentioned in Chapter 10. It explores the various forms of allegorical reading that medieval exegetes employed and shows how both the techniques and the readings they yielded were important strands in the whole fabric of Christian theology. It is being translated into English by Mark Sebanc and E.M. Macierowski; so far three volumes have appeared (Grand Rapids: Eerdmans, 1998–2009) with one more yet to come.

In the 1950s, de Lubac found himself coming under suspicion from the Catholic hierarchy. He was prevented from teaching, and his works were censored. His work on the medieval theological heritage had led him to question some of the most basic building blocks of neo-scholasticism: ideas about the relationship between nature and grace that allowed a neat, systematic distinction between the natural capacities of human being on the one hand and the capacities of human being enlightened by grace on the other. De Lubac believed that such ideas fuelled perceptions of an unbridgeable opposition between Catholic thought and practice and the non-Catholic world (and so, we might say, fuelled perceptions of an unbridgeable opposition between Catholic truth and modernism). De Lubac argued that such a neat and oppositional systematising of the relationship between nature and grace misrepresented Aquinas and broke ranks with the dominant witness of medieval and patristic theology.

In the 1960s, however, de Lubac returned to favour with the Catholic hierarchy – to such an extent that in 1960 he was appointed to the theological commission that was preparing for the Second Vatican Council. At the council itself he served as an official theological expert, with considerable influence over its pronouncements. Finally, de Lubac was offered a cardinalship in 1960 (though he did not accept until a renewed offer was made in 1983).

The Second Vatican Council, held from 1962 to 1965, was to some degree the vindication of the strategy of *ressourcement* – though that was by no means the only current of thinking that influenced the Council's outcomes. The Council set the seal on the Catholic Church's move away from neo-scholasticism; it allowed the liturgy of the Mass to be celebrated in vernacular languages; it encouraged greater attention to the study of the Bible among both clergy and laity; it did much to allow a new approach to ecumenical relations with other Churches, and more positive engagement with other religions. Inevitably, however, the documents produced by the Council were complex compromises between those who wanted to preserve the Church's stand against modernism in all its forms, those who saw the primary resources for renewal in voices and movements from outside the Church and those like de Lubac who believed that deeper continuity with the past of the Church went hand in hand with a greater openness to, and critical engagement with, the modern world. In part because of the balancing of these tendencies in the documents, the implications of Vatican II for Catholic life and thought are still a source of significant disagreement and debate in Catholic theology.

Figure 12.2 Second Vatican Council: Closing Ceremony in St Peter's Square, 9 December 1965

Hans Urs von Balthasar

A friend of de Lubac's, Hans Urs von Balthasar (1905–1988) was another theologian associated with the *Nouvelle Théologie* movement, though it is fair to say that for most of his life he was a more marginal figure in Catholic theology than de Lubac. (He played no significant role in the Second Vatican Council, for instance.) Because von Balthasar had studied philosophy and German literature at university before joining the Jesuit order, his work was shaped by engagement with a more eclectic range of sources than was that of de Lubac and the other theologians of *ressourcement*. The development of his theology was also deeply influenced by his reading of (and friendship with) the Protestant theologian Karl Barth (see Chapter 10).

> According to von Balthasar, an even deeper influence on his work was Adrienne von Speyr, a Swiss Catholic doctor (and the best friend of Karl Barth's brother) who converted to Catholicism with von Balthasar's help, and then began receiving a series of mystical experiences and visions, on the basis of which she dictated book after book to von Balthasar, who eventually published nearly 70 volumes of her work between 1940 and 1953.

Von Balthasar's engagement with the tradition can be seen throughout his many works: in books on Maximus the Confessor, Gregory of Nyssa and Irenaeus, as well as on Henri de Lubac, Karl Barth and others; but also throughout his *magnum opus*, the 'Trilogy' (actually a multi-volume work, comparable in size to Karl Barth's *Church Dogmatics*, but split into three parts: *The Glory of the Lord: A Theological Aesthetics* (7 vols), *Theo-Drama: Theological Dramatic Theory* (5 vols), *Theo-Logic: Theological Logical Theory* (3 vols) and an *Epilogue* (English translations: San Francisco: Ignatius Press, 1982–2004). Like de Lubac, von Balthasar was a theologian who invested a great deal in the attempt to do justice to the saints and theologians of the Christian tradition. He regarded them as living voices who needed to be understood in their own terms (and therefore historically), but also as teachers with whom one can have lively and critical engagement in the present. Also like de Lubac, von Balthasar believed (and sought to demonstrate) that such lively and critical engagement with the past coheres with, and leads to, a broader openness to engagement beyond the walls of the present-day Catholic Church.

Von Balthasar argued that creation and history only exist because the triune God has opened his life wide to make space for them – and the breadth and depth of that space are seen in the distance travelled by the Son into sin, suffering and death. All creation and all of history take place within that space; there is nothing that can take place that escapes from it, or goes further from God than God has already gone on creation's behalf. All things are therefore shaped by and open to the dynamics of

God's life, to the light and life of the God in whom all things cohere. In the light of such a vision, von Balthasar was deeply critical of what he identified as a citadel mentality in the Catholicism of his day – the clear demarcation of the realm of ideas and voices with which it was proper to engage from those that were beyond the pale. As well as being marked by intense engagement with patristic and medieval writers, his work is therefore marked by similarly intense engagement with non-Catholic philosophers, artists, novelists and theologians.

In recent decades, von Balthasar's work has probably received more attention than that of any other Catholic theologian from both Catholics and non-Catholics, and it has moved from the margins of the Catholic Church to official respectability. In 1988, official recognition reached the point where he was about to be made a cardinal but von Balthasar died just a few days before the investiture could be carried out.

The official recognition of de Lubac and von Balthasar, and the continued approbation of their works by recent popes, is taken by some as a warning signal. Critics ask how powerful a resource for *ongoing* reform in the Catholic Church can be provided by their work, when it is such a favourite of a hierarchy that is seen to be going through a relatively conservative period (compared, at least, to the hopes raised for such critics by Vatican II). Von Balthasar's fairly conservative social views, especially his understanding of the role of women in the Church, have come in for particular critical scrutiny.

Engagement with tradition

Much twentieth-century theology has been shaped by renewed engagements with the Christian tradition, by theologians who in different ways have aimed neither at the simple preservation of the past nor at a return to some state of past purity, but at some kind of critical conversation.

Such engagement has by no means been restricted to Catholicism. Protestant theologians who are indebted to Barth, for instance, have often been influenced by his re-engagement with the texts of Protestant scholasticism (see Chapter 2). In seeking to do justice to the witness of the Bible to God's revelation by reading that witness in its own terms (see Chapter 10), Barth increasingly found himself able to draw critically but extensively on the terminology and patterns of presentation of the Protestant scholastics. Their texts provided him with a stock of distinctions and connections that had been minted or adapted in an attempt to speak clearly about the shape of the biblical witness and Barth adopted them insofar as he found them useful for articulating his own understanding of that witness. Such engagement with texts of the Protestant past provided the core of Barth's engagement with the Christian tradition, although it is supplemented in his work by extensive engagement with patristic and medieval texts as well.

Barth's engagement with Protestant scholastic was helped on its way by a compendium of Reformed scholastic texts from the sixteenth to the nineteenth centuries gathered by Heinrich Heppe (1820–1879). His 1861 *Reformierte Dogmatik* has since become available in English translation as *Reformed Dogmatics: Set Out and Illustrated from the Sources*, revised by Ernst Bizer, translated by G.T. Thomson (London: Allen and Unwin, 1950).

We should also mention in this context the impact of Eastern Orthodox theology on modern theological conversations in the twentieth century. In the nineteenth century, it is hard to tell the story of Russian or Greek Orthodox theology in a way that connects it closely to the rest of the story of modern theology (whether Protestant or Catholic), though there were some Russian Orthodox thinkers who engaged with German philosophy – especially the works of Hegel and Schelling. Those works of German idealism, taken in the most religiously pregnant sense possible, were read in the light of the Orthodox mystical tradition, and a distinctive synthesis emerged (see the discussion of Soloviev in Chapter 9).

In the early part of the twentieth century, however, the conversations among Russian Orthodox thinkers – some more in favour and some more critical of this Hegel-flavoured approach – moved westward, as waves of émigrés left Russia after the revolution of 1917. The most influential and impressive of those who, broadly speaking, continued the Hegel-flavoured tradition was Sergei Bulgakov (1871–1944), a Marxist economist who had moved away from Marx and towards the Orthodox Church as the revolution approached. Among those who reacted against this idealist trend in Orthodox thought, the most prominent is probably Vladimir Lossky (1903–1958), a man whose writings did a good deal to introduce the texts and authors of the Orthodox tradition to non-Orthodox audiences in Europe and North America.

Many non-Orthodox writers (the Anglican theologian Rowan Williams is a prime example) have been deeply influenced by this re-engagement with the Orthodox tradition, and that impact has been reinforced by the work of more recent Orthodox writers based in the West, or influential there – John Meyendorff (1926–1992), John Zizioulas (b. 1931) and Kallistos Ware (b. 1934). These and other figures have helped generate interest in various aspects of the Greek and Russian theological traditions, including study of Alexandrian Christology, as well as of figures such as Pseudo-Dionysius, Maximus the Confessor and Gregory Palamas.

Conclusion

There are, of course, ongoing tensions between those who approach figures and movements from the history of Christianity simply historically (trying to understand them as figures or movements firmly embedded in their historical contexts) and those who approach them theologically (engaging with them as conversation partners in the quest for theological truth and faithfulness in the present), but there is also a wide area of complex overlap between the two camps. At the beginning of the twenty-first century, critical engagement with all manner of figures and movements from Christian history is a thriving academic industry and a good deal of modern theological work is carried on by means of detailed study of pre-modern tradition – whether or not the theological work in question counts as traditional*ist*.

Bibliography

Owen Chadwick, *From Bossuet to Newman: The Idea of Doctrinal Development*, 2nd edition (Cambridge: Cambridge University Press, 1987). Explains how the idea of development arose and how it itself developed.

Aidan Nichols, *From Newman to Congar: The Idea of Doctrinal Development from the Victorians to the Second Vatican Council* (Edinburgh: T&T Clark, 1990). Picks up the story where Chadwick left off.

Stephen Sykes, *The Identity of Christianity: Theologians and the Essence of Christianity from Schleiermacher to Barth* (London: SPCK, 1984). Tells the story of various attempts made by modern theologians to identify something constant beneath the changing surface of the Christian tradition – with more focus on Protestant theologians than Chadwick or Nichols.

John Henry Newman, *Essay on the Development of Christian Doctrine* (London: Longmans, Green and Co., 1909). Available online at <www.newmanreader.org/works/development>. Newman's great work on development.

Nicholas Lash, *Newman on Development: The Search for an Explanation in History* (London: Sheed and Ward, 1975). A very thorough and precise study of Newman.

Alfred Loisy, *The Gospel and the Church*, trans. Christopher Home (New York: Scribner, 1904). One of the 'Modernists' who took ideas like Newman's and ran with them in directions he would have found surprising.

George Tyrrell, *Medievalism: A Reply to Cardinal Mercer* (London: Longmans, Green and Co., 1908). Facsimile available at <www.archive.org/details/ medievalismreply00tyrriala>. Another of the Catholic Modernists.

Fergus Kerr, *Twentieth Century Catholic Theologians: From Neoscholasticism to Nuptual Mysticism* (Oxford: Blackwell, 2007). A good guide to Chenu, de Lubac and the rest.

Rowan Williams, A.M. Allchin and Peter C. Bouteneff, 'Eastern Orthodox Theology' in David Ford and Rachel Muers (eds), *The Modern Theologians: An Introduction to Christian Theology Since 1918*, 3rd edition (Oxford: Blackwell, 2005), pp572–588. A good overview of twentieth-century Orthodox theology and its impact on Protestant and Catholic thinking.

Rowan Williams, *Why Study the Past? The Quest for the Historical Church* (London: DLT/Grand Rapids: Eerdmans, 2005). A short book and a fairly easy read, setting out reasons why ongoing engagement with the past might be healthy for modern theology.

Morwenna Ludlow, *Gregory of Nyssa: Ancient and (post)Modern* (Oxford: Oxford University Press, 2007). Taking just one example of a figure from the Christian tradition, Ludlow traces the many different ways in which his work has been appropriated by modern theologians, and raises questions about the kind of engagement with history involved.

Henri de Lubac, *Catholicism: Christ and the Common Destiny of Man* (San Francisco: Ignatius Press, 1988).

13

Confronting evil

AIMS

By the end of this chapter, we hope that you will:

- understand some of the specific forms and contexts in which the 'problem of evil' has arisen for theology in the modern period and how the modern 'problem of evil' is distinctively modern

- know about, and have reflected on the implications of, some of the Christian Churches' responses to Nazism

- understand some of the key features of Dietrich Bonhoeffer's theology.

Introduction

In one of the most famous passages of his memoir *Night*, the death camp survivor Elie Wiesel describes witnessing the hanging by the SS of a young boy. As the boy dies in protracted agony, Wiesel hears a man asking where God is. Wiesel's answer, as recorded in the memoir, is that God is hanging on the gallows.

'Where was God in Auschwitz?' has in many ways been the defining religious question in Europe and North America since 1945. Auschwitz, the German name for the Polish town that was the site of the most notorious of the Nazi death camps, instantly calls to mind the horrors of the **Shoah** (Holocaust). Speaking about the *Shoah*, in turn, makes us think about the massive scale of human-made evil and suffering in modernity. So, asking 'Where was God in Auschwitz?' directs religious people both to a perennial question – the so-called 'problem of evil', the issue of how a good God relates to human evil and human suffering – and to the specific modern contexts in which that question arises.

Figure 13.1 SS officers supervising the building of gallows in the forest near Buchenwald concentration camp

In this chapter, we shall look at some of modern theology's confrontations with evil, taking the *Shoah* as our central focus. We shall look back to see the factors that shaped modern reflections on the 'problem of evil', and forward to see how Christian theology in the second half of the twentieth century confronted the memory of the *Shoah*. In our central section, we shall consider how theologians in Germany and Nazi-occupied Europe confronted the evil of the *Shoah* as it was taking place and how their work has affected later theology.

Shoah or Holocaust? What is the appropriate term to use for the mass killings of Jews in Europe between 1941 and 1945? 'Shoah' is a biblical word meaning 'destruction' or 'storm' (see for example Psalm 35:8, where it is translated 'ruin' in the NRSV, and Ezekiel 38:9, translated 'storm'). It is preferred by many commentators, and is our term of choice, because: (a) there are objections to the sacrificial connotations of 'Holocaust' – a burnt offering; and (b) 'Holocaust' has been used to refer to events other than the mass killing of the European Jews, whereas 'Shoah' is a unique name. The naming of the event is already a political and theological issue, and no term is universally accepted.

Putting God on trial

This chapter is concerned with the problem of evil in modernity. But, of course, evil and suffering – in cataclysmic events that affect whole societies or in the lives of individuals and families – are nothing new and nor are theological struggles with evil and suffering. The theologian Julian of Norwich, for example, wrote her reflections on evil and the goodness of God in fourteenth-century England, in the aftermath of the Black Death and in a context of enormous social turmoil and violence. Many of her words would not seem out of place in contemporary reflections on Auschwitz.

> Deeds are committed which in our eyes are so evil and lead to so much harm that it seems impossible that any good could come out of them. And we cannot rest in the happiness of contemplating God as we should because we dwell on all this evil and sorrow and grieve over it.
>
> Julian of Norwich, *Revelations of Divine Love*, §32 edited by Halcyon Backhouse (London: Hodder and Stoughton, 1987), p62.

So, what is distinctive and interesting about *modernity's* theological confrontation with evil? The question 'Where was God in Auschwitz?' points us to a few possible answers.

There is a well-known story of how a group of Jews imprisoned in a death camp put God on trial, for breaking the covenant God made with the Jewish people and subjecting them to the horrors of the *Shoah*. In the story, the men find God guilty as charged – and then begin their evening prayers.

In the UK, the story was made famous by the *Shoah* survivor Rabbi Hugo Gryn, who placed it at the centre of his reflections on post-*Shoah* Judaism. It has been made into a film written by Frank Cottrell Boyce, starring Anthony Sher (*God on Trial*, BBC, 2008).

The story of the trial of God in the death camp may not be directly related to Christian theological reflection on the 'problem of evil' but it does point us to an important dimension of modern confrontations with evil. Modernity tends to interpret *the reality of evil as* (possible) *evidence against God.*

Evil can be used as 'evidence against God' in at least two senses, both of which are relevant to modern debates. On the one hand, it can be 'evidence' in the scientific sense, evidence that helps us to decide whether a belief is true. So, the existence of evil might be evidence that there is no God (or evidence that God, if God exists, is radically other than God has been thought to be); it is, in other words, evidence against the 'God hypothesis'. On the other hand, as in the Auschwitz story, evil in the world can be the 'evidence' given at God's trial – evidence that leads humanity to convict God of immorality and injustice, and perhaps to convict people who believe in God of complicity in immorality and injustice. In either case, the existence of evidence 'against God' seems to demand a *defensive* response, from or on behalf of God.

To see why this is interesting, and distinctively modern, we can look again for contrast at Julian of Norwich, writing in the fourteenth century. Immediately after the passage quoted above, in which she describes how evil disturbs faith, she writes:

The reason for this is that our minds are so blind, so base and so foolish that we cannot recognise the supreme and wonderful wisdom, the power and goodness of the blessed Trinity.

Julian is genuinely and persistently troubled by evil, but she assumes that both the evil and her troubles about it can only be thought about within a framework of trust in God's goodness. She does not ask, in her confrontation with evil, whether she *should* trust God, or whether she *should* affirm the goodness of God.

The term '**theodicy**' was coined in 1710 by Gottfried Leibniz, who composed a philosophical account of how the goodness of God was compatible with the existence of evil. The term comes from two Greek words – for 'God' and for 'justice', 'rightness' or 'justification'. Theodicy, then, is an attempt to defend God – to prove God right, or to prove belief in God to be reasonable in a context of evil and suffering. Famously or notoriously, Leibniz, in his original theodicy, argued for the conclusion that this is 'the best of all possible worlds'.

Forty-five years after Leibniz published his theodicy, an earthquake struck south-west Portugal, devastating Lisbon, then one of the largest and most beautiful cities in Europe. It was followed by fires and a tsunami. As many as 90,000 people may have died in the earthquake, fires and floods – up to a third of Lisbon's population.

Figure 13.2 Illustration of ships on the sea and buildings on shore in a tumult during the catastrophic Lisbon earthquake

It is interesting to compare reactions to the Lisbon earthquake of 1755 with the impassioned debates about God and suffering, conducted in many media, that followed the Indian Ocean tsunami of 2004.

In the wake of the Lisbon disaster, Voltaire launched a passionate attack on Leibniz and those who followed his lead in their defences of God.

> Come, you philosophers who cry, 'All's well'
> And contemplate this ruin of a world ...
>
> Voltaire, 'Poem on the Disaster at Lisbon'
> translated by Joseph McCabe (1912).

Later, in his satirical story *Candide*, Voltaire caricatured Leibniz and others in the figure of Dr Pangloss, the philosopher who insists that 'everything is for the best in the best of all possible worlds', in the face of all evidence to the contrary.

Leibniz's own work on theodicy may have been largely discredited but the concept of a 'theodicy', a trial and/or justification of God, has not. Modern articulations of the 'problem of evil' still refer back, explicitly or implicitly, to the confrontation between Leibniz and Voltaire. There are some obvious reasons why the trial and justification of God becomes possible in *modernity*. We have seen that the modern 'turn to the subject' places a great emphasis on the subject's ability to make free and autonomous judgements – including, or especially, moral judgements. On the face of it, there is no reason to exempt *anything* from these judgements – even or especially God. Recall Kant's claim that we can only have faith in Jesus as a perfect moral exemplar because *our own* moral reason judges him to be morally perfect. The modern problem of evil is the 'flip side' of this claim. Even if we are *told* that God is good, we cannot accept that on external authority, but have to make our own judgement about it.

Note also an important – and often unacknowledged – shift in how God is imagined, in relation to morality and evil. In modern discussions of morality and the 'problem of evil', God is often assumed to be a moral agent like us, inhabiting the moral world we inhabit – so that, for example, God's 'motives' and the 'effects of God's actions' are at least in principle open to our scrutiny and so that we can ask the question 'to what extent is God morally good?' It can be hard to relate this to traditional Christian accounts of God – accounts on which, for example, Julian of Norwich's theology relies – where God is the *source* of all goodness. God, on these traditional accounts, does not 'possess' goodness (moral or otherwise) as we might possess it. God *is* goodness and we, like all other creatures, exist and are good insofar as we share God's goodness. In that context, the 'problem of evil' is not a problem about to what extent God is good, because there is *no good apart from God*. The problem is about how created things (such as human beings) come to be apart from God, and hence 'no good' – how they fail to share fully in the goodness of God.

When you are studying modern theodicy, it is worth bearing this wider tradition in mind – if only to remind you to ask what assumptions about humanity, God and goodness underlie any given version of the 'problem of evil'. Note also the renewed interest in this wider tradition within contemporary theology, which we discuss a little further on.

There are many clear accounts available of modern *philosophical* debates around the 'problem of evil', and we are not going to repeat them here.

See, for example, Eleonore Stump and Michael J. Murray (eds), *Philosophy of Religion: The Big Questions* (Oxford: Blackwell, 1999), Part 3, for a range of relevant excerpts and a helpful introduction to the issue. Note also the presence, even here, of 'alternative perspectives', including an essay by Desmond Tutu on theology's confrontation with the evils of apartheid.

Modern theology, however, at least since the mid-twentieth century, has generally refused to place the philosophical 'problem of evil' at the centre of its accounts of evil. Some reasons for this might already be clear (for example, the question of whether the God of modern theodicy debates is really the God of Christian tradition); other reasons will become clear later in our discussion. In the rest of this chapter, we look beyond the theodicy debates to a wider range of confrontations with evil in nineteenth- and twentieth-century religious thought.

Humanist confrontations: the evils of belief

In the nineteenth century, discussion of theodicy was connected to a broader questioning of the morality of Christian belief. Opponents of Christianity argued that the human sense of love, compassion and justice was offended by various aspects of Christian teaching. Christian belief was 'inhumane'. This was the age of developing **humanitarianism**, the concern that humanity's increased power over material and social circumstances should be used to alleviate suffering. Questions had been raised before this time about the morality of Christian belief – but in the nineteenth century this became a major focus of concern and a source of religious doubt. Why should humans worship a God to whom they were morally superior – a God who, if everything said about God were true, would be obviously unloving and unjust?

You will see various nineteenth-century critics of Christianity described as 'humanists'. 'Humanist' is a term with a very complex history. It was first coined in the early nineteenth century in Germany, to refer to a system of education that focused on the classics – and the subjects that we would still in English call the *humanities*. Later it was used to describe the movement towards interest in *human life*, its nature and possibilities, that characterised the European Renaissance.

In modernity, 'humanism' also came to refer to philosophies that advocated faith in *humanity* as more basic than faith in God – philosophies that spoke of ethical values, ideals and possibilities that were integral to all human life and could be discovered and fostered by humankind, without divine aid. George Eliot and Matthew Arnold are among the best-known English-language 'humanist' writers, in this latter sense, in the nineteenth century. Contemporary self-declared 'humanists' will often – but not always – be identifying themselves with this form of humanism. For a helpful (if critical) account of the history of the term, see Tony Davies, *Humanism* (London: Routledge, 1997).

George Eliot is a particularly interesting figure among the nineteenth-century moral critics of religion. Her novels explore both the 'anti-human' consequences of religious fanaticism (the tyrannical reformer Savonarola in *Romola*, and the unsympathetic and self-deceiving evangelical Bulstrode in *Middlemarch*) and the humanising, even 'saving', power of rightly ordered religious faith (the Methodist preacher Dinah Morris in *Adam Bede* and the devout and saintly Dorothea Brooke in *Middlemarch*). In Eliot's novels we see every form of religion held up to searching moral interrogation. How, Eliot asks, does religion advance, or hold back, human goodness and human flourishing?

Note also that Nietzsche lampoons Eliot for her desire to hold onto 'Christian' morality while rejecting Christianity; for him, she was an example of people's failure to recognise and celebrate the death of God.

A particular focus of nineteenth-century debate, especially in Britain, was the 'doctrine of eternal punishment' – belief in hell. The significance given to belief in hell shifted dramatically during the nineteenth century. (This is explored in detail by Geoffrey Rowell in *Hell and the Victorians* (Oxford: Clarendon, 1974).) For most of the nineteenth century, it was widely accepted in orthodox Christian circles that belief in hell was integral, not only to Christian faith, but also to social order. Fear of hell, set alongside the promise of heaven, was seen as an incentive for moral and socially responsible behaviour. But at the same time, the justice and goodness of a God who would condemn anyone to eternal suffering grew harder to defend. This was the case, especially, in a context in which attitudes to *earthly* punishment for criminals were shifting, away from simple retribution and towards the rehabilitation of criminals. If criminals on earth were being reformed and rehabilitated, rather than simply made to suffer, how could a just and good God punish people *eternally* without the prospect of reform?

The activities of Western Christian missionaries in non-Christian countries also posed major questions. On the one hand, the doctrine of hell provided part of the incentive for missionary work (converts were being saved from hell). On the other hand, however, greater awareness of the enormous number and variety of non-Christian societies raised sharper questions about the goodness of a God who would condemn all non-Christians to hell.

> Bishop John Colenso of Natal (1814–1883) was one of those missionaries whose experience in the field led him to question the doctrine of eternal punishment. His commentary on the Epistle to the Romans, published in 1861, expressed his view that neither the Bible nor the breadth of Christian tradition required belief in hell. Colenso was controversially deposed and excommunicated (and later reinstated) in the wake of the publication of his critical commentary on the Pentateuch.

Belief in hell was not, of course, an isolated doctrine. It was particularly closely linked, in nineteenth-century eyes at least, to theologies of the atonement; hell was the punishment that human sin deserved and from which Christ saved humanity. In both Britain and America, the Unitarians were at the forefront of nineteenth-century critiques of belief in hell – and they linked this to the denial of substitutionary accounts of atonement. Moral objections to the doctrine of atonement itself were less prominent in nineteenth-century critiques of Christianity, although they have come to the forefront in the twentieth century. Christian feminist theologians, and others, who describe penal-substitutionary theories of atonement as 'divine child abuse' are following in this tradition of the moral critique of religious doctrine.

> The description of certain accounts of atonement as 'divine child abuse' already has a long and controversial history. It was used by the feminist theologians Joanne Carlson Brown and Rebecca Parker in 1989 (Brown and Parker, 'God So Loved the World', in Joanne Carlson Brown and Carole R. Bohn (eds), *Christianity, Patriarchy and Abuse* (New York: Pilgrim Press, 1989)), and has appeared frequently in debates around Christian feminism. More recently, the prominent evangelical Steve Chalke came under sustained attack for using the expression 'cosmic child abuse' in his critique of penal-substitutionary theories of the atonement.

Humanist confrontations: human goodness and human evil

The eighteenth and nineteenth centuries' moral critiques of Christian doctrine relied, implicitly or explicitly, on a belief in *human* goodness and the possibility of human progress. Humanity was obviously capable of love, compassion and justice – and more so, when not hampered by oppressive or immoral doctrines. Humanity was visibly progressing, not just scientifically but also morally. Not only 'humanism', but also humanitarianism and campaigns for the moral improvement of humanity, flourished in the nineteenth century. This was when societies for the 'prevention of cruelty' to children and animals were founded (notoriously, in Britain the latter was several decades earlier than the former). Anti-slavery movements (which we discuss further in Chapter 15) gained some of their force by drawing attention to the immoral and 'uncivilised' practices associated with slavery; humanity needed to progress beyond such 'barbarism'. Temperance movements and campaigns around 'vice' and prostitution (see our discussion of Josephine Butler, Chapter 9) spoke of moral improvements not only in the individual but also in society.

It is no accident that many of these nineteenth-century movements for human moral progress were strongly associated with Evangelicalism, with its focus on conversion and on holiness of living. But beyond Evangelical circles, there were many who interpreted Christianity as, in its essence, a force for the moral advance of humanity.

It is commonly suggested that this widespread optimism about human progress ended with the First World War, when the members of 'civilised', Christian nations inflicted suffering on each other on a scale that was previously unimaginable. Karl Barth developed his dialectical theology as a response to the crisis that these events provoked in European thought about civilisation, humanity and religion.

If the First World War was the first major challenge faced by twentieth-century theology, in the North and West at least, this means that the twentieth century began with the problem of *human* evil – 'how can people do these things?' This question arises even more sharply in the aftermath of the *Shoah* and the other genocides of the twentieth century. As many commentators have put it, perhaps the most pressing question is not 'where was God in Auschwitz?' but 'where was humanity in Auschwitz?'

More specifically, Christians reflecting on the First World War had to acknowledge that it had been fought between Christian nations and supported by leading Christian thinkers; and Christians reflecting on the *Shoah* had to acknowledge that it had taken place in Christian Germany and that many of the perpetrators were professing Christians. We should also note that a new, specific and urgent question about the morality of Christian belief arose after the *Shoah* – to what extent did Christianity, not merely in the immediate context of Nazism but throughout its long history, fuel **anti-Semitism**? Christian responses to this challenge are discussed in Chapter 16.

As usual, the truth is more complicated. Belief in 'progress' did not just continue unchallenged until 1914 and then suddenly end. On the one hand, many interpreters of nineteenth-century scientific and social change were far from optimistic. Take, for example, Matthew Arnold (a prominent humanist, see above) in 'Dover Beach' (1867), reflecting on a time of dramatic shifts in culture and belief:

> Ah, love, let us be true
> To one another! for the world, which seems
> To lie before us like a land of dreams,
> So various, so beautiful, so new,
> Hath really neither joy, nor love, nor light,
> Nor certitude, nor peace, nor help for pain;
> And we are here as on a darkling plain
> Swept with confused alarms of struggle and flight,
> Where ignorant armies clash by night.

On the other hand, in the period immediately after the First World War, the formation of the League of Nations, the growth of the international ecumenical movement and numerous other international movements expressed and enacted optimism about the possibility of transforming human relationships and the conditions of human life for the better.

The more general question is how, in the twentieth century, has Christian theology enabled people to judge and resist human evil, and how has it failed to do so (or, worse, itself contributed to the evil)? In the next section, we will look briefly at some well-known examples of theology developed and used in resistance to Nazism and will consider their wider influence and implications for theology's confrontation with evil.

When reading the next section, you may find it helpful to have access to some background material on the history of Nazism and the *Shoah*. There is, of course, an enormous volume of literature on the subject. Laurence Rees' introductory works *Auschwitz: The Nazis and the Final Solution* (London: BBC, 2003) and *The Nazis: A Warning from History* (London: BBC, 2006) are possible places to start, as is the website of the United States Holocaust Memorial Museum, <www.ushmm.org>.

There is also plenty of material on Christianity under Nazism – see the Bibliography at the end of this chapter.

Theology for resistance to evil: Christians against Nazism

The Confessing Church and the *Barmen Declaration*

In 1933, Hitler came to power following an election that gave the Nazis a substantial majority in parliament, and promptly passed the Enabling Acts suspending the constitution and granting himself dictatorial powers. In the same year, there were nationwide elections for the governing body of the Protestant Church in Germany. Here, again, there was an overwhelming victory for the Nazis – or rather, the 'German Christians', the pro-Nazi organisation within the Protestant Churches. These Church elections brought the national Protestant Church into close alignment with the Nazi state. Some of the implications of this development rapidly became clear; there were moves to exclude Christians of Jewish descent from 'German' congregations and to prevent them from serving as pastors.

A group of young Church leaders, concerned about the growing power of the 'German Christians', formed the Pastors' Emergency League. This group were the nucleus of the 'Confessing Church' – a national body in direct opposition to the state-sanctioned Church. A key document for the Confessing Church was the 1934 *Barmen Declaration*, largely produced by Karl Barth. Barth was very important for the opposition to Nazism, though as a Swiss citizen he was both protected from any dangerous personal consequences of his political stance and unable to have much direct influence on events in Germany.

The *Barmen Declaration*, then, established a platform for opposition to Nazi domination of the Protestant Church. A few key features of the document are worth considering as we ask about the nature of theological 'confrontation with evil'.

- It is uncompromisingly *christocentric*. 'Jesus Christ, as he is attested to us in Holy Scripture, is the one Word of God whom we have to hear, and whom we have to trust and obey in life and in death' (First article).
- It repeatedly poses a choice between allegiance to Christ and allegiance to 'other lords', 'other powers' or other sources of revelation.
- It asserts the *freedom* of the Church, grounded in loyalty to Christ, to proclaim the Word of God, and contrasts this with attempts to use the Church for political ends:
    'The Church's commission, which is the foundation of its freedom, consists in this: in Christ's stead, and so in the service of his own Word and work, to deliver to all people, through preaching and sacrament, the message of the free grace of God. We reject the false doctrine that ... the Church could place the Word and work of the Lord in the service of self-chosen desires, purposes and plans.'
- In this context, it affirms the vital importance of the *separation of Church and state*.

The key point about *Barmen* is perhaps not so much its theological content as its political effect – the effect of restating ('confessing') these particular beliefs at this time and calling on others to do the same. The declaration demanded a decision from all Christians – to recognise what their faith required and to act on it by rejecting the Nazi-dominated Church. Note the *binary* character of its language, the stark choices it poses. The Confessing Church pastors believed that they were confronting a *status confessionis* - a situation in which 'confessing' (affirming) Christian faith *could only mean* adopting a particular stance.

The *Barmen Declaration* and the formation of the Confessing Church have inspired various subsequent declarations, similarly intended to call on Christians to take a stance against a perceived evil. Most notably, Lutheran and Reformed Churches in the 1970s and 1980s declared the apartheid regime in South Africa to be a *status confessionis* and said that opposition to that regime was required of all Christians and all Christian communities.

Dietrich Bonhoeffer

One of the theologians who in 1934 called most forcefully for Christians to declare a *status confessionis* – a situation in which the heart of Christian faith was at stake – was Dietrich Bonhoeffer.

Bonhoeffer (1906–1945) is one of the twentieth century's best-known theologians. The interpretation of his work is inevitably (and more obviously than for most of the theologians we have discussed) tied up with the interpretation of his life. After being a leading figure in the Confessing Church and training its pastors, he became involved in a conspiracy to assassinate Hitler and replace the Nazi government. For several years he worked as a 'triple agent' in the German secret service, trying to make links with Allied governments on behalf of the conspirators and helping with the rescue of groups of Jews. Along with other conspirators – including several members of his own family – Bonhoeffer was arrested and imprisoned in 1943. He was executed in April 1945, a few months before the end of the war.

Before the Nazi rise to power, Bonhoeffer was an extremely promising – and productive – academic theologian. He is best known, however, for the works he produced in the context of opposition to Nazism, and best of all for his fragmentary writings from prison.

What theological thinking arose from and shaped Bonhoeffer's 'confrontation with evil'? First, as we might expect given his association with the *Barmen Declaration*, his theology is consistently christocentric. He repeatedly affirms that God is to be found and understood *only* in Jesus Christ and that the truth about humanity and the world is also to be found and understood only in Christ. On the face of it, this could look like a very narrow vision of humanity and the world and a way to limit theological concerns. Bonhoeffer, however, turns it around; he asks the question 'how do we interpret *each and every aspect of reality* in relation to Jesus Christ?' Or, more succinctly, as he put it in his letters from prison: 'who is Jesus Christ for us today?'

Figure 13.3 Dietrich Bonhoeffer

The focus on Jesus Christ in asking these questions forced Bonhoeffer – as he saw it – to beware of using any general principles or explanatory frameworks to understand a real person or situation. Jesus Christ is a person, not a system of ideas; and a genuine encounter with a living person breaks down any attempt to make a system out of reality.

Consider this situation: you have heard a few facts about a person. You know how old she is, where she comes from, what work she does, what music she listens to, what clothes she wears. On that basis, you can make all sorts of further pre-judgements about her – how she will behave, what you can say to her, how she will relate to the other people you know. You can fit her into your 'system', your pre-existing ways of classifying people. You might think: I've *got* her now, I don't even need to meet her, I know all about her. I know what she is.

But perhaps, if you do meet her, you will stop thinking about her in terms of her place in your system, stop wanting to classify her, and be able to relate to her not as what she is but as *who* she is. Perhaps you will start to think that your earlier claim to 'know all about' her was wrong or unjust.

For Bonhoeffer, one of the implications of christocentrism is that ultimate reality is personal. Knowing the truth is more like 'encountering a person' than 'understanding an idea'.

There is a direct confrontation here, in Bonhoeffer's thought, with Nazi totalitarianism. The Nazi state was, as he experienced it, an attempt to impose a 'system' on reality, to reduce people and their relationships to their functions in the system and to destroy everything that failed to fit in. To put it another way, Nazism was an enacted lie – first telling a lie about how the world worked and then violently reshaping the world to fit with the lie.

Compare the account of totalitarianism given by Hannah Arendt in *The Origins of Totalitarianism* (Orlando: Harcourt, 1979), for example p384.

For Bonhoeffer, then, placing 'Christ at the centre of life' (another of his well-known slogans) is a move with significant ethical and political implications; it is not simply about interpreting things truthfully, but about acting responsibly. In his *Ethics* (his last, unfinished, piece of academic work), Bonhoeffer is particularly critical of the systems of morality, inspired by Kant, that divide the world or human life into 'spheres' – the public and the private, the religious and the secular, the 'official' and the personal. He argues that, under Nazism, this 'thinking in terms of spheres' has become a way of avoiding responsibility and it is, in any case, contrary to the Christian belief in God's reconciliation of the *whole* world in Christ.

Bonhoeffer's christocentric theology led him, for many years, to hold that Christians should renounce violence – a difficult and counter-cultural message in the context of a highly militarised and violent state. What did it mean for him to participate in the conspiracy to assassinate Hitler? One of his key theological and ethical insights here was that to act *responsibly* in a given situation might in fact be to do something that was 'morally wrong'. Being 'right' according to my principles – or even according to God's commandments – might be less important than doing the will of God in a particular situation. At the very least, a Christian might be called to take the risk of incurring guilt and trust in God's forgiveness.

> This is a highly controversial area of Bonhoeffer's thought; for a thought-provoking account of it by a pacifist theologian, see James McClendon Jr., *Ethics* (Nashville: Abingdon, 2002), Chapter 7. For this chapter's discussion, one important point to note is how hard Bonhoeffer works to *avoid* setting himself up as the 'judge' of his own actions, let alone of God's, even in a context where he is making all sorts of judgements about good and evil in his historical situation.

So far, Bonhoeffer sounds like a critic of modernity – of the modern systematisation of knowledge (and the totalitarian ambitions it made possible), of Kantian-inspired ethics, of attempts to 'judge' God. However, he is really trying to *think through* modernity, positively as well as negatively. The modern world, he writes in his prison letters, has 'come of age'; it no longer needs God to explain the inexplicable, to fill gaps in knowledge or to prop up society and morality.

> Bonhoeffer was almost certainly thinking of Kant's essay 'What is Enlightenment?', and subsequent discussions of it, here; compare Kant's famous claim that 'Enlightenment is man's emergence from self-imposed immaturity' (see Chapter 3).

The modern world does not need God and pushes God out – but, says Bonhoeffer, God in Jesus Christ *was* pushed out of the world. The powerful God, the God who supplies explanations, fills gaps or keeps social systems going, is not the God in whom Christians believe.

Bonhoeffer's thought emerges from a specific and extreme confrontation with evil, but it has often been used as a starting-point for later theological engagements with the 'problem of evil'. In particular, Bonhoeffer's christocentric focus on the weakness of God, and his rejection of the idea that God is only necessary or useful to fill the gaps in human knowledge, can be used to challenge the modern project of theodicy.

Roman Catholic resistance to Nazism: the example of Bishop Galen of Münster

Political support for Nazism was, on the whole, less widespread among German Roman Catholics than among Protestants. The reasons for this were complex; importantly, German *nationalism* was much more closely associated with Protestantism than with Catholicism (Martin Luther was often described – including by the Nazis – as a German national hero). The German Catholic political party did seek political alliances with the Nazis in the 1930s, with the active support of the Vatican. Once the Nazi government was formed, an agreement (the *Concordat* of 1933) was reached with the Vatican to secure – and at the same time significantly to restrict – the position of the Catholic Church in the Nazi state.

During the Nazi period there were numerous instances of Roman Catholic resistance to specific Nazi policies and to the form of the Nazi state itself. The papal encyclical *Mit Brennender Sorge* ('With Burning Concern'), distributed in Germany in 1937, criticised both the government's restriction of Church activities, and the attempts to eliminate the 'Old Testament' from Christianity and from religious education. It also put forward a clear basis for the critique of Nazi policies from the existence of a universal, divinely-ordained and objective *natural law*, which could not be swept aside in the service of particular national or communal interests.

Some of the specific implications of the encyclical's arguments can be seen in the sermons of Bishop August von Galen of Münster, who became a focus of Catholic anti-government protest in the 1940s. Bishop Galen spoke, for example, against the denial of individual rights in a police state:

> I, as bishop and as exponent and defender of divinely appointed justice and moral order, which gives to each individual those original rights and that liberty before which it is God's will that all human opposition must cease ... am called to defend courageously the authority of justice ... The right to live, to be unmolested, the right to liberty is an indispensable part of every ordered community life.
>
> Sermon of 13 July 1941, in Heinrich Portmann, *Cardinal von Galen*, trans. R.L. Sedgwick (London: Jarrolds, 1957), pp239–246.

Figure 13.4 Bust of August von Galen in Münster

Bishop Galen's most famous protest – one of the few instances of internal protests that may have brought about changes in Nazi government policy – was against the 'euthanasia' programme of 1940–1941. The state-organised killing of people with disabilities (the first use to which the infamous poison gas Zyklon B was put) reached the attention of the Catholic authorities rapidly because Catholic-run hospitals and children's homes faced the demand that they should hand over some of the people in their care to the euthanasia programme. In August 1941, Bishop Galen described the euthanasia programme as it had begun to affect people in his own diocese, and declared:

> 'Thou shalt not kill.' God engraved this commandment on the souls of men long before any penal code laid down punishment for murder, long before any court prosecuted and avenged homicide ... Because of His love for us God has engraved these commandments in our hearts and has made them manifest to us. They express the need of our nature created by God. They are the unchangeable and fundamental truths of our social life grounded on reason, well pleasing to God, healthful and sacred.
>
> Sermon of 3 August 1941.

Galen's sermon was widely distributed, and protests followed. The euthanasia programme was halted or significantly changed shortly afterwards (although there are debates over the extent to which Galen's intervention was responsible for this). Of most interest for our purposes here is Galen's appeal – mirroring that of *Mit Brennender Sorge* – to a divinely-instituted moral law rooted deep in, and able to be perceived from, human 'nature'. Nazi policies and the Nazi state, as Galen analyses them, are profoundly *unnatural*.

> Similar arguments were in fact used by Bonhoeffer in his unfinished *Ethics* (much of which was written while he was staying at the Catholic monastery of Ettal). It is particularly interesting to see 'nature' invoked in the theological confrontation with Nazi evil, because appeals to 'nature' and to the orders established by God in creation were also used by *pro*-Nazi theologians to justify Nazi racial policies.

In the final section of the chapter, we look at some attempts since 1945 to engage theologically with the question 'where was God in Auschwitz?' and with the wider question of how to relate belief in God and the experience of evil and suffering. As we will see, many of the themes that emerge from Christianity's confrontation with the evils of Nazism are taken up in the aftermath of Nazism and form part of the ongoing theological conversation about confronting evil. We focus particularly on a set of debates – that often refer back, whether accurately or not, to Bonhoeffer's work – around divine **impassibility**, the idea that God cannot suffer.

God suffering evil

The Crucified God

At the centre of Christianity is an image of suffering – the crucifixion of Jesus. What does this image say to the question 'where was God in Auschwitz?'

The most influential theological voice on this subject since the 1960s, at least in Europe and North America, has been that of Jürgen Moltmann. Moltmann's life confronted him directly with the distinctive appearance of the 'problem of evil' in twentieth-century Europe. Born in 1926 in Germany and brought up in a secular household, he was conscripted into the German army in 1944, aged 18. Following the German surrender in 1945, he spent three years in prisoner-of-war camps – during which time he converted to Christianity. In his subsequent career as a Protestant pastor and academic theologian, he has been a powerful advocate of theological engagement with social and political questions – including the question of how to remember and respond to the horrors of 1939–1945. In *The Crucified God* (1967), Moltmann finds the beginnings of a theological answer in Luther's assertion that 'there is no other God for us than … the man on the cross', and in Hegel's later recognition that the 'death of God' was the fulcrum of Christian theology.

> Despite the similarity of terminology, Moltmann has very little time for the US movement called 'death of God theology', which was at its brief peak in the late 1960s, and of which the best-known representatives are Thomas J.J. Altizer and William Hamilton.

Moltmann's work responds to a tradition of thinking about the problem of evil that he calls 'protest atheism' – a term he uses to describe those whose unwillingness to believe in God arises, not from the illogicality or irrationality of the idea, but from the sense that a God, whose plan for the world permitted evil and suffering on the scale on which we experience them, could not be worth worshipping. Ivan Karamazov, in Dostoyevsky's *The Brothers Karamazov*, is the most famous and powerful literary spokesperson (before the fact) for what Moltmann terms 'protest atheism'. In the chapter 'Rebellion', Ivan describes in graphic detail a series of incidents of appalling cruelty to children, recalls the Christian promise of a final 'harmony' that reconciles all things, and then declares:

> I don't want harmony. From love for humanity I don't want it. I would rather be left with the unavenged suffering. I would rather remain with my unavenged suffering and unsatisfied indignation, even if I were wrong …
>
> Fyodor Dostoyevsky, *The Brothers Karamazov*
> Trans. Constance Garnett (New York: Barnes and Noble, 2004), p227.

This is not really a philosophical statement of the problem of evil; it catches the emotional and existential force of what it is like to be confronted by horrific suffering and injustice. It comes closer to Elie Wiesel's anguished cries from Auschwitz – and they in turn come strangely close to the psalms of lament in the Hebrew Bible.

We might say that the target of 'protest atheism' – as indeed of Voltaire's protests after the Lisbon earthquake – is not God *per se,* but *any* general framework of explanation that 'explains away' particular suffering, rendering it unimportant or forgettable. Especially after the *Shoah*, the twentieth century has seen intense interest in *remembering* evil and suffering, in detail and with an emphasis on the victims' stories.

Consider the memorials throughout Europe to those killed in the wars of 1914–1918 and 1939–1945, with the slogan 'Lest We Forget'; and the US memorials to the Vietnam War; the institution of 'Remembrance Day' and more recently 'Holocaust Memorial Day'; or the widely-publicised Vatican statement on the *Shoah*, entitled simply 'We Remember'. Prominent in many of the memorials to twentieth-century suffering is the naming of the victims (sometimes with photographs or other 'identifying' material). The naming of *particular* suffering, the suffering of *individuals*, prevents the absorption of the many different stories into a single, abstract '[problem of] evil'.

Remembering the *Shoah* and other instances of mass human-made suffering is often presented as an ethical obligation apart from any religious framework. Sometimes remembering is given a purpose beyond itself – 'so that this does not happen again'; but sometimes it is advocated in its own right.

The call to remember stems in part from a Jewish – and Christian – emphasis on remembering and re-narrating the history of the people of God, including instances of horrific suffering (the destruction of the Temple, the crucifixion of Jesus).

As Johann-Baptist Metz writes, Christian theology cannot lose sight of the 'dangerous memory' of the crucified Jesus; but this means that it cannot be satisfied with any way of telling the story of the world that forgets, ignores or explains away the suffering of history's losers (see Metz, *Faith in History and Society*, trans. David Smith (London: Burns & Oates, 1980)).

This in turn suggests that there might be good theological reasons for Christians *not* to engage in theodicy – at least, not insofar as theodicy involves the 'justification' or explanation-away of particular instances of suffering.

'Protest atheism', Moltmann says, is onto something with its refusal to give up on the memory of suffering. Christianity has at its heart the same refusal – Christians do not give up on the memory of the crucified Jesus. For Moltmann, Jesus' crucifixion is central to Christian thinking about God and the world; it should be the 'frame' for everything Christians say about God. Taken seriously, the crucifixion is a radical challenge to how most people (including in practice most Christians) understand 'God'. Under the influence of Greek philosophy, Moltmann claims, God is interpreted as *a-pathetic*, non-suffering, not affected by anything in the world. This in fact is a betrayal of Christianity's Jewish inheritance – within which God is first and foremost a God present in history, identified with the fate of God's people and sharing their sufferings.

Furthermore, Moltmann argues, the impassable God cannot be believed in honestly without trivialising human suffering – and also trivialising divine love. A God who could not be affected by anything could not really love anything, and would hence be 'poorer' than any human being. Furthermore, a God who 'stood by' while the *Shoah* happened would be a God unworthy of worship. Moltmann quotes Wiesel's account of 'God ... hanging on the gallows' and responds that 'any other answer [to the question "where is God in Auschwitz?"] would be blasphemy'.

How does the memory of the crucified Jesus help in the confrontation with contemporary evils? For this to be the basis for a meaningful response, it matters enormously that Jesus is not 'just another suffering human being'. Speaking of the crucified *God* makes the memory of suffering, the vindication of the sufferers and the eventual transformation of the world to overcome sin and alienation, part of God's own life. God's very being is, as it were, at stake in the drama of world history. God's 'solution' to the problem of evil lies in the future, although it is decisively revealed and anticipated in the resurrection of the crucified Jesus. Moltmann, then, calls for a re-examination of our concepts of God in the light of the crucified Christ – after Auschwitz.

Debating God's impassibility

The fellow-sufferer who understands.

Process and Reality (New York: Macmillan, 1929), p532.

Alfred North Whitehead (1861–1947), the British mathematician turned philosopher and theologian, coined this influential description of God in the context of his philosophy of *process*. For Whitehead, and for the many later thinkers (particularly in North America) who have taken up his work, process is more fundamental to reality than is substance or being. Reality is made (to put it simply) not of things, but of events and processes. God's reality, in turn, has to be understood, not only as unchanging substance, but as a process involved with other processes. God 'guides' the world-process, without fixing the outcome of any specific event – and God responds to what happens within the world-process.

Whitehead, when he re-described God in this way, was not directly seeking a response to the 'problem of evil' – but his vision of God as 'fellow sufferer' has found many resonances and parallels among Christian theologians attempting to respond to the evils of the twentieth century. Many later proponents of *process theology* set their thought in direct opposition to the traditional Christian belief in God's impassibility – that God, as God, cannot 'suffer' anything from God's creation. Influential figures in process theology, besides Whitehead, include Charles Hartshorne, Schubert Ogden and John B. Cobb, Jr.

Process theology – and wider movements in Western theology that take up its ideas – treats (what is often referred to as) 'classical theism' as untenable in the contemporary world. Divine impassibility – and associated doctrines of divine immutability, transcendence and omnipotence – is for the process theologians not only untenable in the light of the modern scientific worldview; it is *morally* untenable, because it presents a God who creates a world of suffering and remains aloof from and unaffected by that world. Thus far, the arguments of process theologians sound similar to those of Moltmann. In both cases, moreover, the answer is sought in a radical questioning of (what is taken to be) the established understanding of 'God'.

Moltmann, as we have seen, looks to Christology and Trinitarian thought to transform what we mean by 'God' and hence how we understand the 'problem of evil'. Process theologians, on the other hand – particularly mindful of the issues about divine causality discussed in Chapter 11 – look to metaphysics, and particularly to Whitehead's questioning of the priority of substance. A God who is involved in the world process, not as an outside agency that controls it but as a force within it and responding to it, cannot be 'blamed' for evil and suffering; the standard question 'how can an all-powerful and good God allow evil?' is met by rejecting the claim that God is 'all-powerful' – and adding to this the claim that God's exertion of 'power' in the world is conditioned by the freedom of created beings, such that God Godself 'suffers' the destructive consequences of creatures' freedom.

Belief in divine impassibility and immutability is not, however, dead – nor are many of its defenders afraid to confront the modern 'problem of evil'. In recent years, there has been a resurgence of ideas about God and God's relationship to creation that bear more relationship to the wider, pre-modern theological traditions we discussed earlier. Various theologians have insisted that God is not best understood as an agent like us, albeit one with vastly greater powers – and that this gives us a different perspective on 'impassibility'. Impassibility, they argue, does not mean that God is unfeeling and uncaring, but rather that God does not have needs. God's life is (always and from the beginning) a life of perfect loving communion; and the world exists only because God wills joyfully and entirely freely to share that life with others.

If one asks where evil fits into this picture, in which God is the sustaining source of the being and goodness of everything there is, and there is no good apart from God – the first answer is simply that it *does not* fit in. Evil is, for this way of thinking, seen as a 'privation', a lack, 'no good'. It is a hole in the picture of God and God's good creation – something that does not belong and has no place in that picture. All that one can say by way of explanation, without giving evil more of a 'place' in creation than it deserves,

See Thomas Weinandy, *Does God Suffer?* (Notre Dame: University of Notre Dame Press, 2000) for a robust defence of God's impassibility and critique *inter alia* of Moltmann. Oliver Davies, *A Theology of Compassion* (London: SCM Press, 2001) combines an extended (and dense, though rewarding) engagement with the question of God's presence in Auschwitz with a reaffirmation of theological tradition.

For other examples of theological re-engagements with the tradition of evil as 'a lack of good', see Kenneth Surin, *Theology and the Problem of Evil* (Oxford: Blackwell, 1986) and Terrence W. Tilley, *The Evils of Theodicy* (Washington: Georgetown University Press, 1991).

is that God has so made the world that such holes, such privations, are not prevented from existing. The second answer that such theologians give, however, is that the perfect life of goodness that God shares with creation is a life of *redeeming* and saving love: it is a life that makes good out of no-good. Evil is not 'explained', but it is met, redeemed and overcome.

In the twenty-first century, theology continues its confrontation with multiple evils, natural and human-made – indeed, in an age of massive ecological degradation, natural and human-made evils are becoming harder to separate. The condemnation of religion as *itself* a human-made evil, which we saw in nineteenth-century humanist thought, has gained new force in public debates in recent years. One question that this chapter's discussion raises is whether the confrontation with evil – as a 'problem' to be solved – is really, on Christian terms, a good place from which to *start* doing theology. On the other hand, looking at the example of Christianity in Nazi Germany, we can see that Christian encounters with the extremes of natural and human evil prove a crucial test of theology's capacity to speak meaningfully about God.

Bibliography

Theology, the Churches and Nazism

Jack Forstman, *Christian Faith in Dark Times: Theological Conflicts in the Shadow of Hitler* (Louisville: Westminster John Knox, 1992).

Klaus Scholder, *The Churches and the Third Reich* (London: Fortress Press, 1987).

Robert A. Krieg, *Catholic Theologians in Nazi Germany* (London: Athlone Press, 2004).

Ernst Christian Helmreich, *The German Churches under Hitler: Background, Struggle and Epilogue* (Detroit: Wayne State University Press, 1979).

Richard Steigmann-Gall, *The Holy Reich: Nazi Conceptions of Christianity, 1919-1945* (Cambridge: Cambridge University Press, 2003).

Robert P. Ericksen and Susannah Heschel (eds), *Betrayal: German Churches and the Holocaust* (Minneapolis: Augsburg Fortress, 1999). Both this and the above focus on 'pro-Nazi' Christianity and 'pro-Christian' Nazism.

Dietrich Bonhoeffer

The best English edition of Bonhoeffer's works is the Augsburg Fortress series (usually abbreviated to DBWE), edited by Clifford Green *et al.*, and translated by Ilse Tödt *et al.* Various older translations exist and are usable. The most relevant primary sources for this chapter are:

Discipleship (DBWE 4, 2003)

Ethics (DBWE 6, 2009)

Letters and Papers from Prison (DBWE 8, 2010).

Useful secondary sources include:

Eberhard Bethge, *Dietrich Bonhoeffer: Theologian, Christian, Contemporary* (London: Collins, 1970). The definitive biography, long but worth it!

Ferdinand Schlingensiepen, *Bonhoeffer: Martyr, Theologian, Man of Resistance* (London: T&T Clark, 2009). A more recent biography.

Stephen Plant, *Bonhoeffer* (London: Continuum, 2004). Strongly recommended introductory text.

John de Gruchy (ed.), *The Cambridge Companion to Dietrich Bonhoeffer* (Cambridge: Cambridge University Press, 1999).

Joel Lawrence, *Bonhoeffer: A Guide for the Perplexed* (London: T&T Clark, 2010). Another very well-written and clear introduction.

James McClendon Jr., *Ethics* (Nashville: Abingdon, 2002). See Chapter 7 on Bonhoeffer, pacifism and resistance.

'Confronting evil' in theology after 1945

We have not attempted to give a comprehensive bibliography on the problem of evil in philosophy and theology; we list works that connect directly with the discussion in our chapter.

Jürgen Moltmann, *The Crucified God*, new edition (London: SCM, 2001). A classic, reprinted with an introduction by Richard Bauckham, leading scholar of Moltmann's work.

John B. Cobb and David Ray Griffin, *Process Theology: An Introductory Exposition* (Louisville: Westminster John Knox, 1976). Classic outline of process theology by two of its major exponents.

David Bentley Hart, *Where was God in the Tsunami?* (Grand Rapids: Eerdmans, 2005). Theological engagement with the problem of natural evil in relation to twenty-first century events.

Stephen T. Davis (ed.), *Encountering Evil: Live Options in Theodicy* (Edinburgh: T&T Clark, 1981). Includes contributions from process theologians.

John Hick, *Evil and the God of Love* (London: Macmillan, 1986). Well-known and much-debated attempt at contemporary theodicy.

Kenneth Surin, *Theology and the Problem of Evil* (Oxford: Blackwell, 1986).

Terrence W. Tilley, *The Evils of Theodicy* (Washington, DC: Georgetown University Press, 1991).

Thomas Weinandy, *Does God Suffer?* (Notre Dame: University of Notre Dame Press, 2000). Restatement of the doctrine of God's impassibility.

14

Feminism, gender and theology

AIMS

By the end of this chapter, we hope that you will:

- know what is meant by 'feminist theology' and have thought about why it might be important and influential

- understand some of the debates within and around feminist theology, particularly concerning the relationship between feminism, the Bible and Christian tradition

- understand how recent and contemporary feminist theology relates to various developments in nineteenth-century thought (including, but not only, nineteenth-century feminism)

- have thought about how feminist theology is *modern* and how it is *postmodern*.

Introduction: Beyond God the Father

Feminist theology is generally thought of as a twentieth-century phenomenon, consisting of a powerful challenge to **sexism** and misogyny within Christian tradition and the subsequent efforts to work out how that challenge might be met. In this chapter, we first look at the challenge of feminist theology as it was put forward most clearly in the second half of the twentieth century, and then ask about where that challenge came from and where it might be going.

In 1973, at the height of the women's liberation movement, Mary Daly's *Beyond God the Father: Towards a Philosophy of Women's Liberation* was published. It has been recognised as one of the key texts of twentieth-century **feminism**. Engaging with a broad sweep of intellectual history, it provided an account of why the women's movement was necessary, and where it was going. One of its major targets was religion and its role in sustaining sexism. This combination of religious and feminist thought was a new development in the 1970s debates.

An early and enthusiastic reviewer, Lois Gehr Livezey, wrote: '*Beyond God the Father* is a distinctive contribution to theological discussion because it represents a feminist perspective; it is a distinctive contribution to feminist discussion because it represents a theological perspective' (Livezey, *Journal of Religion* 55/4 (October 1979), pp478–479, here p478).

Mary Daly (1928–2010) was a lecturer in theology at Boston College, a Roman Catholic institution. Her previous book, *The Church and the Second Sex* (1968), had already caused controversy within the theological world – but *Beyond God the Father* marked a decisive turning-point. Daly declared herself to be 'post-Christian' and signalled her rejection of all *man*-made religion.

Beyond God the Father makes intriguing reading, even for those who also find parts or all of it infuriating or misguided. Daly thought that existing language and existing conventions of philosophical argument, no less than existing forms of religion, were helping to support **patriarchy** and sexism. The women's liberation movement had to break or invert these forms. Daly writes in aphorisms, uses 'serious' puns that question everyday assumptions about what words mean and experiments with language.

Figure 14.1 Mary Daly

Daly's style is often reminiscent of that of Nietzsche and her motivations are, in many ways, similar. She, like Nietzsche, wants to call into question not just particular 'truths', but the whole system that produces and authorises things as 'truth'. As we will see, a key feature of Daly's work, and that of other feminist theologians, is the claim that sexism is an all-pervasive and systematic problem. For her, changing or challenging a few specific ideas will not end sexism; we need to change *the way we think*. Hence her playing with language, and her subversion of all expectations about how 'serious' philosophical and theological argument works.

One of Daly's best-known aphorisms sums up her assessment of the connection between religion and sexism: 'If God is male, then the male is God.' In other words, the maleness of God in Christianity (in particular) reinforces the dominance of men and the suppression of women in society. Daly's critique of the patriarchal structures of the Church, developed in *The Church and the Second Sex*, goes alongside a critique of theological language and symbolism. Both are, in her view, structured in such a way as to deny power, goodness or agency to women.

Some key terminology for studying this area

The word 'feminism' was coined in the mid-nineteenth century – accounts of its origins vary, but it was first used in English around 1850. Before reading further, we suggest you write down your own working definition of the word; then look up a few dictionary definitions and compare them with yours. Think about any significant differences that emerge – for example, over whether feminism is being defined as an *idea* or as a political *movement*, and whether it is about 'women' or about 'the equality of the sexes'. You will probably find that definitions vary, because the meaning of 'feminist' is contested.

The *women's liberation movement* is one of the terms commonly used for feminist writing and political activism in the second half of the twentieth century, in Europe and North America.

Sexism and *patriarchy* are closely connected terms. Sexism refers to discrimination on the basis of sex – *usually* to discrimination against women. Patriarchy (literally 'rule of the father') refers to societies, organisations and systems in which power is held by (some) men. Feminist thinkers, including feminist theologians, generally argue that patriarchy is a key dimension – although not necessarily the only dimension – of injustice in human societies. They may differ in their views on the origins, nature and extent of patriarchy.

Sex and *gender* are also closely connected terms, and the relationship between them is more controversial. The easy way to make the distinction is to say 'sex is about biology, gender is about society'; your sex is determined by (for example) your chromosomes and genitalia, your gender by (for example) your name, how you dress and behave, how people treat you and how you fit into the system of family relationships. Many thinkers argue that this distinction is not really clear-cut. The important point to note, though, is that it is usually confusing to say 'gender' when you mean biological maleness or femaleness. (Some people do this to avoid using the word 'sex' – but their squeamishness is misplaced.)

Feminist theology looks, at first glance, like a twentieth-century phenomenon. It goes alongside one of the most dramatic changes to the 'face' of theology in the twentieth century – a major increase in women's access to theological education and to the power to contribute to theological debate in the academy and the Churches. Daly's work has obvious links to a number of important analyses of sexism and patriarchy that appeared in the second half of the twentieth century. The title of Daly's first book refers directly to one of these – Simone de Beauvoir's *The Second Sex* (1949). Other key early works for the women's liberation movement include Betty Friedan, *The Feminine Mystique* (1963) and Kate Millett, *Sexual Politics* (1968).

Beyond God the Father was accompanied, and followed, by a number of significant theological works by feminist thinkers. They developed critical analyses of Christian institutions, practices, beliefs and symbols – in the interests of freeing women (and, as many feminists would argue, men) from the situation of patriarchy. Some of these theologians and critics, such as Daly, argued (and continue to argue) that Christianity and feminism were simply incompatible. Others argued (and continue to argue) that the challenges of feminism, the challenge to reveal and end the injustice of patriarchy, could and should be met from *within* Christianity, through the re-thinking of Christian tradition.

For a good introduction to the debates between these two groups of feminist theologians – 'post-Christian feminists' and 'Christian feminists' – see Daphne Hampson (ed.), *Swallowing a Fishbone? Feminist Theologians Debate Christianity* (London: SPCK, 1996).

Note, incidentally, that while most well-known feminist theologians are women, and while there have been real debates about the nature of men's involvement in the feminist movement more generally, you should not assume that all feminist theologians are women (nor, of course, that all women theologians are feminists!).

So where does the emergence of feminist theology – and of feminist critiques of religion – fit into the story of modern theology? Is it part of the trajectories of religious thought we have been tracing within 'modernity', or is it a reaction against them? We begin by looking at the *critical* motivation for feminist theology and its links to developments in the nineteenth century.

Feminist suspicion, women's liberation

Much as she would (with some justification) object to being linked to historical 'masters', at least some of Daly's intellectual tools come from the nineteenth-century 'masters of suspicion'. We have already noted the similarities between her approach and Nietzsche's. What she shares with Marx and others is a critical analysis of religion as a human production that serves particular human political interests. As we have seen, she reads the 'male God' of Christianity as an ideological support for male domination – a way of making the patriarchal order of society seem 'natural' and 'obvious'. She, and other feminist critics of Christianity, can easily find numerous examples of how the portrayal of God as male – and, linked to this, the maleness of Jesus – has been explicitly, as well as implicitly, used to justify a subordinate position for women in society and in Church institutions.

One obvious example, which has continuing relevance, is the debates over women's leadership within the Churches. Feminist critics of the Churches would attack, not only the explicit arguments that are put forward against women's leadership and/or priesthood – 'a female cannot represent the male Christ' – but also the way that the representation of God as male reinforces the idea that power and authority belong to males.

Such a feminist approach assumes that it is useful to read theological arguments, texts and symbols suspiciously – asking about their political functions and their roles in systems of power. It does not necessarily reduce theological arguments, texts and symbols to *just* their political functions. So, for example, *Christian* feminist theologians might be interested, not just in pointing out that the maleness of Jesus is used to support patriarchy in arguments about women's leadership, but in arguing about whether that way of talking about Jesus' maleness is theologically sound.

Many of the most important works of feminist theology in the twentieth century directly acknowledge their links to (other) theologies of liberation (see Chapter 15), and to the modern practice of reading religious tradition 'suspiciously' for its political and social implications. For example, Rosemary Radford Ruether's *Sexism and God-Talk* (London: SCM, 1993) presents a Christian feminist theological vision that centres on the 'prophetic' dimension of Jewish and Christian tradition – the voice that speaks out against injustice and challenges those religious hierarchies and systems that maintain injustice. Feminist theologians have been critical voices within the movements of liberation theology, drawing attention to the pervasive injustice of sexism in religion and society.

This, however, sounds as if feminist theology's main inspiration is drawn from critics of religion – such that feminism comes as an external, 'modern', challenge to religious tradition. However, as we will see in the next section, the situation is rather more complicated.

First wave, second wave

As we have seen, in the late twentieth century, it was not at all obvious that feminism and Christianity could or should go together. Everyone involved in the debate – post-Christian feminists such as Daly, Christian feminists such as Ruether and the commentators on their work – has tended to treat the feminist 'challenge' as something that came to Christianity from outside and not as an integral part of Christian tradition. For many conservative Christians it was and is perceived as a 'modern' secular threat to Christianity.

If we look back to the earlier history of feminism, however, it is less obvious that feminism is external to Christianity. Debates around gender equality and the roles of women and men have often been conducted as *theological* debates – that is, both feminists and their opponents have conducted the argument from *within* Christian tradition, drawing on Christian theological resources.

A further note on terminology: Histories of feminism often refer to 'first wave', 'second wave' and (sometimes) 'third wave' feminism. The 'first wave', in the nineteenth and early twentieth centuries, is associated particularly with campaigns for women's suffrage, and other forms of political and legal equality for women. The 'second wave' is what we have discussed above as the *women's liberation movement* in the second half of the twentieth century – taking up the concerns of the 'first wave', but adding a stronger emphasis on how the structures of patriarchy affected all aspects of women's and men's lives. 'Third wave' is often used to refer to contemporary feminist thinkers who engage explicitly with postmodern ideas and concerns, and with the intersections of race, class, colonialism and gender.

   The key point to note for our purposes is that what is read and discussed as 'feminist theology' today usually comes from the *second wave* of feminism – but the *first wave* also produced theological work, and in fact engaged much more widely with Christian beliefs, texts and institutions.

   Note also that it could be argued that feminism, and even feminist theology, began *before* the 'first wave', and before the word 'feminist' was used. See, for example, our discussion of Mary Wollstonecraft in Chapter 9. To give an even earlier example, Margaret Fell in 1666 wrote an extended defence of women's leadership in Christian communities, which prefigures many of the arguments used by later feminist theologians. See Margaret Fell, *Women's Speaking Justified, Proved and Allowed of by the Scriptures* (1666), available online at <www.qhpress. org/texts/fell.html>.

   For an introduction to the relationship between 'first wave' and 'second wave' feminist theology, with discussions of key figures from the 'first wave' and earlier, see Ann Loades, *Feminist Theology: Voices from the Past* (Cambridge: Polity Press, 2001).

There were feminist interpretations and criticisms of Christian texts and traditions in the nineteenth and early twentieth centuries. However, they were often not being expressed in the places where we might look first for 'theology', and the reasons for this are linked to wider features of religious life in modernity.

Part of the background to first-wave feminism was the widespread and pervasive idea of (upper- and middle-class) women as maintainers of the home, belonging to the private sphere and hence not able to take part in public life. The division between private and public spheres, which we have encountered several times in our discussion of modernity, was also (at least by the mid-nineteenth century) a *gendered* division. Religion played an important part in this portrayal of gender roles. The private sphere, maintained by women, was the focus of religious life. There was a strong association, not only between women and domesticity, but between women and religious faith; women, in their roles as guardians of the home, nurtured their families' faith and instilled moral values in them. In this context, women's emergence from 'the home' and their participation in public life could be seen as a threat to the spiritual and moral health of the community.

> A notorious example of this image of women's domestic-and-religious role is Coventry Patmore's poem 'The Angel in the House' (1854). Virginia Woolf, as a twentieth-century feminist writer and the inheritor (as she saw it) of the nineteenth century's problematic legacy for women, famously declared that she could not begin to write until she had killed the 'Angel in the House' (Woolf, 'Professions for Women', 1931 available at http://s.spachman.tripod.com/ Woolf/professions.htm).

By the same logic, women's public religious voice was significantly constrained – even though 'in private' women were supposed to be more religious than men. Few women were publishing academic theology, and few women were in Church leadership. (Of course, feminist theology does not have to be done by women. In practice, however, there is little feminist theology by men from this period.) Much early 'feminist theology' appears in contexts and genres other than the academic book or lecture – contexts and genres that were more easily available to women in the light of the constraints on their public voice.

Literature is one key example. Women's novels and poetry from the nineteenth century are a key source for feminist religious thought. Marian Evans (George Eliot) articulated her critical accounts of Christianity and its shaping of women's lives through her novels. Christina Rossetti, who was involved with several feminist groups in London, explored religious themes and themes of sex and gender extensively in her poetry.

> A good example of Rossetti's poetic exploration of Christianity and gender is 'Goblin Market' (first published 1862). The text is widely available online – see for example <www.victorianweb.org/authors/crossetti/gobmarket.html>.

Rossetti's best-known work is probably the hymn 'In the Bleak Midwinter'. Most people do not realise how many of today's widely-used hymns were written by women in the nineteenth century – using one of the forms of religious expression that was most widely recognised and accepted as appropriate for women. Hymns were seen as expressions of women's personal and emotionally-charged faith, and as suitable for use in private devotion and religious instruction in the home. It is generally hard to find *feminist* themes in these hymns – although it can be argued that the very fact of women producing theological texts, for wider publication and use, was a form of resistance to male religious authority.

First-wave feminism did, however, produce numerous challenges to the restriction of women's public voice. One important arena in which 'first wave' feminist theology developed was the campaigns for women's suffrage, particularly in Britain and America – and the associated campaigns around women's education and employment rights and the reform of family law. As with the anti-slavery campaigns (see Chapter 15), religious arguments were invoked on all sides of these debates.

It is not surprising that many of the participants in the early feminist campaigns incorporated very critical analyses of the religious establishment into their work – in particular, critical analyses of the silence of the Churches on issues affecting women's lives, and of the use of Christian texts and traditions to justify women's subordination. However, these analyses were often linked to re-readings of texts and traditions. For example, the writings of the Grimké sisters (see also Chapter 15), Lucretia Mott and Susan B. Anthony – key campaigners for women's rights in the USA – all demonstrate the strong links between their interpretations of the Bible and of Christian teaching and their political activism. Themes beloved of 'progressive' religious thinkers in the modern era include the creation of humanity, male and female, in the image of God; the appeal to God's authority over against human (male/patriarchal) authority; and Jesus' disruption of social and religious hierarchies.

More broadly, many participants in first-wave feminism were, like Josephine Butler (see Chapter 9), inheritors of the nineteenth century's evangelical revivals. They believed that Christian faith could and should produce radical transformation, not only in the individual's 'private' life but also in her or his interactions with society. In the USA, the 'Second Great Awakening' in the early nineteenth century was strongly associated with social activism as well as personal transformation. Conversion in this and similar revivals meant, among other things, being set free to do good in the world – and to follow one's calling to do good, even in the face of social and institutional opposition. Campaigns for women's rights were only one part of a wider programme of action for social transformation in which many of the first-wave feminists were involved.

The most obvious example in the USA is the interconnection of anti-slavery and women's rights campaigns. This was a conflicted area – many campaigners for women's rights (such as those listed above) were also anti-slavery campaigners, but within the anti-slavery movement there was also significant opposition to women's political activism – and after the US Civil War there were bitter disputes within the women's movement over the relative priority to be given to the civil rights of African-Americans and of women.

The famous account of Sojourner Truth's speech to the Akron Women's Convention in 1854 highlights some of the tensions around the links between the women's movement and the anti-slavery campaigns.

Figure 14.2 Sojourner Truth

Sojourner Truth (1797–1883), a former slave who had become a travelling preacher and campaigner, caused a disturbance when she arrived at the public discussion of women's rights (according to the account written some years later by the chair of the meeting, Matilda Joslyn Gage):

> The leaders of the movement trembled on seeing a tall, gaunt black woman in a gray dress and white turban, surmounted with an uncouth sun-bonnet, march deliberately into the church, walk with the air of a queen up the aisle, and take her seat upon the pulpit steps. A buzz of disapprobation was heard all over the house ...

The following day, after a session in which various ministers opposed to women's suffrage spoke about:

> superior rights and privileges for man, on the ground of 'superior intellect' ... because of the 'manhood of Christ; if God had desired the equality of woman, He would have given some token of His will through the birth, life, and death of the Saviour' ... [because] of the 'sin of our first mother'.

Sojourner Truth delivered a speech in which she both directly challenged the arguments against women's rights and exposed the myth of idealised womanhood.

> I have ploughed, and planted, and gathered into barns, and no man could head me! And a'n't I a woman? I could work as much and eat as much as a man – when I could get it – and bear de lash as well! And a'n't I a woman? ... Den dat little man in black dar, he say women can't have as much rights as men, 'cause Christ wan't a woman! Whar did your Christ come from? ... From God and a woman! Man had nothin' to do wid Him ...
>
> Elizabeth Cady Stanton, Susan B. Anthony and Matilda J. Gage (eds), *History of Woman Suffrage*, vol I (Rochester: Susan B. Anthony, Charles Mann, 1881), pp114–117.

Elizabeth Cady Stanton (1815–1902) stands out among first-wave feminist thinkers because of the nature of her engagement with religious themes. Stanton was one of the fiercest critics of Christianity within the suffrage movements. In her view – as, later, in Daly's – religion in general, and Christianity in particular, constituted one of the major barriers to women's social and political advancement. Christian teaching was and always would be degrading to women.

Figure 14.3 Elizabeth Cady Stanton with Susan B. Anthony

Stanton was also, however, responsible for editing a landmark work of early feminist engagement with theology, the *Woman's Bible* (1895). Deliberately following on from the much-discussed publication of the 'Revised Version' of the Bible in 1888, Stanton gathered a 'Revising Committee' of women with thorough knowledge of the biblical texts (supported by various levels of academic training) and with feminist concerns. The text they produced offers commentaries on every book of the Bible insofar as it relates to women. The articles include, for example, detailed discussion of issues of translation, analyses of the narratives and their symbolism, social and historical commentary on the interpretation and use of the texts, theories about their origins and purposes. Rather than confining feminist engagement with religion to 'feminine' spheres (such as literature or hymns), and rather than addressing religious questions in the context of specific political campaigns, Stanton and her committee were introducing feminist concerns directly into the 'male' sphere of biblical commentary.

In its time, the *Woman's Bible* was enormously controversial – not least within the women's suffrage movement itself. The National American Women Suffrage Association, for example, felt it necessary to pass a resolution denying all official connection with the *Woman's Bible*. The book was widely interpreted – with much justification, given Stanton's own views as expressed in the introduction – as a wholesale attack on the Bible in the name of women's rights.

However, the individual articles by the various members of the 'Revising Committee' give a rather more complex picture. Some focus, not on the sexism of the Bible itself, but on sexist translations or misleading traditions of interpretation. Some focus on female characters who are portrayed positively and bemoan the lack of emphasis on these figures within Christian tradition. In other words, while some of the articles in the *Woman's Bible* clearly 'attack' the Bible, others can be construed as 'defences' of the Bible against what these commentators see as patriarchal misinterpretation, and attempts to argue from the Bible for women's equality and rights. Some, that is, seem to prefigure post-Christian feminism, others to prefigure Christian feminism.

For an example of the former, see Stanton's comments on the female characters in Genesis:

> In woman's struggle for freedom during the last half century, men have continually been pointing her to the women of the Bible for examples worthy imitation, but we fail to see the merits of their character, their position, the laws and sentiments concerning them. The only significance of dwelling on these women, and this period of woman's history, is to show the absurdity of pointing the women of the nineteenth century to these as examples of virtue.
>
> *Woman's Bible*, p53.

For an example of the latter, see Lillie Devereux Blake's comments on the narrative of 'the Fall': 'Reading this narrative carefully, it is amazing that any set of men ever claimed that the dogma of the inferiority of woman is here set forth ...' (*Woman's Bible*, p26).

The *Woman's Bible* draws attention to a key area of tension within feminist theology, to which we have already referred. Are feminist theologians criticising sexism and patriarchy in order to *reform* Christian tradition or in order to *reject* it? More than this, can the critique of patriarchy be inspired and motivated by Christianity, rather than only directed against Christianity? In other words, can feminism be a movement internal to Christianity, a form of Christian *self*-criticism?

Reject or reconstruct?: the example of biblical interpretation

The interpretation of the Bible continues to be a focal point for the working out of these tensions. If we compare feminist theology with (other) liberation theologies (see Chapter 15), one of the main points of difference that emerges is the ambivalent attitude to the Bible and biblical interpretation. It is simply harder to find gender justice in the Bible than it is to find economic justice. The books of the Bible were, obviously, written in patriarchal societies. At the very least, they reflect these societies, their social structures and their assumptions (for example, in the limited range of roles and the limited power available to female characters). In several cases, as the writers of the *Woman's Bible* noted, they appear explicitly to affirm and uphold patriarchal structures and assumptions. So the question for feminist theologians is: can feminist thought and practice work *within* the community that reads this Bible – as a movement of reform – or must feminists end up rejecting the Bible and, with it, Christianity?

For those feminist thinkers (such as Daly or, before her, Stanton) who argue for a 'post-Christian' position, the patriarchal character of biblical texts is one of the most obvious reasons to move away from Christianity altogether. Within Christianity, women will always be subjected to a patriarchal norm, because the Bible will always be normative; and women will always be surrounded by stories, images and terminology that demean them. At the same time, feminist theologians who want to remain within Christianity have continued, not only to draw attention to those biblical texts that are more 'positive' for women, but also to use the tools of modern biblical scholarship to develop new interpretations of 'problem' texts.

Some have argued, for example, that certain texts are reforming or even radical *in their original contexts*, and that a contemporary reading needs to take account of the original context. The modern interest in the historicity of the Bible is used to challenge or undermine traditional readings for feminist purposes. Others go further and argue that we need to take a suspicious approach to the formation of the biblical canon, asking how the selection and presentation of material may have served the interests of patriarchy and obscured messages of gender equality.

This suspicious approach to the formation of the biblical canon is itself prefigured in the *Woman's Bible*. See, for example, Stanton's comment on Genesis 2: 'It is evident that some wily writer, seeing the perfect equality of man and woman in the first chapter, felt it important for the dignity and dominion of man to effect woman's subordination in some way' (p21).

The twentieth-century scholar most strongly associated with this latter argument is Elisabeth Schüssler Fiorenza, best known for her feminist interpretations of early Christian history and critical re-readings of the New Testament canon. Fiorenza's argument is that Christian *readings* of the New Testament have been shaped by the assumption that patriarchy is natural and normal. Christians reading the New Testament have, for example, simply assumed that Jesus' disciples and the leaders of early Christianity were men, unless they found textual evidence to the contrary. Fiorenza asks what happens if we read the New Testament assuming that women and men held equal status within early Christianity. The results, in her work, include the positive reinterpretation of certain texts (texts that can be seen to record and affirm women's leadership, once that is what the reader 'expects' to see) – but also the suggestion that other, patriarchal, texts are signs of early attempts to conceal or deny women's role.

To see how Fiorenza's method works, look at two New Testament texts, which are examples of the two types she discusses: Mark 14:3–9 and 1 Corinthians 11: 3–16. Ask yourself, in each case:

- How would you interpret each of these texts if you believed that it was written in and for a community in which all the leaders were men?
- How would you interpret each of these texts if you believed that it was written in and for a community where women and men were equally likely to be leaders?
- Then, looking back to Chapter 10, ask yourself: how much do or should our beliefs about the Bible's 'original context' matter anyway?

Fiorenza's *In Memory of Her: A Feminist Theological Reconstruction of Christian Origins*, 10th edition (New York: Crossroad, 1994) is a good place to start exploring her interpretations of these and other New Testament texts. (Note the reference, in the title, to Mark 14:9.)

Feminisms modern and postmodern

Reframing sex and gender

Fiorenza's approach to biblical interpretation is a good example of the uneasy relationship that feminist thought in general and feminist theology in particular has with modernity. On the one hand, Fiorenza is using modern methods of biblical criticism. She is working as a historian, reconstructing the original contexts of biblical texts, using historical methods to produce interpretations that challenge or disrupt theological tradition. She is also using 'modern' ethical standards, of justice and equality, to judge the texts and their interpreters. Her explicit aim is progress towards a more just community and a more just world, and this is a key criterion for evaluating theology and biblical interpretation.

But this in turn means that Fiorenza is explicit about the 'partial' character of her interpretations. She is not attempting to adopt the neutral, objective, scientific position associated with the first proponents of modern biblical scholarship. In fact, she is demonstrating that this supposedly neutral position is and was shaped by patriarchy. Her feminist suspicion is directed, not just at Scripture and theological tradition, but (perhaps even more) at modern scholarship. Other contemporary feminist biblical scholars, both from the North and from the South, are more explicit about their rejection of the 'modern' emphasis on neutrality and objectivity, and about their critique of how modern approaches to biblical scholarship excluded the voices of women (and others who were not part of the Western academic establishment). See, for example, Musa Dube, *Postcolonial Feminist Interpretation of the Bible* (St Louis: Chalice Press, 2000), to which we also refer in Chapter 15.

Feminist thought both arises from the modern project and reveals the limits of the modern project. The links between Mary Daly's work and Nietzsche's, to which we referred earlier, should alert us to this, because Nietzsche's suspicious critique of the search for truth was directed at the modern project as well as at religion. From a feminist point of view, it is necessary to be (at least a little) suspicious of overarching claims to determine truth, emanating from systems or institutions shaped by patriarchy – be that the Christian Churches or the modern academy.

Many characteristically modern ideals are, in fact, foci of debate within the feminist movement. A good example is equality. To what extent is equality really a goal of feminism? Is it right for women to seek 'equality' with men – when the role of men has itself been shaped by patriarchy? To put it another way: should feminists accept modern definitions of what it means to be human and seek recognition of women's humanity on those terms or should they, instead, try to challenge the definitions of humanity? Is it true that, as the often-quoted quip goes, 'women who seek to be equal with men lack ambition'?

Most of the feminism of the 'first wave' is often characterised as *liberal* feminism, motivated by modern 'liberal' ideas about humanity. For example, early feminists embraced the idea of human rights and claimed them for women; they assumed that it was vitally important to be free to participate in the public sphere by voting and campaigned for women's suffrage. Theologically, claims about the equality of human beings before God, and an account of how human being related to God that de-emphasised gender difference, helped to support these arguments.

> Alison Jaggar's categorisation of feminisms, distinguishing between 'liberal', 'romantic', 'radical' and 'socialist' feminism, has been influential and is still very useful. See Alison M. Jaggar, *Feminist Politics and Human Nature* (Lanham: Rowman & Littlefield, 1983), Chapter 1.

Even in the first wave of feminism, however, there were already very extensive debates about whether women's participation would *change* and disrupt the public sphere and whether the dominant stories about humanity reflected only a male point of view. Theologically, there were also strong narratives about the importance of women's embodied distinctiveness.

> J. Ellice Hopkins, to whom we referred in the section on Josephine Butler in Chapter 9, is an intriguing example of an early feminist theologian whose attack on gender injustice was linked to a very strong emphasis on sexual difference. Several of the *Woman's Bible* contributors also emphasise the distinctive virtues, power or capacities of women – either as they appear within the biblical text or as the biblical text seems to suppress them.

Placing an emphasis on sexual difference has obvious advantages for feminist theology. It can be a way of resisting the modern construction of a supposedly-universal (but actually privileged male) human subject – and, along with that, resisting the way in which that 'universal' vision of humanity left no room for real *religious* difference. It can be a way of upholding Christian claims about the goodness of human embodiment, in the face of modern denigrations of the body and its passions. On a practical level, women are clearly not always helped by systems that ignore or downplay sexual difference – for example, if their needs as mothers are not taken seriously.

Many second-wave feminist theologians have been influenced by the work of Luce Irigaray (b. 1932), a French feminist philosopher and psychoanalyst with a strong interest in religious symbolism and language. Irigaray's starting-point is not equality but sexual difference and her work focuses on, among other things, the need for women to develop language and symbolism in which they can speak *as women,* and the far-reaching implications of acknowledging sexual difference as a basic dimension of human existence. For examples, with discussion, of Irigaray's writings on religion, see Morny Joy *et al.* (eds), *French Feminists on Religion: A Reader* (London: Routledge, 2002).

At the same time, an emphasis on sexual difference does not obviously help to move theology in the direction in which feminist theologians have hoped to go. 'Complementarity' has become a key and contested term in debates around the role of women in Christianity. Drawing on biblical texts and on arguments from natural law, both Catholic and Protestant theologians have developed accounts of men's and women's 'different but equal' roles before God. In many cases, these accounts justify the exclusion of women from leadership and the subordinate position of women within marriage as aspects of women's divinely-ordained 'difference'. Within Roman Catholicism, a central document for these discussions has been the encyclical *Mulieris Dignitatem* (On the Dignity of Women), issued in 1988 by Pope John Paul II. *Mulieris Dignitatem* contains both a repudiation of injustices done to women and the warning: 'In the name of liberation from male "domination", women must not appropriate to themselves male characteristics contrary to their own feminine "originality".' The differentiated functions of men and women (which includes, of course, the exclusion of women from ordination) are strongly affirmed in a clear attack on (one account of) what 'modern' feminism was trying to achieve.

Ironically, Mary Daly is also opposed, for very different reasons, to the idea that women should 'appropriate to themselves male characteristics' while seeking their liberation. For Daly, it is profoundly counterproductive for women to try to take up male/patriarchal forms of power or to claim that sexual or gender difference does not matter. This is a political and social argument, but also a theological one. Daly thinks that the feminist project needs to begin by discovering what *different* ways of being human women can create, when they free themselves from patriarchal oppression. For her, there is no 'gender-neutral' option, in religion or society, and no space that is free from struggles over patriarchy. In a context where patriarchy distorts everything, 'equality' is a meaningless idea.

Beyond this, Daly's attack on the 'male God' of Christianity – the 'Godfather' – is also an attack on women's attempt to achieve equality in the image of a male God and a call for women to re-imagine God. Many subsequent feminist thinkers have also perceived a need for re-imagining and renaming God, rethinking core Christian narratives and symbols, and re-forming religious practices, with a focus on *women's* voices, experiences and needs.

> The 'women-church' movement, from (around) the 1980s onwards, was, and is, one location for this feminist theological work. Women-church is used to describe various communities within the Christian Churches (primarily, within the Roman Catholic Church), formed around feminist insights and experimenting with visions of a non-patriarchal Christian community. In origin, it was a grassroots movement in a close relationship with (academic) feminist theology. The place of men within 'women-church', and its relationship with Church institutions, have been contentious. One major result of women-church has been the development of feminist and women-centred liturgies. See Rosemary Radford Ruether, *Women-Church: Theology and Practice of Feminist Liturgical Communities* (New York: HarperCollins, 1986).

Pluralising women's voices

But is the idea, advanced in Daly's work as in numerous other major texts of second-wave feminism, that patriarchy affects every aspect of life and of religious thought

> Kwok Pui-Lan criticised Daly on this basis in her essay 'Unbinding our Feet: Saving Brown Women and Feminist Religious Discourse' (in Laura E. Donaldson and Kwok Pui-Lan (eds), *Postcolonialism, Feminism and Religious Discourse* (London: Routledge, 2002).
> Sojourner Truth's speech at the Akron convention (see above) provides one example, from the first wave of feminism, of a challenge to the idea that 'woman' is a unitary category. Sojourner Truth's 'And an't *I* a woman?' draws attention to the gulf between her experience – in a patriarchal and racist society – and that of the white women on whom the Convention focused. Their status as idealised guardians of the domestic sphere, angels in the house, relied on the labour of enslaved African women. Significantly, however, Sojourner Truth also makes common cause with – and contributes her theological arguments to – the struggle for 'woman's [political] rights' in which the white women are engaged.

still, in some ways, too 'modern'? One criticism that has often been made of Daly is that she is, in effect, substituting her own new 'grand narrative' for the grand narratives of modernity. Critics have attacked, in particular, her analyses of the situation of non-Western women – analyses that, it is argued, do not take enough account of Daly's own position as a relatively privileged white woman from the global North. Daly, they say, analyses all societies as if patriarchy were the same everywhere and as if patriarchy were the only problem women face – where she herself, a white woman, might in fact be part of *another* problem for women facing racist or colonial oppression.

The challenge from **womanist** theology to second-wave feminist theology has been especially important. Womanist theology, arising from the experience and reflection of black women in the USA and elsewhere, has drawn attention to the many ways in which white feminists' accounts of women's oppression and women's struggles simply fail to recognise the effects of racism – and fail to speak of the realities of black women's lives. For example, as Jacquelyn Grant points out, white feminist theological controversies over the maleness of Jesus Christ do not reflect the priorities of black women. Women who are not struggling to gain equality within the privileged elite but rather are struggling to survive and flourish in a situation that repeatedly denies their humanity, develop christologies that may emphasise (for example) the presence of Jesus alongside those who struggle for justice, rather than the 'likeness' or otherwise of certain groups of people to Jesus.

See Jacquelyn Grant, *White Women's Christ, Black Women's Jesus: Feminist Christology and Womanist Response* (New York: American Academy of Religion, 1989). See also our discussion of womanist theology in Chapter 15.

Feminist theology's recognition of women's diversity is reflected in the title of a major recent volume of feminist biblical scholarship – Carol Newsom and Sharon H. Ringe (eds), *The Women's Bible Commentary* (Louisville: Westminster John Knox, 1992; expanded edition 1998). Where Stanton and her colleagues spoke of 'woman' in the singular – implying that all women really shared the same interests, concerns and needs – feminist theology now is much more likely to speak of 'women' in the plural. There is then, of course, an ongoing question (which does not only arise in theology, but is part of wider debates within feminism) about whether and how it is useful to make *any* general claims about 'women' or to bring different women together as part of one feminist movement.

For this and other reasons, it is much harder in the early twenty-first century – the time of feminism's 'third wave' – than it was in the 1980s to describe 'feminist theology' as a single coherent movement. It is, however, clear that feminist tools of analysis and feminist concerns are still being used worldwide in theology. Furthermore, since feminist theology has historically been closely connected with feminist activism and as global campaigns continue against sexism and gender-based discrimination, occasions for feminist theological work will continue to arise.

The intersection of modern and postmodern, 'universal' and 'particular', global and local, in contemporary feminist theology cannot be described systematically. Partly for this reason, feminist theology continues to be one of the spaces in which the legacy of modernity for theology, and for specific communities who do theology, is worked through.

Bibliography

Introductions to feminist theological thought

Daphne Hampson (ed.), *Swallowing a Fishbone: Feminist Theologians Debate Christianity*. (London: SPCK Publishing, 1996). An extended and very readable debate between Hampson, as a 'post-Christian' feminist, and five Christian feminist theologians. An excellent introduction to the key concerns of second-wave feminist theology.
Serene Jones, *Feminist Theory and Christian Theology: Cartographies of Grace*. (Princeton: Augsburg Fortress, 2000). Besides Jones' own constructive work, contains some very helpful introductions to key aspects of feminist theory.
Ann Loades, *Feminist Theology: Voices from the Past* (Cambridge: Polity, 2001).
Susan Parsons (ed.), *The Cambridge Companion to Feminist Theology* (Cambridge: Cambridge University Press, 2002). See chapters on major methodological and substantive issues in feminist theology.
Elizabeth Cady Stanton and others, *The Woman's Bible* (New York: Prometheus, 1999).

Some major 'second-wave' primary texts

Mary Daly, *Beyond God the Father: Towards a Philosophy of Women's Liberation*. (Boston: Beacon Press, 1973).
Elisabeth Schüssler Fiorenza, *In Memory of Her: A Feminist Theological Reconstruction of Christian Origins*. (London: SCM Press, 1995).
Daphne Hampson, *Theology and Feminism* (Oxford: Blackwell, 1990).
Sallie McFague, *Models of God: Theology for an Ecological Nuclear Age* (London: Augsburg Fortress, 1987).
Phyllis Trible, *Texts of Terror: Literary-Feminist Readings of Biblical Narratives* (Minneapolis: Augsburg Fortress, 1984).
Delores Williams, *Sisters in the Wilderness: The Challenge of Womanist God-Talk* (Maryknoll: Orbis Books, 1993).

Useful collections of shorter primary texts

Morny Joy, Kathleen O'Grady and Judith L. Poxon (eds), *French Feminists on Religion: A Reader* (London: Routledge, 2002).

Ursula King (ed.), *Feminist Theology from the Third World: A Reader*. (London: Orbis Books, 1994).

Janet Martin Soskice and Diana Lipton (eds), *Feminism and Theology* (Oxford: Oxford University Press, 2003). Includes material by Jewish as well as Christian feminists, in a range of genres.

More specific secondary material

Christine Bolt, *The Women's Movements in the United States and Britain from the 1790s to the 1920s* (New York: Harvester Wheatsheaf, 1993). See pp55ff on the role of religion in first-wave feminism.

Rebecca Chopp, *The Power to Speak: Feminism, Language, God.* (New York: Wipf & Stock, 1989). Looks at the wider theological implications of feminist theological work.

Julie Melnyk (ed.), *Women's Theology in Nineteenth-century Britain: Transfiguring the Faith of their Fathers* (London: Routledge, 1998). Looks at first-wave feminist theology.

15

Liberating theology

AIMS

By the end of this chapter, we hope that you will:

- understand, and be in a position to assess, the central ideas and concerns of twentieth-century 'liberation theology', in Latin America and elsewhere

- understand what is meant by 'contextual theology' and 'postcolonial theology', and why they are important

- understand how these twentieth-century theologies draw on, develop or challenge some aspects of nineteenth-century thought.

Introduction: the Medellín conference

Our starting point for this chapter is the entry onto the world theological scene of one of the most influential theological movements of the twentieth century.

In 1968, the Roman Catholic bishops of Latin America met in Medellín, Colombia. The countries from which they came were the former colonies of Spain and Portugal. Independent for the most part since the nineteenth century, these countries were struggling to emerge from economic and political dependence on the USA and Europe. Many of them were under military rule and economically dominated by foreign companies; most were marked by widespread poverty, enormous differentials of wealth, violence and political repression. Most of them were predominantly Roman Catholic; the Roman Catholic Church was a pervasive presence and force in Latin America.

The bishops gathered at Medellín felt they had been called to look at the situation of Latin America with new eyes. The Second Vatican Council (1962–1965) had called the Church to engage with the political and social challenges of modernity. The council's Pastoral Constitution on the Church in the Modern World (often referred to by the first words of its Latin text, *Gaudium et Spes,* 'Joy and Hope') called for the transformation of unjust political structures, the affirmation of the dignity of all human beings and, above all, for Christians to stand in solidarity with the poor. For the Latin American bishops, this was a clear call for the Church to take a stand in the polarised and violent political situations of their countries. In a statement that marked a decisive theological shift for Latin American Catholicism and had worldwide repercussions, they declared their intention to take the 'preferential option for the poor'.

The Medellín documents made clear that this was not simply a case of 'the Church' dispensing charity or aid to 'the poor'. Rather, the poor *were* the Church. Solidarity with the poor meant placing *their* voices, aims and struggles at the centre of what the Church did. This required, not just a different set of theological teachings but a different way of doing theology. Medellín affirmed and gave an additional spur to the establishment of small grassroots communities of Catholics – the *comunidades ecclesiales de base* (CEBs) or 'base communities'. These were groups of poor and marginalised people gathering for Bible study, theological reflection and joint social and political action.

The bishops at Medellín were calling for new ways of doing theology and new ways of being the Church – but they were also putting forward a distinctive understanding of *salvation* and of the work of God in the world. Salvation is about liberation from sin and the deathly effect of sin – but, for the Latin American theologians, sin was to be found in the structures of society, politics and the economy, as well as in individual actions. To be liberated from 'structural sin' was to experience social and political transformation. The promise of salvation, as they interpreted it, was a promise of full human flourishing in a just and well-ordered society. Jesus' life was oriented towards, and foretold, this social and political transformation. As Leonardo Boff, one of the key figures in early liberation theology, put it: Jesus 'preaches ... an authentic global and structural revolution: the kingdom of God'.

Latin American 'liberation theology' was born from the Medellín conference – from the impetus given by the Second Vatican Council for a political and theological re-positioning of the Roman Catholic Church in Latin America. The concepts and approaches developed in Latin America in the wake of Medellín have been widely studied and have exerted a wide influence. But this is not the only source of modern 'liberating theology'. In this chapter, we shall look at the Latin American example, but we shall also look forwards and backwards in history to find other examples of theology allied with movements for political and social transformation.

One particularly well-known and well-documented 'base community' was that at Solentiname in Nicaragua, established by Ernesto Cardenal and made famous in his book *The Gospel in Solentiname*.

Figure 15.1 Ernesto Cardenal

Cardenal transcribed, from his recollections, the Solentiname peasants' discussions of biblical texts. His accounts show how closely the Bible, community and political action were linked for the base communities. It also conveys the egalitarian character of the base communities; Cardenal, the priest, is only one voice in the dialogue of interpretation. This is part of the discussion of Luke 18:38 (in which a blind beggar calls out 'Jesus, Son of David, have mercy on me'):

> 'I bet that the blind man had already heard the news that Jesus was around there ... and when they told him it was Jesus, he shouted because he wanted to see and because of his faith in Jesus as a liberator.'
> 'That "have pity on me", only a person can say it who feels very humiliated, very poor. He was begging beside the road. There are rich people that are blind but this was a blind beggar.'
> 'When he calls him Son of David he's calling him a leader of the people. He's being subversive.'
> 'Sure, like suppose we get to a city, San Carlos for example, and we shout "Hurray for President so-and-so", who's not the president, right?'
> 'To have him called Son of David wouldn't be very pleasing to some people.'
> 'And here it says they shut him up.'
>
> Ernesto Cardenal, *The Gospel in Solentiname*
> (Maryknoll: Orbis, 1976), vol 4, p71.

Doing theology with Marx?

'Those who sup with Marxism should use a long spoon,' wrote Pope John Paul II to the Latin American bishops in 1979. It was certainly disturbing to many Christians, particularly those who (like John Paul II, formerly Karol Wojtyla) had lived under or alongside the communist regimes of Eastern Europe, to hear theologians and priests quoting Marx with approval. For many Christians, Marxism was by definition anti-Christian. Yet Marxist analysis was a key tool of Latin American liberation theology, and has been an influence on theological work throughout the world. How did this double meaning of Marx for twentieth-century theology arise?

Marx himself has been classed alongside Nietzsche, Feuerbach and Freud as one of the great 'masters of suspicion', the thinkers who claimed to uncover religion's guilty secrets. He was also, as we saw in Chapter 5, a student of Hegel's work who saw his thought as developing from and beyond the Hegelian approach. Like other 'left Hegelians', Marx interpreted the Hegelian dialectic as a story about revolutionary change. He saw, in modern industrialised society, unsustainable contradictions and

Figure 15.2 Karl Marx

alienation; workers were 'alienated' from their work and the products of their work. The 'reconciliation' of this condition of material alienation would come through revolutionary change in economic conditions.

Where did religion fit into this? Marx analysed religion as **ideology** – as the set of ideas, images and stories that helped to sustain a particular political and economic *status quo*. In an age of capitalism, religion arose from and supported the capitalist system. It was one of the means by which people were able to ignore or forget the real contradictions with which they lived. Most famously, Marx declared that religion was 'the opium of the people'. For the poor who were exploited under capitalism, religion was the drug that dulled their pain and allowed them to escape from the harsh reality of their situation. Marx's analysis of Christianity focused on the ways in which it arises from particular historical circumstances and helps to support particular political interests.

Marx did not say that religion was 'opium *for* the people', that was Lenin. The difference is significant. Marx focused on how 'the people' formed religion *for themselves* as a way of coping with their alienation. Lenin focused on how the elite classes taught religion to the poor, in order to maintain the *status quo*.

So what did the liberation theologians, particularly in Latin America, take from Marx? They saw that Latin American society was in an intolerable and unsustainable condition, permeated by injustice and violence. They also saw that there were various ideologies – including Christian ideologies – propping up unjust regimes and enabling people to tolerate the intolerable. They used Marx to help them do the critical, 'suspicious' work of naming social evils and unmasking the lies that were being told to conceal those evils.

Unlike at least some European Christians, the Latin American bishops did not believe that Marxism necessarily implied atheism. They argued that Marxist analysis enabled them to identify false and evil religion – and that true Christianity, standing with God on the side of the poor, would not fall foul of Marx's suspicious analysis. Crucially, these theologians rejected or qualified the Marxist claim that the material conditions of human existence – especially the economic conditions – provide a *complete* explanation for religion (and other aspects of cultural and intellectual life). Religion is, obviously, shaped by material and social conditions but this does not mean that God does not exist, or even that God does not act in and through religious life. The history of Jesus and of the Church can still, even if we use Marxist analysis, be read as the history of *God's* work.

In fact, for Latin American liberation theology and for those theologies influenced by it, Marx's **materialism**, far from leading to atheism, offered a necessary theological corrective. As we have seen, liberation theology emphasises the social and material aspects of the future Kingdom of God. 'Liberation from sin' involves liberation from sinful political and economic systems. So Marx's critique of religion in general becomes, in Latin American liberation theology, a critique of those forms of religion that do not take the material realities of human life seriously enough.

Even in Europe and North America, Marx has been used with approval by theologians in the twentieth century. The basic understanding that religious teachings come from, and help to support, particular political and social situations has been widely recognised and used. It is now more widely acknowledged that theology is partial – it speaks of and from only 'part' of human existence, and it is 'partial' in that it supports the values and priorities of particular groups. It has become harder (for example) to speak theologically about 'humanity' in general without acknowledging one's own, particular and partial, human location.

> Look back at the texts and thinkers discussed in Section A, and ask yourself, firstly where there is evidence of *their* political and social 'partiality', and secondly where there is evidence of *our* partiality as authors – in our selection and presentation of historical material.

Having said this, it is undeniable that Marxist-inspired readings of religion, especially in Europe and North America, have often been inhospitable to theological thought. Marx's own assumption of atheism makes it easy for those who take up his thought to adopt a stance of 'methodological atheism' – to assume that the *best*, or even the only valid, interpretations of religion are those that explain it in purely human or natural terms.

Earlier 'liberating' theologies

Latin American liberation theology makes prominent use of the language and narratives of Exodus. God's action in freeing the Israelite slaves and leading them to a new land is seen as definitive of God's character and God's work in history. Jesus' life and mission is read alongside the narrative of Exodus and its associated promise of future liberation. God in Exodus hears the cry of the poor and acts to transform their situation. For readers of the Bible in Latin America, texts such as this fed into the hope for radical social and political transformation *within* history.

The Latin American liberation theologians were not, however, the first modern Christians to find in the Bible a promise of freedom from present injustices. For example, in the nineteenth century, debates in Britain and North America over the institution of slavery were conducted, in part, through biblical interpretation. Defenders of slavery argued that the institution of slavery was assumed in the biblical narratives, laws and injunctions, both in the Hebrew Bible and the New Testament. Campaigners for the abolition of slavery often took the Exodus narrative – together with affirmations of the equality of all humanity in the sight of God – as their central text and rallying cry.

Furthermore, for many abolitionists, biblical language about the future 'day of the Lord' and the coming of the kingdom of God spoke directly of an impending social upheaval, a day when the injustice of slavery would be swept away and the sins of a slaveholding society punished.

The nineteenth century saw, however, not only theologies against slavery by white abolitionists, but also theologies *from* slavery – enslaved Africans (especially) in America reflecting on, and speaking, their situation through Christian theology. Studies of slave sermons and slave songs reveal how biblical stories and images were used to give voice to revolutionary hopes – for freedom, for dignity, for recognition as children of God, for God's intervention to overturn the established order. Much attention has been devoted, especially since the mid-twentieth century, to the theological content of the 'spirituals' composed by black enslaved Christians, and to the theological imagination evident in other aspects of slave culture. The pivotal importance of the black Church in the civil rights movement and in the ongoing life of African-Americans ensures that this inheritance remains a major source of creative theological thought.

Angelina Grimké's *Appeal to the Christian Women of the South* (New York: American Anti-Slavery Society, 1836) is a striking example of the theology produced by white abolitionists – striking, in part, because it was written by a Southern woman from a slaveholding family, at a time when women's participation in political debate was itself a matter of controversy.

Figure 15.3 Angelina Grimké

Grimké's appeal to 'Christian women' from the slaveholding states to reject slavery is based, in part, on the 'first charter of human rights' that she finds in Genesis 1, in which humanity, created in the image of God, is given dominion over the Earth but not over other human beings. Equality, she claims, is 'a Biblical principle'. She rehearses a (by then) familiar set of arguments around biblical justifications for slavery – arguing, for example, that 'Hebrew' slavery, even if it is accepted by Jesus, was in no way comparable to American chattel slavery. More to the point, however, she lends to her appeal the force of numerous biblical texts that speak of God's retribution on unjust rulers and societies, and God's vindication of the oppressed.

As Dwight N. Hopkins notes, 'the Exodus of slaves from bondage to freedom ... becomes an overarching hermeneutical reference frame' in black theologies of liberation both before and since the end of slavery (Hopkins, 'Black Theology of Liberation', in Ford with Muers (eds), *The Modern Theologians* (Oxford: Blackwell, 2004), pp451–468, here p453). Both the imagery of Exodus and other biblical narratives of reversal and liberation, and the understanding of God that emerges from these narratives, are prominent in African-American 'liberating theologies'. Also shared with Latin American liberation theology is an emphasis on material, social and political well-being as integral to Jesus' work of salvation. 'Freedom' in African-American thought and theology means more than simply freedom from external constraint – it means the freedom to *be fully human*, in community with others, living the life that God desires for the human beings made in God's image.

The classic study of 'slave religion' is Albert Raboteau's *Slave Religion: The 'Invisible Institution' in the Antebellum South* (Oxford: Oxford University Press, 1978, reprinted 2003). In the twentieth century, black theology of liberation from the USA (and elsewhere) has often drawn on 'slave religion' as a key resource. See for example Dwight N. Hopkins, *Down, Up and Over: Slave Religion and Black Theology* (Minneapolis: Fortress, 1999). A collection of essays edited by Cain Hope Felder, *Stony the Road We Trod: African American Biblical Interpretation* (Minneapolis: Fortress, 1991), gives a good introduction to some of the central interpretive principles of African-American theology.

James Cone is generally regarded as the founding figure of contemporary black theology of liberation. His major work *Black Theology and Black Power* (Maryknoll: Orbis, 1969) set an agenda for black theology that allied it closely with Latin American liberation theology – although, as we have seen, Cone did not need to rely on sources outside the African-American community for his biblical hermeneutic. Cone summoned the Churches, black and white, to a radical decision for the marginalised and oppressed, and to prophetic action against the pervasive injustice of racial discrimination.

Since Cone's work, black theology of liberation has rapidly grown in significance and diversified. Particularly important, and an ongoing issue, is the work of **womanist** theologians – African-American women writing and reasoning about God from their distinctive contexts and experiences. For example, Delores S. Williams' *Sisters in the Wilderness: The Challenge of Womanist God-talk* (Maryknoll: Orbis, 1995), one of the pioneering texts of womanist theology, poses a challenge to the dominant language of 'liberation' in black theology. Williams argues that for African-American women 'survival', finding ways to live and flourish even under the worst oppression and

COLGATE UNIVERSITY

Figure 15.4 James Cone

hardship, is a more fruitful starting-point for theological reflection. As we shall see, theological challenges to the language of 'liberation' are not confined to womanist theology.

Voices from the margins

A key emphasis of liberation theology in the twentieth century has been the recovery and the bringing to the foreground of marginalised theological speakers, thinkers and writers. Theology itself, as a practice, has to undergo the kind of overturning of which the biblical texts beloved of liberation theologians speak, in which the mighty are put down from their thrones and the humble exalted. The right to speak of God and be heard by others – to do theology, to enter the theological conversation – is itself part of an integral vision of liberation. Theologies from the margins, from communities outside the social, political and educational elite, will often be very different in form and genre from 'mainstream' theologies – and in many cases less likely to be preserved in writing. It is clear that tensions can arise between – on the one hand – the identification of specific themes, narratives and paradigms for liberatory theology, and – on the other hand – the commitment to privileging the theological voices of marginalised people. What happens when the theological reflection of marginalised people does not fit with the paradigm of liberation theology? What should we say, for example, when (as has arguably often been the case since the heyday of liberation theology) impoverished

> Thus, for example, Ada María Isasi-Díaz, a pioneer of **mujerista** theology –
> theology from the voices and experiences of Hispanic women – writes that 'to
> do *mujerista* theology is one of the key ways in which I contribute to and
> participate in the struggle for fullness of being, for liberation' (*En La Lucha:
> Elaborating a Mujerista Theology* (Minneapolis: Fortress, 1993), pxi). In the past,
> Isasi-Díaz writes: 'Theology ... was lacking ... a platform for the voices of Hispanic
> Women' (p1); to make these voices heard is itself a liberatory work.

urban people in Latin America reject liberation theology's claims about the material
and political nature of the kingdom of God and look deliberately to a more 'otherworldly' and 'spiritual' vision of salvation?

In such a situation it could, of course, be argued, using Marxist analysis, that the
theological thought of the victims of oppression is quite likely to be 'opium of the
people' – theology that enables them to endure their situation, rather than motivating
them to change it. It is not very convincing (although it might be convenient for those
who are in positions of power) to claim that poor people do not want economic justice
or that slaves do not want freedom, simply because they are not at this moment
struggling for justice or freedom but just finding ways to cope.

Latin American liberation theology, along with many other forms of 'liberating
theology', made extensive use of the models of consciousness-raising and
emancipatory pedagogy developed by Paulo Freire and others. Underlying Freire's
work is the idea that an oppressive system can destroy the capacity of those whom
it oppresses to think about, or name, alternative possibilities. Not only the bodies
but also the minds and spirits of oppressed people are, in a certain sense, held
captive. So ideas that resist the dominant story are not necessarily 'ready-made' in
the minds of victims of oppression. Communities have to be formed and processes
set up whereby people who have never been invited to tell their own stories or to
analyse their situation can start to do so. The base communities, discussed above,
were examples of the Church providing such communities of consciousness-raising
and emancipatory learning.

The story of the origins of black theology of liberation in 'slave religion' suggests
that consciousness-raising can take many forms and need not be explicitly linked to a
particular anthropological or political theory. Enslaved Africans, reading the Bible –
and hearing their fellow slaves reading, preaching and singing from it – discovered
narratives and images that did not fit with the version of Christianity or the account
of their place in the world that they had been taught by their 'masters'. As in Latin
America, the Bible, interpreted by communities of marginalised people, was a key
source of resistance to the dominant theological and political narrative.

In both of these examples – as in the example from Ada María Isasi-Díaz, above – note that the process of doing theology is part of the process of liberation. Liberation theology is not simply about saying what *ought* to happen (the captives should be freed, the poor should receive justice) – it is part of the process *by which* this happens (people are freed from oppressive ideologies, the voices of the poor are heard). But this in turn means that liberation theology does not simply speak from a context of 'oppression' or 'injustice' – it speaks from, and to, a context in which people are acting to *overcome* oppression and injustice.

Latin American liberation theologians, and many others, use the concept of **praxis** to describe the relationship between theology and social-political action. 'Praxis' refers to a circular movement – from theological reflection, to action to transform a context, to theological reflection on the new situation and so forth. Theological reflection interprets and challenges what is going on in the world – but what is going on in the world also tests the truth and adequacy of theological reflection. Theology that does not 'work' towards the transformation of the world is not good theology. Compare Marx's famous slogan: 'Philosophers have only interpreted the world, in various ways; the point is to change it.'

The term *contextual theology* is used to refer to theological work that explicitly arises from and speaks to a specific social and political context, often drawing on the methods and approaches of liberation theology. Contextual theologies will not always have the same *content* or *interpretive principles* as liberation theology (for example, the Exodus narrative might not be a key text for all contextual theologies; and not all contextual theologies will identify 'liberation' as a central theological theme for the communities in which they are developed). They will share the insight that theology always 'makes sense' in and for some particular community in its context – and that theology is a means of social and political transformation.

See Sigurd B. Bergmann, *God in Context: A Survey of Contextual Theology* (Aldershot: Ashgate, 2003). Bear in mind what we said earlier about the 'partiality' of *all* theology. In the same way, we could say that all theology is contextual. Note, for example, the information we provide about each thinker's context, in each chapter of Section A. We assume that each person's theological work 'makes sense' *in and for its context*. The point about twentieth-century contextual theology is not that it is in some way *more* 'in and for its context' than the dominant European and North American theologies of the nineteenth century – but that it explicitly acknowledges its context.

Many voices, many cultures

The Medellín conference was significant, not only because of its clear call to the Church in Latin America and worldwide to take the 'preferential option for the poor', but also because it drew worldwide attention to theological work being done in the global South. Prior to the mid-twentieth century, academic and Church theology – what we might call 'official' theology – was dominated by theologies developed, written and taught in the global North and the West. Theology was, of course, being *done* worldwide but there was – and still is – a global 'imbalance of theological power' that mirrored imbalances of political and economic power. The theological voices of people in the global South have often been given a low status within Church and academic institutions. Medellín, and Latin American liberation theology more generally, was an example of theologians from the global South doing theology in and for their own context.

The second half of the twentieth century saw a great flowering of contextual theologies, particularly from the global South. Some, but not all, of these can be described as 'liberation' theologies. Their priorities and key themes vary, as might be expected, with the specificities of their contexts and with the social and cultural locations of the theologians.

For example, in Korea the development of *minjung* theology has close parallels with liberation theology. It focuses on marginalised people as theological and political subjects – the *minjung* are the non-elite 'masses', the ordinary people whose voices and history are central to *minjung* theology. It reads Jesus as one of the *minjung*, who brings the fullness of salvation – social and material as well as 'spiritual' – to his suffering people. Features of the Korean context that give rise to *minjung* theology include the history of occupation by Japan, the brutality of post-war military regimes and the hardship that accompanied Korea's industrialisation.

The challenges of poverty, structural inequality and political repression are found in, and confronted by, contextual theology in many Asian countries. However, Christianity in much of Asia has to engage with a further significant feature of its context – its existence as a minority religion, often viewed as a 'Western' religion, in a context of religious pluralism. Hearing theological voices from Asia means hearing how Christians negotiate the relationship of Christianity to non-Christian cultures, and how they attempt to develop theologies that are both authentically Chinese, Sri Lankan (and so forth) and authentically Christian. Concerns about cultural identity, in a world still dominated in many ways by the West, play an important role in the development of these contextual theologies.

Contextual theologies in Africa have also taken up, to a greater or lesser extent, the themes of liberation theology, while at the same time developing themes specific to the African context. In South Africa, under apartheid – a system of strict racial segregation and structural discrimination against the black majority, in place between 1948 and 1994 – theologies of liberation developed with close links to black theology in the USA, discussed above. Faced with a Church that sanctioned apartheid and produced theological justifications for it, both white and black Christian critics of apartheid engaged in critical and constructive theology as part of the liberation struggle.

Chung Hyun Kyung, an important proponent of *minjung* theology, is discussed further in our Chapter 16 on theology and religions. Kim Yong Bok is probably the *minjung* theologian whose work is best known outside Korea.

For another influential liberation theology, this time from Sri Lanka, see Aloysius Pieris, *An Asian Theology of Liberation* (Edinburgh: T&T Clark, 1988). Pieris includes a discussion of the relationship between Christianity and non-Christian religions, and how this might contribute to a theology of liberation.

The (Hong Kong) Chinese theologian Kwok Pui-Lan is one of the best-known advocates of **postcolonial** theology from East Asia – see our discussion below. (Note for Western readers: East Asian personal names usually begin with the family name. The Korean and Chinese theologians named here should be referred to and indexed as Chung, Kim and Kwok respectively. However, if you are looking for them, it is worth checking in the 'wrong' place, since errors are common!)

Elsewhere in Africa – and in South Africa itself since the end of apartheid – the language and themes of liberation theology have often been secondary to (for example) questions about the African identity of Christianity, the relationship of Christianity to African traditional religions or the mission of Christianity in Africa. The urgent need to articulate Christianity in African terms has gone alongside the call to respond theologically to the major challenges facing African Christians in the late twentieth- and early twenty-first centuries.

In the wake of numerous atrocities – most notably, the Rwandan genocide and the crimes of the apartheid era – there has been the need for theological reflection on difficult questions of forgiveness and reconciliation, and also on the ways in which the Churches permitted or contributed to these atrocities. The HIV/AIDS pandemic, a worldwide phenomenon but most acute and widespread in Africa, has posed an acute pastoral and theological challenge to the African Churches. In many parts of Africa, the question of Christian responses to Islam is of urgent and material, not merely theoretical, importance. Most recently, debates within global Church communions around attitudes to homosexuality have drawn much attention from African theologians (see our further discussion below).

There has been extensive debate among African theologians about the relationship between '(South African) black theology of liberation' and 'African theology' – between the models of 'liberation' and 'inculturation', as they have often been described. Underlying the debate are several complex issues. For example, how meaningful is 'African' as a label – why, how and for what purposes is it possible to speak about 'Africa' as a whole? What are the criteria by which 'good' theology can be judged and who has the authority to make these judgements? How much stake should black/ African theology have in particular theoretical accounts of what it means to be African, of the nature of political liberation, and so forth?

Some major works of African theology include John Mbiti, *Concepts of God in Africa* (1970); Kwesi Dixon, *Theology in Africa* (1986); Kwame Bediako, *Christianity in Africa: The Renewal of a Non-Western Religion* (1995); and Mercy Amba Oduyoye, *Daughters of Anowa: African Women and Patriarchy* (1995). A good, if now somewhat dated, overview is Bénézet Bujo, *African Theology in its Social Context*, trans. John O'Donohue (Eugene: Wipf & Stock, 2006 – originally published 1986).

Diversity in contexts: gender and sexuality

The discussion of African and Asian contextual and liberation theologies, above, refers at several points to the work of women theologians. It is important to acknowledge women's role in shaping contextual theologies. It is also important to see that their work raises questions for these contextual theologies. For the contexts in which theology is done are not only shaped by colonialism, racism and global inequality; they are also shaped by sexism and patriarchy (see Chapter 14 for more on these terms).

Women in the global South, or who are part of racial minorities in the global North, are often said to experience 'double jeopardy' – more than 'double', if they are also poor, living with disabilities or otherwise disadvantaged. Theological work that only looks at one possible source of oppression or disadvantage may ignore or further marginalise people who live in conditions of multiple oppression.

> The term 'double jeopardy', as used in this context, was popularised by Frances M. Beale in her pamphlet *Black Women's Manifesto: Double Jeopardy, To Be Black and Female* (New York: Third World Women's Alliance, 1969).

So, as we discuss in Chapter 14, white feminists from the North have often been criticised for speaking about 'women's experience' as a whole, as though the multiple forms of oppression and marginalisation, that affect different women in different ways, did not matter. Conversely, liberation theologies have been challenged to take gender and sexuality seriously and to avoid performing their own exclusions and marginalisations.

For example, African women theologians have challenged appeals to 'traditional' African values and practices in some anti-colonial discourse. They argue that this can be misused by male elites to reaffirm sexism and patriarchy. Feminism – and with it many vital concerns about women's social, political and economic well-being – can easily, and wrongly, be dismissed as a 'Western' cultural imposition. A genuinely liberating theology in this context requires more than a confrontation between (for example) 'Africa' and 'the West' – it requires an analysis of what, in the theological thought of both 'Africa' and 'the West', genuinely serves the flourishing of both women and men.

> The Ghanaian theologian Mercy Amba Oduyoye writes: 'African women recognise cultural plurality and the necessity to honour and celebrate difference as long as practices do not entail injustice and violence. But they would like to see this not only across cultures but also within them ... "[The] past" is often misused for the subjugation of women, while traditional values that are advantageous to women ... are overlooked' (*Introducing African Women's Theology* (Sheffield: Sheffield Academic Press, 2001), p9).

The tools and language of the theology of liberation have been widely taken up to challenge the exclusion and stigmatisation of gay and lesbian people within and beyond the Christian Churches. Gay, lesbian and **queer** theologies have been particularly controversial since their inception in the late twentieth century. This is partly because they pose a more direct challenge to certain established patterns of biblical interpretation than do other liberation theologies, but also because homosexuality (and heterosexuality) has become a symbolically central issue in the 'culture wars' in the USA and beyond. The relationship between the wider cultural movement of 'gay liberation', on the one hand, and liberation theology, on the other, has itself been controversial.

Theologies reflecting on gay, lesbian and queer lives and identities share with other liberation theologies an emphasis on 'unheard voices', on resistance to a dominant and dominating theological narrative, and on the dangers of theology's alliances with existing systems of power. Here, the dangerous system of power is the social, cultural and legal system that enforces heterosexuality as the norm, and denies the full humanity of people who do not fit that norm. Beyond this challenge to *heterosexism*, gay, lesbian and queer theologies have challenged Christian theology's distrust of the body and particularly of the erotic and the sexual. They build on 'classic' liberation theology's emphasis on the *material* nature of salvation, and argue that this calls for attention to the reality of embodied and sexual experience.

There is now an enormous literature on 'theology and sexuality'. Examples of works that draw on, or explicitly engage in dialogue with, liberation theology are Robert Goss, *Jesus Acted Up: A Gay and Lesbian Manifesto* (San Francisco: Harper, 1993) and Marcella Althaus-Reid, *Indecent Theology* (London: Routledge, 2000). For a useful historical overview of gay, lesbian and queer theology – including a critical discussion of the relationship between theology and 'gay liberation' – see Elizabeth Stuart, *Gay and Lesbian Theologies: Repetitions with Critical Difference* (Aldershot: Ashgate, 2003).

Theology and postcolonialism

Postcolonial thought and theory starts from the history of colonialism and imperialism – the appropriation, by powerful nations or groups of the lands, resources, cultures and ideas of other nations or groups. Postcolonial thinkers try to identify the ongoing effects of this history and to work out how to reverse or transform them.

The second half of the 'long nineteenth century' is often described as an 'Age of Imperialism', during which the newly-developing European nations enriched themselves by claiming possession of land and resources in Africa and Asia (the formation of 'colonies'). The political process of *decolonisation*, by which the 'colonies' became self-governing, occurred (in the main) from 1945 onwards.

'Colonialism' usually refers specifically to the policies by which a powerful nation or group retains control over other nations or foreign lands.

Of course, imperialism and colonialism have very long histories. Think of the Roman Empire – or, perhaps more importantly for our discussion, of the sixteenth-century Spanish and Portuguese colonisation of what became 'Latin America'. Nor are imperialism and colonialism European phenomena – Korea, for example, was part of the Japanese Empire in the early twentieth century.

Postcolonial theory, however, suggests that 'decolonisation' is an ongoing process. The Age of Imperialism left a legacy of distorted attitudes and relationships that need to be transformed if the injustice of colonialism is to be overcome. Postcolonial thinkers seek, first, to work out how colonialism has affected ideas and beliefs – including theological ideas and beliefs – both in the former colonies and in the former colonisers. Beyond this critical move, they seek to develop approaches to thought – including theological thought – that will move beyond the injustices and distortions of colonialism.

What might a postcolonial analysis of the authors we studied in Section A look like? Postcolonial thinkers might ask critical questions, for example, about Hegel's attempt to give a philosophical account of *world* history centred on the history of Europe – and how this links up to colonialist attempts to make all of the world's peoples and resources serve European interests. For another example, they might note Schleiermacher's development of the category 'religion' and ask whether non-European religious practice is being judged by European standards – or discussed only in order to 'prove' the superiority of European religion and culture. Think about these and other possible examples and ask yourself how important a challenge postcolonial thought poses to a theological tradition based on these nineteenth-century thinkers.

Postcolonial theology is not, then, concerned mainly with structures of injustice and oppression within one society; it is concerned with *global* structures of injustice and oppression. Taking a postcolonial perspective brings in additional questions that were not prominent in liberation theology. Questions of 'race', national and cultural identity, multiculturalism and the status of 'minority' religions and traditions come to the fore in postcolonial theology. Also highly significant, and more obviously connected to liberation theology, are questions of representation. Who is allowed to speak for whom, to represent whom, to interpret whose religious tradition? In contexts where the colonial powers have often claimed the right to define and represent colonised people (as, for example 'noble savages', 'exotic Orientals', 'primitive religions'), how and on what terms are people able to start defining and representing themselves?

As with liberation theology, the re-interpretation of the Bible has been a key source of postcolonial theological thought. Postcolonial thinkers are interested in colonialism within the Bible itself – the extent to which the biblical narratives authorise or promote colonialism; and they are interested in how colonial aims have shaped biblical interpretation, particularly Western biblical interpretation, through the centuries. What happens, for example, if we read from the perspective of the 'colonised' peoples of the Bible? Do we see that the mainstream tradition of interpretation has ignored this perspective, and hence been able to use the Bible to justify colonialist ambitions?

We can see how divisions may open up between postcolonial theology and the earlier tradition of liberation theology if we go back to the Exodus narrative. For landless labourers in Latin America and for African slaves in America, this story speaks of a God who frees them and grants them what they need for their dignity and flourishing – land of their own. But in a postcolonial context, read from the perspective of the indigenous peoples of Canaan, this story is much more troubling. It seems to provide the justification for the violent appropriation of other people's land and the eradication of their religious and cultural traditions.

> There are several good introductions to, and overviews of, postcolonial biblical interpretation available. See R.S. Sugirtharajah (ed.), *The Postcolonial Biblical Reader* (Oxford: Blackwell, 2006), and other works; Musa Dube, *Postcolonial Feminist Interpretation of the Bible* (St Louis: Chalice Press, 2000).
>
> For an account of how indigenous people in America might read the Exodus narratives, see Robert Allen Warrior, 'Canaanites, Cowboys, and Indians: Deliverance, Conquest, and Liberation Theology Today' in David Jobling *et al.* (eds), *The Postmodern Bible Reader* (Oxford: Blackwell, 2001), pp188–194.

Liberating theology: where now, what next?

Liberation theology in its original location in Latin America is no longer the major force it was in the 1960s and 1970s. Social and political changes and shifts in patterns of Christian practice in Latin America (for example, the enormous growth of Pentecostalism) and generational change mean that the ground-breaking work of the early liberation theologians can now sound very dated. On liberation theology's own terms, this should perhaps be expected. Theology needs to change with changing times and contexts if it is to continue to be not only 'words about liberation' but a force for and of liberation. Looking worldwide, we can see that liberation theology has changed assumptions about what theology is, who can or should do it, and what its aims and criteria might be.

> The titles of books in the series Reclaiming Liberation Theology (SCM Press) indicate the wide range of topics on which the insights of liberation theology are seen as relevant in the twenty-first century: for example, *Beyond the Spirit of Empire* (Nestor Miguez, 2009); *Desire, Market and Religion* (Jung Mo Sun, 2007); *Liberation Theology and Sexuality* (Marcella Althaus-Reid, 2009); *Theology, Liberation and Genocide* (Mario Aguilar, 2009); *The Rise and Demise of Black Theology* (Alistair Kee, 2008).

We finish with two examples of contemporary global theological conversations in which the effects of 'liberating theology' can be seen, and within which its controversies remain alive.

In the early twenty-first century, debates over attitudes to homosexuality, particularly within the worldwide Anglican Communion, provide some indication of how complex global theological conversation has become. Many of the terms and ideas we have introduced in this chapter are invoked in these debates – often in multiple and contradictory ways.

Thus, for example, as we have seen, theologies of liberation are developed by gay and lesbian Christians (mainly, but by no means exclusively, in the West), to name and transform the homophobia of society and the Churches. But then, the language of postcolonialism, and accusations of 'imperialism' directed against the Churches of the North and West, is used by African and Asian Christians who oppose what they see as 'Western' rejection of traditional teaching against homosexuality. Sensitivity to contextual difference, and to the theological voices of many different Christian communities, is advocated – but then critical questions are raised about who is allowed to represent or speak for any given Christian community. Sometimes the questions at stake can be portrayed as questions of competing interests. Is this a struggle in which theology must take sides, as the Medellín bishops called the Church to take sides with the oppressed – with the difference that in this case there are several groups claiming to be 'the oppressed'? At the same time, much theological work has been done and is being done on the nature of reconciliation, peace and Church unity in this fragmented and often highly polarised global conversation.

Arguably more urgent in the early twenty-first century, although at the time of writing less widely discussed than questions around homosexuality, is the challenge of global environmental degradation and the threat of climate change. The Churches, and Church-based organisations, have had a significant role in pointing out how climate change exacerbates global injustice, as the people of the South suffer the effects of overconsumption and unsustainable lifestyles in the North. Liberation theology is increasingly being drawn on to develop theologies of ecological justice, in which the exploitation of non-human nature is challenged alongside the exploitation of other human beings.

Bibliography

In such a broad and diverse field, it is only possible to be indicative, not comprehensive – we have tried to list a few foundational or representative texts for various liberation theologies, as well as some useful introductions. We recommend the online bibliography and other resources available at <http://liberationtheology.org>.

Latin American liberation theology

Leonardo Boff, *Jesus Christ Liberator* (London: SCM, 1978).

Enrique Dussel, *Ethics and Community* (Tunbridge Wells: Burns & Oates, 1988).
Gustavo Gutierrez, *Theology of Liberation* (Maryknoll: Orbis, 1973).
Juan Luis Segundo, *Liberation of Theology* (Maryknoll: Orbis, 1976).
Jon Sobrino, *The True Church and the Poor* (London: SCM, 1984).
    Christology at the Crossroads (London: SCM, 1978).

Womanist theology

Karen Baker Fletcher *et al.*, *Deeper Shades of Purple: Womanism in Religion and Society* (New York: New York University Press, 2006). A useful overview.
Monica A. Coleman, *Making a Way out of No Way: A Womanist Theology* (Minneapolis: Fortress, 2006).
M. Shawn Copeland, *Enfleshing Freedom: Body, Race and Being* (Minneapolis: Fortress, 2010).
Delores S. Williams, *Sisters in the Wilderness: The Challenge of Womanist God-Talk* (Orbis: Maryknoll, 1996).

Black theology

James Cone, *A Black Theology of Liberation* (Maryknoll: Orbis, 1990 – originally published 1970).
Cain Hope Felder, *Stony The Road We Trod: African American Biblical Interpretation* (Minneapolis: Fortress, 1991).
Dwight Hopkins, *Down, Up and Over: Slave Religion and Black Theology* (Minneapolis: Fortress, 1999).

African theology

Bénézet Bujo, *African Theology in its Social Context*, trans. John O'Donohue (Eugene: Wipf & Stock, 2006 – originally published 1986).
Kwame Bediako, *Christianity in Africa: The Renewal of a Non-Western Religion* (Maryknoll: Orbis, 1995).
John Mbiti, *Concepts of God in Africa* (London: SPCK, 1970).
Mercy Amba Oduyoye, *Introducing African Women's Theology* (Sheffield: Sheffield Academic Press, 2001).

Mujerista theology

Ada María Isasi-Díaz, *En La Lucha: Elaborating a Mujerista Theology* (Minnapolis: Fortress, 1994).

Korean liberation theology

For more on Asian liberation theology, see Chapter 16.

Chung Hyun Kyung, *Struggle to be the Sun Again: Introducing Asian Women's Theology* (London: SCM, 1991).

Kim Yong-Bok, *Minjung Theology: People as the Subject of History* (London: Zed Books, 1984).

Postcolonial theology and biblical interpretation

Musa Dube, *Postcolonial Feminist Interpretation of the Bible* (St Louis: Chalice Press, 2000).

Kwok Pui-Lan, *Postcolonial Imagination and Feminist Theology* (Louisville: Westminster John Knox, 2004).

R.S. Sugirtharajah (ed.), *The Postcolonial Biblical Reader* (Oxford: Blackwell, 2006).

Queer theology

Marcella Althaus-Reid, *Indecent Theology* (London: Routledge, 2000).

Elizabeth Stuart, *Gay and Lesbian Theologies: Repetitions with Critical Difference* (Aldershot: Ashgate, 2003).

Useful overviews, collections and secondary sources

Sigurd Bergmann, *God in Context: A Survey of Contextual Theology* (Aldershot: Ashgate, 2003).

Ursula King (ed.), *Feminist Theology from the Third World: A Reader* (London: SPCK, 1994).

Rebecca Chopp, *The Praxis of Suffering: An Interpretation of Liberation and Political Theologies* (Orbis: Maryknoll, 1986).

Virginia Fabella and Mercy Amba Oduyoye (eds), *With Passion and Compassion: Third World Women Doing Theology* (Orbis: Maryknoll, 1986).

Christopher Rowland (ed.), *The Cambridge Companion to Liberation Theology* (Cambridge: Cambridge University Press, 1999).

16

Christianity among the religions

AIMS

By the end of this chapter, we hope that you will:

- understand why and how the question of how Christianity relates to 'other religions' is a modern question

- know about some of the important events and trends that have affected how that question is asked and answered now

- know about an influential twentieth-century categorisation of Christian approaches to non-Christian religions, and be able to evaluate its usefulness

- understand why relations with Judaism, and differently with Islam, raise distinctive theological questions for Christians in modernity

- have thought about how social and cultural context affects Christian theological responses to non-Christian religions.

Introduction

In the twenty-first century, we are so used to the idea of studying 'religions' that we may forget that there was a time when 'religions' did not exist – or at least, a time when Christianity was not one example of a class of things called 'religions'. Of course, Christians have always had to negotiate, explain and reflect on their relationships to those who did not worship the God of Jesus Christ, but it is only in the modern period that this has been understood as involving an encounter between several different 'religions'. The study of 'religions', and hence the idea of (for example) 'interreligious dialogue' or 'theology of religions', is a modern phenomenon.

We still use the term 'religious orders' for orders of monks, nuns and friars, and refer to their members as 'religious'. This preserves the older sense of the word 'religion', from the Latin *religio*, 'to bind'. Members of religious orders are bound to a particular community and rule of life.

> A classic text on the history of (the idea of) 'religion' is Wilfred Cantwell Smith, *The Meaning and End of Religion* (New York: Macmillan, 1963; republished by Fortress Press, 1991). An intriguing theological critique of the idea of 'religion', conceived as a direct response to Cantwell Smith, is Nicholas Lash, *The Beginning and End of 'Religion'* (Cambridge: Cambridge University Press, 1996).

Nevertheless, though a relatively recent development, this way of thinking has become deeply embedded in late modernity and questions about the nature of 'religion' and about the relationship between 'religions', have become ever more prominent. This chapter begins by working with the framework that treats Christianity as one among many 'religions' and goes on to suggest reasons why that framework might need to be questioned or challenged in contemporary theology. Our first focal point for considering 'Christianity among the religions' in the modern period is the Second Vatican Council in 1962–1965, which has already been discussed in several chapters of this book; and we end with a visit to the World Council of Churches Assembly in 1991, a centre of recent controversy about Christian encounters with non-Christian 'religions'.

Vatican II: the Church among the religions

Nostra Aetate ('In Our Time'), subtitled 'Declaration of the Relation of the Church to Non-Christian Religions', has been one of the most important documents to emerge from the Second Vatican Council. It is a document clearly shaped by the Council's emphasis on *aggiornamento*, 'bringing up to date' through openness to sources of truth beyond the Church. The title of the document itself emphasises 'bringing up to date' – this is a document for *our time*, responding explicitly to the insights, opportunities and needs of modernity.

Encounters between the Christian Churches and non-Christian 'religions' are not, as such, a modern phenomenon. *Nostra Aetate* recognises the long history of such encounters – and in particular the history of violent conflict between religious communities before and during the modern period. It then sets out, on theological grounds, a basis for non-conflictual relationships between the Roman Catholic Church and non-Christian religious communities.

Nostra Aetate sets out the foundations for a theology of the religions in its claim that human beings share:

> the unsolved riddles of the human condition, which today, even as in former times, deeply stir the hearts of men: What is man? What is the meaning, the aim of our life? ... What, finally, is that ultimate inexpressible mystery which encompasses our existence: whence do we come, and where are we going?

Focusing on these 'unsolved riddles', *Nostra Aetate* discusses how partial answers to them have been sought and found in non-Christian religious traditions. It establishes, more or less explicitly, a hierarchy of non-Christian religious life. Beginning with the 'perception of a hidden power which hovers over the course of things' found among 'various peoples' throughout history, it progresses to a discussion of religious traditions within 'advanced cultures'. Hinduism and Buddhism are named, and some Hindu and Buddhist beliefs and practices are discussed in positive terms, before a general positive comment on the ways proposed by other religious traditions to 'counter the restlessness of the human heart'.

Nostra Aetate then gives more extended consideration to Islam (or, as the English translations at the time expressed it, to 'the Moslems'). It notes commonalities of worship, belief and practice, referring to several core aspects of Islam (such as submission to God, prayer and belief in the Day of Judgement) as points that must be held in 'esteem' by the Church. The most extended section, and probably the most influential, discusses Judaism.

Nostra Aetate made, or made possible, several important steps in the relationship between Christianity and other faiths – and not only within Roman Catholic contexts. Some of the moves made in this document had a long theological history; others can be traced more easily to the immediate context of Vatican II. In the next two sections, we focus first on Christian approaches to 'other religions' in general, and second on the specific and rather different issue of Jewish-Christian relations. We then provide a further section, almost but not quite anticipated in *Nostra Aetate*, on relations with Islam.

Theology of religions: defining the issues in the contemporary world

Contemporary students of the theology of religions, or of interreligious dialogue, are likely to come across the very influential typology categorising theologies of religion as either inclusivist, exclusivist or **pluralist**. This is a very common way of categorising – often, too neatly – Christian theologians and thinkers in terms of their attitudes towards non-Christian religions.

The typology was used by Alan Race in *Christians and Religious Pluralism* (1983) and was taken up and amended by Gavin D'Costa in *Theology and Religious Pluralism* (1986). It is set out in most introductory books and essays on the 'theology of religions'. In his later work, D'Costa has criticised the typology and argued that it is theologically insufficient – see for example his *The Meeting of Religions and the Trinity* (2000).

For an overview, see Gavin D'Costa, 'Theology of Religions', in David F. Ford with Rachel Muers (eds), *The Modern Theologians*, 3rd edition (Oxford: Blackwell, 2004). Refer to the third edition of *The Modern Theologians* for this chapter, if you can – the earlier editions do not incorporate more recent challenges to the typology.

There are several interconnected versions of the 'inclusivism–exclusivism–pluralism' typology and it is quite important to be clear about the version you are using. When the typology was first developed, it was a way of dealing with issues about the *truth* of non-Christian religious claims. Very quickly, however, it was taken up and used to deal with issues about the *salvation* of non-Christians.

Very roughly, when you are thinking about religious truth:

- 'Exclusivists' believe that truth is only found within Christianity.
- 'Inclusivists' believe that the full truth is found within Christianity, but other religions express, indirectly or incompletely, the truth that Christianity tells fully.
- 'Pluralists' believe that the claims of many [or all] religious traditions are true.

When you are thinking about who is saved:

- 'Exclusivists' believe that salvation is only available through faith in Christ and membership of the Christian community.

- 'Inclusivists' believe that everyone who is saved is saved through their relationship to Christ, but this may include people who do not have explicit faith in Christ – including members of non-Christian religious traditions.
- 'Pluralists' believe that salvation is available through many (or all) religious traditions, without any necessary link to Christ.

To avoid some common mistakes and oversimplifications, note that it is possible to occupy different positions on the two typologies. Someone might, for example, think that non-Christian religions indirectly tell the truth about God ('inclusivist' about truth), but still think that salvation is only for Christians ('exclusivist' about salvation). Note, also, that the 'salvation' version of the typology is not about whether you believe that *everyone* is saved (universalism) – that is a rather different argument. Logically, you could be a pluralist without being a universalist – for example, 'all good people from all religions are saved, but bad people are not'.

Remember also that, as always with typologies, these are 'ideal types' – it is very hard to find good and uncontroversial examples for each category. One example, however, is fairly clear – and it should, hopefully, become more obvious if you look back to the discussion of *Nostra Aetate* in the light of the definitions given above. The Jesuit theologian Karl Rahner was a particularly influential 'reforming' voice at Vatican II and *Nostra Aetate* has strong links to his theology of religions. Rahner is

Figure 16.1 Karl Rahner

famous – or notorious, depending on your point of view – as a key proponent of theological inclusivism. In fact, it would be easy to argue that the category was designed specially to fit him and the post-Vatican-II theologies of religion he inspired.

The idea of 'anonymous Christians' is one of Rahner's most famous and most controversial contributions to the theology of religions. Within Rahner's thought, it is possible to talk about people who are really saved through their relationship to Jesus Christ (and who in that sense are 'Christians') without them or anyone else knowing it. Members of other religions – or, for that matter, atheists or agnostics – could be 'anonymous Christians'. This is not a statement about what they believe (as if he were trying to second-guess the 'real meaning' of other people's beliefs), it is a statement about God's relationship to them and theirs to God.

There are plenty of criticisms of Rahner's inclusivist theology of religions. Some of them are based on criticisms of the underlying theology and anthropology. For example, some have criticised his focus on the individual human subject, in his or her interior depths, as the 'place' where God's revelation happens (rather than, for example, a focus on human beings in community and history). Talking about 'anonymous Christians' tends to *individualise* the issue of interreligious relationships. This can be helpful (for example, it stops Christians generalising about 'Islam' and forces them to pay attention to real individual Muslims) – but it can also be problematic (relationships between communities and institutions *do* also matter). Rahner can be criticised from the 'pluralist' side for patronising and/or offending non-Christians by incorporating them into a Christian story of salvation – 'you're saved by Jesus Christ, you just haven't realised it yet'. (He did recognise, incidentally, the possibility that inclusivist paradigms might be applied from within non-Christian religious traditions – Buddhists might regard Christians as 'anonymous Buddhists'.) He can also be criticised from the 'exclusivist' side for failing to give enough importance to the unique history of Jesus Christ.

An unequivocal – because self-described – example of 'pluralism' is the well-known work of the British theologian John Hick. Hick's argument, as it has developed over the years, is centred on the transcendence of God (or, as he later put it in order not to exclude *a priori* those traditions that do not speak of God, to the transcendence of 'the [Eternal] One'). If God transcends all human attempts to describe or specify God, no religious tradition can be said to provide a full, complete or 'best' account of God and all religious traditions can be understood as attempts to speak about a reality that is, in the end, inexpressible.

One of the most common criticisms of this kind of pluralism is that it is itself a form of exclusivism, or perhaps inclusivism – at least epistemologically, if not soteriologically (see above). That is, it relies on a prior idea of 'the truth' that is (supposedly) common to all religions – say, the 'transcendence of the Eternal' – and religions are 'true' only insofar as they conform to that prior idea of the truth.

It is much easier to understand why Rahner can talk about 'anonymous Christians' if we take a step back into his theological claims about what it is to be human.

Rahner argues that ordinary human experience is inherently open to a horizon, a backdrop, of absolute mystery. When we reflect on it, we see that every particular thing we do, or think about, or become, is limited. We *know* that we are limited – and in knowing that we have limits, we automatically see that there is a 'beyond our limits'. That recognition of a horizon 'beyond our limits', beyond every particular thing we could ever be or know or do, is the first way we know God. The implication of this is that everybody who reflects seriously on their ordinary human experience will come to some knowledge of God – as the 'ultimate inexpressible mystery which encompasses our existence', to use *Nostra Aetate*'s terms.

Already we have the basis in Rahner's work for an inclusive model of *truth* – Christianity and non-Christian religions can both be talking about the same 'ultimate inexpressible mystery' of God. To get to an inclusive model of salvation, we need another of Rahner's theological moves. Rahner argues that, because God is the God who loves and gives Godself to humanity, human beings do not just encounter the 'horizon' of their being as distant and threatening. They encounter it as something that comes to meet them and offers them love. Jesus' life, death and resurrection are at the centre of this gift of love, and its unconditional acceptance – but the gift itself is universal, offered to every person.

So, for Rahner, God offers Godself in love to every person, *whether he or she knows it or not*, and every person's life constitutes a response to that offer, acceptance or rejection of God's love, *whether he or she knows it or not*. A life can be a real response to God's grace without that person realising it. There is no reason to assume that acceptance of God's grace, and hence the relationship to God that constitutes salvation, is limited to Christians. The 'anonymous Christians' are the people whose lives, whether they know it or not and whether anyone else knows it or not, are lived within the relationship of love that God's grace, in Jesus Christ, makes possible.

Rahner specifically does not say that everyone is saved in this way – an offer of love can, after all, be rejected. Part of the point of the 'anonymous Christians' idea is that we simply do not know who is saved – although, Rahner says, Christians may, indeed should, hope that *everyone* is.

Pluralism has been described as a characteristically modern – and, in some of its manifestations, postmodern – approach to the plurality of religions. Looking back to the beginning of this chapter, and to other chapters in this book, we can start to see why. First, we should note that Hick explicitly links his understanding of the inexpressible transcendence of God to Kant's idea of the 'thing in itself' – which we cannot perceive or experience because we cannot escape the basic structures that shape all our thought and experience. Recall, also, some of the political implications that we discovered in Kant's philosophy – the separation of a 'private' sphere of revealed or traditional religion from a 'public' sphere of rational thought, which is echoed as Hick de-emphasises the 'revealed' and traditioned differences between religious traditions. We will see in the next section that Kant's thought does have practical implications for how we can – and cannot – think about interreligious relations.

Second, a statement like 'all religions lead to God' or 'all religions contain truth' relies on knowing what a 'religion' is – and on being able to distinguish 'religion(s)' from other forms of human life and other sources of truth. This is not just a pluralist move, of course. *Nostra Aetate* also assumes that we can place 'religions' in a common category and distinguish them from various other things – nations, societies, political systems and so on. But this, as we suggested at the beginning of the chapter, has not always seemed so obvious.

In the next few sections, we look more closely at the development of modern understandings of 'religion'. At the end of the chapter, we return to two more recent and more controversial articulations of the place of Christianity 'among the religions'.

One of the criticisms of the whole exclusivist/inclusivist/pluralist typology is that – at least as it was first used by Race – it is designed to tell a story of progress. It is easy to write about these categories as if exclusivism belongs to the 'bad old days' and pluralism is the new way forward. 'Pluralist' is more readily used as a self-description than 'inclusivist' or 'exclusivist' – you will find more theologians claiming to be 'pluralist' than claiming to be 'exclusivist' (and those whom others would describe as 'exclusivist' would not always claim the label for themselves, which is why we have not provided an example here).

Alongside the other in modernity

Some histories of Christian attitudes to interreligious dialogue give the impression that the encounter with non-Christian communities was something new and surprising for Christians in the modern period. Of course, this is not true. Even in medieval European Christendom, Islam and Judaism were present as significant 'others' – whether Muslims and Jews were seen as dialogue partners, potential converts, neighbours or enemies.

Our discussion of the modern accounts of religion focuses particularly on Christianity and Judaism, and we begin by turning again to *Nostra Aetate*. Probably the most influential section of *Nostra Aetate*, at the time and since, has been its very extensive discussion of Judaism. The stated theological and anthropological basis of this entire section differs significantly from that of the rest of the document. Christianity is connected to Judaism not through a general desire for answers to 'unsolved riddles', but through a specific shared history. The 'bond that spiritually ties the people of the New Covenant [Christians] to Abraham's stock [Jews]' is traced through the biblical narrative of salvation history. The document cites several biblical texts emphasising the irrevocability of God's covenant with the Jewish people and the close relationship between this covenant and the reality of the Church. It also explicitly names and repudiates various manifestations of Christian **anti-Judaism** – for example, blaming all Jews for the death of Jesus – and repudiates **anti-Semitism** along with all forms of prejudice based on 'race, colour, condition of life, or religion'.

Anti-Judaism is usually used to refer to religion-based hatred, denigration or condemnation of Jews, and *anti-Semitism* to refer to race-based hatred/ denigration/condemnation of Jews. On these definitions, anti-Judaism goes back a long way, but anti-Semitism was invented in the nineteenth century, when theories of race were developed. (In fact, the *term* anti-Semitism was coined in the 1870s, and was a positive self-description.)

It is, as always, not quite that simple, because religion and membership of a 'people' (by birth, family membership, etc.) are interlinked for Jews – and for Christians talking about Jews. In any case, 'religious' attacks on Jews ('the Jews killed Christ') have often been linked to more general, and not obviously 'religious', attacks ('Jews are murderers'). So, many writers on the 'history of anti-Semitism' see very strong continuities between Christian anti-Judaism and racial anti-Semitism.

Other terms relevant for discussions of Jewish-Christian relations since Vatican II include:

- *Supersessionism*: the belief, either stated explicitly or implied, that Christianity replaces Judaism, that the Church replaces Israel or that the covenant of God with Israel is superseded by the covenant made in Jesus Christ, etc. Note that this is a term invented in the twentieth century to define a problem, i.e. calling someone a supersessionist is never complimentary!
- The *deicide charge*: the idea that Jews are/were responsible for, and guilty because of, the death of Christ.

At this stage it is most important to note that *Nostra Aetate* treats Jewish-Christian relations as qualitatively different from all other relationships between Christianity and 'other religions'. Judaism is not simply at the 'top of the hierarchy' of non-Christian religions, it is a different *kind* of 'other religion', which is in an important sense not separate from Christianity.

> The Vatican's Commission for Religious Relations with the Jews, established in the wake of *Nostra Aetate*, was and is linked to the Secretariat for Christian Unity (now the Pontifical Council for Promoting Christian Unity). In other words, relations with Judaism were placed, institutionally, alongside relations with the non-Catholic Christian Churches. Relations with Islam, by contrast, were and are under the Secretariat for Non-Christians (now the Pontifical Council for Interreligious Dialogue).

Thus, Jewish-Christian relations sometimes look like an exception to the normal 'rules' of interreligious relations, but they can also be seen as a starting-point for shaping Christian attitudes to interreligious relations. As *Nostra Aetate* acknowledges, Christians interpreting the Bible and their own history simply cannot avoid saying something about their relationship to Judaism. This is true in general terms, but – as we will see – it is true especially in the period we are studying.

Judaism and Christianity become religions

The category of 'religion' and the idea of many 'religions' became useful in modernity, not just when religious differences appeared but when these religious/theological differences came to be seen as a threat to social order. As we have suggested in other chapters, this can most obviously be linked to the 'Wars of Religion' in Reformation Europe and their aftermath. Modern European concerns about religious difference originate with differences between Christians. However, they have major implications for the relationships between Christianity and other faith communities – first of all, for the Jewish communities in the 'Christian' states of Western Europe.

Jews throughout Europe suffered increased persecution and violence in the late medieval and early modern period. The reasons for this are widely debated, as is the dating of the period of intensified persecution. Some scholars point to theological trends (such as greater emphasis on the unity of the Church and of Christendom, and the move to interpret Judaism as a 'heresy'); others point to economic and social trends (such as rapid social change and urbanization, producing greater insecurity and a fear of difference).

Figure 16.2 Lisbon massacre

In this context, many developments in the aftermath of the Wars of Religion can be seen as positive for the situation of Jewish communities in Europe. For example, this period saw the rise of the idea of religious toleration as a way beyond religious war. John Locke in his famous *Letter Concerning Toleration* (1689; edited by James H. Tully (Indianapolis: Hackett, 1983), p23) argues, in the context of a discussion of the 'mutual toleration of Christians in their different professions of religion' for Jews (and also 'Pagans' and 'Mahometans') to be given full civil rights and freedom of public worship alongside Christians of all denominations.

Did modernity mean the beginning of a new era of peace between religious communities? If we look again at some of the key developments in modern accounts of religion, and ask about their implications for the attitudes of European Christians – and European Christian states – to Jews and Judaism, we can see reasons both to support and to reject that thesis.

The era of Jewish emancipation in Europe is normally regarded as beginning in the aftermath of the French Revolution, with the admission of Jews to full citizenship in 1791. Crucially, citizenship was granted to Jews on condition that they took the oath of loyalty to the state, and renounced thereby 'all privileges in their favour' – the 'privileges' being a certain degree of communal autonomy and self-government that had traditionally been given to Jewish communities in France (as elsewhere in Europe). This move in France set the pattern for the gradual emancipation of Jews in Europe throughout the nineteenth century; Jews acquired rights as individual citizens and states ceased to give official recognition to Jews as a distinct community.

We do not have space here to discuss the very significant intra-Jewish debates and developments that accompanied emancipation (for example, the development of Reform Judaism), nor the contributions of individual Jewish thinkers to the Enlightenment's rethinking of religion. Most importantly, Moses Mendelssohn (1729–1786) was a key voice in the debates about the implications of modernity and Enlightenment, particularly in relation to religion. His own essay in answer to the question 'What is Enlightenment?' appeared a few months before Kant's. See Alexander Altmann, *Moses Mendelssohn* (Oxford: Littman, 1998).

For further discussion of the process and implications of emancipation for Jewish communities in Europe, see Pierre Birnbaum and Ira Katznelson, *Paths of Emancipation* (Princeton: Princeton University Press, 1995) and Jacob Katz, *Out of the Ghetto* (Cambridge, MA: Harvard University Press, 1975).

This pattern fits well with what we have already said about the changing accounts of *Christian* 'religion' in the nineteenth century. In our discussions of nineteenth-century 'religion', we have seen several key distinctions emerging, all of which have implications for Christian attitudes to Judaism.

In Kant, for example, we saw the distinction between rational religion ('within the limits of reason alone') and revealed religion. Religion 'within the limits of reason alone' was in principle available to *any* rational person, and would be the *same* for any rational person; revealed religion belonged to particular communities. Rational religion could be explained and debated in the public sphere; revealed religion (which included anything that related to scriptural interpretation, collective worship, laws other than 'moral' laws) had for most purposes to remain 'private'. This distinction also enabled Kant, as he saw it, to distinguish between the essential and the inessential aspects of religion; the essential aspects were the rational, public and universal aspects. Other thinkers, such as Schleiermacher, gave different accounts of the 'essence' of religion, but agreed that it made sense to distinguish between the essential and the inessential, the core and the periphery.

In principle, this way of looking at religion applied (and still applies) equally to any and every religion. However, it assumed and reinforced several assumptions about 'religion' that do not obviously work as well for Judaism as they (might) do for Protestant Christianity. The 'essence' of religion, the really important part of any religion, tends to be located by these nineteenth-century thinkers in an individual's experience or beliefs, rather than (for example) in a community's life. It tends to be located in something that could or should be common to all human beings, rather than in a specific story that affects specific people.

This is not just a theoretical issue about how to define religion – it is a political issue, about the place and power of different religious communities. Nor is it just an issue about Christianity and Judaism – it sets the scene for later accounts of how 'religions' can relate to one another. (For example, look back to the last section and consider how a 'pluralist' approach to interreligious dialogue fits, not only with Kant's philosophy of the 'thing-in-itself' but with his account of the essential and inessential aspects of religion.)

An exercise: think about any context in which the term 'religion' is used and *more than one* religious community is (supposedly) included under this term. The most obvious example as we write this is 'religious education' in schools, and public debates about the place of 'religion' in education.

Ask yourself: What is being assumed here about what 'religion' is and how it works? What aspects of 'religion' are being emphasised? Do you think these assumptions apply equally, and these aspects are equally important, to (all) Christians, Jews, Muslims, Sikhs, etc.?

And how modern is this presentation of religion? Is religion being defined in terms of beliefs and opinions? Is it individual or corporate? Is it something that can be explained and debated in public or is it confined to the private sphere?

One specific aspect of modern accounts of religion has particular implications for Christian views of Judaism. As we might expect from modernity's emphasis on progress, many nineteenth-century stories about 'religion' are, implicitly or explicitly, stories of progress in religion. (Again as we might expect, these are particularly common in Protestant accounts.) Stories of progress in religion told by Christians, however, are unlikely to represent Judaism in a positive light. Judaism appears repeatedly, in nineteenth-century texts, as the past that Christianity has left behind on its way to a more free, more rational and more universal form of religion. Hegel is an obvious example of a thinker for whom Judaism is mainly an earlier stage on the way towards the 'religion of truth and freedom', Christianity.

It is important to remember, again, that Jewish thinkers were major participants in debates about religious 'progress'. A particularly interesting and important exchange was that between the Protestant theologian and scholar of early Christianity Adolf von Harnack (1851–1930) and the Jewish philosopher Leo Baeck (1873–1956). Harnack's very popular *Essence of Christianity* (1901; English translation by Thomas Bailey Saunders, New York: Putnams, 1903) presented a history of Christianity in which Judaism was used throughout for negative contrast; Judaism for Harnack was the form of religion that Christianity had to 'escape' or move beyond. Baeck, a liberal thinker identifying with both Judaism and the Enlightenment, wrote first a critical response to Harnack and then his own *Essence of Judaism* (1905; English translation by Victor Grubweiser and Leonard Pearl, New York: Macmillan, 1936). Baeck identifies Judaism's 'essence' in ethical life and in the response to God's holiness; Judaism, in his account, becomes not a prison that Christianity needed to escape from, but a high standard that Christianity unfortunately abandoned.

A postscript: Leo Baeck was imprisoned in Theresienstadt (Terezin) concentration camp in 1943. He survived the camp, and moved to London after 1945. The Progressive Jewish rabbinic college in London is named after him.

Rethinking religion after the Shoah

Representations of Judaism as an outdated or dead religion, coming from European thinkers in the nineteenth and early twentieth century, often make chilling reading after the *Shoah* ('Holocaust', see Chapter 13 for notes on this terminology). We discuss wider theological engagements with the 'problem of evil' during and after the *Shoah* in Chapter 13. In this section, we look specifically at the implications of the *Shoah* for Jewish-Christian relations and for Christian understandings of Judaism.

Christian anti-Judaism has, as we have said, a long history. It is natural to look to this history as an explanation for the mass killings of Jews in 'Christian' Europe in the twentieth century. Scholars disagree, however, about the extent to which Christian anti-Judaism as such can be 'blamed' for the *Shoah*. The relationship between Christian anti-Judaism and racial anti-Semitism (see above) is a very complex one – and the debate also becomes entwined with wider debates about the causes of the *Shoah*.

What is certain, however, is that the aftermath of the *Shoah* saw an urgent reassessment within the Christian Churches of Christian attitudes to, and relationships with, Judaism. Even if Christian anti-Judaism did not carry the historical blame for the *Shoah*, it was clearly unacceptable. Many of the Churches in Germany issued 'confessions' of Christian failure to prevent the mass killing of Jews, and repudiations of anti-Judaism.

See the bibliography at the end of Chapter 13 for further reading on Christian Churches' and theologians' associations with Nazi policies. See also Susannah Heschel, *The Aryan Jesus: Christian Theologians and the Bible in Nazi Germany* (Princeton: Princeton University Press, 2008) and Richard Stiegmann-Gall, *The Holy Reich: Nazi Conceptions of Christianity 1919-1945* (Cambridge: Cambridge University Press, 2004).

In an example of how Christianity features in wider historical debate about the *Shoah*, Daniel Goldhagen, *Hitler's Willing Executioners: Ordinary Germans and the Holocaust* (London: Abacus, 1996), includes some discussion of the role of Christianity in forming anti-Semitic attitudes among ordinary Germans. Goldhagen's much-debated thesis is that the majority of non-Jewish Germans were 'willing executioners' of Jews.

As *Nostra Aetate* makes clear, however, ending Christian anti-Judaism would need more than a simple affirmation of tolerance and respect for all religions and races. The nineteenth-century stories of religious 'progress', in which Christians wrote Judaism out of history, were the modern version of a much older pattern in which Christianity has been defined in relation to, and often over against, Judaism. *Nostra Aetate*'s clear repudiation of the deicide charge and its affirmation of the Jewishness of Jesus and the Jewish origins of Christianity were important and influential moves towards reforming Christian 'theologies of Judaism'.

Among the many major Christian theological engagements with Judaism that have appeared since 1945 are Rosemary Radford Ruether, *Faith and Fratricide* (New York: Seabury Press, 1974); Paul van Buren, *A Theology of the Jewish-Christian Reality* (London: HarperCollins, 1987); R. Kendall Soulen, *The God of Israel and Christian Theology* (Minneapolis: Fortress Press, 1996). For a useful collection of extracts on recent developments in Jewish-Christian relations, see Helen Fry, *Christian-Jewish Dialogue: A Reader* (Exeter: University of Exeter Press, 1996).

One lesson we can learn from reflecting on Jewish-Christian encounters since 1945 is that it is important not to assume that interreligious relations are *symmetrical*. It is misleading, for example, to assume that Christians and non-Christians have the same understanding of the relationship, its importance or its possible consequences. Thus, for example, we have seen that there are many reasons why Christians since 1945 have 'needed' or 'wanted' to engage with Judaism – but it is not so obvious that Jews should need, or want, to engage with Christianity. Christian thinking about, and with, Judaism goes on alongside Jewish thinking about, and with, Christianity, but the two do not necessarily map onto each other.

> The statement *Dabru Emet: A Jewish Statement on Christians and Christianity* (2000), and the very extensive debates around it, highlighted some of the historical barriers to Jewish-Christian dialogue (from a Jewish perspective) and raised the question of how Jews should respond to changes in Christian thought and attitudes since 1945.

Much of the urgency in Christian thought about non-Christian religions, in the contemporary world, is focused on Christian-Muslim dialogue and to three-way conversations between all the 'Abrahamic' traditions. In the next section, we take this as an example of how the place of Christianity 'among the religions' is being negotiated in practice in particular social and historical circumstances.

Global, plural, particular, theological: contemporary Abrahamic conversations

The difference that history and context can make to interfaith relations has become rapidly clear on a global scale in the twenty-first century. A series of terrorist attacks by groups claiming 'Islamic' identity – as well as continuing conflict in Israel/Palestine and elsewhere in the Middle East – has directed attention in interreligious dialogue towards the encounters between Islam, Christianity and Judaism.

The current theory and practice of Jewish-Christian-Muslim relations exemplifies many of the issues we have discussed in this chapter. The relationships between these religious communities are not equal and not symmetrical – either theologically or historically. Nor are these religious communities really separate from each other – either theologically or historically. Looking back at *Nostra Aetate*, we see a clear affirmation that Islam and Christianity are linked (by stories – of Abraham, Jesus and Mary – as well as by beliefs or 'values'); but we also see Judaism placed in a different, closer and more complex relationship to Christianity. Specific, and different, relationships to Judaism and Christianity are also 'built into' and much debated within Islam.

Some Jewish-Christian-Muslim dialogue in recent decades has had specific and urgent political and ethical aims, and has focused on making sense of particular contexts and problems in interreligious relations.

A good example is the First Alexandria Declaration of the Religious Leaders of the Holy Land (2002), which begins:

> *In the name of God who is Almighty, Merciful and Compassionate, we, who have gathered as religious leaders from the Muslim, Christian and Jewish communities, pray for true peace in Jerusalem and the Holy Land, and declare our commitment to ending the violence and bloodshed that denies the right of life and dignity.*
> *According to our faith traditions, killing innocents in the name of God is a desecration of His Holy Name, and defames religion in the world.*

It is worth noting that this declaration, while centred on 'ending the violence', is also a theological statement, with its shared invocation of the 'name of God who is Almighty, Merciful and Compassionate'. Even the implicit assumption that Jews, Christians and Muslims speak of the *same God* is a significant move; Christian polemicists used to speak of Allah as a Muslim 'idol'. The Alexandria Declaration has been the basis for a wider process of consultation and dialogue – at grassroots level as well as among 'religious leaders'.

Some other developments in Jewish-Christian-Muslim dialogue focus more on the exploration of *differences* – differences of theologies, ways of life, interpretations of scriptural texts and so forth. An emphasis on difference arises partly as a reaction against the modern trends we discussed earlier – the trend towards coming up with definitions of, or stories about, 'religion' that failed to recognise just how different the different 'religions' could be. At least some contemporary practices of interreligious dialogue are trying to get away from the need to define the essence of 'religion', or of each of the 'religions', before dialogue or study can begin. We might say that the dialogue of life – the unofficial interreligious dialogue that goes on when people from different religious traditions live alongside each other, and that does not depend on a prior theory about how religions 'ought' to interrelate – has been given more official and academic forms.

Conversations between Jews, Christians and Muslims, however much they emphasise differences, are recognisably grounded in shared narratives and shared theological claims. What happens when the contextual encounter of Christianity and other 'religions' reaches beyond the Abrahamic traditions? Our final section considers a still-controversial example of the theological outworking of such an encounter.

One example is *scriptural reasoning* – the practice of shared study, by Jews, Christians and Muslims, of their own and each other's scriptures. Scriptural reasoning and similar activities have developed in a range of settings – academic, civic and 'religious'. Normally, they involve sustained work by small groups, and are focused not on producing 'conclusions' or resolving differences, but rather on enabling new understandings in the participants of their own and others' traditions. Although there have been several attempts by Jews, Christians and Muslims to describe the theoretical – and theological – implications of scriptural reasoning, it does not *rely* on a particular theological understanding of the relationships between the traditions and their scriptures. (For example, looking back to earlier in the chapter – there is no particular reason why a person engaged in this kind of shared study would have to be an 'exclusivist', an 'inclusivist' or a 'pluralist'.) Various materials on scriptural reasoning are available online – see <www.scripturalreasoning.org>.

Christianity among the religions: global contexts

The World Council of Churches (WCC) Assembly in 1991 is best remembered for the plenary address by the Korean theologian Chung Hyun Kyung.

Figure 16.3 Chung Hyun Kyung at the 7th WCC Assembly in Canberra, Australia, 1991

Speaking on the theme 'Come Holy Spirit – Renew the Whole Creation', Chung interwove figures and terminology from non-Christian East Asian religions with invocations of the Holy Spirit, calling on the Holy Spirit's aid in the transformation and purging of *han*. Chung appealed in her address to the pre-Christian, shamanic practice of *han-pu-ri* – the purging of anger, hopelessness and despair.

> With humble heart and body, let us listen to the cries of creation and the cries of the Spirit within it.
> Come. The spirit of Hagar, Egyptian, black slave woman exploited and abandoned by Abraham and Sarah, the ancestors of our faith …
> Come. The spirit of indigenous people of the earth. victims of genocide during the time of colonialism and the period of great Christian mission to the pagan world …
> Come. The spirit of Jewish people killed in the gas chambers during the Holocaust …
> Come. The spirit of Vietnamese people killed by napalm, Agent Orange, or hunger on the drifting boats …
> Come. The spirit of Mahatma Gandhi, Steve Biko, Martin Luther King Jr, Malcolm X, Victor Jam, Oscar Romero, and many unnamed women freedom fighters who died in the struggle for liberation of their people …
> Come. The spirit of the Liberator, our brother Jesus, tortured and killed on the cross.
> I come from Korea … For me the image of the Holy Spirit comes from the image of *Kwan Yin*. She is venerated as goddess of compassion and wisdom by East Asian women's popular religiosity. She is a *bodhisattva*, enlightened being. She can go into Nirvana any time she wants to, but refuses to go into Nirvana by herself. Her compassion for all suffering living beings makes her stay in this world, enabling other living beings to achieve enlightenment. Her compassionate wisdom heals all forms of life … Perhaps this might also be a feminine image of the Christ who is the firstborn among us, one who goes before and brings others with her?

Chung's use of the image of *Kwan Yin*, the East Asian goddess of compassion and wisdom, to envision the Holy Spirit, with the suggestion that this was also a 'feminine image of the Christ' caused particular controversy – but her whole approach to non-Christian beliefs and practices was criticised from many directions. Representatives of the Orthodox Churches suggested that their participation in the WCC was at risk if more presentations such as Chung's could be expected. Representatives of many Protestant denominations were equally concerned.

How might we describe Chung's approach and why was it controversial? She does not obviously fit the categories of exclusivism, inclusivism or pluralism. She does not, in this address, make any *general* claims about the location of truth in non-Christian religious traditions, nor about the possibility of salvation outside Christianity. In linking *han* and the Holy Spirit, *Kwan Yin* and Jesus Christ, she is (in her terms) simply doing Christian theology from a Korean context.

The description that was most often used by Chung's critics was **syncretism**. Syncretism, in religious contexts, is the bringing together of (elements from) different religions, belief-systems or symbol-systems. Concern about syncretism generally stems from the idea that it is bound to create a *new* 'religion' that belongs authentically to neither tradition. It is fair to say that 'syncretism' is a dirty word for most Christian writers on interreligious relations.

Yet Chung herself was happy to accept the 'syncretism' label, and to acknowledge that her theology combined Christian and non-Christian elements. Her syncretistic approach, as she sees it, reflects a way of working that is basic to Asian spirituality in general and Asian women's spirituality in particular. Thus she raises the question: who decides what is and is not acceptable in 'interreligious relations'? Furthermore, she draws attention to possible clashes between 'official' accounts of what is and is not possible in interfaith relations, and the everyday practice of people living in religiously plural situations.

Michael Barnes SJ, *Theology and the Dialogue of Religions* (Cambridge: Cambridge University Press, 2002), uses the term 'dialogue of life' to refer to the kinds of interfaith encounters and reflections on the relationships between faiths that develop when people from different religious communities live alongside each other.

Chung's address locates the interaction between Christianity and Korean religious traditions in the context of struggles against poverty and oppression. Like other liberationist theologians (see Chapter 15), she does theology *for* social and political transformation – and justifies this theologically by speaking of the work of the Holy Spirit in healing and liberating the whole of creation. The relationship between Christianity and other religions is worked out, for her, by discerning the Holy Spirit in particular instances of 'compassion and wisdom for life' to whatever religious tradition they pertain. In recent years, it has often been argued that religious traditions can be united through social action or through their ethical claims.

Chung also speaks from a non-Western context, and one where the spread of Christianity is a relatively recent phenomenon. Within the modern period, as we discuss in Chapter 15, Christianity beyond the West was often – explicitly or implicitly – an instrument of Western colonial power. In many contexts to which Christianity

The Global Ethics foundation and movement, led by the Roman Catholic theologian Hans Küng, seeks 'to bring to light those moral values on which the great religions of the world, despite all their differences, tend to converge and which, by reason of their convincing meaningfulness, prove themselves to be valid standards with which secular thinking can also agree' (Joint press statement following dialogue between Hans Küng and Pope Benedict XVI, September 2005). Here, the appeal to a convergence on 'moral values' seems to rest on beliefs about humanity's natural or universal ability to understand what is good – and perhaps to go back to Kant's account of the rational and moral core of religion.

However, it is not necessary to believe that there can be a universal or 'global ethic', to believe that good interfaith co-operation around ethical issues is possible and necessary. There are many examples of more ad-hoc 'interfaith' work involving Christians, starting from the *fact* of ethical agreement on a particular issue but not necessarily drawing wider theological conclusions from it.

was originally brought by Western missionaries, theologians in the twentieth and twenty-first centuries have reconsidered the relationship between Christianity and other 'indigenous' religious traditions. For these thinkers, the theological question 'where is Christ beyond Christianity?' is also a pressing question about cultural identity and history – 'where is Christ in our cultural inheritance? How do we as Christians interpret our culture's non-Christian texts?' Asian theologians, working in contexts of religious diversity where Christians are often a small minority, have made important, and often controversial, contributions on this and related questions; Raimundo Panikkar and Aloysius Pieris are two of the best-known examples.

Chung, in an interview many years after her presentation, commented: 'The Orthodox Church talks about my presentation as syncretism, but when I look at them and the German theologians who criticised me, they are as syncretistic as I am, only our ingredients are different' (interview by Stephen Brown for the World Council of Churches, Harare 1998, <www.eni.ch/assembly/0560.html>). Here she draws attention again to the importance of different histories and contexts – and to the question of who holds the power to define the boundaries of Christianity. The 'syncretism' (the adoption of pre-Christian symbols and practices) that shaped European Christianity, Chung argues, is now concealed or regarded as unproblematic because of the dominant power of European Christianity.

Perhaps, in the light of these global conversations, the place of Christianity among the religions is now best thought about in ways more 'postmodern' than 'modern'. In other words, the aim may not be to show how all religious traditions fit a single narrative (be it exclusivist, inclusivist or pluralist, about salvation or about truth), but recognising and working with the depths of difference within and between religious traditions. What kind of *theology* of religions arises from such an approach to life 'among the religions' is an ongoing question.

Bibliography

Theological engagements with religious plurality

Michael Barnes, *Theology and the Dialogue of Religions* (Cambridge: Cambridge University Press, 2002). Contains extended discussion of Judaism and of Indian religions.

Gavin D'Costa, *The Meeting of Religions and the Trinity* (New York: Continuum, 2000).

Gavin D'Costa (ed.), *Christian Uniqueness Reconsidered: The Myth of a Pluralistic Theology of Religions* (Maryknoll: Orbis, 1990). A direct response to Hick and Knitter, below – reading both of them gives a good introduction to recent debates on the subject.

J.A. DiNoia, *The Diversity of Religions: A Christian Perspective* (Washington, DC: Catholic University of America Press, 1992).

John Hick, *God and the Universe of Faiths* (London: Macmillan, 1977). Key early text for 'pluralist' approaches, although Hick's position has shifted since it was written.

John Hick and Paul Knitter (eds), *The Myth of Christian Uniqueness: Towards a Pluralistic Theology of Religions* (Maryknoll: Orbis, 1989).

Hans Küng, *A Global Ethic for Global Politics and Economics* (London: Oxford University Press, 1997).

Nicholas Lash, *The Beginning and End of 'Religion'* (Cambridge: Cambridge University Press, 1996).

Aloysius Pieris, *An Asian Theology of Liberation* (Edinburgh: T&T Clark, 1988). Major early constructive treatment of religious pluralism in an Asian context.

Jewish-Christian, and 'Abrahamic', relations

J. Kameron Carter, *Race: A Theological Account* (Oxford: Oxford University Press, 2008). See Carter's discussion of the formation of modern ideas of 'race' through Christian theologies of Judaism.

Kenneth Cragg, *Call of the Minaret* (Oxford: Oxford University Press, 1956). Influential work 'ahead of its time' in taking a positive approach to Christian-Muslim relations.

Helen Fry, *Christian-Jewish Dialogue: A Reader* (Exeter: University of Exeter Press, 1996).

Tikva Frymer-Kensky *et al.*, *Christianity in Jewish Terms* (Boulder: Westview, 2000). Jewish scholars engage with Christian theological themes – includes Christian responses.

Edward Kessler and Neil Wenborn (eds), *A Dictionary of Jewish-Christian Relations* (Cambridge: Cambridge University Press, 2005). Very useful for historical overviews and key figures.

Rosemary Radford Ruether, *Faith and Fratricide* (New York: Seabury Press, 1974).

R. Kendall Soulen, *The God of Israel and Christian Theology* (Minneapolis: Fortress, 1996).

Paul van Buren, *A Theology of the Jewish-Christian Reality* (London: HarperCollins, 1987).

The website of *A Common Word* is a good place to start for understanding contemporary Christian-Muslim conversations: <www.acommonword.com>.

17 Becoming postmodern

AIMS

By the end of this chapter, we hope that you will:

- understand some aspects of postmodern philosophy

- be aware of some of the ways in which theologians have appropriated that philosophy

- be familiar with various forms of postliberalism in theology

- have reflected upon the impossibility of neutral overviews of the theological world.

Decoding the world

Discussions of postmodernism are, in our experience, frequently bewildering, so we are going to begin with an extended analogy with the hope that it will help readers grasp as clearly as possible the nature of the ideas we are discussing.

Imagine a wartime decoding team, working together in a series of huts somewhere on a secret military installation. Today, as on other days, they have received various coded messages to crack – including one from a very high priority source. The coded message reads:

AMSHENOXPNBFNSHEDZXHNJEXWNYS

Imagine that the code breakers know that this code is a simple substitution cipher, so that their task is to find which letter of the alphabet each letter of this code stands for. Several code-breakers scurry off to work on the code. Before long, code-breaker Anne returns. 'I've discovered', she says, 'that if you make the following substitutions, you can begin to read the message' – and here she hands the Commanding Officer the following sheet:

Code	A	B	D	E	F	H	J	M	N	O	P	S	W	X	Y	Z
Text	T	-	L	R	-	A	-	H	M	Y	S	E	-	I	-	Y

Message: THE ARMY IS m--m EARLY iam-ri-m-e

Anne admits that some of this is gibberish – but it's possible that some of the message was garbled in transmission and she thinks the rest looks promising. 'The army is early – but I can't work out how early, or what it is early for, sir.'

Code-breaker Brian has been looking over Anne's shoulder. 'Hang on a minute,' he says, scribbling furiously. 'Try this.'

Code	A	B	D	E	F	H	J	M	N	O	P	S	W	X	Y	Z
Text	T	-	-	R	-	A	B	H	M	Y	S	E	D	I	G	C

Message: THE ARMY IS m N-mEAR – CiAMBRIDmGE

'There are still some garbled letters in there, sir, but it's looking clearer: The army isn't early, it's *near Cambridge*. I've got more of the message than Anne, and you'll see I don't have that problematic double coding she had – with both O and Z coding for Y. There's still some work to do, but ...'

The Commander Officer begins to get excited, sensing that his team are onto something. He sets them all to work to see if they can refine the code further and perhaps find a variant that clears up some of the remaining garbled letters. The code-breakers scurry back to work – but, in the corner, code-breaker Claire has been working away silently all this time. She now approaches the commanding officer. 'Sir', she says, 'I have something completely different. If you use *this* set of substitutions' – and she hands him this sheet:

Code	A	B	D	E	F	H	J	M	N	O	P	S	W	X	Y	Z
Text	W	B	G	N	U	A	?	E	T	D	I	C	R	O	H	?

'Then you get *this* message:'

   Message: WE CAN'T DO IT BUT CAN G-O at- NORTH -

'You see', she says, 'I've no more garbling than Brian – do you think *I'm* on to something?'

In the confines of this code room, there is no clear way of choosing between Claire and Brian. Before Claire had spoken, it looked as though the task was one that was yielding to incremental progress, with successive code-breakers refining and adjusting the table of substitutions to help eliminate the remaining gaps in the code, and each new proposal building on what went before and improving on it – reducing the remaining fractures and enigmas. Brian's proposal may have had to unpick a little of what Anne had suggested, but his proposal was recognisably in continuity with hers.

Once Claire has joined in, however, it is clear that that is not the game we are playing. Two completely different pathways for analysis have now opened up. Within each pathway we might have a fairly clearly defined sense of 'better' and 'worse' – but what about the choice between pathways?

Neither pathway can, yet, claim a total interpretation. In each there are letters that have not been decoded, or letters that have been decoded but that do not seem to fit the message – each of which acts as an irritating reminder of the incompleteness of the decoding. To put it more poetically, each of those undecoded letters or ill-fitting decodings acts as the tell-tale reminder, or trace, of the absent total interpretation.

One way of beginning to understand some of the characteristic claims of postmodernism is to see us as engaged, constantly, in decoding the world. We order and categorise it, and try to make sense of it – we give experiences and objects labels, we tell stories about causes and effects, on every level from the mundane minutiae of everyday existence to the broader sweeps of our philosophies of life. A confident nineteenth-century thinker (one who was not steeped in the writings of Nietzsche, at least) might have agreed that there were all sorts of gaps in his society's decoding of the world, but have been confident that at least some of those gaps were being filled. He might have thought at very least that it was possible, in the round, to compare decodings and identify them as better and worse, and that the better decodings were on the way to a complete and true decoding. He might think this even if he also thought of such a complete decoding as a goal that finite creatures could never fully attain – a 'God's-eye view' imagined as an ideal to guide the work of ongoing decoding. The gaps and question marks left in his and his society's current decoding would be irritants prompting progress towards that goal.

Postmodernism is, in part, the breakdown of this picture of things. It involves the recognition that there are multiple incompatible decodings of the world (or multiple incompatible pathways of decoding) and that they can't all be arranged on a single scale of 'better' and 'worse'. The gaps and question marks left in any one decoding are no longer simply irritants prompting progress; they are reminders of the existence of those other incompatible pathways. The idea of a total, God's-eye interpretation now acts not as a lure and a goal, but in a more purely negative way, as an image that reminds us of a completeness that we do not and cannot ever have. Each gap or question-mark in our decoding is a potential reason for throwing that whole decoding into question and skipping over to a different pathway – not better or worse in any absolute sense than the pathway we are on, but capable of making sense of this particular gap or question mark, at the expense of the creation of gaps and question marks elsewhere. And to the extent that such a transition will not be a matter of making things clearly better or clearly worse, we might call it a matter of play – playing with the code one has been given.

It might be objected that the code-breakers in my analogy do have ways of choosing between decoding pathways if they can go outside the code room, to check (for instance) whether there is in fact an army near Cambridge. A postmodern philosopher might reply that when we turn by analogy to our whole way of interpreting the world, there is nowhere left outside the code-room: our world *is* the code-room. We can certainly conduct empirical checks to help us make decisions between interpretations – but an empirical check is a check against some experience that we are able to identify as pertinent and to discuss (to write about in a scientific paper, for instance); it must be a check, in other words, against experience or evidence that we have already managed to categorise and to name, and therefore to fit into our decoding. There is no such thing, the postmodern philosopher might say, as a check against completely undecoded experience – and so an empirical check might be a great way of working *within* some decoding pathway, making an existing decoding better or showing that another is worse, but it isn't a magic wand that enables us to choose *between* pathways.

Postmodern philosophy, then, speaks about various aspects of this situation:

1) *The end of metanarratives.* This can mean both the end of the overarching ('meta') story of progress towards a complete interpretation, but also the undermining of the belief that any one decoding – however all-encompassing an interpretation it might appear to provide – is a step on the high road to such completeness, rather than one more bid for decoding in a whole set of incompatible and equally plausible bids.
2) *Non-foundationalism.* This is, roughly speaking, the realisation that the process of interpretation cannot begin with secure islands of achieved decoding and build incrementally from there in the direction of completeness. What might look retrospectively like secure foundational decodings to those working within one pathway may well look like mistakes to those working within a different pathway.
3) *The roles of power and rhetoric.* If the choice between alternative pathways of decoding cannot be made by measuring them in some secure way as better or worse, then those who advocate a particular decoding will need to advance it by other means. Direct coercion is one method (power), but postmodern philosophers also focus on subtler ways in which people are lured, perhaps without realising it, into alternative ways of seeing things (rhetoric) – a messy matter of politics and desire, advertising and evangelism, more than of evidence and rationality.
4) *Deconstruction.* To speak again very broadly, this term refers to a way of reading texts that looks for the garbling and the question marks: looking for the ways in which the deployment of an apparently clear bit of decoding has created gaps and inconsistencies, and perhaps covered up those gaps and inconsistencies for the sake of appearing plausible.

Postmodern philosophy

The overview just presented is an attempt to synthesize multiple different strands of recent philosophy into something like an overview – even though this kind of comprehensive synthesis is not a very postmodern thing to do! Although there are some affinities with the work of Nietzsche (see Chapter 7), the rise of this kind of postmodern philosophy is more often associated with a range of much more recent thinkers, such as Jean-François Lyotard, Michel Foucault and Jacques Derrida.

Jean-François Lyotard (1924–1998) wrote *The Postmodern Condition* in 1979. He examined the fragmentation of academic inquiry that resulted from the slow evaporation of the big pictures – the metanarratives – that had held diverse inquiries together. Those inquiries, he argued, can no longer present themselves as attempts at the refinement of a single coherent and comprehensive worldview, even though they are still mostly carried out *as if* such a worldview existed.

Michel Foucault (1926–1984) examined the processes by which ways of seeing (decodings, in our language) are propagated – not by the straightforward triumphs of evidence and rationality that they *present* as their justification, but by messier processes of power politics. He explored shifts in whole systems of practice and feeling (for example, our attitudes toward crime and punishment) that have in one sense been quite arbitrary, but which have come to seem unavoidable and natural.

Jacques Derrida (1930–2004) ranged very widely in his work, but he is best known for pioneering deconstruction. Taking almost any text, he would identify the codings that appear to structure it (noting that a text works, say, in part by means of a neat, unquestioned opposition between male and female). He would then look at how that coding is actually played out in the text, how it is made to seem inevitable and natural, but how there are gaps and questions, strange reversals, hints of other possibilities – in particular, how there are hints of difference between all those things that are assumed in the text to be identical and hints of similarity between all those things that are claimed to be simply different. Hints might be found buried in allusions, connotations or etymologies, and Derrida's characteristic move is to stop in its tracks a text that is rushing to some obvious conclusion and to play with it until the confidence tricks that it uses to appear straightforward, meaningful and effective are uncovered.

We have concentrated on French postmodernists here, but you could look instead to various English-language authors for other thinkers raising similar questions. You could, for instance, visit the *Stanford Encyclopedia of Philosophy* at <plato.stanford.edu> and look at the article on Richard Rorty, or the discussion of Alasdair MacIntyre in the article on Virtue Ethics. Where do they fit into the picture?

Theological appropriations

One form of postmodern theology was generated by the dissemination of these postmodern ideas – especially Derrida's – among theologians in the United States and elsewhere. There are plenty of theological resonances in the language that Derrida uses, and that made questions about the theological implications of his work, and about the implications of postmodern philosophy more generally, very enticing.

The prospect for a theological appropriation of postmodern philosophy, particularly in its Derridean, deconstructive form, does not seem good, however. We noted above that a *modern* philosopher might trade on the idea of a 'God's-eye view', with 'God' being the name for the one who is imagined to possess a total decoding – the full and uninhibited understanding which our own thought is supposed to be approaching. 'God' is the possessor of the God's-eye view to which we believed our successive decodings approximated and which our incremental improvements in decoding were supposed to allow us to approach. The gaps and inconsistencies in our present encodings are seen, in such modern philosophy, as temporary problems and as spurs to greater efforts as progress; they are barriers we expect to overcome on the way to a God's-eye view.

> How does this portrayal of modernity's God relate to the portrayal of God we have seen from various modern theologians? How does it relate, for instance, to the God of Kant, or of Hegel, or of Kierkegaard, or of Harnack, or of Barth?

In postmodern philosophy, however, that God vanishes, and so postmodern philosophy can appear to be profoundly atheological or atheistic. It appears to be, in a somewhat Nietzschean sense, a theology of the death of God. The gaps and question marks in our decodings are no longer lures to renewed labour of incremental progression; they are not signs pointing to God, but reminders of God's absence – reminders that there is not and cannot be any 'God's-eye view'. Many theological appropriations of this kind of postmodern philosophy are therefore animated by the question, 'What becomes of God if we take this philosophy seriously?'

Mark C. Taylor

Mark C. Taylor (b. 1945) was one of the earliest theologians to try to answer this question, in his book *Erring: A Postmodern A/theology* (Chicago: University of Chicago Press, 1984). The subtitle might give a clue as to the direction in which he travels. He agrees that we cannot now believe in a God who is a transcendent guiding star, orienting our intellectual progress – but the word 'God' might name instead something we encounter in our wandering, in our transitions from pathway to pathway, in our discoveries of the incompletenesses and errors of our decodings. It is almost as if the God who is imagined to sit majestically at the pinnacle of human achievement is replaced by a mischievous figure, only ever seen out of the corner of one's eye, who repeatedly overthrows our presumption that our decoding is the only real decoding. God's word, God's revelation (if we can call it that) has now become 'the script enacted in the infinite play of interpretation' (p103), in the 'perpetually transitory and forever nomadic' journeys that we take (p11), now that we no longer hold on for a total interpretation. In other words, the only view we can gain of the whole of things, of the way in which all things hold together – the only kind of 'God's-eye view' we can gain – is the view we gain as we play with decoding after decoding, and are tipped from one to another and then to another by the gaps and inconsistencies we find. This new God's-eye view is the view that there is no overview, only the endless possibility of decoding differently. 'God' is a name we might use for the impossibility of completeness that haunts all our decodings, and the gaps and question marks in those decodings might be thought of as the riddles of this playful God, throwing all our decodings into question, without ever becoming present. Taylor's a/theology is therefore a ringing, playful affirmation of a situation in which 'instead of expressing a single story or coherent plot, human lives tend to be inscribed in multiple and often contradictory texts' (p3) – a world of 'the ineradicable duplicity of knowledge, shiftiness of truth, and undecidability of value' (p16).

Taylor is particularly interested in what he calls the 'death of the self' – that is, in the way in which the loss of a secure and stable decoding includes the loss of any ability to securely and stably define what is mine over against what is not mine. Any such distinction, far from being unavoidable, natural and foundational, is more or less arbitrary, and close deconstructive attention will show all the gaps and question marks that bedevil it (or 'begod' it, we might better say). Taylor insists, however, that the fruit of the death of the self is not annihilation but compassion, which flows from the realisation that the boundary between myself and the other is not an absolute distinction.

If the boundary between 'mine' and 'not mine' is going to be deconstructed, that will also affect what we think of authorship – because the difference between what 'I' wrote, and what 'I' didn't write is going to be eroded. 'My' footnotes and acknowledgements are pointers to the fact that in everything I can identify as *my* writing we can also identify the voices of others. It is also true, though, that in everything you identify as my writing, you are in fact reading your *own* decoding of what I wrote: you are the co-author of everything you think is mine. The acknowledgements page in *Erring* therefore begins this way:

> If authorship is never original but is always a play that is an interplay, then clearly 'I' did not write this text. Or at least 'I' alone did not write it. Like all works, this 'book' (if it is a book) has been (and will continue to be) co-authored by many people and various institutions. To name any of these fellow writers is to attempt to bind a fabric that is boundless ... (pxi)

He does, however, go on to thank his friends and colleagues in the normal way.

Kevin Hart

Kevin Hart (b. 1954) is another theologian who has appropriated deconstruction, most influentially in his book *The Trespass of the Sign: Deconstruction, Theology and Philosophy* (Cambridge: Cambridge University Press, 1989). Hart draws deeply on the Christian theological tradition to show that the 'God' who is the target of some atheological (or 'a/theological') versions of deconstruction (the 'God' of the 'God's-eye view') is not in fact the God of the Christian mystical tradition – the God of Pseudo-Dionysius, of Meister Eckhart, of Teresa of Avila and so on. The deconstructive critique of the God of the God's-eye view does not meet Christian theology head on – and so should not lead Christians to atheism but to a renewed engagement with their tradition's deepest thinking about God.

For Hart, we cannot simply replace the God who was the transcendent goal of our decoding with the God of playful wandering between decodings. Deconstruction is not the kind of philosophy that can consistently provide us with such an overarching vision – a new kind of overview to replace the one we have lost (even if it is the overview that says there are no overviews). Rather, deconstruction has its place not as a total view, but as a discipline of speech – an ongoing practice by which we purge our language, including our theological language, of the recalcitrant imprint of the idea of a graspable God. In this view, deconstruction has an affinity with what we saw in Chapter 10 of Karl Barth's and Rudolf Bultmann's determination not to speak of a God who can be delivered into the grasp of our understanding, and a still stronger affinity with the paradoxical strategies used in the apophatic strand of the Christian mystical theology to indicate *in* speech that God is always *beyond* speech.

The work of Denys Turner (b. 1942) approaches this connection from the other direction – from a primary expertise in the interpretation of the texts of Christian mysticism. His main work on that mysticism is the 1995 book, *The Darkness of God: Negativity in Christian Mysticism* (Cambridge: Cambridge University Press, 1995), but he has explored the connections to postmodern philosophy more directly in a 2003 essay on 'Atheism, Apophaticism and "Différance"' in Jacques Haers and Peter De Mey (eds), *Theology and Conversation: Toward a Relational Theology* (Leuven: Leuven University Press, 2003), pp689–708.

Postliberalism

Such engagements with Derrida and deconstruction are not the only form of theological response to postmodernism, broadly construed. A somewhat different pathway from that being explored by the likes of Taylor and Hart is often labelled 'postliberalism'. That is a term with a complex history but it has come to be used to describe a form of theology associated with the theologians George Lindbeck, Hans Frei and David Kelsey, who taught together at Yale in the 1970s and 1980s, as well as with numerous theologians among their students and among those they influenced, and with others whose work in some respects resembles theirs.

One of the most helpful attempts to delineate postliberalism has come from the commentator James Fodor, who has identified nine characteristics that can be seen in most theology identified as postliberal (see 'Postliberalism' in David Ford and Rachel Muers (eds), *The Modern Theologians: An Introduction to Christian Theology Since 1918*, 3rd edition (Oxford: Blackwell, 2005), pp229–248).

1) Postliberalism is one of the forms of recent theology engaged in a conscious retrieval of pre-modern elements of Christian theology (cf. Chapter 12) – not least because it finds in some of those pre-modern resources better ways of pursuing one or more of the remaining eight characteristics given below.

2) Those identified as postliberals tend to see theology as a form of inquiry undertaken primarily for the sake of the Church, and to be somewhat self-conscious about explaining and reflecting upon that fact. Postliberal theologians are often, therefore, interested in probing what it means for an academic discourse to be bound up with, and responsive to, a particular community.

3) They often regard narrative as a crucial mode of thought and expression. Sometimes that has meant an interest in specific biblical narratives (see the discussion of Hans Frei in Chapter 10) – but it has also often meant a focus on the narrative form of the Christian gospel. The gospel is not a system of ideas, but a story about God's ways with the world, within which believers are to locate the stories of their communities and of their own lives. For postliberals, the meaning that concepts of Christian theology have is primarily the meaning they gain in the course of this story.

4) Postliberalism involves a focus on, and celebration of, the peculiar 'grammar' of Christian faith. That is, the Christian Church is seen as having its own habitual ways of making sense (of decoding the world and itself), embodied and passed on in characteristic practices and patterns of life. Theology is interested in the formal and informal rules that structure these recognisable Christian patterns of action, speech and thought – the rules that a native inhabitant of this community naturally follows – just as a linguistic ethnographer might try to piece together the implicit grammatical rules followed by the native speakers of a particular language.

5) Theologians regularly identified as postliberal normally regard themselves as having the task of taking stock of the existing patterns of thought, speech and action of the Church, and correcting those in the light of the criteria of discrimination that the Church itself points to. It is a matter of course correction

within a particular pathway, rather than an attempt to stand outside all pathways of decoding, deciding which is best or constructing a new one from scratch.

6) The first couple of generations of postliberal theologians tended to be Protestant – though postliberalism has now spread more widely.

7) Postliberal theologians have tended to take a non-essentialist approach to religions. That is, they have tended to be sceptical about the strategy of defining religion in general, and then of demonstrating the ways in which Christianity and other religions are examples of that definition. In particular, postliberals have rejected the strategy, associated with Schleiermacher, of identifying all religions as particular modifications and expressions of the feeling of absolute dependence.

8) Postliberals have tended to be non-foundationalist. That is, they have tended to insist that there is no way of standing outside all pathways of decoding in order to decide objectively between them. If pushed to give criteria for choosing between competing decodings, they might point to a decoding's capaciousness (its ability to make sense of as wide a range as possible of the salient data – the data of scripture, tradition and experience), its resilience (its ability to respond to difficult questions and challenges) and its habitability (the extent to which it makes for a context in which human lives can be lived, and be sustained across the generations, and provide its inhabitants with resources to meet the challenges of a changing and crisis-ridden world). However, what counts as salient data, or as a response to a challenge, or as sustainable human life might differ from decoding to decoding, so even these criteria are only of limited use.

9) Finally, postliberal theologians have tended not to regard it as their primary duty to convince people outside the Christian community of the truth or plausibility, or even of the possibility, of Christian claims – because they do not want to show that Christian theology makes sense within some other, non-Christian framework of thinking (see characteristics 4 and 5 above). They may well, however, be interested in smaller-scale connections, resemblances and overlaps between Christian habits of thought, speech and action, and the habits of other communities.

Such theology is 'postmodern' primarily by virtue of characteristics 8 and 9 – its non-foundationalist and non-apologetic character. The 'liberalism' that postliberalism is 'post' is portrayed by postliberals as a matter of Christianity having been squeezed in to a framework provided by a philosophy or pattern of understanding – a decoding – that was supposed to be universal, neutral and available to any rational human being. Liberal theology was foundationalist to the extent that the truth, plausibility or meaning of Christian claims was defined by that non-Christian philosophy; it was apologetic to the extent that it was decisively shaped by its attempt to demonstrate to any rational human being that Christian claims did make sense, or were plausible or true, on the basis of that philosophy. Postliberalism rejects both these moves – and is, paradoxically, aided to some extent in doing so by the (non-Christian) critique of foundationalism put forward by secular postmodern philosophers.

George Lindbeck

George Lindbeck (b. 1923) was widely regarded as having provided a manifesto for postliberal theology in his book *The Nature of Doctrine: Religion and Theology in a Postliberal Age* (London: SPCK, 1984) – although neither he nor others who were identified as postliberals saw it that way. The book derived from Lindbeck's experiences in ecumenical discussion – he had been involved in Lutheran-Catholic dialogues for some time – and in particular from his attempts to make sense of dialogues in which both sides claimed to be being faithful to their traditions, but nevertheless found doctrinal rapprochements possible that would have horrified their traditional forebears. What is doctrine, if it can be handled in this way?

Lindbeck distinguished three main ways in which Christian doctrine can be understood. First, there is the 'cognitive-propositional' account of doctrine, in which doctrines are more or less plain statements of fact, and can be handled as such. The theology of Charles Hodge (see Chapter 8) would be a good example of this approach. Second, there is the 'experiential-expressivist' account of doctrine, in which doctrines are partial and inadequate expressions of religious experiences or deep patterns of religious feeling that are ultimately beyond all adequate expression. The theology of Charles Hodge's sparring partner, Horace Bushnell would be a good example (see Chapter 8 again). Lindbeck argued that neither of these accounts does justice to what he saw take place in ecumenical discussion – and that each has in any case been shown by postmodern philosophers to face deep conceptual problems.

Lindbeck approaches his third and favoured option, the 'cultural-linguistic' account of doctrine, by way of a more general account of religion (and if you are wondering how that fits with the seventh characteristic, noted above, you have hit upon one of the reasons why the book was not necessarily the manifesto for postliberalism that people took it to be). What if we think of religions neither as belief systems (the cognitive-propositional approach) nor as patterns of deep feeling (the experiential-expressivist approach) but as something like cultures, in the social anthropological sense: the ingrained habits of speech, thought and practice that characterise a particular people or society. The task of theology will then not primarily be a matter of systematising and arranging beliefs, nor a matter of delving into and expressing feeling, but of something like ethnography – the attempt to set out this people's way of doing things, their way of talking and their ways of thinking.

If we adopt this view of religions as something like cultures, Lindbeck suggests, we might see doctrines as providing something like a 'grammar' of believers' language. The people who share the culture of Christianity, for instance, have a particular way

Lindbeck's intellectual debts here are not so much to the likes of Lyotard, Foucault and Derrida, but to the social anthropologist Clifford Geertz (specifically, his book *The Interpretation of Cultures: Selected Essays* (New York: Basic Books, 1973)), and behind him to the later work of the philosopher Ludwig Wittgenstein. Wittgenstein argued in his *Philosophical Investigations* that 'the meaning of a word is its use in the language' – i.e., that the task of uncovering the meaning of some word is primarily descriptive, focused on the practices within which a word is used (*Philosophical Investigations*, trans. G.E.M. Anscombe *et al.*, 4th edition (Oxford: Blackwell, 2009), §43). What Wittgenstein actually says is: 'For a *large* class of cases of the employment of the word "meaning" – though not for *all* – this word can be explained in this way: the meaning of a word is its use in the language.' Geertz, as an ethnographer, was engaged in precisely this kind of descriptive task: looking at the patterns of practice that give the words of particular cultures their meaning.

of speaking about God and can recognise when people are speaking their kind of language about God and when people are not – just as native speakers of English can normally recognise who is and is not a fellow native speaker. A doctrine is an attempt to set out the rules of this people's speech – to describe some part of its underlying pattern.

To understand any given doctrine, one first of all needs to understand how it functions as a grammatical rule for this people's speech and action. If we take the doctrinal statement, 'Jesus is Lord', for instance, then we will need to understand how the name 'Jesus' gains its meaning in the context of a whole weave of practices of Bible-reading, of hymns, of sermons and all the other means by which the figure who bears this name is identified by believers. We will then need to understand what 'Lordship' means by understanding the practices and patterns of speech by which these people govern their lives – the practices and patterns of speech involved in living as disciples, in presenting and pursuing their lives as lives of obedience and devotion. 'Jesus is Lord' is, then, a statement in which is crystallised a whole broad pattern of believers' lives: it provides a way of naming the fact that the focus of this people's discipleship, obedience and devotion is the one they identify by the name 'Jesus' – or the fact that the practices by which they identify and describe this Jesus are central to their practices of discipleship, obedience and devotion.

Lindbeck thinks that all doctrinal statements work in something like this way, and that there is therefore an extent to which the precise formula does not matter – it is the broad pattern of life that matters. It may be that a different form of words could capture and convey this pattern of Christian people's life just as well, or even better

– hence the possibilities of faithful doctrinal flexibility that he had noted in ecumenical discussions.

Lindbeck also argued that it is not a straightforward matter to ask whether such a doctrinal claim is true. We cannot ask whether the claim 'Jesus is Lord' is true without understanding the whole weave of practice that is crystallised in it. If anything is going to be true or false, it is the whole weave of practice, the whole cultural-linguistic system, that will be true; the sentence 'Jesus is Lord' considered in abstraction from that whole weave is not capable of being either true or false. Indeed, one can imagine the same sentence woven into a different pattern of practice – where either the patterns of identification of what is meant by 'Jesus' were different, or where the practices by which this people showed what they meant by lordship were different – and gaining a meaning that most Christians today would think was false. (Lindbeck uses the example of a crusader yelling 'Jesus is Lord' to authorise his cleaving of a Muslim's skull; we should presumably imagine that crusader to be a member of a community in which that would be regarded as a characteristic and appropriate action.)

Finally, Lindbeck argues that the weave of practices that constitute the Christian religion, and that give meaning to the terms used in Christian doctrine, include right at their heart practices of reading Scripture. Because reading Scripture is taken by Lindbeck as a defining task of the Christian community, the meanings that doctrinal terms have is derived from the meaning they gain in the course of the narrative of God's ways with the world that Christians read the Bible as conveying.

Hans Frei

In the course of his discussion of scriptural narrative, Lindbeck acknowledges the influence of his colleague Hans Frei (1922–1988), whom we have already met in Chapter 10. Alongside the work on the eclipse of biblical narrative described there, there are two aspects of Frei's contribution to postliberal theology that are important for our purposes.

The first is his investigation of the practices of scriptural reading by which Christians identify Jesus of Nazareth – the practices that give meaning to the name 'Jesus' in such claims as 'Jesus is Lord'. Frei argued, at around the same time that Lindbeck was writing *The Nature of Doctrine*:

1) That the characteristic practices by which the Christian Churches have read the gospels are practices that identify Jesus primarily by reading the Gospel narratives for the story they tell;
2) That these practices of reading, although they are the practices of the Christian Church and are not dictated by any non-Christian philosophy, are practices of

reading that allow the Jesus of the story to appear with a certain objectivity that allows him to stand over against the Church as someone not wholly assimilated into the Church's existing practices;

3) That Christian theology can begin with an obedient descriptive tracing of the patterns and connections of these narratives, and then see where other realities – the community doing the reading, the world within which they read and the God for whose sake they read – fit into these narratives. This is where Lindbeck's point about Scripture's role in shaping the interpretation of Christian doctrine comes from: the meanings that Christian doctrinal terms have is fundamentally the meaning those terms gain in the course of the narrative of God's ways with the world in Christ that Christians find in the Bible.

For all these points, see the essays from the 1980s collected in Hans W. Frei, *Theology and Narrative*, eds. George Hunsinger and William C. Placher (New York and Oxford: Oxford University Press, 1993).

Frei's second contribution relates to this final point. Frei tried to get away from a simplistic opposition between theology subordinated to some external philosophical scheme and theology done in its own terms. Instead of such a straightforward division, he came up with a list of five different positions – five 'types' (in *Types of Christian Theology*, eds. George Hunsinger and William C. Placher, New Haven: Yale University Press, 1992).

For type 1 theology, peculiarly Christian ways of speaking and thinking are only of value if they can be shown to express a truth which is also taught – and taught more directly – by some more general philosophy. Frei points to Kant (see Chapter 3) as an example here. Except as a vehicle for communication to the unphilosophical, the peculiarities of Christian tradition seem entirely dispensable in Kant's philosophy.

For type 2 theology, some more general philosophy still provides the overarching account within which the contribution of the Christian tradition must fit, but the Christian contribution is not thereby made dispensable. Think, perhaps, of Harnack (see Chapter 10): the particular truth taught by the Christian Gospel completes and perfects what can be taught by philosophy.

Type 3 is Frei's attempt to do justice to Schleiermacher (see Chapter 4). For Schleiermacher, two things converge: on the one hand, his understanding of Christianity circles around a basic way of experiencing and living in the world which is unique to Christianity; on the other hand, he believes that secular philosophy is quite capable of talking about the nature of 'basic ways of experiencing and living in the world' in general. However, Frei thinks that for Schleiermacher neither side quite gets to set the agenda. Schleiermacher negotiates between the two sides, but the theology he ends up with is a curious mix – a balancing act – rather than a systematic whole arranged in ways dictated by the general philosophy. Type 3 theology, then, unsystematically balances the description of the peculiar patterns of Christian life and thought with the findings of general philosophy, with neither side having absolute priority.

Type 4 is Frei's favoured type – and it is the type he associates with Karl Barth (see Chapter 10). Type 4 begins with the peculiarities of Christian speech and action – so it can begin with what Christians read in their scriptures about Jesus of Nazareth, and refuse to let the agenda be set in any other way. But the agenda set by that starting point may well be one that includes all sorts of negotiations with other ways of thinking and other patterns of inquiry. So Christian theologians might find that there is a place for historical-critical inquiry (although it will not get to set the terms of the whole debate); they might even find that there is a place for deconstruction (although it won't get to set the terms of the whole debate either).

For type 5, all that theology can be is a description or articulation of the peculiar patterns of thought, speech and action of the Christian community. Christians may talk about anything and everything, but they have no way of asking whether their ways of talking relate to, and perhaps should affect or be affected by, very different ways of talking in other communities. It turns out to be rather difficult to find clear examples of type 5 (though Frei tries rather unconvincingly to place the Welsh philosophical theologian D.Z. Phillips (1934–2006) there) – and we certainly haven't covered any in this book.

Frei's type 4 connects in significant ways to the features of postliberalism identified by James Fodor. If you look back to Fodor's characterisation of postliberalism above, you will see that postliberal theologians are viewed as taking stock of the existing patterns of thought, speech and action of the Church, and not regarding it as their primary duty to convince people outside the Christian community of the truth or plausibility, or even of the possibility, of Christian claims. They are rather associated with interest in smaller-scale connections, resemblances and overlaps between Christian habits of thought, speech and action, and the habits of other communities. To the extent that critics sometimes accuse theologians associated with postliberalism of having too little concern with these connections, resemblances and overlaps, they see it as exemplifying Frei's type 5 rather than type 4.

Stanley Hauerwas

Stanley Hauerwas (b. 1940) is perhaps the most influential – and the most controversial – of theologians classed among the postliberals and his focus falls in rather a different place from that of either Lindbeck or Frei. He is concerned with what you might call the ethical and political shape of Christian life. He does not, however, see the discipline of Christian ethics as a matter of solving certain ethical conundrums, but as describing how it is (or how it should be) that Christian people are formed by the Gospel story to live in certain ways. The condition for choosing and acting well is not that one should be a free moral agent in possession of all the facts, and the right form of calculus that can help you weigh all those facts. Rather, the condition for choosing and acting well is that one should be being formed as a disciple in a community of disciples – learning that the Gospel story is your community's story and your own story. Ethical life is a matter of participation in a story-shaped community that forms one in certain virtues – habits of action and speech that become second nature and which are identifiable *as* virtues in the light of this community's story.

According to Hauerwas, the trouble is that Christians live in a context where very strong forces pull against their formation as Christians. They live in a world shaped by a very powerful alternative story, embodied in all sorts of rituals, carried by all sorts of media, passed on in all sorts of family interactions and pervasive now in the patterns of action and speech in many Churches. The story in question is the 'liberal' or 'secular' story that claims that it is not itself a story but that it is neutral and natural; it is what is left over once we have stopped telling all the particular stories of our different traditions. It is the story that in order to live and decide responsibly, one needs to be freed from particular formation and freed from the stories that particular religious communities tell.

Hauerwas insists that secular liberalism is, despite the ideology it purveys, simply one particular moral formation among others – and that it will more clearly be seen as a particular (and problematic) programme of moral formation if Christians allow themselves to be formed more thoroughly by *their* particular formation. Hauerwas argues that the liberal, secular world needs Christian distinctiveness in order better to recognise its own particularity and questionability.

Hauerwas is sometimes taken to be advocating a withdrawal from the world, with Christians retreating into bunkers where they can cultivate their own identity without interference from, or any chance of interfering with, the wider world. Part of his response to that criticism is to say that, yes, Christians *do* need to learn renewed faithfulness to the story of good news that they tell and, yes, that does mean a deep formation of distinctive life together – and if a bunker is the only place you can do that at present, so be it. But he also argues against the idea that working constructively in the world requires that Christians play by the rules of secular liberalism by accepting the unChristian formation that secular liberalism offers. It is simply not the case, he thinks, that honest and fruitful public discourse is only possible when the particular communities from and for which we speak are ignored or downplayed. It is not the case that we can all get along together only if our particular tradition-shaped identities are contained and controlled as mere private preferences, and public decisions are made on the basis of ways of thinking and talking that are supposedly neutral, belonging to nobody in particular. Only a real acknowledgement of difference makes dialogue possible, and Hauerwas can therefore say that an account like his can 'provide a more defensible account of democracy than that based on the rationalism of modernity' (*The State of the University: Academic Knowledges and the Knowledge of God*, Oxford: Blackwell, 2007, p56).

John Milbank

A political edge as sharp as that found in Hauerwas' work can also be found in the work of the English theologian John Milbank (b. 1952), and in the 'Radical Orthodoxy' movement of which he is the leading figure. Milbank's focus is less on the postliberal repair of the Church, and more on the critique of the patterns of thought of secular liberalism – and then on the exploration of the alternatives that the Christian tradition makes it possible to imagine. And, in contrast to the work of Hauerwas and the others classed among the postliberals, the emphasis of Milbank's critique and of his development of alternatives falls at the level of philosophy or metaphysics – the drama he depicts goes on at the level of the most basic concepts and categories that we use to think about our lives and our world. In order to get to the bottom of the problems with secular liberalism and in order to understand the full impact of Christian thinking we need to think differently about power and possession, about identity and difference, about substance and relation.

Like Hauerwas, Milbank attacks the myth that modern liberal secularity is neutral. He seeks to demonstrate that it is based on a particular, questionable tradition of metaphysical thinking and of moral formation that Milbank argues is ultimately nihilistic and cannot finally handle real difference except by violence or repression. This sharp critique of secularity has often itself come in for criticism. In a recent survey of Radical Orthodoxy, Steven Shakespeare accuses Milbank of dismissing all secular institutions and discourses as 'servants of evil'. He asks:

> Are Greenpeace, Oxfam and Amnesty International simply the agents of savage capitalism? Granted that their ideas about work, nature, rights and so on need to be examined critically, and that these movements are always likely to be compromised, does this mean that they must be utterly rejected?
>
> Steven Shakespeare, *Radical Orthodoxy: A Critical Introduction*
> (London: SPCK, 2007), p125.

It is not hard to find statements by Milbank that seem to beg precisely this question and yet he does not actually claim (despite some of his more extravagant rhetorical flourishes) that such institutions are entirely and only corrupt in the sense that Shakespeare's questions seem to assume. Rather, he is interested in the deep intellectual and political foundations upon which such secular institutions and discourses rest and he claims that even what is good in such institutions and discourses rests, finally, upon deep patterns of thought that undermine or betray that good. As Milbank says, these institutions and discourses are 'threatened by an incipient nihilism' (Theology and Social Theory: Beyond Secular Reason, Oxford: Blackwell, 1990, p154, emphases added). That is, such institutions and discourses are not blatantly evil through and through, but are (often in subtle ways) self-contradictory. Milbank maintains that only a story that tells of peace all the way down – and he thinks that only the Christian story does this – can properly and without contradiction ground the goods that the institutions and discourses Shakespeare cites do indeed pursue. Milbank's claim that only Christianity is able to ground such goods is certainly stated very sharply, but that sharpness does not imply that there is simply nothing of any value to be found beyond the boundaries of Christianity.

Milbank's most famous work, *Theology and Social Theory: Beyond Secular Reason*, begins:

> Once, there was no 'secular'. And the secular was not latent, waiting to fill more space with the steam of the 'purely human' [i.e., a neutrality supposedly available to every rational human being], when the pressure of the sacred [i.e., the particular traditional formation provided by Christianity] was relaxed ... The secular as a domain had to be instituted or *imagined*, both in theory and in practice.
>
> Milbank, *Theology and Social Theory: Beyond Secular Reason*, p 9.

Milbank insists, in line with the postmodern and postliberal thinking described above, that there is simply no alternative to being formed by a particular story – there is no human life in general, only human life as shaped and lived in the light of particular traditions of thought and formation. And there is also no way of thinking about and relating to *that* fact – the necessary particularity and difference of human formations – that is not itself shaped by the particular stories that we tell.

According to Milbank, liberal secularism (including its most recent postmodern forms) can only in the end tell the story of the unavoidable particularity and difference of human formations as a story of arbitrariness, and ultimately as a story of the collision between worldviews and communities in which only unjustified coercion moves people from one pathway to another. Christianity, on the other hand, provides Milbank with a way of telling the story of real difference as a form of participation in the life of God. The world of difference exists because the triune God, whose life is already one of harmonious difference, has opened his life wide to make space for it, and all the differences of history take place within that space, and (precisely to the extent that they are themselves peaceable) participate *as* different in the dynamics of God's already differentiated life.

Milbank and other writers associated with Radical Orthodoxy are sometimes accused of claiming that the Church needs no external criticism – and that only *internal* criticism has any purchase. (See the fourth and fifth characteristics of postliberalism set out above: the accusation rests upon Radical Orthodoxy's sharp insistence upon both these points.) However, that claim needs to be understood quite carefully. Suppose we examine two criticisms of the Church, the first saying that the Church is in the wrong because it underwrites the oppression of women, the second saying that the Church is in the wrong because it contributes so little to the GDP of its host nations. Christians might well respond, without being insular in some corrosive sense, that unlike the latter question, the former is one they have to take seriously *because it is capable of being understood as an internal criticism*, one that can make sense in terms of the Christian story – and that the second criticism is irrelevant or pernicious precisely to the extent that it *cannot* become an internal criticism. External criticisms, that is, are telling for Christianity to the extent that they become means by which Christians are called to look more deeply at the implications of their own deepest commitments.

Conclusion: regimes of theological discourse

Peering into any of the movements we have been discussing in this chapter, or the movements discussed in the other chapters in the second half of this book, is a bit like peering into a separate world that runs by its own peculiar rules. If you were fully part of any one of these movements, you would be familiar with the characteristic ways of talking that distinguish its participants and with the stock of shared reference points that help keep their conversations going. You would, perhaps without being aware of it, know the sort of thing that counts as a good argument for members of this community, and have some sense of the standards of accuracy, objectivity and fruitfulness that help members of this community distinguish between good work and bad. All of this would be supported by your participation in the practices and institutions that sustain this community: you would attend the relevant conferences, read the relevant journals. You might well have become a participant in this movement by one of the standard forms of apprenticeship by which such movements reproduce themselves – perhaps studying for a PhD supervised by an existing member of the movement and embarking on a career trajectory that took you through research and teaching jobs in institutions where this movement is strong. To borrow some terminology rather informally from Michel Foucault, you would be involved in a particular 'regime of discourse': a mutually supporting weave of patterns of thought and speech, practices, institutional arrangements and relationships.

The postmodern theological world is – like the world of any modern academic discipline – made up of the overlapping and interaction of such regimes of discourse, and the whole of the second half of this book could be thought of as a series of glimpses into such worlds and their clashes. Of course, though we might with some plausibility speak of each movement as if it were a world unto itself, these worlds are not pure and walled off from one another. Modern theology is constituted by the unruly mixing and shifting of these movements, and any given individual theologian might be involved in a complex negotiation in relation to several movements at the same time.

The differing postmodern theologies that we have been examining in this chapter might suggest different strategies for negotiating one's way through such a complex theological environment. Should such a negotiation be a matter of 'erring', in Mark C. Taylor's sense: a playful wandering between movements, aware of the gaps and question marks in each that help tip one from movement to movement? Should it simply be a matter of pursuing critically faithful participation in one's own particular intellectual community – as in some forms of postliberalism? Or are there ways in which critically faithful participation in one intellectual tradition can support genuinely open, genuinely peaceable engagement with other traditions of theological thought and practice?

The one thing that all the theologians discussed in this chapter would probably agree upon is that there can be no neutrality, no position from which to gain an overview that is not in fact a position within one or another specific intellectual tradition – and no textbook, not even a *Critical Introduction to Modern Theology*, that can possibly provide such a neutral overview.

Bibliography

Kevin J. Vanhoozer (ed.), *The Cambridge Companion to Postmodern Theology* (Cambridge: Cambridge University Press, 2003). Provides a good introduction to multiple strands of postmodern theological thinking.

Kevin Hart, *The Trespass of the Sign: Deconstruction, Theology and Philosophy* (Cambridge: Cambridge University Press, 1989). A careful account of the relationship between Derridean postmodern philosophy and theology.

John D. Caputo, *What Would Jesus Deconstruct? The Good News of Deconstruction for the Church* (Grand Rapids: Baker Academic, 2007). One of the most engaging and readable accounts of how learning from Derrida can transform theology.

Fergus Kerr, *Theology after Wittgenstein*, 2nd edition (London: SPCK, 1997). A good, clear guide to the impact of Wittgenstein on theology.

George A. Lindbeck, *The Nature of Doctrine: Religion and Theology in a Postliberal Age* (London: SPCK, 1984). Often regarded as the manifesto for postliberalism.

Hans W. Frei, *Types of Christian Theology*, eds. George Hunsinger and William C. Placher (New Haven: Yale University Press, 1992). Sets out the five types of modern Christian theology and argues for 'type 4'.

Mike Higton, *Christ, Providence and History: Hans W. Frei's Public Theology* (London: Continuum, 2004). A detailed account of Frei's work – including his relation to Karl Barth.

Stanley Hauerwas, *A Community of Character: Toward a Constructive Christian Social Ethic* (Notre Dame: University of Notre Dame Press, 1981). Probably the best way into Hauerwas' work.

Samuel Wells, *Transforming Fate into Destiny: The Theological Ethics of Stanley Hauerwas* (Eugene: Cascade, 2004). A very good guide to Hauerwas.

Paul J. DeHart, *The Trial of the Witnesses: The Rise and Decline of Postliberal Theology* (Oxford: Blackwell, 2006). An overview of postliberalism, including the main figures discussed in this chapter.

John Milbank, Catherine Pickstock and Graham Ward, *Radical Orthodoxy: A New Theology* (Oxford: Blackwell, 1999). The Radical Orthodoxy manifesto; not an easy read.

James K.A. Smith, *Radical Orthodoxy: Mapping a Post-Secular Philosophy* (Grand Rapids: Baker Academic, 2004). A clear and helpful guide.

Glossary

alienation
in Marxist thought, the way in which workers are separated from the results of their work because others own the means of production

Anabaptist
a group of Protestant churches that practice adult, or believer's, baptism, as opposed to infant baptism

anthropocentric
focused on human beings, placing them first or at the centre of a theory or theology

anti-Judaism
prejudice against (people of) the Jewish religion

anti-Semitism
prejudice against people who are Jewish, especially when Judaism is regarded as an ethnic as well as religious identity

Arminianism
a Protestant school of thought following the work of Jacobus Arminius (1560–1609), who emphasised the importance of free will

atheism
lack of belief in a god, or belief that there is no god

capitalism
the economic system within which the capital – goods, land and especially the means of production – is concentrated in the hands of a few

christocentric
focused on Christ; placing the person of Christ at the centre

contingent
something which is not necessary or required by the physical laws of the universe, meaning that it has happened, but need not have done

creationism
a group of beliefs that have in common the idea that the description of creation at the opening of the book of Genesis is in some sense a factual account of the origins of the world

deism
belief in God that rejects many aspects of religious tradition; in particular, belief in a creator God who does not interfere with the creation

emancipation
freedom or liberation, especially from slavery

empirical, empiricist
based on observation or the evidence of the senses. Science takes empirical evidence as its basis, and an empiricist will place observation above other methods of gaining information

epistemology
the study of how we come to know things

eschatology
doctrines relating to the 'last things' – what happens after death, and/or the final destiny of creation

feminism
a collection of movements all taking as their key point the concept that women are fully human and should be treated as equal to men

fundamentalism
in scriptural religions, taking the scripture to be basic to belief and literally true; or strict adherence to certain 'fundamental' beliefs taken to be constitutive of religious identity. In modern political parlance it is often used, loosely and inaccurately, to mean those who take relatively extreme views and/or may be prepared to use violence

humanism
a philosophy or worldview that takes humanity, including human priorities and considerations, to be primary. It may be atheistic, secular or religious

humanitarianism
a focus on protecting or restoring the well-being of humans

ideology
a political or philosophical worldview that shapes the actions of an individual or a society

impassibility (doctrine of divine)
the idea that it is impossible for God to suffer

the Industrial Revolution, industrialisation
the historical period (the Industrial Revolution, spanning the eighteenth to nineteenth centuries) and the social process (industrialisation) by which technologies such as steam engines, mills and factories changed communities and economies

liberal, liberalism
a political position associated with an emphasis on individual freedoms and rights

liberationism, liberation theology
in Christian theology, liberation theologies include those from Latin America and other postcolonial contexts, together with feminist and queer theologies, which have in common an emphasis on teachings of the Gospel that seek to free people from economic and social inequality

materialism
in philosophy, the position that everything which exists is material, or that explanations in terms of matter are the most fundamental

mujerista
a term used by some Latin American women in preference to 'feminist', and popularised in theology by Ada María Isasi-Díaz's 1996 book *Mujerista Theology*

nationalism
an ideology that emphasises the role of the nation-state and often incorporates a high level of patriotism

objective
that which is real or true independent of an individual's perceptions

patriarchy
the system of male privilege under which women may be oppressed and treated as inferior

patristic
relating to the Church Fathers or to the period of Christian history during which they wrote (between around 100CE and 450CE)

phenomenon
in philosophy, any thing or event as it 'appears' to observation or experience

Pietism
a renewal movement within seventeenth-century and later Protestantism, which emphasises personal devotion and holiness

Platonism
philosophy derived from, or related to, the thought of Plato; key features may include a distinction between the (imperfect, changeable) experienced world and the (perfect, unchanging) world known through reason or contemplation

pluralism
a position that accepts or encourages diversity within a community or society; also an approach to the theology of religions that affirms all, or many, religious traditions as paths to truth or salvation

postcolonial
perspectives emerging from populations and places that were previously colonised, usually by European powers; critically reflective on the colonial project and its aftermath

praxis
practice; the process of putting something into practice

Presbyterian
a group of Protestant churches historically linked to the teachings of Calvin; the name refers to their method of governance by presbyters (elders) rather than bishops

Puritans
English Protestants who dissented from the Church of England in the late sixteenth and seventeenth centuries, calling for simplified liturgy and stricter personal religious discipline

queer
an umbrella term used to describe those with non-normative sexualities, including people who are lesbian, gay, bisexual, pansexual, polyamorous, and/or practise BDSM (bondage, dominance/submission and sadomasochism)

Radical Reformation
a group of Christian communities from the sixteenth century onwards, notably including the Anabaptists, who were regarded as more extreme in their rejection of and changes to Catholic belief and practice than were the other Reformers (such as Luther and Calvin); the rejection of infant baptism was a key aspect of their teaching and practice

rationalism
appealing to human reason as a primary source of knowledge. In philosophy, often contrasted with empiricism

relativism
the positions that many or all claims, especially of belief or ethics, are true or meaningful only in relation to the context in which they are made, rather than having an objective value

revelation
in theology, those events, ways or realities in which God is revealed to humankind; God's action in revealing God's self

secular
non-religious

secularisation
the process by which religion's impact in the public sphere is lessened

sexism
discrimination on the basis of sex or gender

the *Shoah*
a Hebrew word meaning 'destruction', this is a common alternative term for the genocide of Jewish people conducted by the Nazi government, also known as the Holocaust

solipsism
a philosophy (of which there are several varieties) in which the self is understood to be primary, and the world only a projection of the self

soteriology
doctrines relating to salvation

subjective
dependent on the perceiving or thinking subject

syncretism
the mixing or interweaving of two or more religious traditions. Common in the Greek and Roman pagan contexts, it is usually considered dangerous to monotheism

theodicy
an attempt to solve the problem of evil by showing that the existence of suffering and cruelty in the world is not incompatible with the existence of an omnibenevolent, omniscient and omnipotent God

transcendent
related to 'going beyond'; in theology, God's transcendence is God's property of being beyond and distinct from the world

the Trinity, Trinitarian(ism)
the Christian doctrine that God is three in one, the Father, the Son and the Holy Spirit

Unitarianism
Christian movement rejecting the doctrine of the Trinity; from the eighteenth century onwards, a church organisation, mainly in Britain and North America, based on Unitarian belief

womanism
a movement of black women to combat sexism and racism, and to analyse the ways in which those forms of oppression support one another

Timeline

We have suggested throughout this work that it is useful to have a sense of the historical context of the texts you are reading. It is also often useful to be able to see how the texts and movements covered in the various chapters relate chronologically. This is why we have provided a basic timeline of the period covered by this textbook. As with the rest of the book, our selections of what to include and what to exclude are very much open to debate. (We have, for example, focused mainly on events in Europe and North America, where most of the texts we discuss were written.) We have not attempted to give you a comprehensive picture, but rather a sketch map with gaps – gaps that we invite you to fill as you study this period.

Date	People	Publications	Events	Science, technology, and the arts
1724	Immanuel Kant born			
1725			Great Awakening movement begins in North America	
1726				Swift, *Gulliver's Travels*
1728		Law, *Serious Call to a Devout and Holy Life*		
1729				Moses Mendelssohn born
1730		Tindal, *Christianity as Old as Creation*		
1733		Pope, *Essay on Man*		Bach, Mass in B Minor
1734		Edwards, *New England's Great Awakening*		
1735				Linnaeus publishes work on plant classification
1736		Butler, *Analogy of Religion*		
1737	Thomas Paine born			
1738			Wesley begins preaching in England	
1739		Hume, *Treatise on Human Nature*		
1741		Edwards, 'Sinners in the Hands of an Angry God'		Handel, *Messiah*
1746		Diderot, *Philosophical Thoughts*		
1749				Fielding, *Tom Jones*

Date	People	Publications	Events	Science, technology, and the arts
1751				
1753				British Museum founded
1755		Rousseau, *On the Origins of Inequality*	Lisbon earthquake	Johnson, *Dictionary*
1757		Hume, *Natural History of Religion*		
1758		Helvetius, *De l'Esprit*		
1759		Voltaire, *Candide*		Haydn's First Symphony
1760			French rule ends in Canada	
1762		Rousseau, *The Social Contract*		
1768	Friedrich Schleiermacher born			Arkwright's loom
1770	G.W.F. Hegel born		James Cook lands in Australia	Goethe begins *Faust*
1775			American Revolutionary War begins	Watt and Boulton begin production of steam engines
1776		Adam Smith, *The Wealth of Nations*	American Declaration of Independence	
1778	Voltaire (real name François-Marie Arouet) dies			
1779		Lessing, *Nathan der Weise*		
1781		Kant, *Critique of Pure Reason*		
1783				Blake, *Poetical Sketches*
1784		Kant, 'What is Enlightenment?'		

Date	People	Publications	Events	Science, technology, and the arts
1785		Paley, *Principles of Moral and Political Philosophy*		
1786				Mozart, *Marriage of Figaro*
1787			American Constitution signed	
1788		Kant, *Critique of Practical Reason*		
1789		Bentham, *Introduction to the Principles of Morals and Legislation*	French Revolution	Lavoisier, *Elements of Chemistry*
1791		Tom Paine, *The Rights of Man*		Mozart dies
1792		Wollstonecraft, *Vindication of the Rights of Woman*	Denmark abolishes slave trade	
1793		Kant, *Religion within the Limits of Reason Alone*	Louis XVI and Marie Antoinette executed: Reign of Terror in France	
1795				Metric system adopted in France
1796	Johann Adam Moehler born			Vaccination against smallpox introduced
1797	Charles Hodge born, Sojourner Truth born			Beethoven's 1st Piano Concerto
1798		Malthus, *On the Principle of Population*		Wordsworth and Coleridge, *Lyrical Ballads*
1799		Schleiermacher, *Speeches on Religion*	Napoleon makes himself First Consul of France	
1802	Horace Bushnell born			

Date	People	Publications	Events	Science, technology, and the arts
1804	Ludwig Feuerbach born, Immanuel Kant dies			
1807		Hegel, *Phenomenology of Spirit*	Slave trade abolished in the British Empire	
1809	Charles Darwin born			
1812				Grimm brothers, *Children's and Household Tales* ('Fairy Tales')
1813	Søren Kierkegaard born			
1815	Elizabeth Cady Staton born		Battle of Waterloo; Napoleonic Wars end	
1818	Karl Marx born			
1819				Mary Ann Evans born (she will write as George Eliot)
1822				Matthew Arnold born
1828	Josephine Butler born			
1830		Schleiermacher, *Brief Outline of Theology as a Field of Study*		
1831	G.W.F. Hegel dies			
1832		Moehler, *Symbolik*		
1834	Friedrich Schleiermacher dies			
1836		Angelica Grimké, *Appeal to the Christian Women of the South*		

Date	People	Publications	Events	Science, technology, and the arts
1844	Friedrich Nietzsche born	Robert Chambers, *Vestiges of the Natural History of Creation*		
1846		Charles Finney, *Lecture of Systematic Theology*		
1848		Marx and Engels, *Communist Manifesto*	Year of Revolutions' in Europe	
1851	Adolf von Harnack born			Herman Melville, *Moby Dick*
1853	Vladimir Soloviev born			
1854		Sojourner Truth speaks at the Akron Women's Convention		
1855	Søren Kierkegaard dies			
1856	Sigmund Freud born			
1857			First Indian War of Independence, also known as the Indian Mutiny	Dickens, *A Tale of Two Cities*
1859		Darwin, *On the Origin of Species*		
1860		*Essays and Reviews*		
1861	Brahmabandhab Upadhyay born		Beginning of American Civil War	
1870	William Seymour born			
1871	Sergei Bulgakov born		End of Franco-Prussian War – formal unification of Germany	
1876	Horace Bushnell dies			

Date	People	Publications	Events	Science, technology, and the arts
1878	Charles Hodge dies			
1880				George Eliot (Mary Ann Evans) dies
1881	Pierre Teilhard de Chardin born			
1882				Darwin dies
1884	Rudolf Bultmann born			
1886	Karl Barth born			
1888				Matthew Arnold dies
1895		Cady Staton (ed.), *The Woman's Bible*		
1896	Henri de Lubac born			
1900	Friedrich Nietzsche dies			
1903	Vladimir Lossky born			Wright Brothers achieve first successful plane flight
1904	Karl Rahner born			
1905	Hans Ur von Balthasar born			
1906	Dietrich Bonhoeffer born		Azusa Street revival	
1913	Paul Ricoeur born			Stravinsky, *Rite of Spring*
1914			First World War begins	
1917			Russian Revolution	
1918			First World War ends	
1919			League of Nations formed	

Date	People	Publications	Events	Science, technology, and the arts
1922	Hans Frei born	Barth, commentary on *The Epistle to the Romans* (2nd edition)		
1924	Jean-François Lyotard born			
1925				Scopes monkey trial in Dayton, Tennessee
1926	Michel Foucault born			First 'talking' feature film, *The Jazz Singer*
1928	Mary Daly born			
1930	Jacques Derrida born			
1934		*Barmen Declaration*		
1936			Second World War begins	
1937		Sigmund Freud, *Moses and Monotheism*		
1938		Henri de Lubac, *Catholicism: The Social Aspects of Dogma*		
1945			Second World War ends	
1947			India gains independence from Britain	
1948			Apartheid begins in South Africa	
1949		Simone de Beauvoir, *The Second Sex*		
1953				Double helix model of DNA published

Date	People	Publications	Events	Science, technology, and the arts
1961			Berlin Wall constructed	First human space flight
1962			Second Vatican Council begins, Cuban Missile Crisis	
1965			Second Vatican Council ends	
1967		Moltmann, *The Crucified God*		
1968	Martin Luther King, Jr. assassinated	Kate Millett, *Sexual Politics*	The Medellin Conference	
1973		Mary Daly, *Beyond God the Father: Towards a Philosophy of Women's Liberation*		
1975		Stanley Hauerwas, *Character and the Christian Life: A Study in Theological Ethics*		Microsoft founded
1977		John Hick (ed.), *The Myth of God Incarnate*		
1979		Jean-François Lyotard, *The Postmodern Condition*		
1984		George Lindbeck, *The Nature of Doctrine: Religion and Theology in a Postliberal Age*		
1986		Gavin D'Costa, *Theology and Religious Pluralism*		
1989			Fall of the Berlin Wall	
1994			South African apartheid ends	

Date	People	Publications	Events	Science, technology, and the arts
1995		Delores S. Williams, *Sisters in the Wilderness: The Challenge of Womanist God-talk*		
2001			9/11 attacks on World Trade Center	
2006		Richard Dawkins, *The God Delusion*		

Index